Studies in Regional and Local History

General Editor Nigel Goose

Previous titles in this series

Volume 1: *A Hertfordshire demesne of Westminster Abbey: Profits, productivity and weather*
by Derek Vincent Stern (edited and with an introduction by Christopher Thornton)
(ISBN 0-900458-92-5, £29.99 hb)

Volume 2: *From Hellgill to Bridge End: Aspects of economic and social change in the Upper Eden Valley, 1840–95*
by Margaret Shepherd
(ISBN 1-902806-27-1, £35.00 hb
ISBN 1-902806-32-8, £18.95 pb)

Volume 3: *Cambridge and its Economic Region, 1450–1560*
by John S. Lee
(ISBN 1-902806-47-6, £35.00 hb
ISBN 1-902806-52-2, £18.99 pb)

Volume 4: *Cultural Transition in the Chilterns and Essex Region, 350 AD to 650 AD*
by John T. Baker
(ISBN 1-902806-46-8, £35.00 hb
ISBN 1-902806-53-0, £18.99 pb)

A Pleasing Prospect

Society and culture in eighteenth-century Colchester

Shani D'Cruze

University of Hertfordshire Press
Studies in Regional and Local History

Volume 5

First published in Great Britain in 2008 by
University of Hertfordshire Press
Learning and Information Services
University of Hertfordshire
College Lane
Hatfield
Hertfordshire AL10 9AB

British Library Cataloguing in Publication Data
A catalogue record for this book is available from the British Library

ISBN 978-1-902806-72-3 hardback
ISBN 978-1-902806-73-0 paperback

Design by Geoff Green Book Design, CB4 5RA
Cover design by John Robertshaw, Harpenden, AL5 2JB
Printed in Great Britain by H. Charlesworth & Co. Ltd., Wakefield, WF2 9LP

This book is dedicated to

John Bensusan Butt (1911–1997)

whose perennial delight in the history of his native town
enlivened my postgraduate research and,
affectionately remembered, has accompanied my
labours on this volume.

Contents

Figures

Tables

General Editor's preface

English local history and urban history have grown in stature together during the course of the twentieth century, particularly with respect to the early modern period, the two sub-branches of the historical discipline coalescing in the work of W.G. Hoskins, whose *Industry, Trade and People in Exeter, 1688–1800* was published as long ago as 1935. Hoskins subsequently developed his early modern urban research alongside his rural interests, with a particular focus upon the towns of the Midlands that featured prominently in *Provincial England*, published thirty years later in 1965. There his concern was with the basic economic and social structures of urban economy and society – occupations, economic development, wealth and poverty. In this research Hoskins introduced us to sources that had been little used previously, such as the Exchequer Lay Subsidies, the Hearth Taxes of the later seventeenth century, freemen's registers and borough financial accounts, all of which have now become the stock in trade of the early modern urban historian. He also insisted that we should count, to provide a more quantitative dimension to urban studies that was previously lacking, but which has since become second nature to the historian of England's early modern towns.

A new wave of interest built upon the pioneering work of Hoskins in the early 1970s. Realising that there was still much to be discovered about early modern towns – that current understanding of them remained fragmentary – a group of young scholars came together under the leadership of Peter Clark and Paul Slack to produce an important collection of essays entitled *Crisis and Order in English Towns 1500–1700* (Routledge and Kegan Paul, 1972), a book with a title that caused some misgivings at the time, and continues to do so today. Collectively these essays dealt with aspects of early modern urban economic, social and political life with an enhanced rigour and a greater depth than had been achieved to date. New topics were introduced to the agenda – such as migration, suburban housing and urban ceremony – while more conventional subjects were aired with a freshness and sophistication that inspired renewed interest in urban studies. The book also provided a framework, an interim statement of the overall structure of English urban society that provided a valuable template for further research. Much further research indeed ensued, published in the form of articles which widened the agenda of the urban historian still further, monographs that have traced the development of individual towns, studies of particular urban types, debates about the vitality or otherwise of the English urban sector, and synthetic overviews of English towns in the sixteenth and seventeenth, and in the eighteenth, centuries. The recent publication of the three-volume *Cambridge Urban History of Britain* (Cambridge University Press, 2000) amply testifies to the development of English urban history in the last thirty or so years.

Much work remains to be done, however, and central issues about urban economic and social development remain unresolved. Studies that trace the development of particular towns over an extended time-frame remain relatively rare, while new topics have risen to the top of the historical agenda that require more detailed exploration in local contexts. This brings us to the present study, the fifth volume of the series

Studies in Regional and Local History, Shani D'Cruze's *A Pleasing Prospect: Society and culture in eighteenth-century Colchester*. Colchester possesses a wonderful archive, one that has attracted the attention of several historians, including the present writer. Until now, however, we have lacked a full-blown study of Colchester in the eighteenth century, and it has been largely relegated to the status one of the 'also rans' of eighteenth century urban history, its apparently faltering progress standing in stark contrast to the more rapid urban development associated with the industrial Midlands and the North and the ports of the west coast. Eighteenth-century economic and urban development was, however, diverse, and if the locus of urban dynamism had shifted north and west, towns continued to grow everywhere, and often exhibited a healthy economic and social outlook, responding to expanding production, greater economic integration and commercialisation, and the development of a consumer society. Despite some rationalisation of the urban network, urban consolidation was a feature of the eighteenth century, with the growth of retail outlets, of specialist crafts and new leisure activities ensuring continued urban growth and prosperity. It has been suggested that the 'long eighteenth century' was a golden age for most of Britain's small towns, but it was also a prosperous era for many county towns of the size and status of Colchester. Peter Borsay's 'English Urban Renaissance' was by no means confined to the largest English towns, and Colchester shared in the development of walks, theatres, assemblies, new buildings and improved amenities that have led to this characterisation. Such towns were also the place where we might expect to find the 'middling sort of people', a social category that has risen to such prominence in recent discussions of eighteenth-century social structure, if one that remains almost impossible to define. Outside of London, they have proved particularly elusive, and hence a study such as this that situates them within a specific provincial urban context is particularly welcome. With the 'middling sort' taking centre stage, Shani D'Cruze reconstitutes the social networks of eighteenth-century Colchester associated with family, kinship, gender, space, religion and politics, examining the relationship between individual and family biographies and broader historical change to reflect upon eighteenth-century provincial urban society and culture at large. In so doing, she not only adds to the body of research on eighteenth-century urban communities, but also advances the agenda of urban historical research.

Nigel Goose
University of Hertfordshire
May 2008

Foreword

John Bensusan Butt was born on 6 June 1911, in the attic of 16 North Hill, Colchester, and at the age of two the family moved to the Minories which is where he spent his formative years. He won an exhibition to Magdalen College Oxford, but, unhappy at being forced, as he put it, to study things other than eighteenth-century French history, he left with only a third-class degree. Characteristically, and to his family's dismay, he forsook a conventional career and took up landscape painting. This was in 1934, and John continued to paint, interrupted only by his war service, until 1961. His *catalogue raisonnée* lists over 620 meticulously documented works, mostly in watercolours or in crayon or pencil. He had London shows at the French Gallery (1937), Kensington Art Gallery (1949) and the Leicester Gallery (1957). He was exhibited also at the Ashmolean in Oxford in 1986, and at the Minories Art Gallery in 1962, 1964, and 1975. He wrote extensively on aesthetics and on art history, and amongst his publications are *Recollections of Lucien Pissarro in his Seventies* (1977), *On Naturalness in Art* (1981), and *Gainsborough in his Twenties* (1989). The strongest influence on his painting was that of Lucien Pissarro, the son of the famous impressionist painter Camille Pissarro. Lucien had moved to England and married Esther Bensusan, John's maternal aunt, in 1892.

Painting was interrupted by the Second War when John was conscripted into the Royal Engineers. He took part in the Normandy Landings, where his main job was to draw maps of the terrain for the advancing forces. These maps were both elegant and accurate and some still exist today. Lucien died during the war, and this was a source of great sorrow. John resumed painting after the war, and confined his work almost entirely to landscape or architectural subjects. His painting was firmly *en plein air*, and he preferred the winter to the summer light.

A sense of duty and conviction was no doubt behind John's later career as a champion of Colchester's architectural heritage as well as his increasing involvement in local politics. He was a founder member of the Civic Society which was formed to conserve Colchester's historic buildings. He was the secretary of the Society, and a leading figure. He became a Labour Town and also County Councillor. Some of the more contentious aspects of local politics must have grated harshly on John's sensibilities, but he continued to serve Colchester with zeal and with honour. What little now remains of Colchester's architectural heritage, after the ascendancy of sometimes insensitive developers in the 1970s and 80s, is due in no small part to John's struggle. John was fond of mock eighteenth-century satires, and indeed wrote one about the developers who were then tearing up the Colchester townscape:

> Here neath this costly Tomb lies Tibbetts
> Whose yearly Profits were no Flea-bites
> But pray, do not shrink back in Horror.
> This was paid for by the Borough

John was also an outstanding local historian. He had an encyclopaedic knowledge of eighteenth-century Colchester, and was an authority upon whom many called. He had an enormous handwritten collection of notes and biographical details, largely focusing on Colchester's eighteenth-century citizens, and these extensive researches were for the most part never published. It is thus truly exciting that Shani D'Cruze has published this book, which draws on John's notes and researches. Shani D'Cruze is herself a well-known historian, with a distinguished published *oeuvre*, and an expert on Colchester history, amongst other subjects. So indeed she should be, as she started her own historical research working as John's private assistant, and much of John's archive was put together with her help. This book is a testament to her own talent and also to John's tutelage. She has put into this book some of what John suggested to her, and she has been a champion of his work. However, she has greatly extended that work into a meaningful and coherent narrative, of great subtleness and insight. John might have disagreed with some points but would have applauded others, and would surely have been immensely pleased with its conception and conviction.

The *Colchester Evening Gazette* on 29 November 1993 published a page-long interview with, as the headline put it, 'Gentleman John – traveller, artist, historian and much more – ONE OF A VANISHING BREED OF ENGLISHMAN'. This is only part of his story. He was fundamentally a person with a strong sense of family and tradition, of learning and wisdom. He was one of the wittiest persons I have ever met, and undoubtedly one of the most charming. Many in Colchester have had their lives touched by John in one way or another, and his death on 22 August 1997 was deeply felt. He was, in his time, one of Colchester's most illustrious citizens and the publication of this excellent book, by one of Colchester's most important local historians and one of John's closest friends, is something John would have been very pleased about.

Simon Shorvon
nephew of John Bensusan Butt

The author and publishers are grateful to the estate of John Bensusan Butt for their generous financial support of this book.

Acknowledgements

The completion of this book has been funded by the executors of John Bensusan Butt, to whom my thanks are due for their support. This book owes a large debt of scholarship to the John Bensusan Butt collection of research materials. The companion project to this monograph is the completion of the *John Bensusan Butt Biographical Dictionary of Eighteenth-Century Colchester*, forthcoming during 2008. My work on this book has been aided by the volunteer researchers on that project, Rita and Ken Sharpe and Elizabeth Long. I owe a large debt of gratitude to Paul Coverley and Jane Bedford, the archivists at the Colchester and North East Essex branch of the Essex County Record Office (sadly now closed); their professional skills, their knowledge of the local historical sources and their advice and support have been invaluable. I am grateful for the advice and comments of Nigel Goose, the series editor and to Jane Housham at the University of Hertfordshire Press for her encouragement and patience. Joanne Bailey commented helpfully on the original proposal. Other academic friends, in particular Judith Rowbotham and Efi Avdela have shared some of the knottier problems of the research. My thanks also to Bruce Neville for information from his extensive research into Colchester High Street. June D'Cruze and Jeff St Clair have (as always) been unfailingly there.

Chapter 1

The business of living

Changing fortunes

Colchester is in north-east Essex, on the banks of the River Colne. In the eighteenth century it was a sizeable town of around 10,000 inhabitants. It was the centre of a productive rural hinterland (the grain of East Anglia supplied both regional and the huge London markets) and had a long, if uneven history as a producer of woollen cloth. It was a port and a centre for a range of industries such as malting, milling and salt-refining. Its regular markets, inns, shops and trades attracted custom from the region. Colchester was well placed on lines of communications by sea and land, between London, southern England and continental Europe. Colchester polite society included increasing numbers of (more or less) affluent individuals who chose to move there. The town acquired many of the attractions of polite culture. Its social life was enhanced as it became a garrison town during the Napoleonic period. It was a chartered borough, with its own corporation and courts. Colchester returned two members of parliament on a wide freeburgess franchise, so was of national as well as regional political relevance.[1]

Nevertheless, decline and decreasing national significance have been written into most modern histories of eighteenth-century Colchester. The cloth trade fell off by fits and starts, while the cutting edge of English urban and industrial growth shifted northwards and westwards. The corporation was so shambolic as to surrender the borough charter for twenty years. By the 1840s Colchester was a Tory market town.[2] However, for the twenty-first-century historian processes of de-industrialisation are themselves of interest. Recent historiography of the English eighteenth century also points to leisure, culture and consumption as important loci for understanding the development of modern industrial society. Renewed interest in topics as diverse as the eighteenth-century family, poverty and its management, crime and disorder, as well as the socio-cultural processes of formation of identifiably modern (urban) subjectivities encourage re-examination of Colchester's eighteenth-century history, in particular that of the middle layers of town society.

The eighteenth-century middling sort has proved notoriously difficult to define. Income level, occupation, patterns of consumption, family structure and relationships, property holding and management all contributed to middling identity, but no single factor accounted for it. This was a very diverse social group with numerous gradations of status. French argues that contemporaries used different delineations according to

---

1 J. Cooper *et al.*, *The borough of Colchester, Victoria county history of Essex*, vol. 9 (Woodbridge, 1994), pp. 133–75; G. Martin, *The story of Colchester* (Colchester, 1959); D. Stephenson, *The book of Colchester, a portrait of a town* (Buckingham, 1978); A.F.J. Brown, *Colchester in the eighteenth century* (Colchester, 1969).

2 A.F.J. Brown, *Colchester in the eighteenth century* (Colchester, 1969); A.F.J. Brown, *Colchester 1815–1914*, (Chelmsford, 1980).

social context, something that has made the task of historians harder.[3] In the most comprehensive recent consideration of these questions for the period to 1750, he distinguishes between the internal self-definitions of seventeenth- and early eighteenth-century middlings which were shaped from their locally-focused identities as the 'chief inhabitants' of the parish (or indeed borough) and externally recognisable social, economic or occupational characteristics. [4] My own approaches to what was shared among this heterogeneous group emphasise a nexus of relationships between family, property, credit and office-holding, all matters which, as French argues, focused on localism. However, during the half century following the conclusion of his study, external forces of historical change went some way to shift both the perspectives and indeed the constituency of those who adhered to middling social and cultural patterns in Colchester.

My earlier survey of borough records, newspapers, wills, poll books and administrations for 1735–50 indicated that occupations in Colchester borough included the range of craft trades and amounted to 57.7 per cent of the 1,120 individuals surveyed. There were yeomen and horticulturalists (unsurprisingly present in far greater numbers in the rural parishes), high-street retailers, carpenters and metalworkers, millers, brewers, maltsters and distillers, baymakers and merchants. Of those with known occupations in the borough including the liberties (440 individuals), the baytrade comprised 26.6 per cent, compared to 6.5 per cent of occupations associated with the port at the Hythe, 10.4 per cent in the professions, including physicians, surgeons, apothecaries, schoolteachers, attorneys, scriveners, clergy and non-conformist ministers, and 4.1 per cent gentlemen. These sources under-represented labourers who were only 4.8 per cent of individuals surveyed. Although this sample does not define the middling sort, it indicates its prevalence in local records.[5] Particularly after 1750, the numbers of households in trading and professional occupations nationally increased from around one in seven of the population in 1700 to nearer one in four or five by 1800.[6] Middling incomes ranged from around £50 per year (the minimum necessary to pay poor rates) to around £2,000 per year, though some of the lesser landed gentry commanded only a few hundred

---

3 J. Rule, *Albion's people: English society, 1714–1815* (New York and London, 1992), Chapter 3; H. Barker, *The business of women; female enterprise and urban development in northern England 1760–1830* (Oxford, 2006), p. 8; C. Wiskin, 'Urban businesswomen in eighteenth-century England', in R. Sweet and P. Lane (eds.), *On the town: women and urban life in eighteenth century England* (Aldershot, 2003), pp. 87–110, here pp. 94–5; R. Sweet, *The English town 1680–1840: government, society and culture* (London, 1999), p. 180; H. French, 'The search for the "middle sort of people" in England, 1600–1800', *Historical Journal* (2000), for an overview of the historiography.

4 H. French, *The middle sort of people in provincial England, 1600-1750*, (Oxford, 2007); H. French, 'Social status, localism and the 'middle sort of people' in England 1620–1750', *Past and Present* 166 (2000), pp. 66–99.

5 S. D'Cruze, *The middling sort in provincial England: Politics and social relations in Colchester 1730–1800* (PhD thesis, Essex, 1990), p. 42.

6 P. Sharpe, 'Population and society 1700–1840' in P. Clark and D.M. Palliser (eds.), *The Cambridge urban history of Britain*, Vol. 2, 1540–1840 (Cambridge, 2000), pp. 491–528, here p. 524.

pounds a year and the most prosperous merchants could gross £10,000 annually.[7] The middling sort comprised up to 30 per cent of the population in larger towns.[8] In Colchester, a survey of rateable values suggests a figure of at least 20 per cent middling sort within the town's population in the 1780s and 90s.[9]

Colchester had an impressive past. It had been an important Roman town, fortified to quell the East Anglian tribes and the site of a large temple. The medieval broadcloth industry was damaged following the Black Death here as elsewhere,[10] though better times returned from the late sixteenth century with the introduction of new techniques of woollen cloth manufacture. Colchester's seventeenth-century history was indelibly marked by the events of summer 1648 when the town was occupied by a Royalist army and then besieged for twelve weeks by the Parliamentary forces under General Fairfax. Around 200 houses in six parishes were destroyed, not counting the devastation to churches. St Johns Abbey, St Botolphs and Crouched Friars were laid to waste. Many of Colchester's landmark buildings, including the huge Norman castle and several of its churches remained dilapidated if not ruined into the eighteenth century. The town's troubles continued after the surrender. A heavy fine was raised on the town. Around half of Colchester's population of 10,000 died over eighteen months in the plague of 1665–6, though this population loss was fairly quickly replaced. Brown describes the town in 1670 as accommodating a population of around 9,500 in 2,100 houses. However, the textile depression of 1716 began an

---

7 M. Berg, *Luxury and pleasure in eighteenth-century Britain* (Oxford, 2005) p. 207; Sweet, *The English town*, p. 179.

8 Berg, *Luxury and pleasure*, p. 207.

9 My figure of around 20 per cent middling sort in the Colchester population is based on rateable values shown in Land Tax Assessments for ten Colchester parishes: St Mary-at-the-Walls 1783, St Leonard 1783, St James 1790, St Peter 1778, Holy Trinity 1783, St Nicholas 1792, St Runwald 1783, St Giles 1786, St Botolph 1793, All Saints 1787. The selection was made depending on record availability and the apparent efficiency of the record-keeping. Rateable values remained very constant over the decades, and were the same for parish rates and land tax. Tax payers on property of £1 or £2 per annum rateable value were excluded. Top rateable values could be as high as £40 and £50 for the larger inns, so no clear dividing line could be drawn between middling sort and rentier town gentry. Within these criteria, rate/tax payers (household heads) were assessed as a percentage of the population figures for the parishes in the 1801 Census, less an amount of 30 per cent to account for children, which would in itself tend to an underestimate since population was then growing. These calculations produced a range of between 10.6 per cent of population in St Giles and 22.9 per cent in the prestigious parish of All Saints. These figures were extremes and most parishes produced figures around the average of 13.8 per cent rate payers above the minimum within the adult population. As no clear upper limit can be set to differentiate between the middling sort and the town gentry, this figure is something of an over-estimate of the size of the middling sort. In St James, for example, five rate payers of more than £2 rateable value are listed as 'Esq' and one other is Mrs Wegg of East Hill House. If these can be accounted town gentry, they amount to a little more than 6 per cent of the total rate payers listed in that parish. There is, however, a much more significant under-estimate in that counting rate payers does not include wives and adult children. Rate payers were heads of households, many of whom were married men. Hence around 20 per cent middling sort within the Colchester adult population can be estimated.

10 R.H. Britnell, *Growth and decline in Colchester, 1300–1525* (Cambridge, 1986), pp. 181–205.

out-migration which had resulted by the 1740s in houses being demolished in several parishes. Population growth recommenced only in the 1770s, reaching 11,520 in 1801.[11]

The urbanisation of English society that began in the mid-eighteenth century was a key historical development, then unique in Europe. Population growth in England as a whole was virtually stagnant early in the century so even the slow growth rate of towns at around 5–6 per cent was significant. Although at around 1600 around 8 per cent of the population lived in towns of over 5,000 population, by 1750 the figure was approaching 16 per cent, by 1800 over 27 per cent and by 1841 the proportion was over 50 per cent.[12] Improved rates of agricultural production sustained this larger population and developing communications produced a cohesive urban network and facilitated the marked growth in internal trade. In 1700 Colchester and Norwich were the two largest East Anglian towns (both centres in the cloth trade), followed at some distance by the ports and larger market towns such as Ipswich, Chelmsford and Yarmouth (some 3,000 inhabitants) and satellite textile centres such as Halstead, Braintree, Lavenham and Hadleigh (1,000–3,000 inhabitants). Colchester was therefore the major urban centre in north-east Essex, larger than Chelmsford, the county town. In 1700 the English urban network was dominated by London, the largest metropolis in Europe and by far the largest town in England. Six or seven towns of more than 10,000 inhabitants included regional centres like York, major ports such as Bristol and textile towns in the South West and East Anglia, such as Norwich. Nationally, therefore, Colchester fell into the next ranking, among the twenty-five or so towns with populations between 5,000 and 10,000, compared to the 500 or so English market towns with populations of up to 1,800, and forty or fifty towns of up to 5,000.[13] By 1800, though the giant capital remained the largest single centre, the fastest points of new urban and industrial growth were in the Midlands and the North. Manchester, Sheffield, Birmingham and the Potteries were home to a large sector of the urban population, whereas Colchester had only a little over 11,000 population in 1801.

Provincial urban society is now recognised as a key part of the urban network, where urban culture flourished not as a pale imitation of London, but in lively dialogic relationship with the metropolis. Towns (including smaller towns) were accelerators of social and cultural change. Urban concentration provided better markets for the goods

---

11 P. Morant, *The history and antiquities of the most ancient town of Colchester* (Colchester, 1748), book 2, p. 110, re demolitions; Brown, *Essex at work*, pp. 14–15, 98.

12 E.A. Wrigley, *Poverty, progress and population* (Cambridge, 2004), p. 280; P. Deane, *The first industrial revolution* (Cambridge, 1979), p. 278; E.A. Wrigley and R. Schofield, *The population history of England 1541–1871; a reconstruction* (Cambridge, Mass., 1981).

13 C. Chalkin, *The provincial towns of Georgian England* (London, 1974); C. Chalkin and M. Haviden (eds.), *Rural change and urban growth 1500–1800*, (London, 1974); A. Everitt (ed.), *Perspectives in English urban history* (London, 1973); P. Clark, *Country towns in pre-industrial England* (Leicester, 1981); P. Clark (ed.), *The early modern town* (London, 1976); M. J. Daunton,'Towns and economic growth in eighteenth-century England' in P. Abrams and E. Wrigley (eds.), *Towns in societies* (Cambridge, 1978) , pp. 9–33; P.J. Corfield, *The impact of English towns, 1700–1800* (Oxford, 1982).

and services which were associated with cultures of politeness.[14] Urban society was distinctively gendered; women were the majority of urban inhabitants and had particular visibility and opportunity for work, social association, leisure and pleasure (even where those opportunities amounted to better chances of gleaning a living by begging).[15] A growing body of scholarship on the middling ranks of Georgian urban society delineates the importance and distinctiveness of this social group, though much of this work focuses on London or on larger and faster-growing provincial towns. For example, Hannah Barker's work on Manchester, Liverpool and Sheffield emphasises the dynamic effect middling business, and particularly that of businesswomen, had on those buoyant urban economies.[16] Colchester had its share of businesswomen, from Elizabeth Selly the wealthy brewer who died in 1768 to the numbers of milliners, innkeepers, schoolteachers and women in other trades who were part of the growth of the trading and retail sector in the second half of the century.[17] This study takes a view of eighteenth-century Colchester from the perspective of its middling sort to re-examine the tension between historical processes of comparative urban decline and social modernisation.

Sources

The sources for this book originated in two related projects. My PhD, completed in 1990, investigated the connections between social and political relations among the Colchester middling sort. It used network analysis to map the interactions between individuals in the middling sort and identified figures who as 'community brokers' played important roles in such networks across borough institutions, neighbourhoods and parishes, religious congregations and in kin networks and families. Underpinning this research was a database compiled from a complete search of newspapers, borough records including the borough courts, and wills for

---

14 Wrigley and Schofield, *The population history of England*; E.A. Wrigley, 'Urban growth and agricultural change: England and the continent in the early modern period' in P. Borsay (ed.), *The eighteenth-century town* (London, 1990), pp. 64–75; P. Borsay, *The English urban renaissance: culture and society and the provincial town* (Oxford, 1989); Sweet, *The English town*, pp. 1, 2, 10–12, 194–6; P. Clark *et al.* (ed.), *The Cambridge urban history of Britain* (Cambridge, 2000).

15 Corfield, *The impact*; H. Barker and E. Chalus (eds.), *Gender in eighteenth-century England* (Harlow, 1997); T. Hitchcock, *Down and out in eighteenth-century London* (London, 2004).

16 Barker, *The business of women*; P. Sharpe, 'Gender in the economy: female merchants and family businesses in the British Isles, 1600–1850', *Histoire Sociale — Social History*, 34 (2001), pp. 283–306; M.R. Hunt, *The middling sort: commerce, gender, and the family in England, 1680–1780* (Berkeley and London, 1996); J. Barry and C.W. Brooks, 'The middling sort of people: culture, society, and politics in England, 1550–1800', (London, 1994); J.M. Ellis, *The Georgian town, 1680–1840* (Basingstoke, 2001); Rule, *Albion's people*; J. Ellis, 'Regional and county centres', Chapter 20 in P. Clark *et al.* (eds.), *The Cambridge urban history of Britain* (Cambridge, 2000).

17 *John Bensusan Butt Biographical Dictionary of Eighteenth-Century Colchester* (hereafter JBB BD) (forthcoming 2008), entry for Elizabeth Selly JBB BD/769; S. D'Cruze, '"To acquaint the ladies": women traders in Colchester c.1750–c.1800', *Local Historian*, 17 (1986), 158–62.

the years 1735–50, which was augmented by material from local records across the century.[18]

The second research project is my work in editing and cataloguing the archive of eighteenth-century Colchester history compiled by Mr John Bensusan Butt. His collection of primary source material, accumulated over forty years, has at its core a manuscript biographical dictionary which can identify over 1,000 individuals. Through the accumulation of data from wills, property deeds, local institutional and borough records, published histories, newspapers, correspondence, maps and visual material (including material not on deposit in a public archive), the biographical dictionary contains several hundred extended individual and family histories of the middling sort and 'town gentry', as well as a quantity of less detailed entries.[19] This collection is by no means a complete listing of Colchester traders, professionals and 'leisured' classes. It was accumulated over time through the overlaying of numerous smaller researches and its composition reflects the preoccupations of its compiler. Although some people listed date from the mid-seventeenth century and others had careers lasting well into the nineteenth, the archive is strongest for the middle decades of the eighteenth century. It privileges those with named occupations, who were involved in the borough institutions or who used the local newspaper, the *Ipswich Journal*, to advertise their businesses. It is also stronger on the centre of the town than the Hythe or the liberties – not least because parish rates and Land Tax surveys were listed on a house-by-house basis for many town centre parishes, and alphabetically elsewhere. The material is slanted to the more visible borough records, and pays scant attention to the labouring classes and the poor, though it has the great advantage of tracing individuals from outside the borough who had Colchester associations and of tracking numbers of individuals who migrated out of or into the town. Though there is considerable information on women, the organisation of the data into a biographical dictionary tends to subsume Colchester women into the entries on their male kin. Despite these limitations, the Bensusan Butt archive contains a very rich source of data on eighteenth-century Colchester, particularly for those social groups of at least small property.

This study draws on a database compiled from these two collections of, in all,1,862 individuals in Colchester borough including the liberties named in sources between 1700 and 1810. Of these, 987 have entries in the *Bensusan Butt Biographical Dictionary*. I have used wills as a comprehensive source to round out some of the limitations in the Biographical Dictionary, both from additional notes in the JBB archive and others which are not mentioned there.[20] Using this database as a whole, I have

---

18 D'Cruze, *The middling sort*; S. D'Cruze 'The middling sort in eighteenth-century Colchester: independence, social relations and the community broker', in J. Barry and C. Brooks (eds.), *The middling sort of people, culture, society and politics in England, 1550–1800*, (Basingstoke, 1994), pp. 181–207.

19 The MS material is deposited in the Essex Record Office (hereafter ERO), Acc. C905.

20 The Bensusan Butt (hereafter JBB) archive has notes on 246 wills additional to those of individuals with named entries in the Biographical Dictionary (JBB BD). I have also added 59 wills proved at the local Archdeaconry courts between 1700 and 1720, 154 proved there between 1735 and 1750 as well as 416 wills proved at the Prerogative Court of Canterbury between 1700 and 1810, none of which are noted by JBB.

Table 1.1

Average number of individuals named in sources per decade

	Average individuals per decade	
	1700–49	1750–99
G1: 'town gentry', rentier, esq, 'gent', as well as men with no stated occupation.	29.8	39.2
G2: landed, titled, not necessarily resident but with sustained Colchester connections, e.g. MPs.	4.8	8.2
Land: horticulture and agriculture.	9.0	17.2
Office: includes military, naval, borough, customs.	2.8	10.6
Prof: medical, law, education, clergy, non-conformist ministers.	31.0	78.4
Trade: all trades, crafts, merchants.	142.0	277.0
Women: includes spinsters, widows, wives and those with stated occupations.	17.2	25.2
Overall Averages	33.8	65.11

mapped the numbers of individuals active in Colchester for each decade across the eighteenth century. This survey indicates a clear increase in known individuals in the second half of the century as well as the significant growth in the numbers of professionals, traders, artisans and merchants after 1750. Averages per decade in the first and second halves of the century are summarised in Table 1.1.

Rosemary Sweet argues that later Georgian urban society was 'diverse and in a constant state of flux'.[21] Therefore, the numbers of individuals who persist in the Colchester sources across decades are noteworthy. Ninety individuals first named in the sources in the 1740s can still be traced over ten years later; likewise 73 individuals first appearing in the 1750s and 88 in the 1760s. The 1750s figure decreases due to the suspension of the borough charter at that period. Some long-lived individuals remained entrenched over decades. To take just one example, William Cant, the founder of a dynasty of gardeners (still trading just outside Colchester) was born in 1742, created free burgess in 1765 and died in 1805.[22] Traders and professionals predominate in this sample, which for the most part, is a count of heads of household. The usual size of the middling sort household has been estimated as between four and seven people, including apprentices and servants.[23] Assuming, therefore, around three or four immediate kin in the same household, 90 'persistent' individuals might represent 360 of the Colchester middling sort. Further, if the middling sort comprised around 20 per cent of Colchester's population of a little under 10,000 at mid-century, then 90 persistent individuals might account for around 18 per cent of the middling sort in the town. Not infrequently two or three generations of a family can be identified, including the Cants, the Great family of apothecaries discussed below or the Shillito family of cardmakers reviewed in Chapter 3.

21 Sweet, *English town*, p. 6.

22 William Cant, JBB BD/1141.

23 Sweet, *English town*, p. 182.

Table 1.2

Individuals persisting in the sources for over ten years

Decade	*Trades**	*Prof*	*G1*	*G2*	*Land*	*Office*	*Other*	*Women*	*Total*
1700s	19	6	1	1	1		3		31
1710s	23	5			1	1			30
1720s	29	9		1	1		1	1	42
1730s	48	16		1	2			1	68
1740s	46	28	4		7	4		1	90
1750s	49	15	2	2	2	1		2	73
1760s	60	20	4	3	1				88
1770s	38	12	6	3	5	3	1	1	69
1780s	35	20	2		3	2	1		63
1790s	21	2	3		1	1	1		29
	368	133	22	11	23	12	7	6	583

*see Table 1.1 above for definitions of these categories. Graph shows each category expressed as a percentage of all individuals first appearing that decade.

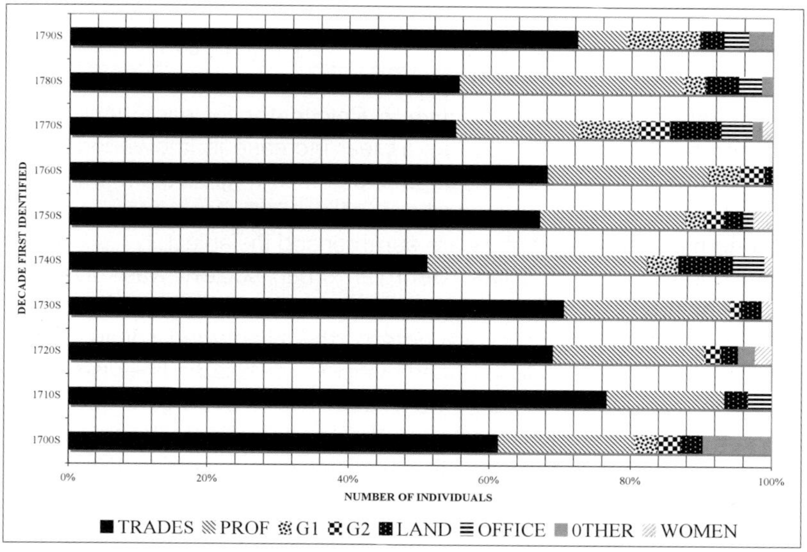

Persistent individuals will necessarily be the most visible in any study which focuses on location. Such stable families left the most legible traces in the local historical record, though in national perspective were probably exceptional. I would argue that such visibility amounted to more than a quirk of my evidence, and does describe something about this specific town. There certainly were people who came and went; Bishop Camplin the coachmaker arrived from London in 1773 and had been imprisoned for debt and left the town by 1777.[24] However, those who stayed anchored the social networks and institutions that coloured the distinct identities of particular provincial towns. Such families were a characteristic component of the Colchester middling sort, where population growth was late and slow and where the staple industry was in decline. The lower figure for persistence in the 1790s (twenty-nine individuals) may be caused by more than the selectiveness of the sources as population growth increased and trade volatility during the French wars took effect.

24 See Chapter 4 below, n. 39.

Structure

The dense and prolific though very particular archive that provides much of the source material for this book allows ideas emerging from current academic research on the eighteenth century to be tested against the 'thick description' of family and individual biographies.[25] Across the chapters which follow, I juxtapose this method against smaller surveys of specific sources, such as the borough petty sessions, wills or mortgages. My intention in this book is to traverse the history of Georgian Colchester from the perspective of its middling sort, and thus to contribute to the now lively field of eighteenth-century urban history an exploration of how middling culture fared as processes of de-industrialisation met with forces of secular economic growth and modernisation in a southern provincial town. This is therefore not a comprehensive social and political history of eighteenth-century Colchester. It lacks in-depth analysis of quarter sessions or London-proved wills (those of the most affluent). It pays more attention to the town centre than the Hythe or the borough liberties and to the town-resident Tory MP Charles Gray than his out-of-town Whig contemporary, Isaac Martin Rebow. It is concerned with gender, though approaches this issue more through discussion of men than women. It is interested in persistence as a characteristic of the Colchester middling sort in a wider urban society more given to instability and change, and in the relationships between the middling family household and business, politics, polite culture and governance.

When researching my PhD as an apprentice historian of gender, I conceptualised and periodised my findings on the men and women of the Colchester middling sort as the immediate prelude to the making of Victorian domesticity and a 'separation in spheres'. Research of the intervening two decades has troubled that conclusion. Returning to the material I see more about violence (in varied forms), about bodies and performance as well as how masculine and feminine subjectivities were produced and reproduced. My earlier emphasis on the middling household family and the contribution of both women and men to its maintenance have been borne out, as has my argument that credit and social connection were vital to middling household survival. What new work has challenged is firstly the reductionist assumption that eighteenth-century Colchester women were automatically empowered in the middling household as well as the notion that public and private were (about to become) distanced and separate structures that regulated an entirely new gender order among the nineteenth-century middle classes. And yet I remain reluctant to take Amanda Vickery's advice to jettison the concepts of public and private altogether.[26] When my source material includes traders who advertised their wares to their 'Friends and the Public' (Chapter 4), a building contractor who fulminates in a business letter that he would not 'favor a whole County to Rob (his) own Family', (Chapter 3) when the right to vote in parliament was a negotiable piece of (private) property, or when the borough corporation was a private institution vis-à-vis the state (Chapter 6), public and private seem to have something to say. Rather than abandon them, I would wish to

25 C. Geertz, 'Thick description' in C. Geertz (ed.), *The Interpretation of cultures* (London, 1975).

26 A. Vickery, 'Golden-age to separate spheres — a review of the categories and chronology of English women's history', *Historical Journal*, 36 (1993), pp. 383–414.

complicate these ideas, reformulating them not as a pair of mutually exclusive opposites, but rather as a culturally recurrent set of juxtapositions that established real but crossable boundaries. The very density of my source material allows the numerous 'micro-sociologies of power'[27] surrounding all these different uses to emerge.

The book will trace a winding course through these issues and questions over eight chapters. Chapter 2 considers the form and something of the uses of urban space both in terms of the architectural changes in the townscape and the design of genteel domestic space as well as contested mappings of urban topography. Chapter 3 addresses the middling family. In the sense of both the household including servants and apprentices and also in wider kinship networks, the family was the key foundation to middling business and culture. The household family depended on and valued the labour and loyalty of all its members, but did this in ways which made rather different and often heavier demands of women than of men. People's key emotional investments were generally vested in their families, which could produce warmth and affection but also tensions, anxiety, conflict and violence. To an extent kinship recognition and obligation was flexible and overlapped with other kinds of social connection. Historiographically, the family has been where the private sphere was once thought to be anchored. This chapter will ask how relations of intimacy, affect and authority played across the juxtaposition of public and private in and around the middling family.

Chapter 4 contextualises middling business and property through an exploration of the mechanisms and reciprocities of credit, both social and financial. Executorships, mortgages and bankruptcies divulge networks of credit and connection, which were public in that they were to do with commerce and business but also private in that they were developed through interpersonal relations and depended crucially on the perceived respectabilities of business and family and thus on the orderliness of intimate relations. Chapter 5 considers polite culture and social association. Genteel material culture underpinned politeness as a social practice. While widely accessible, politeness was a cultural style which required a certain material underpinning. It used gender difference to articulate its social credentials, but invited participation from women and men. It intersected with the eighteenth-century predilection for clubs and associations. Polite culture crossed and re-crossed a social terrain shading between different kinds and degrees of public-ness.

Local politics and government are reviewed in Chapters 6 and 7. The middling sort were necessary to the governance of the town as office holders in the borough and its many other commissions, trusts, charities and parishes. Because the management of parliamentary elections was vested in the borough, office-holding had its own intrinsic politics and was implicated in the political struggles over the parliamentary representation. Men were office holders and voters, but this did not prevent women from having political opinions and involvement, nor from undertaking some of the chores of office. Chapter 6 will consider town governance and locate the middling sort in the history of local politics where political rhetoric of rights and the activities of local political managers were central. The issues raised will be further explored through

27 M.J. Braddick and John Walter (eds.), *Negotiating power in early modern society: order, hierarchy, and subordination in Britain* (Cambridge, 2001).

case studies in Chapter 7.

Chapter 8 examines interpersonal violence and disorderly behaviour. Violence was one technique of local politics and along with drunkenness and wayward sexuality inflected the everyday social practice of (at least some) middling men and women. However, where violence troubled the business of governance it was most often visible as an aspect of popular rather than polite culture. A survey of the petty sessions also demonstrates a shift in the case load across the second half of the century from a predominant concern with the adjudication of interpersonal violence to the administration of the poor law. This trend highlighted the material insecurities of the poor. The axis between the visibility and invisibility of dependency was a salient division between the poor and the middling sort. A conclusion re-surveys Colchester's spatial and cultural terrain in the early nineteenth century by construing the gaze of another of its historians, Borough Chamberlain Benjamin Strutt.

Two tasks remain in this chapter; a survey of Colchester's changing economy will be preceded by some comments on another important factor structuring local society – that of religion.

Grace without enthusiasm

Religion (non-conformity in particular) was perhaps the longest-established form of association which overlaid and exceeded family, contributed to political preference and had its own complex politics. Non-conformity was an important factor in shaping social networks between middling Colcestrians. Non-conformists comprised up to 20 per cent of the population in the eighteenth century, and while being far from the only factor in choice of business and social associates or political party the solidarities of the various non-conformist congregations are evident across middling activities outside religion.[28] It had quietened considerably since its mid-seventeenth-century radicalism, when Colchester was 'swarming with sectaries'.[29] For Anglicans as well as non-conformists, for the first three quarters of the eighteenth century, religious observance was marked by the attainment (in the words of Revd Nathaniel Forster of All Saints) of *Grace without Enthusiasm*.[30] Non-conformity continued to be important in the town, though it had ceased to grow significantly. Despite John Wesley's repeated visits to Colchester, Methodism made comparatively little headway until the following century. Where detailed sources survive (for example for the Eld Lane Baptists or Lion Walk Congregationalists) they show the energies of congregations divided between enforcing doctrinal exactitude and supervising the spiritual and social conduct of their members.

Religion was significant in several overlapping ways to the eighteenth-century Colchester middling sort, and recurs as a factor of social organisation and cultural

28 S. D'Cruze, *'Our times in God's hands', religion and the eighteenth-century middling sort, a study of Colchester,* Studies in Essex history (Chelmsford, 1990), especially pp. 12–19.

29 Cooper *et al.*, *Colchester,* Tudor and Stuart Colchester: religion, pp. 123, 129. Sixteenth-century Colchester also saw persecutions and burnings as radical Protestants opposed Marian Catholicism.

30 N. Forster, *Grace without enthusiasm, a sermon* (Colchester, 1781).

influence throughout the thematic chapters that follow. The old parish boundaries segmented the built area of the town into parishes of different size and importance, from tiny St Runwalds in the town centre to larger and more populous parishes such as St James or St Leonards around the port at the Hythe. The parish was the smallest unit of local government, and the source of poor relief and policing, so parish vestries provided a focus for middling office holders and for the poor. Clergy and non-conformist ministers together were a sizeable group among Colchester's professionals, and included notable sermon writers and scholars. Christian belief systems, although doctrinally 'latitudinarian' were central to eighteenth-century culture.[31] Non-conformist congregations and even Anglican parishes established inclusions and exclusions which were private in relation to the rest of local society. The most significant change in religious culture was the growth of evangelicalism from the 1780s, among both Old Dissenters and Anglicans (particularly in St Peters parish). 'Serious' religion not only had a political effect with the election of the evangelical Robert Thornton as MP in the 1790s, but also tracked back into family and individual subjectivity.[32]

Oysters

In the 1780s, George Reynolds, gentleman innkeeper at the White Hart in Colchester, welcomed travellers to the 'Land of Oysters, Bays and Eringo'.[33] Travel for pleasure was in many ways an eighteenth-century innovation and Reynolds pinpointed the three local products on the tourist route. The first indicates Colchester's maritime aspect as an east coast port and the industrial and commercial activity that developed alongside the coastal trade. The second, the manufacture of woollen cloth, was as indicated the key industry that had shaped the economic and social profile of Early Modern Colchester. The last, eringo, was a quasi-medicinal, allegedly aphrodisiac sweetmeat made from candied sea holly, and can stand for the consumer-oriented retail (and indeed professional) sector which was flourishing by the 1780s. Each of these economic areas comprised an important means of making a living in eighteenth-century Colchester. I will review them in turn.

Oysters did not comprise all of Colchester's fisheries. The shallows and sandbanks around the Essex coast encouraged a proliferation of inshore fishing and there was deep sea fishing for herring, cod and mackerel in the summer.[34] Nevertheless, the native Colchester oyster was a local speciality and the oyster trade was large and valuable for merchants, traders and working fishermen. By the 1830s inshore dredging occupied as many as 2,500 dredgermen in the parishes around Colchester in the summer months. 'Foreign' boats from other east coast ports periodically dredged illegally in the Colne, and Colchester corporation's inefficiency in protecting its fishing

---

31 J. Gregory, 'Christianity and culture: religion, the arts and the sciences in England 1660–1800' in J. Black (ed.), *Culture and society in Britain, 1660–1800* (Manchester, 1997), pp. 102–23.

32 L. Davidoff and C. Hall, *Family fortunes: men and women of the English middle class, 1780–1850* (London, 1987), Chapters 2 and 3.

33 C. Dibdin, *The musical tour of Mr. Dibdin; in which, previous to his embarkation for India, he finished his career as a public character* (Sheffield, 1788), p. 87.

34 H.A. Benham, *Once upon a tide* (Colchester, 1955), pp. 106–8, 110, 114, 124, 149.

rights was a recurrent theme in local politics.[35] Oysters were sent up to London and exported to Dieppe and Dunkirk as well as being traded locally. In 1765 a squabble over the price of oysters was continued publicly between fisherman James Halls and Daniel Manning, innkeeper of the Kings Head Inn. Halls accused innkeepers of selling oysters at 4s 4d per barrel and offered his own at 3s 6d. Halls traded from the High Street as an 'Oyster packer, Dealer in Fish, Rabbets, Lemons &c'. His shop in 1768 was near St Runwalds Church in the Fishmarket, 'where gentlemen may be served with the best Colchester Oysters'.[36]

Colchester's communications with London, the east coast of England and the Continent included packet boats carrying passengers and parcels. There was a weekly passenger service to Ostend from around the 1740s, numbers of slow weekly London packets from the seventeenth century as well as a daily service to Harwich and Ipswich by 1800.[37] The port at the Hythe marked the farthest extent of the River Colne's navigation and by the 1780s was chiefly involved in the coastal shipping trade in corn, coal, lime and timber. One of Colchester's merchants, John Oathwaite, known as 'Humber Jack', shipped woollen yarn to Hull and the developing textile centres of the north each month in the 1770s on the '*Trades Good Hope*, Thomas Wall master'. Wall was organising collection of the yarn from the spinners in the surrounding villages. Oathwaite had come to Colchester in the 1740s and married there, taking over the shipping business then run by Thomas and Sarah Foakes. He left the business to his niece Ann and her husband Daniel Blyth and it later passed to their son Daniel Oathwaite Blyth. In 1816 they acquired three new cutters trading between Colchester, Gainsborough and Hull in place of their brig *Concord* and were also running a packet boat taking passengers and parcels. By 1817 'Oathwaite and Co.' had been trading continuously for forty years and operated maltings at Rowhedge as well as a granary at the Hythe. They continued trading into the 1830s.[38]

The inland coasting trade was vital to the commercial and trade expansion of the eighteenth century, and much of this trade went via London. Huge fleets of colliers brought coal south from Newcastle and Sunderland. Although difficult and dangerous to navigate, the east coast route between London and the north was a major trading artery. Colchester was a staging post in the east coast trade with a number of merchants working the inshore trade in smallish vessels of around sixty tons; numbers of Colchester-owned hoys worked in the grain trade.[39] Agricultural improvement and long-term growth in the production of key foodstuffs, especially grain, was a key precondition for demographic and economic growth. East Anglia was

---

35 Borough Sessions ERO P/Co R 12, 22 August 1738, deposition of Fredrick Nicholson, Wivenhoe, Water Serjeant complaining of threats by dredgermen preventing him from examining Thomas Wright's dredger. For the Colchester fishery; P. Morant, *The history and antiquities of Essex* (Colchester, 1768), Vol. 1, Colchester, book 1, p. 91; Cooper *et al.*, *Colchester*, Georgian politics, p. 163–4; D'Cruze, *Middling sort*, Appendix 6.

36 *Ipswich Journal* (hereafter *IpsJ*) 12 and 19 October 1765, 12 November 1768.

37 D'Cruze, *Middling sort*, pp. 216, 222.

38 JBB BD/627 John Oathwaite, BD/86 Ann Oathwaite Blyth, BD/87 Daniel Oathwaite Blyth, BD/81 Daniel Blyth; Benham, *Tide*, p. 222; *IpsJ* 4 January 1817.

39 Borough Petty Sessions ERO P/Co R 18, 7 November 1774, deposition of Thomas Broom 'Master of the vessel called *Friends Goodwill* belonging to Colchester and employed in the corn trade'.

a major arable producer, in particular for the metropolitan market. Colchester shipped grain to London and elsewhere both from the Hythe and from nearby Wivenhoe at the mouth of the Colne. Colchester's trade grew in the second half of the seventeenth century, shipping out eighty-eight cargos to London in 1684, compared to thirty-eight in 1637–8. In the first quarter of the eighteenth century, Colchester's main outward cargos were woven bays and agricultural produce, though the balance between these two commodities shifted towards agricultural output over the century. Most bays went to London but in earlier decades some were exported to Rotterdam. Inward cargos included coal, wool, wine, tobacco, sugar, oranges, snuff, lemons, ironmongery, fuller's earth and tobacco pipe clay. Hoys arrived from London and Hull with manufactured goods for retail sale. Colchester's china shops often sold both cheese and 'toys', which arrived together as common cargos from the Midlands. Iron, steel and timber came from Sweden and Norway in the 1720s as well as pantiles and brandy from Rotterdam.[40] Colchester was never a port the size of Harwich or Yarmouth; the Colne was never able to take large ships beyond Wivenhoe and the poor maintenance of the navigation was another perennial bone of contention. It suffered when the corporation lost its charter in the middle of the century though later a reinvigorated body of Harbour Commissioners made a rather better job of the navigation (Chapter 6). However, taken together, Colchester and Wivenhoe linked the town into the nationally vital east coast trade. Although primarily an inshore trade, the proximity to the huge entrepôt of London meant that Colchester was also importing tobacco, tea and sugar produced in plantation economies and part of the major international trade flows in commodities and human labour that characterised world trade at that period.

Not all these commodities arrived legitimately. Although rather less spectacular than that on the south coast, where the East Indiamen travelling up the Channel were the key source of supply, east coast smuggling was prolific, given ready access to the Continent and good roads to London. During the first half of the century large, organised operations ran barrels of Amsterdam gin inland from the coastal shallows and on to London.[41] Spirits, wine, tea, tobacco and silk formed the bulk of this illegal trade. Colchester Customs offered confiscated goods for sale in 1787 including 'Brandy 140 gallons, Rum 220 gallons, Geneva 1172 gallons, wine, tea, soap, starch, and orange gourds' and in 1781 they auctioned 5,000 gallons of geneva and 570 of brandy. In 1743 5,900 gallons of old Bordeau and Nantes brandies were sold at Wivenhoe. 'NB the brandy will be put up at Five Shillings per Gallons for the Encouragement of the Bidders.' Hervey Benham argues that smugglers were mostly tradesmen and minor landowners. Robert Chaplin tried in 1779 for running goods valued £26,000 was a victualler in the village of Ardleigh, a few miles from Colchester. Arguably, therefore, the middling sort supplied a good many buyers and sellers of smuggled goods. In 1777 the Customs 'seized out of the Ipswich coach a box of cambrick, containing 112 pieces and sundry bags of fine teas packed up in boxes and

40 N. Goose and J. Cooper, 'Economy', Tudor and Stuart Colchester in Cooper *et al.*, *Colchester*, pp. 85–7; T.S. Willan, *The English coasting trade 1600–1750* (Manchester, 1967), p. 136; J. A. Chartres, *Internal trade in England 1500–1700* (London, 1977); Benham, *Tide*, pp. 33, 37; Cooper *et al.*, *Colchester*, Georgian Colchester: Economy, p. 140.

41 N. Williams, *Contraband cargoes: Seven centuries of smuggling* (London, 1959), pp. 97–105.

hampers; the quantity of tea was upwards of 3 cwt. They are all directed to persons of quality'. In 1713 villagers 'rescued' tea that the Customs had seized on a local farm.[42]

This rescue was one of a number of similar incidents in Essex and Suffolk, and the activities of organised smugglers was sufficiently troubling for the Colchester corporation to petition its MPs for relief in 1779. Such a petition was hardly disinterested, since Colchester was an important centre of Customs operations. A good handful of the Colchester middling sort had Revenue jobs and Captain Daniel Harvey owned and operated a succession of revenue cutters (all named *Repulse*) out of Colchester. [43] In the 1740s his operations amounted to 'quite a little private navy'. Although east coast Revenue officers and ships' crews never faced the extremity of violence that sometimes occurred on the south coast, it could still be a risky business. Several sailors drowned while out chasing smugglers and one of the crew of the Colchester cutter was shot dead in 1742. There were a couple of other fatalities among officers and assisting dragoons in Essex and Suffolk. On the other hand, jobs with the Customs provided useful employment for both working and middling men in the area. Benham argues that the large-scale east-coast smuggling of the earlier eighteenth century, limited rather than significantly challenged by a severely under-resourced Customs organisation, became far more effectively controlled in the period of the French Wars, during and after which smuggling was more to do with marginality and economic hardship rather than the very visible mirror image of legitimate trade that it had been fifty years earlier.[44] Smuggling touches on several ongoing themes of this study; the middling sort as office holders, as both purveyors and consumers of 'luxuries', as well as the greater marginality of the poor by the nineteenth century and the presence of violence in social and economic life.

Over the same fifty-year period, the Hythe became increasingly important as a base for industry. As Stephenson points out, despite the eighteenth-century reverses in textile production,

> Industry was not dead in the town, but increasingly it moved down to the Hythe, so beginning the process by which that area became the hub of the town's industrial life. By the end of the eighteenth century, the Hythe sported coal yards, a salt works, a lime kiln, a foundry and a ship yard.[45]

In terms of function and concentrations of capital, if not of numbers employed, this industry made an important economic contribution. There were an average of 14.2 individuals engaged in industry, commerce and shipping at the Hythe in decades before 1750, and 27.4 individuals per decade thereafter (Table 1.1). The industrial and commercial activity around the Hythe was for the most part controlled by several interlocking networks of merchants, linked by business partnerships, marriage and kinship and often by religious affiliation. It was not uncommon for merchants to spread their capital between the Hythe and the bay trade. Joseph Duffield, alderman and merchant, traded as a cardmaker in the bay trade as well as running a coal

---

42 Benham, *Tide,* pp. 156–60, 185, 173, 166.

43 *Ibid,* pp. 165, 168, 155.

44 *Ibid,* pp. 176. For the wider and more uneven context, Williams, *Contraband cargoes,* pp. 147–203.

45 Stephenson, *Colchester,* p. 91.

merchant's business at the Hythe in a yard leased from 1724 from the corporation. He also ran the Bay Hall and owned the Three Cups Inn.[46]

Later, as large capital was becoming more interested in trade and commerce than cloth production, this coal yard was occupied by Edward Snell.[47] Snell was trading at the Hythe in his early twenties when in 1768 he married Sarah Wood, the daughter of a miller of Great Henny in Suffolk. In 1773 he was operating a lime kiln in partnership with Edward Morley, an established Hythe corn merchant whose father had operated a brig in the coal trade, and had moved into the town centre on retirement.[48] Edward Morley retired to London and died in 1786, leaving over £20,000 to his cousins and the business premises at the Hythe and Wivenhoe to Snell.[49] Meantime Snell had formed a new partnership which his executors continued when he died aged forty-four in 1786, leaving around £6,000 as well as the business. This was inherited by Snell's daughter Sarah and his nephew, Charles Absolom, then a minor. Sarah later married into another Colchester merchant dynasty, the Wallis'.[50] Absolom took over the business in 1794 but died the following year,[51] and so control passed to Sarah and her husband, John Eglonton Wallis, who was also a town-centre grocer and draper. Wallis was bankrupted in 1802, no doubt a victim of turn-of-the-century inflation. His extensive bankrupt sale included: a large 'capital freehold brick fronted messuage' (now 7–9 West Stockwell Street[52]), a high-street shop, a life interest in the Hythe property that derived from Edward Snell, including salt works, cinder ovens, salt pans, counting house and coal yard. Wallis's pastures cottages and a public house in Henny also came from the Snells. The Wallis' were members of Lion Walk congregation and also intermarried with other prosperous non-conformist families. Non-conformity was

---

46 JBB BD/266. Duffield had received farm and town tenement property in his father's will of 1717 (Will Joseph Duffield, All Saints, ERO 8 CR 13). He traded as a cardmaker and had premises in Colchester and with a partner in London (*Essex Review*, Vol. 45, p. 248 for advertisement of 19 October 1719). Hythe Coal Yard Lease, ERO D/DU 518/5, 15 June 1724. In 1728, after the collapse of the Dutch Corporation he also leased the Colchester Wool Hall (Colchester Borough Assembly Book, ERO D/B 5 Gb7, 27 January 1728) with a partner and ran the market there. By his death in 1746 he also owned the large Three Cups Inn. (Will ERO 255 CR 15).

47 JBB BD/267. Thomas and Mary Duffield, siblings of Joseph, ran the yard in the 1740s. They declined the trade in 1750 in favour of William Hickeringill, *IpsJ* 12 May 1750. By 1783 as well as the Granary owned by Morley (rated 5). Edward Snell (JBB BD/815) occupied a house owned by Mrs Hickeringill (rated 7) and two other premises both rated 4, one owned and one rented; St Leonard's rates; Marriage Licence ERO D/ACL 1788, Sarah Snell to J.E. Wallis.

48 *IpsJ*, 8 November 1766, 'The good Brig *Providence* … (carries nearly 108 chaldrons of coal) … (was) … for sale by Mr Edward Morley, merchant in Colchester.' JBB BD/599, Morley's will (National Archives, hereafter NA, PROB 11/1128, proved 22 April 1785) shows him to have retired to St Mary-at-the-Walls, Colchester.

49 JBB BD/600; Will Edward Morley, NA PROB 11/1160, proved 21 June 1787.

50 JBB BD/815. Snell was buried at Great Henny on 28 May 1786 aged 44. His will is NA PROB 11/1143, 3 June 1786.

51 *IpsJ* 24 May 1794 and 25 April, 20 May, 12 September 1795; Will NA PROB 11/1260, proved 20 May 1795; JBB BD/4.

52 Modern house numbers are used throughout.

increasingly common among Hythe merchants as the century progressed. The Freshfields who had earlier run the salt works were Quakers.[53]

The Hythe merchants marshalled the largest reserves of capital in Colchester, particularly after the 1760s. They were a major force on the Harbour Commissioners, a prestigious and influential body founded originally under a statute of William and Mary which from 1780 was undertaking paving and lighting improvements within the town as well as maintaining the navigation. The manufacture and commerce at the Hythe underpinned both economic growth and political influence in Colchester that needs to be set against narratives of the decline of the textile industry and the diminishing prestige of the borough corporation. A merchant's, a ship master's, a Revenue-officer's — or a smuggler's eye view of Colchester and district differed somewhat from the prospect from the Moot Hall door. Maritime Colchester was oriented towards a complex network of waterways and harbours large and small, domestic and foreign, as well as the difficult shipping lanes around the sandbanks of the North Sea. The cat and mouse game of smugglers versus Revenue was played not only at sea and in remote coves and beaches but across an East Anglian hinterland dotted with stashes in safe houses and crossed by the many roads to London. And among the merchants, ship-masters and owners, oyster dredgers and traders, many of the customers and purveyors of contraband goods as well as many of the officers of the Revenue who aimed to control the trade, were numerous members of the middling sort of Colchester and its environs.

Bays

The introduction of the so-called 'New Draperies' in the sixteenth century had revolutionised the production of textiles in Essex and Suffolk. Such new industry stabilised many early modern English towns after a late medieval crisis, and a decline in the older broadcloth manufacture. However, the woollen textile industries throughout southern England were largely at an end by the 1820s and 30s.[54] The techniques of weaving the lighter, long staple New Draperies were brought to Colchester from the late sixteenth century by invited Flemish specialists, known almost universally to Colchester and its historians as 'the Dutch'. 'Dutch' merchants imposed strict quality-control and a system of fines through their monopoly of the market in the Bay Hall at the top of the High Street, a key factor in the success of Colchester bays.[55] The cloth was manufactured on the putting-out system by weavers and spinners (the latter exclusively women and children, the former predominantly men) in their own homes. It is estimated that at the high point of activity before 1700, between a quarter and a third of Colchester's total population was engaged in cloth

---

53 *IpsJ* 13 April 1799, 27 February and 22 May 1802, 19 February 1803; JBB BD/920; D'Cruze. *Our time*; L. Blaxhill, *History of Lion Walk congregational church* (Colchester, 1939).

54 Corfield, *The impact*; P. Clark, *Country towns in pre-industrial England* (Leicester, 1981); Brown, *Colchester*.

55 Morant, *Essex*, Vol. 1, Colchester, book 1, p. 78 for an account of the quality control at the Dutch Bay Hall and the fines or 'Rawbotes' money; N. Goose, 'The Dutch in Colchester', *Immigrants and Minorities* (1982), pp. 261–80.

Table 1.3
Baytrade occupations in Colchester poll books

	Clothiers	Roughers	Weavers	Woolcombers
1768	24	36	224	47
1790	10	5	115	31
1797	4	4	39	4
1820	2	-	34	3
1830	1	-	11	3

From A.F.J. Brown, *Colchester in the eighteenth century* (Colchester, 1969), p. 7.

manufacture.[56] The noise of the looms formed a distinctive background to the working week in the narrow back lanes of the weavers' quarters. Most weavers lived and worked in the town or in villages close by. The spinners were more widely dispersed in the countryside around. Each week the clothier's wagon would call to collect the spun thread and leave the next week's quota of wool to work. Male craftsmen such as woolcombers, roughers and cardmakers were based in their own workshops around the town. Many local watermills were adapted for fulling, though as the trade reduced, the later tendency was to change (back) to corn milling. Baymakers had town houses with large warehouses, whence they controlled the manufacture.[57]

Colchester cloth was sold in Spain, Portugal and Latin America. The light fabric was suitable for warm-climate army uniforms, for nuns' veiling and monks' habits. Though some of the cloth was exported directly via Rotterdam, most undyed bays were sent overland or by sea to London, where factors (merchants) oversaw the final export. The manufacture was a lengthy process, and baymakers' circulating capital was tied over time. Dealing with markets so distant and specialised, disruption frequently occurred as a result of England's foreign wars. Any hostilities with Spain closed the market and let in French competition. Arthur Brown argues that 'from 1700 decline … (in the cloth trade) … was continual, relieved only by booms following the end of each war'. His figures show a collapse in numbers of Colchester weavers from 1,600 in 1707 to 500 in 1784 and 150 in 1807. Cloth-workers voting in Colchester elections show similar reductions (Table 1.3). There is strong demographic evidence for the decline of the trade. The young adults were the first to migrate, predominantly among labouring people.[58] The War of the Spanish Succession to 1713 was a great setback. The post-war recovery proved ineffective and the Dutch Company was dissolved in 1728. However, even as late as 1764 and 1784, renewed post-war booms could look like the return of prosperity.

Trade contraction was marked by recurrent labour disputes with the balance of power in trade relations moving ever towards the baymaker. Disputes over control of the work-process were characteristic of early industrialisation and as a generalisation, capital won out over labour in an ever more complex economy. The weavers' dispute

56 N. Goose, 'English pre-industrial urban communities', *Urban History Year Book* (1982), pp. 27–30.

57 Cooper *et al., Colchester*, pp. 135–8; A.F.J. Brown, *Essex at work 1700–1815* (Chelmsford, 1969); Brown, *Colchester*; ERO D/B 5 Sr188, 11 July 1737, Borough Sessions, Law Inquest Presentment re disturbance due to the noise of the 'Ingine Loombs'.

58 Brown, *Essex at work*, pp. 7, 14–15, 98.

Table 1.4

Last appearances of individuals in baytrade occupations

Last appearance in sources during	*Baymakers*	*Weavers*	*Other baytrade occupations*	*Total*
1700s	12	4	3	19
1710s	7	3	2	12
1720s	5	0	2	7
1730s	6	0	1	7
1740s	5	3	9	17
1750s	6	0	5	11
1760s	4	1	2	7
1770s	7	1	3	11
1780s	8	1	6	15
1790s	5	2	5	12

of 1715 was caused by baymakers attempting to restrict entry to their trade and impose quotas on production to overcome the post-war slump. The weavers struck. A parliamentary enquiry gave victory to the weavers, their last major success, although fifteen years later Colchester quarter sessions regulated wage rates.[59] Revd Philip Morant, the town's eighteenth-century historian, complained at the trade's decline in 1748. From his Tory viewpoint the growth of commerce, with the appearance of more numerous and more elegant shops, smacked of luxury and depravity. As a part of the social group involved in borough administration and, of course, as head of St Mary-at-the-Walls parish vestry, he lamented the passing of the trade as the loss of a means of supporting and managing the town's poor.[60]

In the data compiled here the baytrade features in Colchester sources throughout the century. The denser gathering of source material from the 1740s in the JBB archive means that an average of 28.8 individuals active in the baytrade per decade before 1750 improves to 31.8 thereafter. The trade concentrated as it declined. The poor weavers, never very visible in these sources, were doubtless the first to migrate or take to labouring work, though a good few baymakers, roughers and cardmakers persisted to 1800. Several baymakers were bankrupted in the financial crisis of 1772 and others in the 1790s (Chapter 4). John Baker recommended in his will of 1775 that his wife and executors should not try to continue the trade, though she married another baymaker the following year. Persisting baymakers spread their capital; John Wall's will of 1783 shows that a good deal of his estate was invested in country property in Essex and Suffolk.[61]

The bay trade was still an important local industry at mid-century despite earlier reverses. The trade included a broader range of occupations than Brown's model of a

59 K.H. Burley, *The economic development of Essex in the later seventeenth and early eighteenth centuries* (PhD thesis, London, 1957); A.F.J. Brown, *Essex at work 1700–1815* (Chelmsford, 1969); C.R. Dobson, *Masters and journeymen* (London, 1980); C. Behagg, 'Custom, class and change, the trade societies of Birmingham', *Social History*, 4 (1979), pp. 455–80; J. Rule (ed.) *British trade unionism 1750–1850, the formative years* (London, 1988); J. Langton,'Urban growth and economic change from the late seventeenth century to 1841' in P. Clark (ed.), *Cambridge urban history*.

60 Morant, *Colchester*, book 3, p. 20.

61 JBB BD/910 John Wall, BD/36 John Baker, BD/22 William Argent, BD/396 Benjamin Hall, BD/700 James Robjent 1; Cooper *et al.*, *Colchester*, pp. 135–7.

town characterised by comparatively few affluent baymakers and many poor weavers allows for. Rich baymakers and poor weavers there were a-plenty, but relations between them were buffered by numbers of small baymakers, cardmakers, roughers and multiple-loom weavers. Such artisans often dealt in a small way in wool and thread and put work out to other weavers. Though seventeenth-century prosperity was past, I would argue that, allowing for the setback of the 1720s, the trend towards total extinction in the bay trade accelerated only after the 1760s when competition from Yorkshire had become severe, and the growing Lancashire cotton manufacture was providing an alternative product for warmer climates. The terminal crisis for the trade as a whole arrived only in the 1790s, as the French Wars closed markets for two decades. This period was perhaps more significant than a picture of continual decline from 1700 would tend to suggest.[62] In fact some woollen cloth was made in Colchester until the 1830s. The last woollen cloth factory in Colchester town itself stood on the corner of Moor Lane and East Hill and was run in partnership by Peter Devall and Robert Tabor. This closed on Tabor's death in 1818. It manufactured woollen blankets (in demand in a military town during the French Wars) and also produced some silk cloth. Bourne Mill and another factory on the present site of St Mary Magdalene Church continued to operate until Devall sold the business altogether in 1833.[63]

Eringo

Candied eringo (sea holly) root was first sold in Colchester by apothecary Robert Buxton in the mid-seventeenth century. The recipe passed from Buxton to his apprentice Samuel Great (died 1706). He and two further generations of Greats made eringo a speciality of their apothecary's (and later grocer's) trade. It could still be obtained in the 1860s from a 'maiden lady', a family connection of the Greats, who would make some if requested. Eringo was therefore a curiosity — one of the eccentricities enfolded into Colchester's distinctive urban identity. According to Philip Morant, the town's historian keen to shore up civic pride, eringo was an 'excellent sweetmeat'. Boxes of candied eringo were often presented to visiting dignitaries.[64] The Great (originally from the Flemish, 'Groot') family certainly did well out of it. Their premises throughout the eighteenth century were in the High Street, two doors below the Red Lion, with a sign 'at the Twisted Posts and Pots'. As well as running a successful business, they also owned a collection of paintings, allegedly by Van Dyke, which were another local attraction.[65] The Greats were just one of a number of stable

62 Corfield, *The impact*, pp. 25–7.

63 *Colchester Gazette*, 27 June 1818; H. Laver,'The last days of baymaking in Colchester', *Transactions of the Essex Archaeological Society*, new series, 10 (1906), p. 47; Mark Downe,'Interview with the daughter of the last of the bay makers', *Essex County Standard*, 25 March 1893; ERO Colchester Public Library (hereafter CPL) reference CPL 233, deed of 8 August 1833, Peter Devall to George Round; J. Bensusan Butt, *Essex County Standard*, 22 June 1962.

64 H. Harrod, *Repertory of the records and evidences of the Borough of Colchester* (Colchester, 1865), p. 3; Morant, *Colchester*, book 1, p. 88. For the history and botany of eringo see J.C. Shenstone, 'Flowering plants of the Colchester neighbourhood', *Essex Naturalist* (1887), pp. 32–3.

65 *IpsJ* 31 January 1795,'The Prince of Orange attended divine service at St Peter's Church on Sunday morning. On Monday his Serene Highness viewed the collection of pictures in the

Table 1.5
Growth in trade and professional occupations

	Average individuals per decade	
	1700–49	*1750–99*
Trades:		
Books, printers, music, visual arts	4.0	10.8
Building trades	23.2	35.4
Clothing, hairdressing etc.	14.6	.0
Food and drink including china	17.2	37.4
Furniture and woodworkers	7.8	11.6
Innkeepers	8.2	50.8
Leather and other general trades	4.5	8.4
Metal including clockmaking	16.8	19.8
Horses, carriers, coaching	3.2	8.4
Professions:		
Clergy and non-conformist ministers	9.4	23.4
Education including music masters	4.6	10.2
Law	8.2	22.0
Medical	8.8	22.2

middling families who profited from commercial growth despite cloth trade reverses. Colchester was a centre for clockmaking from the 1600s; the Hedge family continued in the trade until the nineteenth century.[66] At the beginning of the eighteenth century there were silversmiths, milliners, whitesmiths, shoemakers, market gardeners, bakers, butchers and carpenters. As noted above, the trades and professions comprised 68.1 per cent of the 440 individuals in my earlier survey of sources for 1735–50.[67]

As Table 1.5 indicates, by the end of the century Colchester had dancing and music masters, the occasional artist or musician, insurance agents, as well as the (albeit transient) presence of military officers and growing numbers of men and women living on rentier income and patronising the shops, assemblies and other social occasions. The tabulation of average numbers of individuals per decade shown in the sources demonstrates marked increases across both trades and professions between the first and second halves of the century (Figure 1:6). Averages for the professions more than double. As in other towns, including those with far higher growth rates, Colchester saw a pronounced increase in the 'luxury trades'; printers, booksellers, china sellers, milliners, tailors and perukemakers. Among these key growth areas were numbers of women traders, working either as part of a family business, in partnership or trading in their own right.[68]

---

65 *cont.*

possession of Mr. Great, by whom he was presented with a box of Eringo Root which was graciously received.' The Prince was fleeing from the French invasion. The paintings were offered to the National Gallery on 26 April 1854 by William Keymer, heir to the Great family and refused, G.O. Rickwood MS Scrapbook, CPL; JBB BD/367 Samuel Great, BD/368 Thomas Great, BD/201 Rachel Crane, BD/369 Charles Great Keymer.

66 B. Mason, *Clock and watchmaking in Colchester, England* (Colchester, 1969).

67 n. 8 above.

68 S. D'Cruze, 'To acquaint the ladies; women traders in Colchester c1750–c1800', *Local Historian*, 17 (1986), pp. 158–62; Barker, *The business of women*; C. Wiskin, 'Urban businesswomen in

Along with growing numbers of wholesale and retail outlets, Colchester also had its share of markets and fairs. Although some of these had been long established, they were not quaint medieval survivals, but fulfilled a thoroughly modern distribution function in the expanding market economy.[69] The main market day was Saturday when the corn market was held at the Exchange (downstairs from the Bay Hall at the top of the High Street) and the Butter Market, the Gardener's Market, the Fish Market and the Meat Market were arranged in their allotted places down the High Street. Minor markets were held on Wednesdays and Fridays. By the 1820s the market confined itself to Saturday, since by then more shops were available to supply the growing population. A covered market was built behind the Moot Hall in 1813, but traders resisted this attempt to tidy the urban landscape and the market remained in the High Street. Fairs were held in April, June, two in July and the main fair, St Dennis', in October. This last was the main cattle fair and coincided with the mayor-making and general town celebrations. It took until 1840 to remove the cattle market from the town centre.[70]

Road-links, especially to the capital, were improved. Colcestrians could reach London in one day by the stage coach from the 1730s and in six hours in the high-speed post coach by the 1790s. The carrier's wagon rumbled up and down to London throughout the century, through town and village, taking nearly thirty-six hours to make the trip. For the energetic, London was within walking distance. Better road and water transport facilitated trade and improved mobility, particularly for the more affluent population. A few years' residence in London was not incompatible with long-term family settlement in Colchester. Established patterns of domestic service or apprenticeship made it not uncommon for teenagers or young adults to migrate, and certainly among the middling sort, numbers of them returned. John Heathfield had been apprenticed in 1735 to Charles Towson, tinplateman of London for £12. He lived in St Nicholas, Colchester in 1746, and when aged 28 he married Martha Spink. Heathfield then appears to have traded in London for some years, returning to Colchester in 1757 when he set up in All Saints over against the Sea Horse inn, offering brooms and brushes among many other items. At the same time he advertised for an apprentice.[71]

Conclusion

Although in terms of demography and urban ranking the case for Colchester's

---

68 *cont.*

eighteenth-century England', in R Sweet and P. Lane (eds.), *On the town: women and urban life in eighteenth-century England* (Aldershot, 2003), pp. 87–110.

69 Berg, *Luxury and pleasure*, p. 259; P. Morant, *Colchester*, book 1, pp. 80–1; T. Cromwell, *The history and description of the ancient town and borough of Colchester* (Colchester, 1824), p. 182 *et seq.*; B. Strutt, *The history and description of Colchester* (Colchester, 1803), Vol. 2, p. 78.

70 Martin, *Colchester*, pp. 86–7.

71 *Bland's anecdotes*, MS in ERO Acc C905, Box 2, p. 54. JBB BD/424 John Heathfield and *IpsJ* 18 June 1757. On carriers' wagons and coaches, D'Cruze, *The middling sort*, p. 28; MS of lecture, 'Living in style in eighteenth-century Colchester', given by J. Bensusan Butt, 22 February 1967, ERO Acc 905, Box 7; Brown, *Colchester*, p.16.

comparative decline seems clear, this in itself tells us little about urban cultural change and modernisation. Industrialisation and urbanisation affected all of English society and economy and produced growth and increasing complexity in industrial production, the market, commerce, transport networks, the service economy, demography and change in the fabric, size and organisation of urban communities across the country. The historical development of English urban culture involved towns of all sizes and locations, and was equally a product of provincial as well as metropolitan developments. Being a sizeable town comparatively close to London, Colchester stood at the intersection of regional and metropolitan influences. People, things, money, news and ideas as well as the ebb and flow of political manoeuvring moved readily between provincial town and capital. London's influence was huge, but Colchester was far from being a mere suburb of the metropolis. By 1780 Colchester's greater economic complexity and the shifting balance between the textile, commercial and retail sectors was accompanied by social change as local and national developments interacted.

As well as a growing retail sector, and a better transport infrastructure, the material fabric of the town centre changed significantly across the eighteenth century. (Chapter 2) Such developments were embraced by many English provincial towns, large and small, and formed the backdrop to the other proliferating manifestations of polite urban culture.[72] As the economic profile of Colchester changed, the 'persistents' among the middling sort were able to adapt. The Triggs family, who were weavers at mid-century, became prosperous innkeepers and the cardmaking Shillitos (discussed in Chapter 3) became schoolmasters, milliners and wine merchants in the generation of the 1780s and 90s.[73] Not only did this group have the surplus income to indulge in aspects of genteel culture, but they also contributed to its making. They made and sold the clothes, wigs, furniture, food, books, pamphlets and patent medicines that became part of that culture. They supplied the legal, medical, leisure and educational services that it required. They built or re-fronted homes in the desired style. Especially in the Napoleonic period middling men officered the volunteer militias and added a new martial air to their public personas. Across occupational diversity, political and religious difference and a range of income levels there was sufficient common identity: social, family, political and administrative, to make a widely defined middling sort recognisable in the town throughout the eighteenth century whose provincial manners were embedded in new, polite cultural styles.

---

72 P. Borsay, 'The English urban renaissance: the development of provincial urban culture, c.1680–c.1760', *Social History*, 5 (1977), pp. 581–603; P. Borsay, *The English urban renaissance: Culture and society and the provincial town* (Oxford, 1989); C. Chalkin, 'Capital expenditure on building for cultural purposes in provincial England 1730–1830', *Business History*, 21 (1980), pp. 51–70.

73 In Easter 1738, John Triggs the elder, weaver, stood recognisance for his son, John, a woolcomber, for an assault, Borough Quarter Sessions Book ERO D/B 5 Sb5/3. A James Triggs, woolcomber, voted in the 1768 borough election, but by 1772 was landlord of the Griffin in St Runwald with his wife Ann where they bought a case to recover the cost of a quart of beer bought by a counterfeit coin. Colchester Petty Sessions Examination Book, ERO P/CoR 3, 28 February 1772. By 1778 they had moved to the much larger Red Lion in St Nicholas, rated at £50, ERO Q/RPl 1107, Land Tax Assessments for Colchester Borough, 1778. By 1798 the couple had retired to St John's Green, *IpsJ* 21 December 1798. JBB BD/288.

Chapter 2

Status in stone

Town space and urban renaissance

Despite the fact that it was a sizeable and significant town, in 1700 much of Colchester remained confined within its Roman walls, apart from a few streets to the south and east, the habitations at the Hythe (Colchester's port) and ribbon developments down East Hill (Figure 2.1). It was situated on a 'fine eminence'; a gravel hill which encouraged the springs and water courses that provided a good water supply.[1] The River Colne described a wide circuit around the town, bridged at the foot of North and East Hills and again at the Hythe, about a mile east of the main centre. Following the original Roman street grid, Colchester town centre was bisected west to east by a broad High Street running downhill, whose continuation outside the walls was East Hill. At its west end this axis was crossed by another, south to north, comprising Head Street and North Hill. Apart from Botolph Street which wound round outside the town wall to the south-east, linking the High Street to the road to the Hythe, and Gutter Street and Crouch Street, which led into the London road to the south-west, these were the main thoroughfares of the town. Colchester Castle stood behind the main street in All Saints parish at the bottom of the High Street, partly hidden from view by a row of recently built small shops and houses. Larger houses, shops and inns fronted the main roads, while minor lanes divided up the populated areas behind the High Street which contained numerous small houses and shops (especially in the weavers' area around Angel and Bear Lanes) and several larger mansions. Many poorer inhabitants were domiciled in courts and closes, tucked behind the larger streets or to the south in the lanes outside the town walls.[2]

Though Celia Fiennes was impressed by the neatness of the streets in 1698 and in 1722 Defoe thought them 'fair and beautiful', Colchester had a very mixed profile of urban topography. As Defoe went on, 'tho' ... (Colchester) ... may not be said to be finely built, yet there are abundance of good and well-built houses':[3] in other words, practical premises combining domestic and business use for baymakers, rather than the use of architecture to produce the urban prospects that would have pleased polite taste later in the century. The eighteenth century saw a 'renewal and transformation of the (urban) landscape' in English towns, both large and small.[4] In Colchester's case

---

1 P. Morant, *The history and antiquities of the most ancient town of Colchester* (Colchester, 1748), book 1, p. 1; B. Strutt, *The history and description of Colchester* (Colchester, 1803), Vol. 2, p. 1; A. Phillips, *Ten men and Colchester* (Chelmsford, 1985), Chapter 1.

2 J. Cooper *et al.*, *The borough of Colchester, Victoria county history of Essex*, Vol. 9 (Woodbridge, 1994): Georgian Colchester: Topography, pp. 147–53.

3 Cited in G. Martin, *The story of Colchester* (Colchester, 1959), p. 70.

4 P. Borsay, *The English urban renaissance: culture and society and the provincial town* (Oxford, 1989), p. 41.

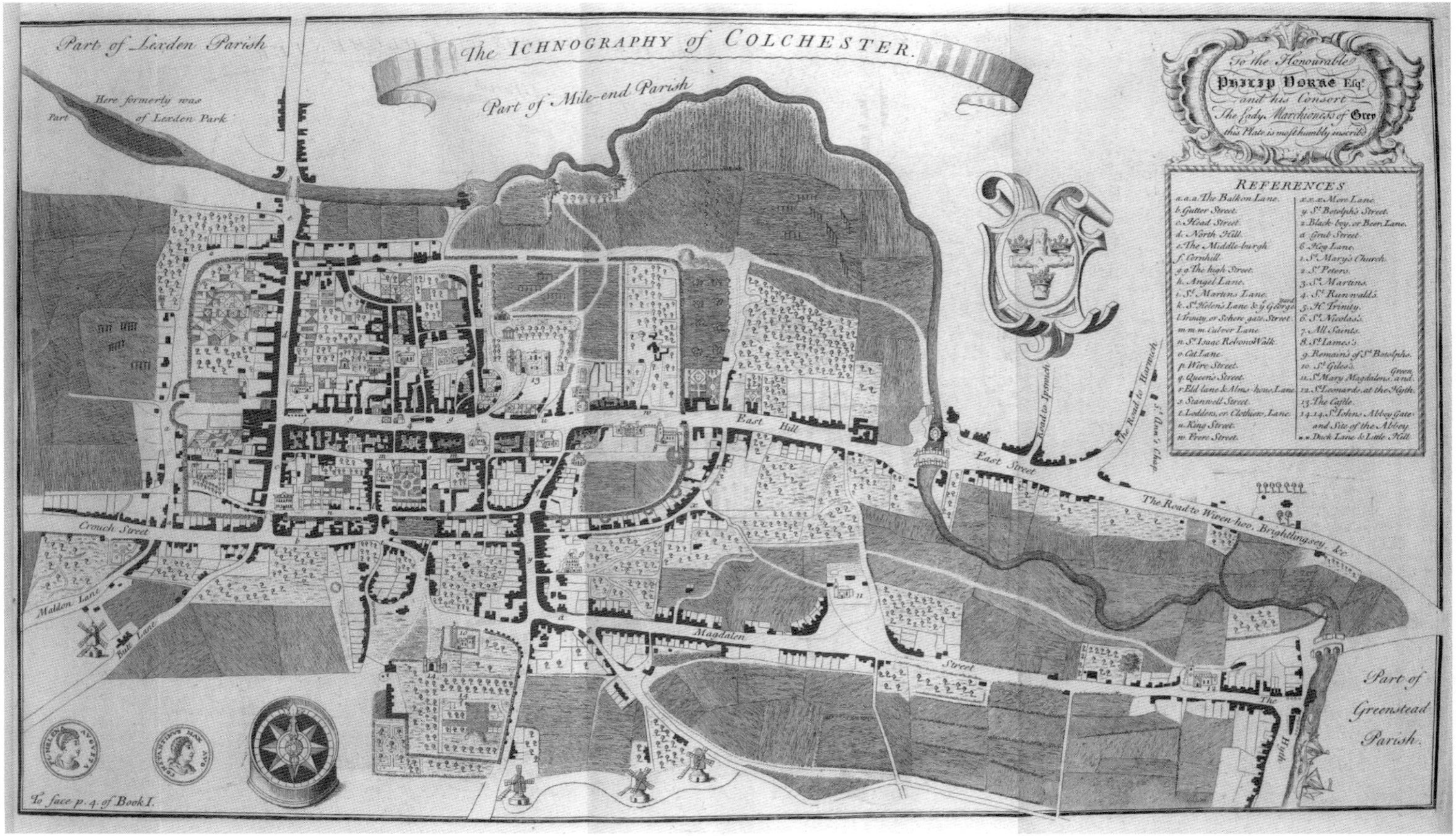

Figure 2.1 James Deane, *Ichonography of Colchester,* 1748. Reproduced courtesy of Essex Record Office

many major buildings including the castle and several churches were dilapidated or partially ruined in 1700. The marks of damage left by the siege of 1648 were by no means eradicated. Early eighteenth-century renovations to St Marys church and later to the castle, St Nicholas and St Peters were undertaken piecemeal, financed by local patrons or owners. However, with the exception of a theatre, built behind the frontage of the Moot Hall in 1764, Colchester did not acquire any completely new prestige public buildings.

The adoption of classical architectural style in place of existing vernacular radically altered the fashionable face of domestic buildings. Light, air and cleanliness were the rational *desiderata* of the urban landscape. Classical architecture was rule-based, and by adopting its principles alongside the wide dissemination of builders' pattern books, provincial builders and architects could readily reproduce the approved style. Colchester builder, William Salmon, was the author of a widely used pattern book, his *Palladio Londoniensis*.[5] Together, owners' renovations (each individual but conforming stylistically) produced distinctive Georgian vistas in central areas of the town. Like other provincial towns, for the most part Colchester adopted simplicity and 'general moderation' in its classical architecture rather than the extravagance of baroque; less perhaps a matter of aesthetic taste and more to do with the practice of local builders working to pattern and the imitation of fashionable style.[6] A new 'capital messuage' was expensive. A builder's estimate for a 'Double Town House' came to £1,100 in the 1740s.[7] Hugh Osborne, a wealthy town gentleman, spent over £4,000 in purchasing, renovating and re-furnishing a mansion in Head Street in the 1760s and 70s.[8] Nevertheless, across the eighteenth century, Colchester acquired a number of elegant new houses and mansions in the classical style. Red brick was most widely used in Colchester, but with the production of 'gault' brick by a supplier in Marks Tey from 1766, numbers of houses in Crouch Street and Lexden Road built in the later eighteenth and early nineteenth centuries are of white brick.[9]

Nevertheless, most of the architectural change in Colchester's urban fabric was through renovation of existing timber-framed buildings. Many were re-fronted, with the original jetted fronts eliminated by building out the lower storey and the whole clad in brick, with new door-cases and windows added. The house now known as the Minories in All Saints (74 High St), then belonging to prosperous baymaker Thomas Boggis received just such treatment in 1776 (Figure 2.2). A central octagonal bay, the height of the house, accommodated the door-case (or 'frontispiece') as well as a two-storey window.[10] Borough Sessions heard many prosecutions for encroachment on the highway by building out under jetted second storeys or adding bow windows or

5 W. Salmon, *Palladio Londinensis or London art of building*, 1st edn, (London, 1734), had reached its eighth edition by 1773; JBB BD/1213; H.M. Colvin, *A biographical dictionary of British architects, 1600–1840* (New Haven, Conn., 1995).

6 Borsay, *The English urban renaissance*, pp. 61–3; Cooper *et al.*, *Colchester*, p. 151.

7 ERO D/DRc 27, James Deane's builders' book.

8 J. Bensusan Butt, 'Typed Boggis Notes III', ERO Acc 905, Box 2.

9 Royal Commission on Historic Monuments for England, *North East Essex*, Vol. 3 (London, 1922), p. 56.

10 J. Bensusan Butt, *The house that Boggis built*, revised edn (Colchester, 1972).

Figure 2.2 Frontage of Thomas Boggis' house, renovated 1776. Reproduced by kind permission of Colchester and Ipswich Museums Service

'pallisades'. A borough committee in 1718 instituted fines of 18d per foot in the main streets and 12d per foot in back streets — but such comparatively low fines did little to halt owners' enthusiasm for architectural improvements.[11] The desire to construct a socially prestigious brick front was generally approved of, and indictments for encroachment on this account were rarely enforced. In 1736 Jonathan Tabor (merchant) was excused for his new front steps in Queen Street and Thomas Hills' extension was overlooked by being respited until the next sessions.[12]

The extent of the consumer demand for architectural renovation is evidenced in the many houses, for example in Angel and Bear Lanes (East and West Stockwell Streets), where owners or occupiers could not afford re-building or re-fronting but simply added modern windows and/or new door-cases to the existing timber-framed fronts. Casement windows cost something like £1 each, and sashes £3.[13] Indeed, timber and plaster construction continued to be used for lower-status houses throughout the century.[14] Overall, therefore, the changes in Colchester's built fabric in the eighteenth century were more to do with renovation of existing buildings than

11 Cooper *et al., Colchester,* p. 149.

12 All examples taken from Borough Sessions Book (ERO D/B Sb5/3) and the Sessions Roll (ERO D/B 5 Sr184) for Midsummer 1736.

13 ERO D/DRc 27, James Deane's builders' book.

14 Cooper *et al., Colchester,* p. 150.

with new building, and with domestic rather than public architecture. Although the most prestigious new mansions cost a pretty penny and were possible only for the town gentry or wealthy merchants or professionals, even modest middling families could participate in the trend by more limited improvements, such as new sash windows.

Urban topography was as much a matter of the spaces between buildings as the buildings themselves. The use of architectural uniformity to organise and frame wider urban environments — streets, squares and sometimes crescents — changed both the style and the nature of urban space, producing ostensibly modern geographies.[15] Colchester owed its broad main streets to its Roman plan. However, the open, light, clean ideal of the urban street proved difficult to achieve in Colchester as in many other towns and cities.[16] Prosecutions for 'nuisances' were a staple of quarter sessions business. Midsummer 1736 Sessions also heard several cases of public nuisance through dunghills. Not all were found, but guilty parties were generally fined sixpence. Erecting posts in the highway was also likely to attract a small fine. Even the great were not immune and Charles Gray MP was fined for this offence on property he owned below the Quaker meeting house in St. Helens Lane.[17] Tanners and other craftsmen pursued their smelly trades close to upscale housing and genteel shops. Several of the ancient town gates remained in 1700 and were only slowly demolished over the century. The shops and shambles of Middle Row including little St Runwalds church, the market hall and the town cage clogged the view down the High Street. The state of the streets remained a problem of governance for much of the century. The High Street was the site of the weekly market including the fish and meat market. In the 1770s rubbish, debris, carts and wheelbarrows as well as pigs still obstructed the passage of polite pedestrians. Only with the Harbour Commissioners' acquisition of powers for urban improvements backed by a rate in 1783, was the paving and the removal of nuisances pursued with any energy. Street lighting came to High Street and other main thoroughfares also in 1783. Nevertheless, throughout the century genteel sensibilities sought out salubrious urban promenades. In 1709 Sir Isaac Rebow improved and gravelled the walk that bears his name and leads from his then house along the top of the southern town wall. St Mary's churchyard was similarly gravelled as a public walk and lime trees were planted.[18]

In 1700, cloth manufacture and horticulture flourished among Colchester's industrial spaces, derelict structures, ruined churches and castle, and the few large half-timbered commercial, domestic and civic buildings such as the Red Lion Inn, the Bay Hall and the Moot Hall in the town centre. Compared to the height of the bay trade in the seventeenth century, housing density had decreased. Houses were demolished in several parishes up until the 1740s. This opened the way for the creation of more orchards and gardens within the town itself. By the middle of the century, for example, there were gardens near the tanyard in St Peters and on the site

---

15 M. Ogborn, *Spaces of modernity; London's geographies 1680–1780,* (New York, 1998), pp. 25, 76.

16 Borsay, *The English urban renaissance,* p. 43.

17 See note 12 above.

18 Morant, *Colchester,* book 1, p. 4; book 2, p 4.

of St James rectory (demolished during the siege).[19] There were extensive market gardens inside and outside the walls, at the bottom of Angel Lane, for example.[20] Behind North Hill the land was used for cultivation and grazing, as well as for tenter fields to stretch newly woven woollen cloth. Much of the area between Holy Trinity church and Head Street was the garden of the ancient half-timbered mansion now known as Tymperleys. The Priory (now Greyfriars) at the top of East Hill was a market garden until a prestigious mansion was built by the Revd and Mrs John Halls at mid-century. Similarly there was cultivated ground within the walls between Balkerne Gate and Head Street. Many other market gardens (a speciality apparently much developed by the Flemish immigrants) surrounded the town behind East Hill and to the south and east.[21]

The genteel 'capital messuage' required its ornamental garden. Revd William Smythies at St Peters planted fruit trees in the garden of his new-built house.[22] Maps of 1748 and 1767 show extensive gardens to houses on North and East Hills, Angel Lane and elsewhere. Those who could afford it enclosed land for gardens, and in so doing marked wider boundaries around domestic space.[23] The maintenance of Colchester's Roman walls was kept up only when landowners did repairs to fence their property. Property deeds show numbers of examples where land was exchanged, walls were built and access rights bought out so that a house should have its garden. George Wegg could not halt the annual cattle fair held on the Berryfield behind East Hill House. He did however successfully do away with everyday intrusions by buying up properties in Queen Street and closing off their back entrances.[24] Charles Gray at Hollytrees was also jealous of his boundaries and bought up neighbouring properties. An emollient letter to him from his neighbour, baymaker Charles Hills, discusses a plan for a bow window:

> Sir,
> My Brother informs me he has had some conversation with you concerning my Summer-House. With respect to having a Bow-Window, I never entertain'd the least thought of such a thing. I only mentioned that it would be a great Addition to the Place. I already think myself greatly obliged to your very kind indulgence in granting me the Liberty to carry it out a few Inches further, but, if, on consideration, you find that even such Alteration will be disagreeable to you in the least, I shall be happy to have it remain in its present state.
> I am,
> Sir, your most obedt Humb Servt
> Charles Hills[25]

---

19 Cooper *et al., Colchester,* p. 152.

20 JBB BD/30 Edward Auston.

21 'Greyfriars' property is in All Saints with some of its grounds in St James. St James rates ERO D/P 138; All Saints rates ERO D/P 200. Revd and Mrs Halls moved into their mansion between 1754 and 1755. Their previous house in Holy Trinity was empty when advertised in *IpsJ* 30 August 1755. See also J. Venn, *Alumni Cantabrigiensis,* (Cambridge, 1922-1927), p. 291; Martin, *Colchester,* p. 54.

22 ERO D/P 178/1/4, Note in front cover of parish registers dated 18 March 1763.

23 J. Ellis,'Georgian town gardens', *History today,* 50, (2000), pp. 38-45.

24 JBB BD/931 George Wegg jnr.

25 ERO D/DRg4/41.

If the urban renaissance in eighteenth-century provincial towns involved the renovation and changing nature of outdoor urban space against the backdrop of classical architectural frontages, in Colchester this meant both streets and gardens. Aspirations towards clean, orderly thoroughfares battled against the costs and the difficulties of enforcing controls of nuisances. Gardens certainly made towns more pleasant places to live and walk in, and in Colchester the amount of cultivated ground increased until early in the nineteenth century when new infill building eroded green spaces.[26] However, to the extent that house demolition and dereliction made the space available for cultivation, the gardens themselves were reminders that the urban economy had shifted. Where those gardens were walled and attached to private houses they enhanced genteel domesticity and opened new spaces for sociability around the home, but also drew boundaries between those who could thoroughly fulfil a polite lifestyle and those who lost out.

Interior space

The urban renaissance did not halt at the front doors of Colchester's rebuilt or renovated homes. Interior as well as exterior space could become genteel if funds and taste allowed. Classical architecture sought to rationalise interior space and subdivide its uses, for those with sufficient resources to command enough rooms and halls to make such differentiation possible. Compared with the multiple uses of domestic space that Weatherill suggests for earlier in the century, and which persisted for the less well-to-do, the classical interior had the potential to shift how domestic space was organised.[27]

Advertisements for house sales can give a good deal of information on the division of domestic space. For example:

> To be sold at Colchester in Essex
>
> A Good New-built HOUSE, with Brick Front, sash'd, with a handsome Frontispiece and good Entrance, with Parlours on each side, one of them neatly wainscotted and hung with a good Paper, a neat Chimney-piece and two Beaufets[28] hung with a good Paper, several Bed-chambers hung with new papers, with all desirable conveniences: a handsome good Dining-room wainscotted in the newest Taste, hung with one of the best Papers, and an elegant Chimney-piece; a Kitchen with Store-room and Pantries &c. Sundry rooms for Servants, a Laundry and Cellars, a good Brew Office with Terras-Cistern and Lead Pump fixed in the Brew Office; in the Yard another Pump well supplied with water; a Garden well laid out, with a good Brick Wall, some good Wall-fruit and Espaliers, a neat Summerhouse and a Grotto, with a curious piece of Roman Pavement in the Garden; Coach-house and Stables and many other conveniences without doors. The above House situated in the best Part of the Town for the Conveniency of Markets &c, a pretty Prospect from the Backside of the House.

---

26 Cooper *et al.*, *Colchester*, p. 153.

27 L. Weatherill, *Consumer behaviour and material culture in Britain, 1660–1760* (London, 1998), pp. 6–15; J. Kross, 'Mansions, men, women, and the creation of multiple publics in eighteenth-century British North America', *Journal of Social History*, 33 (1999), pp. 385.

28 Open cupboards each side of the fireplace.

Many other Recommendations might be advanced in favour of the House; as Bells hung, Locks on Doors &c, the Rooms all being ready to fit up with Furniture directly.

For further Particulars enquire of Henry Lodge in Colchester.[29]

Lodge begins his narrative tour at the entrance — the handsome frontispiece which signifies social status. He is concerned with the reception rooms far more than the bedrooms, which are dealt with fairly quickly before he again pauses in the drawing room. The order of the description suggests that the drawing room is on the first floor. Returning to the ground floor (perhaps by a back stairway) he also spends some energy listing the offices. Satisfactory genteel lifestyles required a household that was also a unit of production-for-consumption. He also mentions the (both ornamental and productive) garden, graced by real and manufactured antiquities. Air, light and water are important as well as central situation in the town. Coach houses and stables indicate the socio-economic positioning of a prospective purchaser.

This house description is one of the very many published in the *Ipswich Journal* over the second half of the century. The JBB archive records twenty-nine advertisements of domestic or retail property for sale or let before 1760, with an additional three advertisements for household goods alone. There were forty-four such house sales in the 1760s (seven for household goods), sixty-two in the 1790s (24 for household goods) and 75 between 1800 and 1810 (28 for household goods).[30] Taken together such descriptions comprise a fragmented yet persistent narrative that reiterated Colchester's credentials as a locus of genteel society and urban renaissance. Such priorities are visually mapped in the plan of Michael Robert Hills' house in Queen Street[31] (Figure 2.3). Hills was the son of a baymaking family who cut his ties with trade and ended his days as a gentleman on a country estate in Earls Colne. The frontage of the house still stands and is not unimposing from the street. On the plan, however, it is dwarfed by the emphatically walled space of the garden, itself subdivided into 'lawn' and the garden proper. A large entrance hall with curved staircase had smaller parlours to left and right. The larger ground floor rooms were to the back of the house, giving onto the lawn rather than the busy street. Wash-house, laundry, greenhouse and yard enclose the main house, all these securely separated from the lawn by a wall. The offices were integral to the functioning of the house as a household, but the 'backstage' labour of domestic reproduction was to be screened from the living area.[32] The more prestigious rooms give onto the garden and were accessed from the large hall, bypassing the smaller parlours.

Where space and affluence allowed there is some evidence of separation between domestic and business or working space. In 1807 the property of Samuel Cooke,

---

29 *IpsJ* 6 May 1769; This was a house rebuilt on the site of the Old Queens Head next to the Moot Hall. JBB BD/538 Henry Lodge.

30 Supplementary Index 1983, 'Sales', in ERO Acc 905, Box 1. Industrial premises, agricultural land and trading stock are excluded. Domestic and retail premises, household goods and furniture are included. Counts only advertisements for Colchester borough and liberties, hence excludes other sales within the social and geographical ambit of Colcestrians.

31 ERO C/T 475/41 c.1789; JBB BD/445 M.R. Hills.

32 Weatherill, *Consumer behaviour*, p. 144.

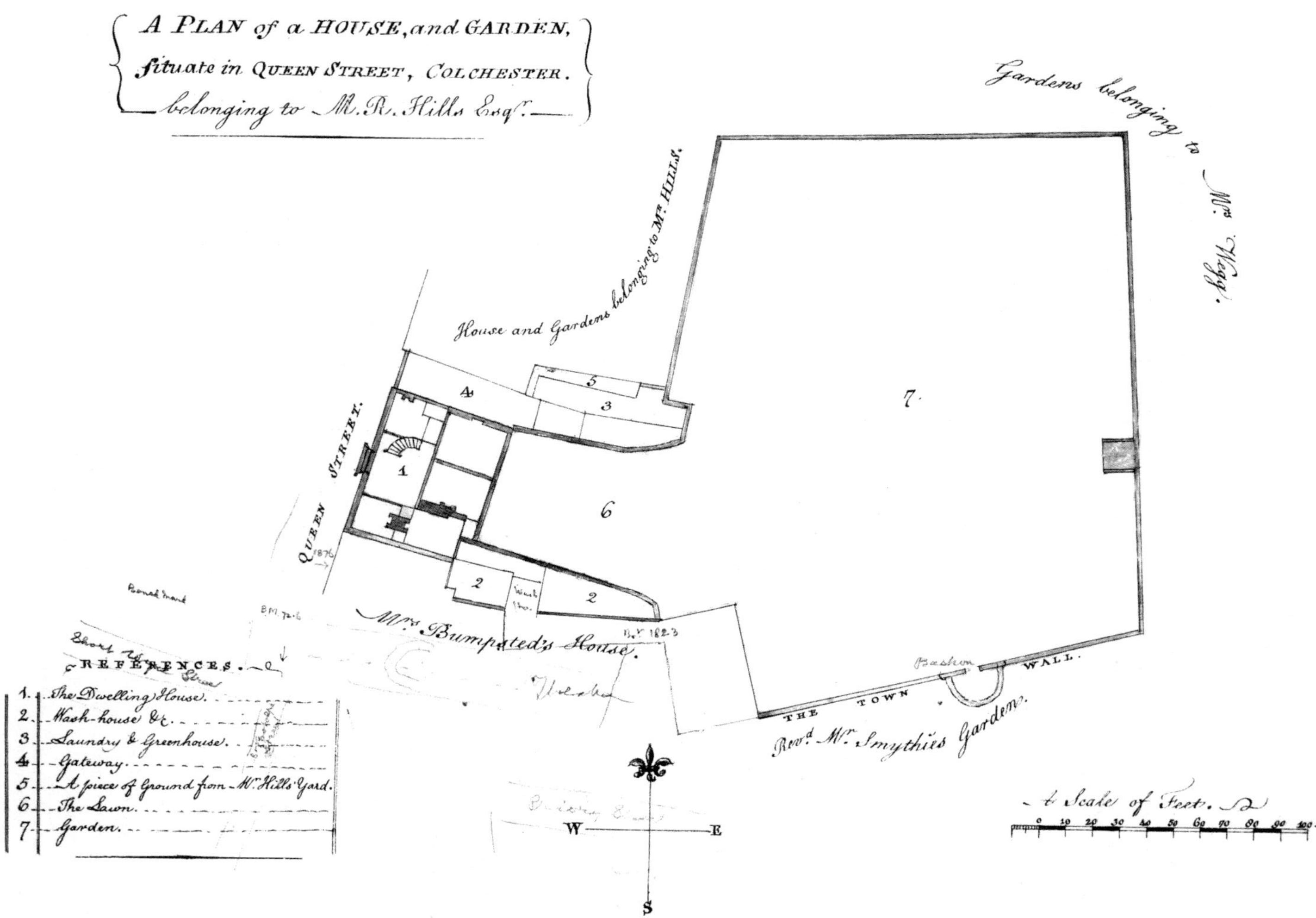

Figure 2.3 Plan of Michael Robert Hills' mansion in Queen Street, c. 1789. Reproduced courtesy of Essex Record Office. ERO C/T 478/41

merchant then deceased was advertised. At his comfortable house on the River Colne at Rowhedge the river frontage across the road from the house had been converted into a walled flower garden, whereas the warehouse was across the river at Wivenhoe.[33] The preference for a garden prospect for the larger reception rooms is repeated in other Colchester 'capital messuages'. The prospect that such rooms afforded was more likely to be formally designed ornamental gardens than the 'naturalised' landscape gardening then being adopted at many country estates.[34] Like the formal promenades in St Mary's Churchyard on along Sir Isaac's Walk, these gardens were spaces for sociality perhaps more than recreating a pastoral idyll. When in 1776 baymaker Thomas Boggis renovated his half-timbered house as well as the classical frontage he had built a garden room with French windows and an elegant curved staircase, an additional parlour and above these a first floor large reception room with a bow window. Revd Richard Daniell (St Martins House) in West Stockwell Street also acquired a garden room designed by James Deane. Such genteel apartments were the setting for much of Colchester's polite social interaction.

Charles Gray's mansion (Hollytrees) also has a garden prospect. Mary Rebow, the MP's wife wrote to her husband in the 1770s when Gray was elderly:

> We meet nothing but fine folks at ye Grays, Mrs Linn & Leson, Mr & Mrs Wegg and the two Misses &c and Mr Smyth, a sweetheart of ye youngest, Mr Mrs and Miss Round and Mrs Keeling ... Old Daddy ... (Gray) ... has got so stout and well as to dress himself out in his Bag Wig to make Mr Hopkins a visit, and to likewise hold a court at Brightlingsea last Thursday.[35]

A local political satire of 1768, couched as a fictitious letter from a lady visiting Colchester, cries:

> But what makes me stark staring mad is, that on entrance to any house, you are instantly ushered into a back room, and there, *sans ceremonie*, fixed to a card-table, among a set of lusty, avaricious old matrons, and battered half-bred beaus, who, though we never play for more than three-pence a fish at Quadrille, often a penny, are as earnest, and quarrelsome as if they had not other pin-money than what they culled out at cards ...[36]

The location of genteel social space towards the rear of the house does something to explain this description; Colchester card parties were not immured in second-rate rooms. It was the quality of the play and the players which made them objectionable. The Colchester pattern differs somewhat from that often adopted in London, where the main reception rooms were on the first floor overlooking the street.[37] The higher premium on the size of metropolitan building plots and the greater preponderance of newer terraced housing stock must in part account for these different provincial spatialities. Genteel domestic social space (including the formal garden) was

33 *IpsJ* 18 January 1807; JBB BD/190 Samuel Cooke.

34 T. Williamson, *Polite landscapes: garden and society in eighteenth-century England* (Stroud, 1995); D. Cruickshank and N. Burton, *Life in the Georgian city* (London, 1990), Chapter 4.

35 Mary Rebow to Isaac Martin Rebow. ERO, Rebow Papers, D/DHt B1, Box 2. The company was composed of town and country gentry, ERO Acc. 905, Box 14, 'Addenda in progress', draft biographical dictionary entry for Charles Gray.

36 *Extract of a letter from a lady in Colchester to her friend in town* (Colchester, 1768), pp. 5–6.

37 Cruickshank and Burton, *Life in the Georgian city*, p. 54.

positioned between the parts of the house accessed most directly from the street (the hallway and front parlours) and the bedrooms, where morning visitors were sometimes entertained. This differentiation hints at the gendering of domestic space, but the links between gender, class and uneven privatisation of domesticity are anything but straightforward. Such reception rooms were by definition not private, but they were secluded from the public thoroughfare and positioned deeper in the house plan than the smaller parlours.[38] They were reached by a journey from the street, through the impressive doorway and the large hall. They could not be casually overlooked and were entered by invitation. However deep in the house plan, they were designed as the sites of 'frontstage' social interaction which called for the presence of both men and women acting out polite gender identities. The composition of James Dunthorne's watercolour of a Colchester card party made the young, attractive, genteel, affluent Mary Keeling its centrepiece.[39] The satire of Colchester card parties uses contrasting and conventional gender stereotypes to mock the card players, both women and men. Lusty, avaricious, elderly and masculine women contended with effeminate beaus for (feminine and trivial) pin money. Polite domestic space saw the intersection of fields of polite culture and domesticity – each gendered but mutually constitutive, rather than separate, spheres.[40]

Such differentiated domestic space might have been desirable but many prosperous middling families and even town gentry occupied older houses that were not so fully renovated to eighteenth-century fashions. The Lechmere sisters, who leased the house owned by the trustees of Winsley's charity, were of affluent clerical stock with family silver to bequeath by will. Their nephew became Borough Recorder in 1790. This seventeenth-century house was originally designed for occupation by a baymaker and only partially 'beautified' early in the eighteenth century. Here, the

38 Lawrence Stone argued that division of domestic space indicated a long-term historical shift towards privacy, L. Stone, *Family, sex and marriage in early modern England,* 2nd edn, (Harmondsworth, 1979). Hanson's morphological analysis of domestic space, of the depth or shallowness of the positioning of different rooms, elides restricted access to rooms with privacy and fairly uncritically maps this against Stone's model of the evolution of the companionate family. J. Hanson, *Decoding homes and houses* (Cambridge, 1998), esp. pp. 66–76. A more nuanced treatment of her methodology by Brown for the seventeenth century confirms her finding of the movement of the parlour from a deep (private) to a more shallow place in the plan of middling-sort houses in London, but is more qualified as to whether the 'shallow' parlour at the front of the house was becoming a space of domestic life away from the places of household labour and/or a place for social mediation between middling households and visitors and thus prefiguring the nineteenth- and early twentieth-century lower middle and working class parlour, F.E. Brown,'Continuity and change in the urban house: developments in domestic space organisation in seventeenth-century London', *Comparative Studies in Society and History,* 28 (1986), pp. 558–90.

39 Weatherill, *Consumer behaviour,* p. 81; Chapter 5 below; W.G. Benham, 'The Dunthornes of Colchester', *Essex Review* 10 (1901), pp. 27–35; John Bensusan Butt, draft biographical dictionary entry for Charles Gray, ERO ACC. 905, Box 14,'Addenda in progress'.

40 Ogborn, *Spaces of modernity,* p. 79, re the mutual constitution of public and private; P. Bourdieu, *Outline of a theory of practice,* ed. R.T. Nice (Cambridge, 1977); L. McNay, 'Gender, habitus and the field – Pierre Bourdieu and the limits of reflexivity', *Theory, Culture and Society,* 16 (1999), pp. 95–117.

largest reception rooms look onto the street. Their rear parlour overlooked not the garden, but the kitchen entrance and yard, and was the route from the offices to the back (servants') staircase.[41] Many trading families lived over the shop and like *Evelina*'s uncomfortably ungenteel trading cousins, the Branghtons, accessed their living space through the business premises. The draper Kendalls, next door to the Red Lion occupied a tall, narrow house over several storeys, with the family rooms between the servants in the attic and the shop fronting the street. Prosperous grocers, Samuel and Maria Carr (11 High Street) occupied a house that was a hybrid between the patterns of affluent fashionable domestic space and practical yet genteel trading premises. They entered their house through the shop, but had improved their premises with an ornate first-floor bow window. Probably their most genteel room was a virtually detached garden room. This was surrounded and overlooked by the backs of other High Street traders, but still owned a large ornate fireplace and walls lined throughout with wooden panelling decorated with (badly) painted landscape views in oils.[42]

Descriptions of houses to let or for sale combined with the remaining material evidence and the few surviving house plans reveal something about the fashionable layout of genteel domestic space, though this remained only an aspiration for many because of the kind of material environment many middling households occupied. Furthermore the social uses of space can never be directly assumed from its layout or even its furnishings and decoration. As Tim Meldrum warns, even the most elaborated architectural intentions could be subverted in day-to-day domestic practice. The footman could always choose to use the front stairs.[43]

For the less prosperous, even among those with middling pretensions, living spaces had even less differentiation. William Blackwell kept the Black Boy Inn in the 1790s. By the time of his death he was living as a broker in St Giles parish. His will shows the potential complications of rights and occupation when domestic space was

---

41 Will of Maria Sophia Lechmere, NA PROB11/1130, proved 4 May 1785, her mother Rebeckah Lechmere, widow, Colchester, NA PROB11/833, proved 19 October 1757; her sister Lucy Lechmere, spinster, All Saints, Colchester, NA PROB11/903, 13 November 1764; plan of Winsley's accompanies JBB's report to the Winsley's Trustees in ERO Acc 905, Box 7.

42 F. Burney, *Evelina, or, a young lady's entrance into the world. In a series of letters* (London, 1779), Vol. 2, especially pp. 79–81 for the Branghtons' table manners, and pp. 117–27 for a visit to Vauxhall Gardens; JBB BD/1012 Robert Kendall, BD/151 Samuel Carr; ERO ACC 905, Box 8, notes on 'Neal and Robards', John Hayes to John Bensusan Butt of 3 November 1989 suggesting that the panels at 11 High Street were of later date that the 1700 suggested by Royal Commission on Historic Monuments for England, *North East Essex*, Vol. 3, (London, 1922), pp. 54–6.

43 Attempts to map the uses of domestic space through house plans and inventories are sometimes over-confident that the historical uses of space can be interpreted from the layout of rooms and even the deployment of things in different rooms, for example A.F. Kelsall, 'The house plan in the later seventeenth century', *Post-Medieval Archaeology*, 8 (1974), pp. 80–92; A. Dyer, 'Urban housing', *Post-Medieval Archaeology*, 15 (1981), pp. 207–18; U. Priestly and P. Corfield, 'Rooms and room use in Norwich housing', *Post-Medieval Archaeology*, 16 (1982), pp. 93–123; even to an extent F.E. Brown, 'Continuity and change in the urban house: developments in domestic space organisation in seventeenth-century London', *Comparative Studies in Society and History*, 28 (1986), pp. 558–90. For a criticism of such approaches, T. Meldrum, 'Domestic service, privacy and the eighteenth-century metropolitan household', *Urban History*, 26 (1999), pp. 27–39, here p. 29.

limited. He divided his house into three parts; the middle (lower room and one chamber over) was left to his wife Sarah. The west and east parts were to be sold for the benefit of his wife and son-in-law James Prentice and comprised on the west one cellar and two lower rooms, two chambers over, kitchen and a passage to the privy; and on the east one lower room, one chamber over, one small kitchen, large yard and small ground.[44] Sarah was presumably to live without the use of domestic offices, lodging rather than keeping house. Tenement properties were often heavily in-mated and living space hardly secluded. For example, the assignment of a lease of properties in East Street over the bridge from Samuel Pooley and Eliz his wife to Henry Hynard of 16 June 1794 recites titles and occupancies back to 1709. The properties consisted of its interleaved ground-floor rooms, chambers over and garrets, with a bewildering array of titles, interests and occupancies.[45] As the discussion of the Shillito family in the following chapter suggests, many respectable middling families who adopted some of the attributes of polite culture had to do so in crowded household space which accommodated one or more businesses as well as domestic life. There is little direct evidence as to how Colchester families achieved this, though foregrounding social rituals such as meals around a laid table, making dedicated space in busy rooms for a shelf displaying china or a few books seem likely tactics. In 1790s London, even before they could afford more than a single room, the young married Francis Place and his wife made a temporal division, finishing their week's work by Saturday lunchtime and then cleaning and domesticating their living space and putting on their good clothes for Saturday evening.[46]

Mapping local history

Urban renaissance involved a prospect of the townscape as a whole and eighteenth-century mapmaking was both a genteel art and a technology of knowledge that delineated and described urban space in culturally satisfying ways. Copeland argues that mapping conventions are necessarily imbricated in prevailing cultural imaginaries; reading a map conjures culturally positioned geographies. Maps make space legible, a process that is suffused with power but not always only power from the 'top down'. Mapmaking in the eighteenth century was a commercial operation and could shape geographies to suit its heterogeneous markets.[47] James Deane labelled the town plan

44 Lived in St Leonards in 1796, cf his bill in the overseers accounts, ERO D/P 245/12/4. His will is ERO 436 CR 19, 1806.

45 Original deed purchased by JBB in ERO Acc 905, Box 7.

46 Weatherill, *Consumer behaviour*, pp. 7–13 ; M. Thale (ed.), *The autobiography of Francis Place, 1771–1854* (Cambridge, 1972), pp. 116, 124, 138.

47 Of the growing literature on the cultural history of cartography I have found particularly helpful: E. Copeland, 'Defoe and the London wall: mapped perspectives', *Eighteenth-Century Fiction* (1998); A. Sills, 'Eighteenth-century cartographic studies: A brief survey', *Literature Compass*, 4 (2007), pp. 981–1002; M.S. Pedley, *The commerce of cartography: Making and marketing maps in eighteenth-century France and England* (Chicago, 2005); C. Withers, 'Eighteenth-century geography: texts, practices, sites', *Progress in Human Geography*, 30 (2006), pp. 711–29; P. Whitridge, 'Landscapes, houses, bodies, things: "place" and the archaeology of Inuit imaginaries', *Journal of Archaeological Method and Theory*, 11 (2004), pp. 213–50; M. Yonemoto, 'The "spatial vernacular" in Tokugawa maps', *Journal of Asian Studies*, 59 (2000), pp. 647–66.

he drew for Morant's 1748 *History*, the *Ichonography of Colchester*. He took the term directly from Serlio the source of much of his architectural inspiration; the *Ichonography* is a mannerist plan of Colchester. The colophon and other decorative elements crowd the top left and bottom right of the map. An elaborately decorated dedication to one of the volume's patrons Phillip Yorke Esq (later Lord Hardwicke) and his wife sits atop the frame of the colophon which lists the town's streets, lanes and churches; Colchester's street plan is subsumed under patronage. The borough arms in a scrolled frame copied from Deane's edition of Vitruvius squeeze into the remaining space in that quarter. The arms so placed signal the absent borough corporation. In the bottom left corner, a compass placed beside the reverse and obverse of a Roman coin, indicates the greater dignity of Colchester's distant past. The roads to Harwich, Ipswich, Wivenhoe and Brightlingsea to the north and east are labelled despite the visual crowding in that quarter of the plan. Crouch Street to the south-west is rather surprisingly not marked as the road to London even though space would adequately allow it. The frame of the map is broken in two places — once to the east to indicate the road to the coast and once at the top left hand to 'let out' the road northwards through Mile End parish. This road leads to the small Suffolk borough of Sudbury (not a significant destination), but a little way outside Colchester the road passes the Severall's Estate. Severalls was corporation property labouring under a ninety-nine-year mortgage originally taken up by Daniel Defoe in 1722 and in the 1740s badly maintained and encroached upon. The gap in the frame marks an absence — a valuable borough estate alienated by an inefficient (Whig) corporation.

Like many town plans of the period, the ichonography is a hybrid between the older 'bird's eye view' and the two-dimensional survey.[48] Deane includes numerous pictograms of all the churches, the ruins of St Botolphs priory and St John's Abbey and, of course, the castle. He also drew several private houses, in large measure making a visual record of his own architectural work; at the west wing of Hollytrees, the renovations to the castle, the east and west wings of East Hill house, St Martin's House in Angel Lane (home of Revd Richard Daniell), as well as the garden ornaments that Deane had undertaken for Gray and George Wegg. A large mansion in Head Street represents the town house of Sir Isaac Rebow, but the pictogram is of a design for a substantial re-build which never in fact took place because the Rebows moved out of town and built Wivenhoe Park with another architect. The pictogram of St Johns priory also shows renovations planned but not completed. The obelisk in the garden of East Hill House was probably never realised.[49] Deane's *Ichonography* is therefore at least in part an imaginary landscape.

The *Ichonography* places the walled town left of centre so as to include the built-up areas at the Hythe, in St Botolphs and around North and East Bridges. Consequently, the actual centre of the plan is the parish of All Saints, containing the castle and the home of Deane's patron Charles Gray — and given Gray's role as county magistrate All Saints was in many ways the administrative centre during the suspension of the charter. The Moot Hall, the seat of (absent) borough government near the top of the High Street has only a small drawing of its entrance arch. A good deal of Deane's own work took place in All Saints where the pictograms also cluster. The conventions of

48 Borsay, *The English urban renaissance*, pp. 181–3.

49 Morant, *Colchester*, book 1, p. 5.

this kind of mapmaking were little bound by (classical) rules of perspective drawing. However Deane's pictograms do play tricks with perspective when viewed together. The tenters for stretching bays in fields around the town and a selection of Colchester's windmills, symbols of industry and agriculture, loom large, particularly the windmills on Golden Hill and Lexden Road that appear in the foreground, hinting at an overall perspective for the pictograms across the plan.[50] However, once the eye is drawn into the centre of the town, Deane's mannerist garden ornaments dwarf both All Saints and St Nicholas churches. Deane's ichonography is therefore not only imaginary, it is also a political perspective centred on All Saints. It cites Colchester's dignities from its Roman past and its political status as a borough, even though the borough charter was in suspension. Its orientation towards the coast and the countryside leaves the cultural and geographical proximity of London as a speaking silence. It emphasises Deane's mannerist architectural contribution to the townscape at the expense of the classical frontages of most of Colchester's architectural improvements. Deane underlines the individuality of Colchester's provincial urban identity[51], but a detailed reading of the ichonography shows that this was a particular, party-oriented reading of that identity.

Deane (1698–1765) had been born and brought up in Colchester. His father, also James, was a builder and surveyor who bought the house, later Winsley's, in 1705 for £120, 'beautifying' and re-selling it in 1708 for £350. James the father also held borough office as a land-looker (surveyor). James the son presumably trained with his father (a younger brother William seems to have moved away from Colchester). From his twenties he had secured the patronage of Charles Gray, whose accounts record loans to Deane and his widowed mother in the mid-1720s.[52] By 1730 Deane was Gray's architect and man of business.[53] As well as overseeing acquisitions, repairs and renovations to numbers of Gray's tenement properties in and around Colchester,[54] Deane designed and oversaw significant improvements to Gray's house (the Hollytrees) and grounds as well as to the Castle itself.[55] Deane designed the new west wing to Hollytrees (1748), the dome and the renovations to the south front of the castle, including the distinctive long windows (1749), the obelisk which stood in the High Street[56] and a gothic summer house for Gray's neighbour at East Hill House,

---

50 K. Farries, *Essex windmills, millers and millwrights*, Vol. 2 (Edinburgh, 1984).

51 R. Sweet, *The writing of urban histories in eighteenth-century England* (Oxford, 1997), pp. 273–4.

52 J. Bensusan Butt, *Magens and Read, Gainsborough and Mayhew, James Deane and Charles Gray* (Colchester, privately printed, 1994), pp. 31–46.

53 Chapter 4, n. 12 below. Among Deane's books there is a small octavo, *Vitruve, reduite en abrege par Mr Perrault* (1681) marked 'ex dono C. Gray armigeri 1732'.

54 ERO D/DR B1, Charles Gray's *General Account Book A*, 1719–68, notes periodic payments to Deane. For example, 1739, p.149, £83 13s 3d for work 'at Thorne's, at Unwin & Wilkerson's, at Grange's, at P. Newton's, at Home, at Mose Hall (Mose Hall Ardleigh, see Morant, *Colchester*, book 1, p. 434), at Berechurch, at Harding, Simpson and Hedges (tenants in All Saints parish), at Harding, Granger and Duffield (also All Saints), Cooper's at Mersea, Shimmens at Wigborough'. See also p. 153, 1740, repairs £26 14s; p.160, January 1751, £31 12s 6d; p.174, 1757, £105 2s 7d and £64 2s 0d. Similar payments continue until Deane's death in 1765.

55 Bensusan Butt, *James Deane and Charles Gray*, p. 40.

56 Later Wire's monument in St Nicholas churchyard.

George Wegg. Deane undertook other work for the borough (on Hythe Bridge in 1736–7), substantial renovations at All Saints Church in 1738 and a new staircase at All Saints Rectory in 1759 — all commissions where Gray's influence extended.[57] Deane's 'Builders' Book' shows a range of costed designs for large and small farmhouses, cottages, barns, a pigeon house and a malt-office as well as garden features (a brick fountain and 'bason') and a 'double town house' reminiscent of the Hollytrees.[58]

Deane lived in a sizeable, 'genteel house, modern built' at the top of St Botolphs Street, and by the time of his death in 1765 also owned rented properties in St Peters and at the Hythe.[59] Through Gray's patronage and employment Deane acquired a viable material independence and a middling lifestyle of some comfort. He owned pictures, prints, drawings 'in fashionable Frames', an eight-day clock, a collection of 'old coins and medals in gold, silver &c' as well as 'two very good Book Cases with Ionic Column and carved Capitals'.[60] His architectural books were willed to Gray and have survived as part of the 'Hollytrees' library.[61] They include Vitruvius and Palladio as well as Batty Langley's *Ancient Masonry*. The most annotated and well-used volume, however, is an English translation of Serlio bought in 1741 in London for 5 shillings.[62]

The influence of the mannerist architect Serlio is evident in much of Deane's surviving work. Mannerism developed out of and in reaction to Renaissance formalism. Balance and proportion were replaced by the creation of elegant but convoluted compositions. Although within European architecture mannerism was soon superseded by the baroque, in England it informed what is now known as Jacobean architecture which combined classical elements freely with decorative detail surviving from Elizabethan design.[63] Hence in mid-eighteenth century Colchester, Deane's gothic summer house, the Italianate dome and long windows inserted into a

---

57 Deane also worked for the Borough. Borough Chamberlain's vouchers (1736, ERO D/B 5 Ab1/33) include £31 17s 2d for work on Hythe Bridge, and (1737-8, ERO D/B 5 Ab1/34) £27 12s 3 1/2d on the new Fairfield Crane there. All Saints parish minutes (ERO D/P 200/8/1, 1686–1753) include 21 February and 14 March 1738 agreement with Mr James Deane and Mr John Walker (carpenters) to take down the north arcade in the church and replace it in wood. The pillars cost £16 16s. In 1759 Deane was paid £140 12s 6d for staircase and parlour in All Saints Rectory, G.O. Rickword, *Essex County Standard,* 18 April 1947.

58 Deane's 'Builders' Book', ERO D/DRc 27.

59 Deane's will, NA PROB 11/911, proved 12 September 1765.

60 *IpsJ* 15 November 1766, household sale after his death.

61 Based originally on the library left to the town by Archbishop Harsnett in the sixteenth century, this book collection formed the basis of the Castle Book Society (Chapter 5). The library later devolved to the Essex Society for Archaeology and History and is now housed in the library of Essex University.

62 Deane's heavily annotated copy of Serlio's *L'Architettura,* in English, is signed on the end-paper: 'J. Deane Novr 27 1741 Pret. 5/- London'.

63 A sixteenth-century Italian architect who later worked on the palace of Fontainebleau, Serlio's *L'Architettura* codified the Roman orders of architecture and its organisation and illustration made it an influential architects' handbook across northern Europe. In style Serlio was a late Renaissance mannerist. J. Summerson, *Architecture in Britain 1530–1830* (Harmondsworth, 1983); *The Columbia Electronic Encyclopedia,* 6th edn, 2003, www.cc.columbia.edu/cu/cup/.

Norman castle, or the (abrupt) stylistic contrasts between the balanced façade of the original Hollytrees mansion of 1718 and the new west wing, made a distinctive architectural statement rather at odds with the more strictly classical contemporary building and renovation in Colchester. Architectural mannerism, in its English variant, was modern but also recuperated less balanced and not necessarily harmonious elements of design from prior centuries. It was a felicitous coincidence of taste that the architect Deane, the historian Morant and their shared patron Gray all shared antiquarian interests.[64] Deane was therefore a natural choice to provide the town map and some other illustrations for Morant's *History of Colchester* (1748).

Morant was preferred to the living at St Mary-at-the-Walls, Colchester in 1738.[65] He was therefore an observer of the final years of the old corporation when, from a Tory point of view, a (virtuous) Tory majority was defeated by Whig manipulation and in the process the borough charter was lost (Chapter 6). Morant and his patron, Tory MP Charles Gray deplored what they saw as the decayed state of Colchester town and borough in the 1730s and 40s, as the reduction in the bay trade coincided with the loss of the charter. Gray as a county JP resident in Colchester was not only caretaking the borough records but also taking over the functions that would otherwise have fallen to borough justices. Their Tory paternalism was affronted by the social problems they perceived without an effective administration to relieve them. Morant's *History of Colchester* is one of the earlier eighteenth-century town histories. The work has an emphatic point of view. The Colchester Corporation is the *bête noire* of Morant's 1748 history. It was published in only a small edition of 200 copies with no more than 80 subscribers. Morant lamented the financial difficulties the project encountered. Rosemary Sweet explains this in terms of the expense of the (large) folio volume and the gentry market that Morant was aiming at; this prestigious volume was intended to enhance the status of the town. However, local politics was an equally important factor in limiting Morant's subscribers. Conspicuously absent from the list are most of the leading town Whigs, in particular the affluent middling non-conformist merchants as well as the gentry Rebows and Martins. Morant's view of Colchester was scholarly and authoritative. It was also political, and the lack of support for the publication from the opposing party in the town implies that it was not uncontested. As suggested above, a fragmented yet insistent counter-narrative was actively being made and remade in the pages of the local paper, as genteel 'capital messuages' and polite social events were advertised and fulsomely described.

Ichonography and Survey

Sparrow's 1767 *Survey of Colchester* is, despite its dedication to the Society of Antiquaries, and in contrast to Deane's ichonography of twenty years earlier, a thoroughly modern representation. The restoration of the borough charter in 1763 and

---

64 For example, Morant consulted Deane about the age of a house on the corner of Pelham's Lane, opposite the Moot Hall, for which a date of 1090 had been suggested. Deane thought it was fifteenth century. Bensusan Butt, *James Deane and Charles Gray*, pp. 42–3.

65 Sweet, *The writing of urban histories*, p. 265; G. H. Martin, 'Morant, Philip (1700–1770) *Oxford Dictionary of National Biography* (Oxford, 2004), http:www.oxford.dnb.com/view/article/19159, accessed 23 July 2006.

the end of the Seven Years War made this a more felicitous decade in Colchester. This survey has no pictograms to trouble the plan view. Instead Sparrow (a London surveyor) emphasised clean delineation of the main streets. He subsumed all 'back offices, courts, yards, gardens both private and common' into dotted shading, concealing all architectural and social messiness including the dwellings of Colchester's working population. The map pays due attention to Colchester's antiquities both Roman and medieval through large etchings around the border and a note on the frequency of archaeological finds. For the most part, however, Sparrow emphasises the town's trade and commerce. He marks the location of the various fairs, the salt works, the two bowling greens and the main inns. Six ships ride at anchor at the Hythe and tenters and windmills occupy the surrounding fields. The dedication blossoms into an illustration of a watermill surrounded by trees. Although a picturesque rural landscape, the eye is drawn to the figure at the centre who is carrying a laden sack of grain to the mill. The Lion Walk non-conformist meeting house is shown, as well as the Anglican churches. The colophon lists attractions for visitors, emphasising the 'Healthfull Air', the 'good Water' and the availability of '... all sorts of Provisions' as well as the manufactures (bays and oysters). The borough arms appear supported by female figures representing Religion and Virtue. Religion, a personification of the town's patron Saint Helena, bears a rugged cross reflecting that on the borough arms. Virtue, with helmet, spear and attendant lion, appears in the form of Britannia. Colchester is celebrated as an English town. Sparrow's Colchester also retains its connection with London — the London Road is indicated, the colophon specifies the distance (51 miles) and the obelisk in the High Street is noted to give 55 miles to London. Unlike Deane, Sparrow emphasises factuality; though there is a visualisation of the Abbey Church at the bottom of the sheet copied from Morant, a note explains 'N.B. this Church is not in being'. The castle dome is indicated as modern and attributed to 'Charles Gray Esq, the present possessor'.

James Deane's anti-classical and indeed gothic architectural vision was consonant with the historical narrative of decline that Morant, Gray, and we may presume Deane perceived in the Colchester of their day. Gothicism is a cultural trope that signals the disruption of orderly progress from the past into the present.[66] Even as they celebrated Colchester's history and provincial urban identity, Morant *et al.* lamented the luxurious and disruptive modernity of Georgian Colchester, which was transformed into optimism and prosperity in Sparrow's Survey. They did so, of course, at the same time as participating in the comfortable urban lifestyle that the middling sort as a whole helped to create materially, socially and culturally. The urban renaissance was, as Brewer comments, hardly a unified process.

---

66 M. Russo, *The female grotesque: risk, excess and modernity* (New York, 1994), p. 8; R. Mighall, *A geography of Victorian gothic fiction: mapping history's nightmare* (Oxford, 1999), p. xviii; P. Stallybrass and A. White, *The politics and poetics of transgression* (London, 1983).

67 Cooper *et al.*, *Colchester*, p. 166.

Different maps

If representations of urban space were both culturally positioned and contesting, once the uses of space and the positioning and movement of bodies are taken into account, spatiality becomes an heuristic perspective from which to view Colchester's society. There were different kinds of mapping at work. The division of the town into parishes defined neighbourhood, ecclesiastical and administrative entities. Parishes shaped patterns of association both for the middling office holders and the poor for whom the parish was the source of relief (Chapter 8). Colchester High Street, increasingly the space for genteel promenades and shopping, was organised on market day according to the different commodities which were sold in different parts of the long street. At the same time it became the space inscribed by the mechanisms of borough justice. Until 1823 convicted thieves were whipped in public, though after 1730 most of the bodies so displayed were men's.[67]

Performativity, or occasionalism as Peter Burke refers to it, is a concept that has underpinned a good deal of valuable work in social and cultural history. Performance — social action directed (in some sense) towards an audience — seeks to convey cultural meaning. Therefore spatial practices depend on the interaction of performativity and spatially. To act thus in one space may not produce the same meaning as to do so in a different space, in fact actions that are unexceptionable in one location may be surprising, shocking or resistant in another. De Certeau distinguishes strategic spatial practices which reinforce and are enabled by dominant power relations and established structures, from those tactical practices which read and use space against the grain.[68] The corporation frequently made use of the High Street for a strategic display of civic dignity. It was a very deliberate parody of such processions when in 1736 a couple of hundred people elected a 'Mayor for Gin' and 'paraded about the town'.[69] In 1789 the king's recovery from his period of dementia was celebrated by a procession of the robed corporation, the charity children and the members of the Angel Lodge of Freemasons down the length of the High Street to hear a sermon preached at St James. The celebrations continued with illuminations and a return up the hill to a dinner at the White Hart.[70] As Darnton suggests, early modern processions provided corporeal enactments of normative social hierarchies. This procession was hardly an accurate reflection of Georgian Colchester society. It was highly selective and imagined the town in the (middling, masculine and patriarchal) guise of the borough. The inclusion of the children (objects of town philanthropy) and the masons (with their masculine associational culture and civic Christianity), along with the corporation, underlined a stable, ordered urban identity.[71] The Peace of Versailles of 1783 which promised a return of prosperity to the bay trade was greeted by a formal announcement by the mayor from the Moot Hall steps and a

---

68 P. Burke, 'Performing history: the importance of occasions', *Rethinking History*, 9 (2005), pp. 35–52, M. de Certeau, *The practices of everyday life* (London, 1984).

69 Chapter 8 below, n. 19.

70 *IpsJ* 2 May 1789.

71 R. Darnton, 'A bourgeois puts his world in order: the city as a text', in R. Darnton, *The great cat massacre and other episodes in French cultural history* (New York, 1984), pp. 107–43, here pp. 116, 124.

few days later an impressive procession by the woolcombers. Far too large and costly to be an impromptu display of artisan enthusiasm, the mounted procession accompanied by fifes and drums included the martial and manly figures of Castor and Pollux, Jason and the Argonauts (celebrated by the woolcombers because of the Golden Fleece) as well as the wool trade's patron saint Bishop Blaize and the union flag. Allegorical figures of Peace, Plenty and assorted shepherdesses also presumably added feminine decoration. Two months later the weavers mounted a second procession which included a moving platform where 'demonstrations of their trade' were re-enacted under the patronage of a personification of Henry II.[72] In the seventeenth century when an estimated third of the town's population worked in the wool trade such demonstrations would probably have been less of a spectacle. In some contrast the bonfire and fireworks to celebrate the Prince of Wales' birthday in 1759 had been more informal, populist and oppositional. It took place outside the town centre in the poor weavers' parish of St Giles. Lauding the heir and his political faction at that late stage of George II's reign was hardly an innocent gesture.[73]

Performativity contributes to the production of cultural identity; to convey meaning by spatially located action calls for the adoption of a plausible subject position (a prisoner in the dock or a mayor on the bench). This in itself depends on how bodies, things and places can be imagined, in Whitridge's phrase, on the 'intricate topologies of bodies and things'.[74] Rituals of domesticity gave meaning to the artefacts of middling consumption and articulated familial intimacies in the spaces of home. (Chapter 3) The bankrupt whose credit had run out confined him or herself within doors and then participated in the formal performance of creditors' meetings in the semi-public space of one of the town centre inns (Chapter 4), spaces which were used for a wide variety of social association, not least the conviviality of political clubs. As Chapter 5 will argue, politeness was about sociability and appropriate bodily deportment in genteel spaces. Political life also ranged across formal and informal spaces; the corporation's procession to St Peters Church at mayor-making, the turmoil of the hustings, or strategic discussions (and the scurrilous gossip) in parlours, offices and coffee houses (Chapters 6 and 7). As the history of local politics demonstrates the formal ceremonial of the Moot Hall could be disrupted by riot, especially given a Recorder in the 1780s who could leap off the aldermen's bench and seize the protesters by the collar, or spring onto a grain wagon and quell rioters with his whip. And of course, there is a rich historiography of the performativity of the grain riot itself.[75]

---

72 *IpsJ* 1 March and 31 May 1783.

73 Lexden and Winstree Petty Sessions, ERO P/LWr/1, Depositions of Sarah Bunner, Elizabeth Thursby, 8 June 1759.

74 P. Whitridge, 'Landscapes, houses, bodies, things: 'place' and the archaeology of Inuit imaginaries', *Journal of Archaeological Method and Theory*, 11, (2004), pp. 213–50, here abstract.

75 The Recorder was Frank Smythies: see Chapters 6–8. On riot, established sources include: E.P. Thompson, 'The moral economy of the English crowd in the eighteenth century', *Past and Present*, 50 (1971), pp. 76–136; L. Tilly,'The food riot in France', *Journal of Interdisciplinary History*, 1 (1971), pp. 23–58; J. Walter and K. Wrightson, 'Dearth and the social order in early modern England', *Past and Present* 71 (1976), pp. 22–42; J.D. Walter,'Grain riots and popular attitudes to the law: Maldon and the crisis of 1629' in J. Brewer and J. Styles (eds.), *An ungovernable people: the*

Conclusion: micro geographies

Urban improvement formed the backdrop for urban renaissance. Classical architecture, rationality, organisation of domestic space and the proliferation of gardens as well as the progress in cleaning up and lighting the streets by the end of the century were all part of Colchester's local history, and the composite narrative of the local press was consonant with the optimistic and progressive mapping of the town drawn and sold by Thomas Sparrow in 1767. However there remains the other narrative of decline. As Geoffrey Martin sums it up, underneath the urban renaissance and the burgeoning of polite culture there remained an 'older and shabbier Colchester, the town of the declining cloth industry, the commoning free burgesses and the nameless poor'.[76] As in other provincial towns the transformation of urban space and architecture was incomplete; modernities were multiple and contestable. The industrial and the smelly remained always close at hand, as did the 'visceral proximity between the rich and the poor'.[77] Colchester's streets were badly paved for most of the century and the market proved unshiftable. The streets were also the place where people begged.[78] Inmating and the medieval legacy of haphazard interior spaces meant that domesticity had to make shifts and compromises in the spaces available. One significant appropriation of that other story was that mapped in party interests by Morant and James Deane.

Cheap political satire has provided a very squint view of polite leisure in Colchester's card rooms. However, this chapter has made only small headway in discovering how the space of the town was lived, particularly the tactical traversing of space by the marginal and the disempowered. Colchester, like every other Georgian town was the site of myriad and substantially irrecoverable micro-geographies where social practice inscribed itself onto urban space. The micro-geographies of the poor between court and alley via the market, the alehouse and the pump make some

---

75 cont.

English and their law in the seventeenth and eighteenth centuries (London, 1980), pp. 47–84; G. Rudé, *The crowd in history; a study of popular disturbances in France and England 1730–1848* (London, 1981); J. Bohstedt, *Riots and community politics in England and Wales 1790–1810* (Cambridge, Mass., 1983); J. Bohstedt,'Gender household and community politics: women in English riots, 1790–1810', *Past and Present*, 120 (1988), pp. 88–122; More recently, articles in A. Randall and A. Charlesworth (eds.), *Markets, market culture and popular protest in eighteenth-century Britain and Ireland* (Liverpool, 1996). Debate around the Thompson model includes, D. Williams,'Morals, markets and the English crowd in 1766', *Past and Present*, 104 (1984), pp. 57–73; A. Charlesworth and A.J. Randall,'Comment: morals, markets and the English crowd in 1766', *Past and Present*, 114 (1987), pp. 200–13; J. Bohstedt, 'The moral economy and the discipline of historical context', *Journal of Social History*, 26 (1992), pp. 265–84; P. King,'Edward Thompson's, contribution to eighteenth-century studies — the patrician plebeian model re-examined', *Social History*, 21 (1996), pp. 215–28.

76 G. Martin, *The Story of Colchester* (Colchester, 1959), p. 80.

77 Ogborn, *Spaces of modernity*, p. 25; T. Hitchcock, *Down and out in eighteenth-century London* (London, 2004), p. 49.

78 T. Hitchcock,'Begging on the streets of eighteenth-century London', *Journal of British Studies*, 44 (2005), pp. 478–98.

showing in the discussion of local petty sessions courts in Chapter 8. During the Napoleonic period the bodies of military deserters were brought into sharp textual focus when their physical descriptions were circulated and noted in petty sessions. Nineteen-year-old, five-foot-tall Charles Kelly, 'a black' who played tambourine in the Royal Bucks militia band (an embodied refutation of the military manliness of the freeborn *English* volunteer forces) only made it from Lexden into Colchester before he was caught.[79] A few unreliable, but nevertheless allusive fragments of anecdotal evidence are also recoverable. The cockle-seller Blind Kibble tramped regularly up from Wivenhoe calling, 'Salt and good Pinpatches ho!' St Leonards workhouse was the place to cross the road and avoid Old Nann the 'idiot woman, dumb with tongue too large for her mouth' and St Giles was the place to go to see the ever-laughing Petticoat Jack 'who wore a petticoat instead of breeches, with a cocked hat and a round wig'.[80]

But one or two middling individual and family geographies can be recuperated. The Taylor family moved from Lavenham to Colchester in 1795, when father, engraver Isaac Taylor, was invited to become minister at Stockwell Independent Chapel.[81] According to the autobiography of his daughter Ann, Colchester was then a 'nice old town ... clean, open and agreeable'. The Taylor daughters worked at engraving and developed their own talents for writing. Ann Taylor's account of her teenage years in Colchester is heavily home-centred. The Taylors were not affluent and their house was old and full of a young family. Ann Taylor's recollections of domestic space reflect on how much time was spent in the engraving workshop which served as social as well as working space. Their house in Angel Lane (in a neighbourhood earlier crammed with artisans of the cloth trade) was

> ... nearly in the centre of the town in a street which, though narrow and disagreeable at one end, became wider, and owned several excellent houses at the other. Ours was among the excellent houses, but it was not one of them. It was just respectable, and would just hold us.[82]

Ann Taylor Gilbert (writing in her old age) transmuted wealth and poverty into aesthetic values of disagreeableness and excellence and positioned the Taylors socially and spatially at a respectable in-between. The Taylors soon improved that important adjunct of domesticity, an ornamental garden with 'grass plots, and winding walks of good Essex gravel, a white seat, a vine-covered arbour, besides laburnums and lilacs

---

79 ERO P/CoR 25, 9 May 1804, deposition of William Davey, private in Norfolk Militia. See Chapter 6 below, n. 54. This was not the only black soldier in the turn-of-the-century garrison. At around the same period, broker William Fenton complained to petty sessions of assault 'by a Black Man servant to Captain Massey of the Royal Artillery now in Colchester barracks'. *Essex County Standard* 17 May 1963.

80 *Bland's Anecdotes*, ERO Acc 905, Box 2, pp. 12–16.

81 L. Davidoff and C. Hall, *Family fortunes, men and women of the English middle class, 1780–1850* (London, 1987), pp. 60–9; L. Davidoff, 'Life is duty, praise and prayer', *Fawcett Library Papers*, 4 (1981); J. Bensusan Butt, 'Jane and Ann Taylor as engravers', *East Anglian Magazine*, 21 (1961), pp. 682–3; J. Gilbert (ed.), *The autobiography and other memorials of Mrs Gilbert*, 2nd edn (London, 1876).

82 J. Gilbert (ed.), *Mrs Gilbert*, pp. 93, 103.

that warm my heart to think of. ...'[83] Sixty years earlier that garden would have thumped to the sound of the weaving looms, so noisy that they kept people awake at night. The Taylors contributed to the 'gardening' of Colchester spaces that previously held the living space of working people and the working space of textile and other trades.[84]

The teenage Taylor children secured for themselves makeshift personal space for play and writing within the house. Ann's sister Jane wrote in her attic bedroom, whose small window commanded a view of the countryside and of the stars. The workshop also had a view of Mile End Church. Such prospects leapt over the poorer parts of the weavers' neighbourhood at the bottom of Angel Lane.[85] Ann's imaginative mapping of the town also moves between its central High Street ('a gay promenade') and the surrounding fields, woods and villages to the north and west which were the regular sites of evening walks. Jane Taylor and her friends read poetry by moonlight 'amongst the picturesque fragments of the old town wall on the Balkerne Hill'.[86] Ann Taylor's re-imagined and recuperated geography of her teenage years in Colchester was a necessarily partial (in both senses) mapping of the town. About two thirds of the town is ignored. The autobiography's mental map of Colchester has nothing to say of the central parts of the town across the High Street, nor of the larger populous districts of St Botolphs and the Hythe. Her geography is completely untouched by the grotesque bodies of Old Nann or Petticoat Jack. The Taylors never came across black military deserters in their country rambles to Lexden. Ann's recuperated perspectives are centred on domestic space which she positions between town and countryside and between rich and 'disagreeable'. The definitive prospect is that through Jane's attic window, framing the landscape from the perspective of the introspective and creating subject, where the watching writers were positioned between family life and the friendly countryside. It is to family life and its meaning for the Colchester middling sort that the discussion will turn in the next chapter.

---

83 *Ibid.*, p. 93.

84 ERO D/B 5 Sr187 Borough Sessions Roll, Law Inquest Presentment, Midsummer 1737: 'The worst noice we had in all our walk was the People said the Ingine Loombs were a Disturbance they made such a noise they could not Sleep for them so you are to judge whether they are Presentable or no.'

85 Gilbert, ed. *Mrs Gilbert*, pp. 119, 102.

86 *Ibid.*, p. 107.

Chapter 3

Kin and connection

Isaac Slythe: family in public and private

> ... I think it is my Duty to do everything I can with Justice for my family; I see no reason why I should favor a whole County to Rob my own Family.[1]

In 1783 Isaac Slythe thus invoked his family in a letter about commercial matters and public business. He had been commissioned to rebuild the House of Correction at Halstead and this letter accompanied a sizeable bill for £681 9s 3½d. Complaining of the cost and scarcity of brick, Slythe was asking for 20s per rod over his original estimate 'and if I have not that allowed, I had better never to have seen the Jobb'. This privileging of family over the concerns of the county was certainly a rhetorical flourish, but a consciously chosen one. Family and the county are at the same time both opposed to and connected with each other. His commercial activities, he implied, enabled him to meet his responsibilities to provide for his family. By discursively substituting his family's interests for his own individual monetary interests, Slythe positioned himself as both a family man and a man of business; indeed the two were contiguous elements of masculine middling identity, as was social connection. Name-dropping, Slythe also cited the opinion of William Mayhew,[2] the Colchester Borough Recorder, that the county had broken its agreement over the job, and proposed a meeting at Chelmsford. But neither was business to be separated from more informal social practice. The letter concludes, 'I must beg your Acceptance of a Barrell of Oysters which I shall send by Coach. I am, Sir, Yours to command. Isaac Slythe.' Slythe's arguments did have some success. The County justices allowed him £40 extra as prices of materials had risen.

Recent reassessments of the history of the family have refined and complicated the proposition that a separation of public and private spheres from the later eighteenth century characterised the formation of Victorian middle-class domesticity as an area of social and cultural life distinct from the public worlds of work, business, the professions and politics.[3] To argue that such social fields were gendered does not

---

1 ERO Q/SBb 314/8; N. Briggs, *John Johnson Architect and County Surveyor for Essex* (Chelmsford, 1991) pp. 113–14.

2 For Mayhew, see Chapters 6 and 7 below.

3 The key study in women's and gender history remains L. Davidoff and C. Hall, *Family fortunes, men and women of the English middle class, 1780–1850* (London, 1987). See also L. Davidoff, *Worlds between: historical perspectives on gender and class* (Cambridge, 1995), pp. 18–40; C. Hall, *White, male and middle class: explorations in feminism and history* (Cambridge, 1992); L. Davidoff *et al., The family story: blood, contract and intimacy, 1830–1960* (London, 1999). Earlier meta-narratives linking domesticity, privacy and modernity include L. Stone, *Family, sex and marriage in early modern England*, 2nd edn (Harmondsworth, 1979); R. Chartier (ed.), *Passions of the renaissance*, eds. P. Aries and G. Duby (Cambridge, Mass., 1989). The recent debate in gender history includes L. Davidoff,'Gender and the"great divide"— public and private in British

imply that men lost involvement in the home nor that all women (or even all middle-class women) were exclusively immured there, despite the strictures of conduct literature and the very real frustrations of women who wanted access to political, educational or professional opportunities that were closed to them. Public and private are best understood as relational, mutually constitutive and historically situated categories. The eighteenth-century middling sort were crucially defined by their relationship to family, as the basis of their material, cultural and public identities. Isaac Slythe's point about his family would have been generally understood. In a comparatively institution-poor society, the middling household was the core of work, consumption and social reproduction, and households were connected through (often selective) networks of kin. People commonly used the term to describe their immediate household, including servants, apprentices and other residents.[4] Elizabeth Wood, who ran a successful school for young ladies at Dedham (three miles from Colchester), clearly identified the two. In 1749 she advertised that a recent epidemic of smallpox was now gone from the school and 'out of thirty two of my Family that have had that Distemper but one person has died of it, which was my Housekeeper, a woman very far advanced in years'.[5] For Elizabeth Wood, her family included her servants as well as all the paying pupils at her school.

This is not to argue that family was less significant, or that family forms necessarily generated less emotional investment for other socio-economic groups in the eighteenth century. However different levels of wealth and status meant that family was differently configured. Upper-class families generally had a geographically wider purview; the management of land and attention to national agricultural markets, the social season with its migrations to London or resort towns, not to mention their political activities and their placing in patronage networks meant that their interests were regional and national as well as local. The landed household was a site of production, but its produce (as opposed to that of the landed estate) was directed towards household consumption rather than to the market. Greater affluence meant a

---

3. *cont.*

gender history', *Journal of Women's History,* 15 (2003), pp. 11–27; M. Ryan, 'The public and the private good — across the great divide in women's history', *Journal of Women's History,* 15 (2003), pp. 10–27; A. Vickery, 'Golden-age to separate spheres — a review of the categories and chronology of English women's history', *Historical Journal,* 36 (1993), pp. 383–414; for revisionist work, R. Shoemaker, *Gender in English society 1650–1850: the emergence of separate spheres?* (London, 1998); T. Meldrum, *Domestic service and gender 1660–1750: life and work in the London household* (Harlow, 2000); E. Foyster, *Marital violence: an English family history, 1660–1857* (Cambridge, 2005); J. Bailey, *Unquiet lives: marriage and marriage breakdown in England, 1660–1800* (Cambridge, 2003); H. Barker, *The business of women: female enterprise and urban development in northern England 1760–1830* (Oxford, 2006). See also D. Castiglione and L. Sharpe (eds.), *Shifting the boundaries: transformation of the language of public and private in the eighteenth century* (Exeter, 1995), in which especially J. Brewer, 'This, that and the other; public, social and private in the seventeenth and eighteenth centuries' in pp. 1–18; also H. Barker and E. Chalus (eds.), *Gender in eighteenth-century England* (Harlow, 1997), pp. 19–26 for a summary overview of the debates.

4 N. Tadmor, 'The concept of the household-family in eighteenth-century England', *Past and Present,* 151 (1996), pp. 111–40.

5 *IpsJ,* 2 December 1749.

different relationship to the domestic infrastructure, not least the delegation to servants of much of the work of child rearing as well as domestic reproduction more generally.[6] The families of the poor, by contrast, were engaged in a constant struggle for material and social survival in an economy of makeshifts. While the support of close kin was a key resource, economic deprivation destabilised family structures. Crucially the intervention of the poor law and philanthropy brought poor families under their scrutiny and could as often separate families as preserve them intact (Chapter 8). Poor households could also be sites of production, as in the East Anglian textile trade for example, but this labour was always determined by external market forces and earning a subsistence on piece rates rather than the dynamics of small business and the prized if fragile independence that control of even small capital brought.[7] Therefore if family was an important organiser of social relations in all levels of society, the dense overlaying of material, social and affective relations in the middling family was distinctive.

Middling family interests and the husbanding of family property were prioritised over individual choice. Individuals occupied different and unequal positions within households and kinship groups according to gender, age and other kinds of status. Authority over servants and apprentices was contiguous with authority over junior co-resident kin and that of adult men over women and children.[8] Some individuals therefore had a good deal more autonomy than others; in particular male adult heads of household like Isaac Slythe. It is unlikely that he took much advice from his household or kin before he took on the sizeable building contract for the Halstead House of Correction at a time when crucial materials were scarce and expensive. Very often, where the middling sort built wider social connections, they used quasi-familial practices (the exchange of greetings and news, the leaving of small legacies, the sending of a barrel of oysters) to cement more and less unequal social relationships. As Chapter 4 will argue, the vital maintenance of social and financial credit was in many ways an extension of such practices towards patrons, business associates and friends. Overall, current historical opinion sees more continuity than change in such family patterns over time.[9] The evidence from Colchester indicates that such changes built upon rather than turned away from family as an organiser of social association. Family is in many ways an ongoing theme of this book.

---

6 K. Wrightson, *Earthly necessities: economic lives in early modern Britain* (New Haven, CT, 2000), pp. 277–82.

7 S. King and A. Tomkins (eds.), *The poor in England 1700–1850; an economy of makeshifts* (Manchester, 2003), especially articles by Hanly, Hindle and Lloyd; B. Lemire, *The business of everyday life: gender, practice and social politics in England, c.1600–1900* (Manchester, 2006), Chapters 1 and 2.

8 B. Hill, *Servants: English domestics in the eighteenth century* (Oxford, 1996), pp. 2, 5, 115–27; M.R. Hunt, *The middling sort: commerce, gender, and the family in England, 1680–1780* (Berkeley and London, 1996); Bailey, *Unquiet lives*, pp. 62, 110.

9 J.M. Bennett, 'Women's history: a study in continuity and change', *Women's History Review*, 2 (1993), pp. 173–84; N. Tadmor, 'The concept of the household-family'; A. Vickery, *The gentleman's daughter: women's lives in Georgian England*, (New Haven and London, 1998); B. Lemire, *The business of everyday life*; M. Doolittle, 'Close relations? Bringing together gender and family in English history', *Gender and History*, 11 (1999), pp. 542–54.

So who and what did Slythe mean by his family? Although earlier generations of the family are hard to trace, they may have come from Ipswich, Suffolk into Essex.[10] By the early 1770s Slythe was trading as a brickmaker in Halstead, Essex, and expanded his business to Colchester from 1779.[11] He had married Elizabeth and seems to have had at least two teenage children at this point.[12] The Slythes lived at first outside the town centre, on the road to the Hythe where Slythe had a stonemason's yard, though in 1785 this house was sold and they moved into the High Street, opposite the Three Cups inn. This was a smart address, previously occupied by a surgeon. The substantially rated house was nicely re-fronted with well-designed windows and the premises extended backwards to yards and stables giving onto Culver Street. Although Slythe did business here, the heavier trade remained at the Hythe and a yard he operated at the bottom of Angel Lane.[13] In 1789 Slythe's daughter Mary married another Colchester stonemason, James Walker.[14] Slythe's son James married Sarah Tabor in 1793. James followed his father's trade, working at first in partnership and from 1797 independently.[15] These marriages underlined both religious and occupational connection. James Slythe continued to trade as a stonemason in Colchester until his death in 1815. From the 1790s he was working in partnership with his brother-in-law.[16] The Slythes and the Tabor family were members of Lion Walk

---

10 *Boyd's Marriage Index*, 1710 Isaac Slithe married Su. Walton, Ipswich St Clements. JBB BD/1253 cites a settlement order of James Slythe and Ann his wife from St Clements, Ipswich to St James, Colchester, 26 September 1763.

11 NA IR1 Apprenticeship Indexes, 58/106, Thomas Osborne apprenticed to Slythe, £3 3s, 1772. NA PROB 11/965 will of William Turner, Halstead, gentleman, proved 19 March 1771 states that Slythe was his tenant in Halstead. Slythe advertised from Colchester; *IpsJ* 8 May 1779, 27 May 1780, 29 June 1780.

12 Table tomb, Lion Walk Independent Chapel commemorates: Isaac Slythe d. 24 December 1800, aged 65, Elizabeth, his first wife, d. 16 November 1784, aged 48, Jane, his second wife, d. 25 November 1792, aged 56, James (his son), d. 8 January 1816, aged 51, plus 5 infant children.

13 *IpsJ* 25 June 1785: 'A new built modern Brick'd house with sash-windows between the High Town and the Hythe, Colchester to be sold. Apply Mr Slythe who will show the premises.' He announced on the same date that he had opened a shop opposite the Three Cups, for customers to whom his Hythe shop was 'inconvenient' and has again opened his Halstead shop 'to accommodate his country friends'. Barn floors 4 gns per 100 feet at a few days' notice. JBB ms note in BD/1253 indicates that this was 22 High Street, for which see N. Lloyd, *A history of the English house from primitive times to the Victorian period* (London and New York, 1975), fig. 547 re varied design of windows. *IpsJ* 30 June 1792, for Slythe's yard at the bottom of Angel Lane.

14 James Walker of St Peters Colchester, mason, aged 28 married Mary Slythe aged 26, of St Runwalds, 1789, marriage licence ERO D/ACL 1789. There had been some earlier trade rivalry between Slythe and the stonemasons' firm of Walker and Eburn in the early 1780s; *IpsJ* 8 June and 29 June 1782.

15 International Genealogical Index; James Slythe married Sarah Tabor, St James, Colchester, 24 April 1793. *IpsJ* 27 May 1797 James Slythe, stonemason, near the Barracks, Colchester, separated from partnership with Father. Barn floors £4 10s per square, Rickstones 10s a pair, 'several marble chimney pieces to be disposed of very cheap'.

16 In 1803 Walker and Slythe were paid £148 1s 7d for repairs to the tower of St Leonards, Hythe. ERO D/P 245/5/2, St Leonards' churchwardens' bills and receipts. *IpsJ* 25 July 1812, James Slythe took on a new builders' yard near the Castle Inn (All Saints) selling Italian marble. *IpsJ* 13 January 1815 announced his death.

Congregational Chapel. Isaac Slythe's first wife, Elizabeth, had died in 1784 and was buried at Lion Walk. He was remarried in 1787 to Jane Grainger.[17] She owned lands in Wethersfield, and the marriage settlement aimed to reserve some of this property within her own birth family. She made a will in 1788 which, while leaving the bulk of her property to her husband, reserved £20 to her brother Samuel of Sible Hedingham, and £100 apiece to his two sons Joseph and George. These legacies were gradually reduced by codicils, until shortly before her death in 1792, her attorney, non-conformist William Francis, lent £60 to cover them, since Isaac Slythe declared he was at the time in need of substantial capital and Jane was then 'sick and infirm'. She died the following November and Slythe remarried within eighteen months. Slythe was in need of the capital because he had been expanding his business. As well as undertaking smart houses in Colchester, the previous year he had completed some extensive improvements at Twinsted Hall and in June of 1792 had gone into partnership with two other stonemasons in Ipswich.[18]

Consequently, an important part of what family consisted of for Isaac Slythe was that it was a source of capital and personnel for his business (his wife's money and his son's and son-in-law's labour). His social connection and support extended via family into both trade and religious associations, particularly through the solidarities among Lion Walk congregationalists. It can be safely assumed that his family (especially, of course, his wives, daughter and domestic servants) did all the largely unacknowledged social, physical and emotional labour that was necessary for his domestic comfort. A substantial High Street tradesman would have required a parlour as well as a workshop. Lacking informal sources, such as diaries or personal letters for these individuals, what cannot be assessed is Slythe's own emotional investment in his family and the tenor of family relationships. There is no historical record of what Jane Slythe's feelings were as her personal funds were subsumed into her husband's business and her ability to leave her nephews a reasonable legacy was foreclosed. Legally she had little power to prevent it, whatever her personal views. Certainly her trustees and her lawyer concurred and drew on the authority conferred on them in law to divert the money. The reasons why James Slythe left the business partnership with his father in 1797 also remain obscure. It turned out to be a (deliberately?) wise move,

---

17 Isaac Slythe, aged 40 married Jane Grainger at Wivenhoe, marriage licence ERO D/ACL 1787. Marriage Settlement 3–4 April 1787, where the trustees were Revd Giles Hobbes of Lion Walk and the evangelical Revd Robert Storry of St Peters. The lawyer was non-conformist William Francis. JBB report on deeds of 16 North Hill for Sidney and Minette Partner, 1995 in ERO Acc. 905, Box 10.

18 *IpsJ* 9 July 1791 reports Slythe's commission for brickwork and masonry at the church at Twinsted near Sudbury, Suffolk, newly founded by Sir James Marriott, Judge of the High Court of the Admiralty to his design. Slythe had lately built 'one straight and one circular portico or viranda (sic) ... and ... a cenotaph and screen of four Corinthian columns with an entablature ... in the entrance of an avenue to a wood' to Marriott's design. Slythe 'deserves much credit for his work, and excellence of the materials, which are of the best Portland stone, and the shafts of the columns all of one piece'. *IpsJ* 8 September 1792 Auction of Slythe's new-built house, middle of North Hill (no.16), 'elegantly finished in the present taste'. *IpsJ* 23 June 1792, partnership of Slythe, Roper and Doughty, stonemasonry, in St Matthews Street, Ipswich, have taken premises of William Lane and wharf in St Peters parish. Also *IpsJ* 6 March 1794.

since Isaac had apparently over-extended himself with the Ipswich venture and went bankrupt in 1799. He died the following year.[19]

The answers to such questions cross and re-cross boundaries between public and private, between business and home, between kin and colleagues, between commercial and family capital. Self-regulating non-conformist congregations were in some measure private vis-à-vis the world of commerce and the legal regulation of insolvency, yet religious connections coloured the organisation of business. The linked dichotomies of public and private framed the view of social life from any subject position, and shifted their emphasis according to particularities of social situation as well as wider historical change. The middling family, per se, cannot be assumed to have been 'private' — it was far too complex an institution and the foundation of credit.[20] It was where the middling sort located both the care and maintenance both of their property and their affective relations.

Property and remembrance

The eighteenth-century middling sort had a distinctive relationship to their material property. In an age of small business, variable professional incomes, no limited liability, restricted capital and scarce specie, small producers and professionals occupied an anxious economic environment. The maintenance of business credit was all important, but always vulnerable to market fluctuations, the vagaries of health and mortality, mistakes of judgement or unexpected drains on family capital. Especially because working relationships were also often affective relationships within the household family or kin networks, the emotional temperature of defending and building a secure material underpinning could be high. Business credit and social credit (economic and cultural capital in Bourdieu's terms) were mutually constituted (Chapter 4).[21] Social respectability and adherence to family norms helped secure cash credit; emotional disharmony had direct material effects.[22] At the same time, as Maxine Berg and others have argued, the middling sort were key consumers of the growing manufacturing sector. Although in the seventeenth- and early eighteenth-centuries not all households who could afford it chose to acquire the kinds of fashionable goods that conferred social status, over time middling culture was increasingly marked by the prudent acquisition of 'luxury' domestic items; textiles, furniture, long case clocks and particularly from the second half of the century, china and ceramics.[23] Colchester

---

19 *IpsJ* 23 March, 25 May, 2 November 1799, for his bankruptcy. *IpsJ* 24 December 1800 announced his death.

20 Hunt, *The middling sort;* C. Muldrew, *The economy of obligation: The culture of credit and social relations in early modern England* (Basingstoke, 1998).

21 L. McNay,'Gender, habitus and the field — Pierre Bourdieu and the limits of reflexivity', *Theory, Culture and Society*, 16 (1999), pp. 95–117; P. Bourdieu, *Outline of a theory of practice*, ed. R.T. Nice (Cambridge, 1977); P. Bourdieu, *Distinction: a social critique of the judgement of taste* (London, 1979).

22 Bailey, *Unquiet lives*, p. 62.

23 H. French, *The middle sort of people in provincial England, 1600–1750*, (Oxford, 2007), Chapter 3; H. Berry,'Prudent luxury: the metropolitan tastes of Judith Baker, Durham gentlewoman', in R. Sweet and P. Lane (eds.), *On the town: women and urban life in eighteenth-century England*

middling households acquired the range of such times from oyster knives to Scotch and Turkey carpets, and a washing machine.[24]

The middling household based its claims to respectability on orderly affective relations and domestic social practice such as tea drinking, socialising, (frequently) reading, or family religious observance. Taken together such practices shaded between public and private. Some involved the household family or only some of its members, others included other kin, friends and acquaintance. Such practices called for a more elaborate domestic infrastructure than in earlier centuries and sometimes dedicated times or spaces. This in itself generated its own rituals of sweeping, cleaning, washing, arranging, tidying, shopping, food preparation, gardening, as well as all the needle work (sic) that made and mended clothes and household textiles. Physical comfort became an increasingly important aspect of domestic life.[25] Amanda Vickery has explored the emotional and personal value that gentry women placed on their personal and household possessions. The amount and quality of goods that came within the ambit of middling consumption was more circumscribed. Nevertheless, trading and professional families seem to have taken a not dissimilar pride in their furniture, linen, plate, clothes, clocks, watches, china and sometimes their books, pictures and musical instruments. Their preference for the consumption of such items over other kinds of expenditure was distinctive.[26]

The drawing up of a will, which for most involved consulting an attorney or scrivener and assembling the necessary witnesses, must have been a significant life event. The transfer of property on death was a key moment and a potentially worrying one. Family survival called for the careful husbanding of property in safe hands. The ongoing welfare of dependents needed to be secured as far as possible, but this imperative was potentially in tension with the claims of family members whose labour had contributed to the family's capital and also the (secondary) need to consolidate the family's position in its wider networks of kinship and friendship by distributing small legacies and remembrances.[27] Will-making (and proving) was far

---

23 cont.

(Aldershot, 2003), pp. 131–56; M. Berg and H. Clifford (eds.), *Consumers and luxury: consumer culture in Europe 1650–1850,* (Manchester, 1999); M. Berg and E. Eger (eds.), *Luxury in the eighteenth century, debates, desires and delectable goods* (Basingstoke, 2003); for a review of the literature on luxury and consumption, L. Klein, 'Luxury in the eighteenth century: debates, desires and delectable goods', *History Workshop Journal* (2004), pp. 289–93.

24 Household accounts of Susan and Horatio Cock, ERO D/DEt/F38; J. Bensusan Butt, *The house that Boggis built* (Colchester, 1972), p. 25 for the household possessions of Thomas and James Boggis.

25 J.E. Crowley, 'The sensibility of comfort', *American Historical Review,* 104 (1999), pp. 749–82.

26 L. Weatherill, *Consumer behaviour and material culture in Britain, 1660–1760* (London, 1998).

27 A. Owens, 'Property, gender and the life course: inheritance and family welfare provision in early nineteenth-century England', *Social History,* 26 (2001), pp. 299–317; A. Owens, 'Inheritance and the life-cycle of family firms in the early industrial revolution', *Business History,* 44 (2002), p. 21; R.J. Morris, 'The middle class and the property cycle during the Industrial Revolution' in T. Smout (ed.), *The search for wealth and stability* (London, 1979), pp. 91–113.

from a universal practice; only something like 7.7 per cent of those dying as adults in Colchester at the end of the eighteenth century left a will that was proved. However, comparing the numbers of wills proved for inhabitants of the populous, town-centre St Peters parish at this period with the numbers of traders and professionals in that parish, the proportion of will-makers rises to 22.7 per cent overall or 31 per cent of middling men.[28] Despite these limitations, wills remain an important source to assess both social relationships and the interactions between individuals, families and property.

Eighteenth-century Colchester wills were proved either in London at the Prerogative Court of Canterbury or at the local archdeaconry courts. Wills proved in London tend to be those of more affluent individuals, particularly in the second half of the eighteenth century. The numbers of Colchester wills proved in London increased from 84 in 1680–99 (20 women will-makers, and 64 men) to 166 in 1800–19 (63 women, 103 men). Proportionately fewer wills were proved in London in the 1720s and 30s, both men's and women's when numbers increased in the archdeaconry courts. These accounted for fewer Colchester wills than the London courts in the later seventeenth and early eighteenth centuries (76 between 1680 and 1699, 59 between 1700 and 1719). Thereafter the archdeaconry courts proved more Colchester wills than the London courts (Table 3.1).

The central concern of will-makers was to distribute property within the immediate family, so as to preserve that property for the next generation.[29] As studies of

---

28 201 Colchester wills were proved at the Archdeaconry courts and a further 145 at the Prerogative Court of Canterbury between 1780 and 1799; 346 in total. Burial registers for the large town-centre parish of St Peters show 759 deaths between 1780 and 1799. Subtracting those recorded as 'son of' or 'daughter of' (the register uses this formulation regularly to record infant or child deaths) this results in an estimated 436 adult deaths; that is 21.8 adult deaths per annum. A note in the registers gives the 1800 population at 1,085. An adult death rate of 22 per 1,000 can be approximated. (This falls within the scope used by Wrigley and Schofield, 1981, p. 16.) W. Page and H. Round (eds.), *The Victoria County History of Essex* (London, 1907), Vol. 2, p. 353 gives 10,087 population in the town parishes in 1801. At 22 adult deaths per 1,000 of population this produces an estimate of 222 adult deaths per annum, hence 4,440 over a 20-year period. The 346 Colchester wills represent something like 7.7 per cent of all adult deaths at this period. The 1790 Land Tax Assessments for St Peters show 92 households rated at more than £2 per year — an absolute minimum figure for a middling establishment. The assessments show only heads of household, generally male so can be doubled to account for wives (181). Any overestimate due to single householders will be more than compensated for by an inbuilt underestimate through neglecting 'adult' (working) children in the household. Given an 1800 population of 1,085 in St Peters, this results in an approximate 181 adult middling sort or town gentry per 1,000 population. An adult annual death rate of 22 per 1,000 gives an expected annual mortality among this group of 3.96, hence 79.2 over the 20 years 1780–99. The actual figure for wills proved at the Archdeaconry Courts (excluding the most affluent, who proved their wills in London) by individuals buried in St Peters in this period is 18, or 22.7 per cent of adults from households rated over £2. If only male wills are included the figure improves to 31 per cent.

29 N. Goose and N. Evans, 'Wills as an historical source' in T.E.A. Arkell (ed.), *When death do us part: understanding and interpreting the probate records of early modern England* (Oxford, 2000), pp. 38–71, here p. 44; A. Owens, 'Inheritance and the life-cycle', p. 21.

Table 3.1

Colchester wills proved in London and locally

Proved in London	Male testator	Female testator	All
1680–99	64	20	84
1700–19	49	12	61
1720–39	60	9	69
1740–59	58	28	86
1760–79	84	43	127
1780–99	95	50	145
1800–18	103	63	166
Proved Locally			
1680–99	60	16	76
1700–19	47	12	59
1735–50	125	47	172
1780–99	155	45	201
1800–29	151	53	204

sixteenth- and seventeenth-century England would lead one to expect,[30] only a comparatively narrow range of kin were recognised by most will-makers, and kinship networks were to a degree selective. Extended kin and friends tended to receive minor remembrances in wills, unless there were no immediate family available to inherit the bulk of the property. The most frequent will-makers were middling males, but the nature of their wills suggests that the document was very much part of a family's strategy for future survival. Direct offspring and surviving marital partners were prioritised as guardians of family property, but other kin (especially nieces and nephews) were selected where wives and children were not present. My earlier quantitative study of wills proved in the archdeaconry courts indicates that between 1735 and 1750, in a less bureaucratic society this pattern seems to have been so accepted that proportionately fewer proven wills (27.1 per cent) left property only to wives and children, than in the early 1800s (37.8 per cent). Before 1750, 24.3 per cent of men's wills and 8.2 per cent of women's named no immediate family, whereas only 7.4 per cent of men's wills and 14.7 per cent of women's did so between 1800 and 1829.[31] Over the same period, however, the practice of leaving small legacies to a wider range of distant kin and friends also declined. In wills naming wife and/or children before 1750 there are an average of 3.1 legacies outside the surname set and 1.9 after 1780. An average of 9.1 legatees of different surname are named in wills before 1750 which do not name the nuclear family, compared to 3.1 later. Middling wills tended to dispose of larger amounts of more diverse, and more mobile kinds of

30 The established studies include, K. Wrightson, *English society 1580–1680* (London, 1982); K. Wrightson and D. Levine, *Poverty and piety in an English village; Terling 1525–1700* (New York, San Francisco, London, 1979); D. Levine, *Family formation in an age of nascent capitalism* (New York, San Francisco, London, 1977); P. Laslett, *The world we have lost* (London, 1965); P. Laslett and R. Wall, (eds.), *Household and family in past times* (Cambridge, 1972). More recently, K. Wrightson, *Earthly necessities: economic lives in early modern Britain* (New Haven, CT, 2000); compare L. Davidoff *et al.*, *The family story: blood, contract and intimacy, 1830–1960* (London, 1999).

31 S. D'Cruze, *The middling sort in provincial England: politics and social relations in Colchester 1730–1800* (PhD thesis, Essex, 1990), pp. 46–56.

capital after 1780 and in changing economic conditions more frequently used formal legal devices such as trusts and the advice of (male) business and professional connections. It was not only among the smaller estates proved at the archdeaconry courts that formal property transfer and the concerns of immediate family became more important. In London-proved wills, an increase in spinster will-makers after 1780 (from 9 between 1760 and 1779, to 14 between 1780 and 1799, to 24 from 1800 to 1819) also evidences the greater need to transfer property formally.

The next chapter will look further at estate administration and executorships in relation to middling business and professions. Here I wish to explore the meanings of property transfer in wills by looking in more detail at a particular kind of bequest, that given in kind rather than cash. I will do so by focusing on archdeaconry wills and therefore on testators with comparatively smaller estates to disperse, at a period (1735–50) when the non-monetary bequest was more common than it subsequently became. Somewhat more locally-proved Colchester wills mentioned household goods at the turn of the nineteenth century than earlier (57.1 per cent before 1750, compared to 66.7 per cent before 1800 and 65.6 per cent thereafter). More testators left books (8.3 per cent after 1800) but fewer made direct bequests of their clothes (17.1 per cent before 1750, 3.9 per cent after 1800).[32] Although the majority of bequests throughout the century were either of real property (houses and land) or expressed in cash terms, a significant minority of legacies were of specific, named household or personal items.

A survey was made of the fifty-seven (25.7 per cent) Colchester wills between 1735 and 1750 which left such bequests (Tables 3.4 and 3.5). General bequests of 'all household goods' or 'all personal estate' were not included, since I sought to explore the leaving of specific things (my bed with the blue hangings) or kinds of things (my clothes). Such bequests made a particular link between a material artefact and a social relationship and can reveal something more about the material environment of the middling sort as well as the cultural and affective meanings of family and friendship among this group. Likewise I excluded remembrances left in cash (£10 for mourning) but included the few instances where executors were charged with the purchase of gloves, rings or clothes for particular people alongside instances where mourning rings earlier received by the will-maker were handed on again in their own will. Both men and women made these sorts of bequests, roughly in same proportion that they made wills. Sixty-two women made wills (38.8 per cent of the 222 locally proved wills between 1735 and 1750) and nineteen women left non-monetary bequests (33.3 per cent of those who did so). Therefore, this was not a specifically female practice, though there are a notable handful of wills left by elderly single or widowed women who seem to distribute their personal possessions item by item. However, the patterns of items distributed and of recipients do vary by gender.

In men's wills, the legatees for such bequests show a pattern similar to, but more extended than, bequests in general. By contrast, women gave far more non-monetary legacies to friends (31.6 per cent), in-laws (around 16 per cent), grandchildren (10.5 per cent), parents (15.8 per cent) and other kin (over 20 per cent) (Table 3.2). Women made more bequests to siblings than men. Men made more bequests to nephews

32 *Ibid.*, p. 67.

Table 3.2

Recipients of non-monetary bequests, 1735–50

	Female wills %	*Male wills %*
children	26.3	31.6
siblings	31.6	21.1
nephews/nieces	5.3	18.4
wife	0	13.2
other kin	15.8	10.5
cousin	5.3	7.9
servants	0	5.3
friends	31.6	5.3
son/dtr-in-law	5.3	2.6
sister/bro-in-law	10.5	2.6
grandchildren	10.5	2.6
parents	15.8	2.6
uncle/aunt	5.3	0

and nieces as substitutes for their own children and a few left items to servants. Overall, women will-makers recognised more diverse networks of kinship and friendship through non-monetary bequests (something that other women will-makers achieved by leaving cash, of course). Bequests to kin by marriage are more numerous in women's wills, and although the kinship links in this sample have not been systematically traced, legatees with different surnames not named as relations (coded here as 'friends') were frequently also kin.[33]

More men left furniture than women (47 per cent compared to 31 per cent including beds and bedding). A small number of married men made specific named legacies of items of furniture (beds in particular) to their wives. This seems to be a practice along the line of securing a widow her 'thirds'.[34] Such legacies restricted a widow's access to the household goods and furniture she had cared for throughout her marriage but also often seemed to reserve the best items for her (Table 3.3). Women distributed silver and clothing somewhat more frequently than men. The bequest of clothing does have a slightly different resonance than other items. Unsurprisingly, people left clothes to legatees of their own gender. Beverley Lemire has found that people not infrequently wore the clothes they stole so it is very likely that people wore the clothes they were left. However, given the value of clothing and the extensive market in second-hand clothes, it is possible that legatees may have been more ready to convert clothes into cash than furniture, clocks or engraved silver. Most silver was left in the form of household items such as teaspoons, though a minority of men left watches. There were few bequests of china or ceramics (included here under 'other'); before the last decades of the century more affluent, London-

33 A London-proved example is the will of Hannah Nuttall, who left many legacies to kin and connections among Colchester non-conformists. NA PROB11/1051, proved 10 March 1779; JBB BD/626; D'Cruze, *'Our times in god's hands', religion and the eighteenth-century middling sort, a study of Colchester,* Studies in Essex history (Chelmsford, 1990), p. 17.

34 J. Cox and N. Cox, 'Probate 1500–1800: a system in transition' in T.E.A. Arkell (ed.), *Till death do us part: understanding and interpreting the probate records of early modern England* (Oxford, 2000), pp. 14–37, here p. 23; A.L. Erickson, *Women and property in early modern England* (London, 1993), p. 238.

Table 3.3
Items left as non-monetary bequests, 1735–50

	Female wills %	Male wills %
silver	57.9	47.4
clothes	57.9	42.1
bed/bedding	26.3	26.3
furniture	5.3	21.1
other	15.8	18.4
jewelry	10.5	15.8
linen	5.3	13.2
books	0	5.3
mourning clothes	5.3	0
mourning ring	5.3	0

proved wills were most likely to bequeath china.[35] Silver items were often engraved and jewellery including handed-down mourning rings were clearly seen as family heirlooms. One widow left her dead husband's sword to a nephew. The few itemised mourning bequests were left by women, not men. Only men left books and on the whole bequeathed a greater diversity of items. The small number of bequests of men's working tools have also been included under 'other'.

The London-proved wills of the women of the Lechmere family, who lived at Winsleys (Chapter 2) show interesting patterns of bequest. In 1745 widow Rebeckah Lechmere left cash legacies to her two adult, unmarried daughters in their own control, sufficient to provide an independent income. She also made them trustees for monies to provide the interest to two other daughters then widowed and to reserve the capital for their children. She left a fair amount of other property in cash between married sons, daughters and grandchildren. In her will of 1764, her daughter Rebecca left fewer legacies, but similarly in cash and reflecting the same extended family patterns of distribution. However, when the last surviving daughter, Maria Sophia Lechmere made her will in 1785, as well as some cash legacies she also bequeathed the family silver to her married sister Elizabeth Grimwood and the 'bed and bedding in the servant's garret' to her friend Mrs Hannah Hubbard.[36] Non-monetary bequests

35 B. Kowaleski Wallace, 'Women, china and consumer culture in eighteenth-century England', *Eighteenth-century Studies* 29 (1995), pp. 153–167; M. Berg, *Luxury and pleasure in eighteenth-century Britain* (Oxford, 2005), pp. 227–9; A. Vickery, 'His and hers: gender, consumption and household accounting in eighteenth-century England' 1 (2006), pp. 12–38; L. Weatherill, *Consumer behaviour*, p. 8. Colchester had a 'china warehouse' from at least 1765, run by John Keeling three doors above the Red Lion (39 High Street), *IpsJ* 8 and 15 June 1865, 30 May 1767; JBB BD/702 John Rogers, BD/482 John Keeling, BD/587 Ann Minks, BD/185 Joseph Coney. Colchester wills leaving bequests of china include James Deane (see Chapter 2 above n. 45) who asked that a large china bowl presented to him by Joseph Eyre of Dedham (the composer) be returned to him. JBB BD/226, Mrs Julian Dare, among many bequests of itemised household goods and clothes left Lucy Carr, her neighbour's daughter, 'my Best Tea Spoons and Tea Tonges, two Dozen of Blue and White China Plates and Six Dishes', neighbour James Boggis 'two of my China Bowls', his brother Thomas Boggis 'my Pair of China Sauce Boats with the Plates belonging' and her nephew John Jacob Morley 'all my China Fruit Baskets', NA PROB 11/1132 proved 19 August 1785. In 1792 William Hitchcock, carpenter (will ERO D/ACR 18/396, proved 4 February 1792) left his china to his granddaughters.

often indicated the complete or partial break-up of the household, but at the same time the transfer of these items into other households (of adult children, other kin or friends) established a symbolic continuity. Both men and women made such bequests but there were some differences both in the kinds of goods they left and their choice of legatee. Men's more privileged position as the legal owners of most household property is apparent. Spinsters and widows (and some widowers and bachelors) were more likely to be distributing the remnants of a now dispersed household, and remembering a wider selection of kin and friends. Non-monetary bequests underline the middling-sort's concern for their material household goods and personal possessions and also make visible the value placed on the wider family, even while the core of family property was handed down through the household family wherever possible.

Wills indicate what measures people took for their property when they lacked a household family. Bachelor Peter Alvis of All Saints parish divided his estate between distant kin and numerous neighbours.[37] Likewise wills can show how other kinds of connections, in particularly religious ones, could buttress existing kinship networks or create fictive ones. Where bequests spilled outside family, they could also delineate networks of patronage or other sorts of connection. George Wegg left over sixty mourning rings, a good many to his neighbours, the middling tradesmen of All Saints and St Nicholas.[38]

Nevertheless, middling wills were written mostly in accord with normative models of family.[39] Historically, families have been created in the imagination as much as in the genes. The recognition of individuals as family creates exclusions as well as inclusions. The idealisation of particular familial roles structured by gender, age and connection may well be important to family life, even though such roles are struggled over in lived experience.[40] When Jonathan Feedam left his wife sole control of the estate, 'relying on the fidelity of Ann my dear and loving wife to educate, bring up and otherwise provide for' his six children, the text may well have reflected his sentiments. However, the language was that of his lawyer, Samuel Wall who witnessed the will.[41] George Davis left a life interest in his estate to his 'loving wife, Sarah' but the bequest was conditional on her giving up the bond he gave on marriage.[42] Although the use of such rhetorical devices had cultural significance it is unwise to rely on positive declarations of family affection as directly reflecting lived

36 Wills of Rebeckah or Rebecca Lechmere, widow, Colchester, NA PROB11/833, proved 19 October 1757; Lucy Lechmere, spinster, All Saints, Colchester, NA PROB11/903, 13 November 1764; Maria Sophia Lechmere, spinster of Colchester, NA PROB 11/1130, proved 4 May 1785.

37 ERO D/ACR 15/139, proved 21 April 1743. See also JBB BD/16.

38 NA PROB 11/1035, proved 17 September 1777; JBB BD/931.

39 N. Tadmor, 'Women and wives: the language of marriage in early modern English biblical translations', *History Workshop Journal*, 62 (2000), pp. 1–28 for the reinforcement of marriage as the appropriate model of domestic relations in religious discourse.

40 L. Davidoff *et al.*, *The family story*, pp. 93–8.

41 ERO D/ABW 96, proved 27 May 1749.

42 ERO D/ABR 170/28, 1790.

experience, though the opposite case can be more revealing. Wills can show up points of tension, instances of failure, disappointment, conflict, or authority contested. Richard Morton wanted his household goods to go to his wife 'without controversy amongst my children'.[43] Susan Constable left all her estate to her son Thomas, specifying that 'Elizabeth the now wife of Thomas Constable shall not be entitled to thirds or dower or any claim on my estate but to be wholly at the disposal of Thomas without any claim from Elizabeth.' This might be just a scrupulous lawyer's drafting, but it might also indicate trouble between a mother and son's (second?) wife. When Susannah Newton left a messuage to her mother to enable her to provide 'thereout according to her discretion for my unfortunate reputed Daughter or Child Susanna the spurious offspring of that ungrateful & perfidious villain Edward Jones of Colchester ... Grocer.' there is a better chance that this view of Edward Jones was her own, even though the will was again written by a lawyer well known for his colourful language (William Mayhew, later the Borough Recorder).[44] Priscilla Hutton left a reversionary interest in her estate to her son-in-law James Laming, but if he 'should elope from his wife as he offing said he would, I impowr my dauter with her brother to sel the said houses and dispose of the money as she shall think fit without him'.[45] A neighbour wrote out this will for Priscilla Hutton so in this case it seems fairly certain that this tells us something about that family.

Susannah Newton was not the only will-maker to incorporate an illegitimate child into her family,[46] though not all illegitimate children were so readily included. John Dykes left Mary Richardson his housekeeper £40 she was owed in wages. Her daughter, 'now a nurse child at Edward Jays in St Mary-at-the-Walls, gardiner, registered as Mary Dikes' was left the interest on two thirds of his estate until she was twenty-one. Thereafter a third of the estate went to his wife 'if she be living on condition she does not go to law' with his executors, a third to the child Mary and a further third to her mother Mary Richardson if the executors considered she had 'done a Motherly part by her child'.[47] Even such a revealing source as wills frequently leaves only incomplete and tantalising traces in the record. If John Dykes' sexual relationship with Mary Richardson caused a separation from his wife, as seems likely, the reconstitution of household family he made was deliberately incomplete.[48] Leonore Davidoff has commented on the elisions between wife and servant status of women in nineteenth-century households and something rather similar seems to be going on

---

43 ERO D/ACR 15/258, proved 22 October 1747.

44 ERO D/ACR 15/147, proved 26 October 1743. Edward Jones never married. JBB BD/481. For William Mayhew see Chapters 6 and 7.

45 Alias Spencer, Hutting, St Botolphs, ERO D/ACR 18/335, proved 16 January 1790.

46 Robert Blyth, apparator of the Bishop of London left a gilt watch to his daughter Mary by his first wife, and a 'time piece' to natural daughter Elizabeth by present wife who received the bulk of the estate to bring up the children. ERO D/ABR 30/121, proved 4 February 1807.

47 ERO D/ACR 16/45, proved 4 July 1753.

48 N. Tadmor, *Family and friends in eighteenth-century England: Household, kinship, and patronage* (Cambridge, 2001), pp. 19–20.

here.[49] Mary Richardson was not fully acknowledged as mother, and the will makes a point of suggesting that she did not wish to be one (which might of course be true). The child, Mary, seems to have been called by her father's name, was to be provided for and would inherit something on adulthood. However, she was excluded from the household.

Wills remain a very rich source to explore the intersections between property and family among the eighteenth-century middling sort. Nevertheless, they provide only scant and slippery traces of lived experienced. Questions about family, authority, intimacy and affect (as well as the ways that the lives of particular families crossed and re-crossed between public and private) can be addressed more successfully by drawing on the few local instances where personal sources such as correspondence or autobiography survive. Although other such evidence can describe some of the darker side of family life (for example the early reminiscences of Mary Wollstonecraft), Colchester personal sources tend to describe family in a more positive light.[50]

The Taylors: writing the family

Regular and prolific correspondents, diarists or autobiographers among the Colchester middling sort tended to live in households where literate culture was a means of everyday expression accomplished with facility rather greater than that needed to acquire a basic education, keep sound accounts or conduct business correspondence, hold a minor office, or even to keep a parish school. As Margaret Hunt has argued, all these kinds of literacy were central to how the middling sort set about maintaining order and respectability, and across the country there are many surviving examples of middling self-writing authored by women and men where basic and functional literacy had been developed further.[51] Within a single (if sizeable) town these will inevitably be few. Colchester examples tend to be from later in the eighteenth century and originate in households where literacy, education and religious commitment were conjoined. Hence the best-described middling households are by that fact exceptional. The social imaginaries of households that were reflected upon and written about were inevitably shaped in part by that process of observation.[52] This is not to say that households

---

49 L. Davidoff, 'Mastered for life: servant and wife in Victorian and Edwardian England' in L Davidoff, *Worlds between*, pp. 18–40; see also D. Cooper and M. Donald, 'Households and "hidden" kin in early nineteenth-century England: four case studies in suburban Exeter, 1821–1861', *Continuity and Change*, 10 (1995), pp. 257 *et. seq*; E. Higgs, 'Women, occupations and work in the nineteenth-century censuses', *History Workshop Journal*, 23 (1987), pp. 59–80.

50 E. Nixon, *Mary Wollstonecraft; her life and times* (London, 1971), pp. 4–6.

51 Hunt, *The middling sort*, Chapter 7. Perhaps the fullest eighteenth-century autobiographical source to give more of the texture and tensions of the household is D. Vaisey (ed.), *The diary of Thomas Turner* (Oxford, 1985). For discussion of this N. Tadmor, 'The concept of the household-family in eighteenth-century England', *Past and Present*, 151 (1996), pp. 111–40; see also J.D. Marshall, *The autobiography of William Stout* (Manchester, 1967). My use of the term 'self-writing' derives from F. Nussbaum, 'Eighteenth-century women's autobiographical commonplaces' in S. Benstock (ed.), *The private self; theory and practice of women's autobiographical writings* (London, 1988), pp. 147–76, here p. 149.

52 L. Davidoff, *Worlds between*, p. 5 and p. 15, n. 5.

were severed from print culture unless people were given to dashing off gossipy letters or to painstaking spiritual self-examination; as John Brewer has argued the spread of print was enabling ever more people to become readers even if not writers.[53] Neither does it imply that pre-existing social realities were passively acted upon by the process of writing; the exchange between the social and psychological dimensions of family life was necessarily dialogic. Hence, although the writing practices of families such as the Taylors and the Twinings might be more prolific than in most middling households in the town, nevertheless they can speak to wider social imaginaries of the middling family. As Isaac Slythe's letter which opened this chapter indicates, the family got into middling writing of many types and in ways that are consonant with the descriptions of those most given to pen and ink.

The Taylor family, introduced in Chapter 2, derived their income from Isaac Taylor's ministry at Stockwell Chapel, their work as engravers and eventually also as authors.[54] The Taylor parents, Isaac and Ann, produced eleven children, six of whom survived. Their large family strained limited finances and the health and energies of Ann Martin Taylor who nevertheless kept up her intellectual partnership with her husband and was an author in her own right. All the Taylor children were educated at home, with additional teaching at the day school for the boys. Ann Taylor, writing in her old age, remembered her parents as enthusiastic exponents of domestic practices which were to become so characteristic of the nineteenth-century middle class, even though all family members, male and female, worked to earn income in the family business and the older children were paid wages as well as board. From their mid-teens each child was trained in engraving work and assisted their father in his workshop. Women's labour in a family business or even as independent traders was not only central to the success of the household family but was also a distinctive component of middling culture, certainly until the 1820s, for most except the most affluent bourgeoisie.[55] The Taylor daughters, Jane and Ann, who also wrote popular children's books, poetry and adult moral tales, alternated between engraving and housework. They rotated these duties between them, the engraver for the week being known as 'Supra' and the housekeeper as 'Infra'.

The Taylor daughters thus had a clear idea of the hierarchy of their duties, as well as a deep emotional attachment to home and family strengthened by their religious faith. As Jane Taylor later wrote, life was 'Duty, Praise and Prayer', all of which centred on the Angel Lane household. The religious tone of the household seemed also to have transmuted any social or emotional problems into spiritual ones. Ann's text glosses her mother's domestic anxieties and her sister's irritation with the monotony of engraving work. In 1802 Ann Taylor was very ill with the smallpox which had already killed her youngest brother, Decimus. Her illness was perceived by both Ann and her father as an opportunity for developing spiritual grace. As she recovered he 'watched for fruit' and finally persuaded her to take up full membership of the chapel

53 J. Brewer, *The pleasures of the imagination: English culture in the eighteenth century* (London, 1997), Chapter 4, esp. p. 187.

54 J. Gilbert (ed.), *The autobiography and other memorials of Mrs Gilbert*, 2nd edn (London, 1876).

55 H. Barker, *The business of women*; P. Sharpe, 'A woman's worth: A case study of capital accumulation in early modern England — women and property relationships in medieval and early modern England', *Parergon*, 19 (2002), pp. 173–84; J. Bailey, *Unquiet lives*.

congregation.[56] Not only the work of mother and daughters as housekeepers, but also of the daughters and sons as engravers, enabled father Isaac Taylor to maintain a dual occupation of engraver and non-conformist minister. His domestic duties involved the spiritual and practical education of his children. The contingency of public and private is exemplified in this as well as in the way that scientific lessons were expanded to include an audience of many of the daughter's friends and contemporaries, thus becoming semi-public, fee-earning occasions.[57] The Taylor household had trade, domestic, religious and educational uses. It was the workplace of family members engaged in engraving, intellectual and domestic work. It was operated by the parents and older children with one or two domestic servants, two apprentices and often a few pupils. The Taylors were part of a coterie of religiously, socially and intellectually like-minded middling families who seem to have shared a similar affective investment in family and kinship. Ann Taylor described this social world as a series of overlapping 'family circles'. On their first night in Colchester the Taylors stayed with baymaker James Mansfield and his family. The Mansfields were Unitarian non-conformists and assembled a party to welcome the new minister and his family. Ann Taylor was struck by how closely related the company was, almost all being cheerily referred to as 'cousin'.[58] Families are everywhere in her narrative, even among the household cats.[59] Ann Taylor Gilbert's family romance was written in old age and is committed to portraying the spiritual virtues of the well-ordered middling family household. Nevertheless it does convey the social and affective components of non-conformists' friendship and familial networks that were working to provide material support and business associates for men such as Isaac Slythe.

The Twinings: gossip and affect

It was not only non-conformists who valued the household family and extended kin networks. Thomas Twining came from the London tea-dealing family. His first association with Colchester was through attending Colchester Grammar School, which he entered in 1754. After university at Cambridge he took holy orders and obtained his first living as curate of Fordham, just outside Colchester in 1764. In 1772 he was appointed rector of White Notley in Essex (near Braintree) though he never resided there, and in 1788 of St Mary-at-the-Walls in Colchester. Although worth only £90 a year, he sought the Colchester living because it brought with it a residence in town and close to his own and his wife's relations. Having secured the Fordham

---

56 Gilbert, *Mrs Gilbert*, p. 149.

57 *Ibid.*, pp. 99, 102. L. Davidoff, 'Life is duty, praise and prayer', *Fawcett Library Papers*, 4 (1981) ; L. Davidoff and C. Hall, *Family fortunes*, especially pp. 59–69, 478, and Chapter 3, note 114, p. 494, for detailed bibliography of works about and by the Taylors; J. Bensusan Butt, 'Jane and Ann Taylor as engravers', *East Anglian Magazine*, 21 (1961), pp. 682–3; J. Bensusan Butt to Christina Duff Stewart 12 August 1969, ERO Acc 905, Box 12, for review of the Taylor ephemera, teaching aids and other items then held in the Hollytrees Library; S. Bowerbank, 'Taylor, Jane (1783–1824)', *Oxford Dictionary of National Biography* (Oxford, 2004), www.oxford.dnb.com/view/article/27039, accessed 18 March 2007.

58 JBB BD/560 James Mansfield.

59 Gilbert, *Mrs Gilbert*, p. 197.

Figure 3.1 James Godby, *Thomas Twining*. Published by T. Cadell and W. Davies, after William Evans, after John James Halls; stipple engraving; published 21 August 1816; NPG D14265. Reproduced courtesy of the National Portrait Gallery, London

curacy, the same year he had married Elizabeth, the daughter of Revd Palmer Smythies of St Martins (Twining's late schoolmaster). This connected him with the extensive clerical and political Smythies family, that included a number of Colchester clergy, a surgeon and Francis Smythies the energetic Town Clerk and leader of the borough corporation party in the 1780s and 90s (Chapters 6 and 7, family tree at Figure 3.2). Also living in Colchester were John and Hester Mills and Hester's mother. Mills was a tea dealer and later a banker with smart premises at the top of High Street. He had been a part of the Twining firm in London and had married into the family; Hester Mills was Thomas Twining's cousin.[60]

Thomas Twining was a regular and prolific letter writer. Given his education and profession, Twining was able to write in a number of styles, but reserved an informal, chatty voice for his correspondence with family and friends. He used this voice to gossip about learning, local politics and society, and to talk about his domestic life. The letters to his young (and sickly) brother Daniel are deliberately playful and consequently describe the rather jolly family life of the young married Twinings at Fordham and during their stays at Elizabeth's father's in Colchester. Cleaning, gardening and visiting, as well as Elizabeth's irregular practice in reading French (Dan was also struggling to develop his French) are typical subject matter. A family joke about eating too much pudding runs through the domestic chatter. Twining also

60 S. Lane-Poole, 'Twining Thomas (bapt. 1734 d. 1804)', rev. A. Chahoud, *Oxford Dictionary of National Biography* (Oxford, 2004), www.oxford.dnb.com/view/article/27910, accessed 20 March 2007; R.S. Walker (ed.), *A selection of Thomas Twining's letters 1734–1804: a record of a tranquil life*, two vols (1991–2); JBB BD/804 Palmer Smythies, BD/583 John Mills.

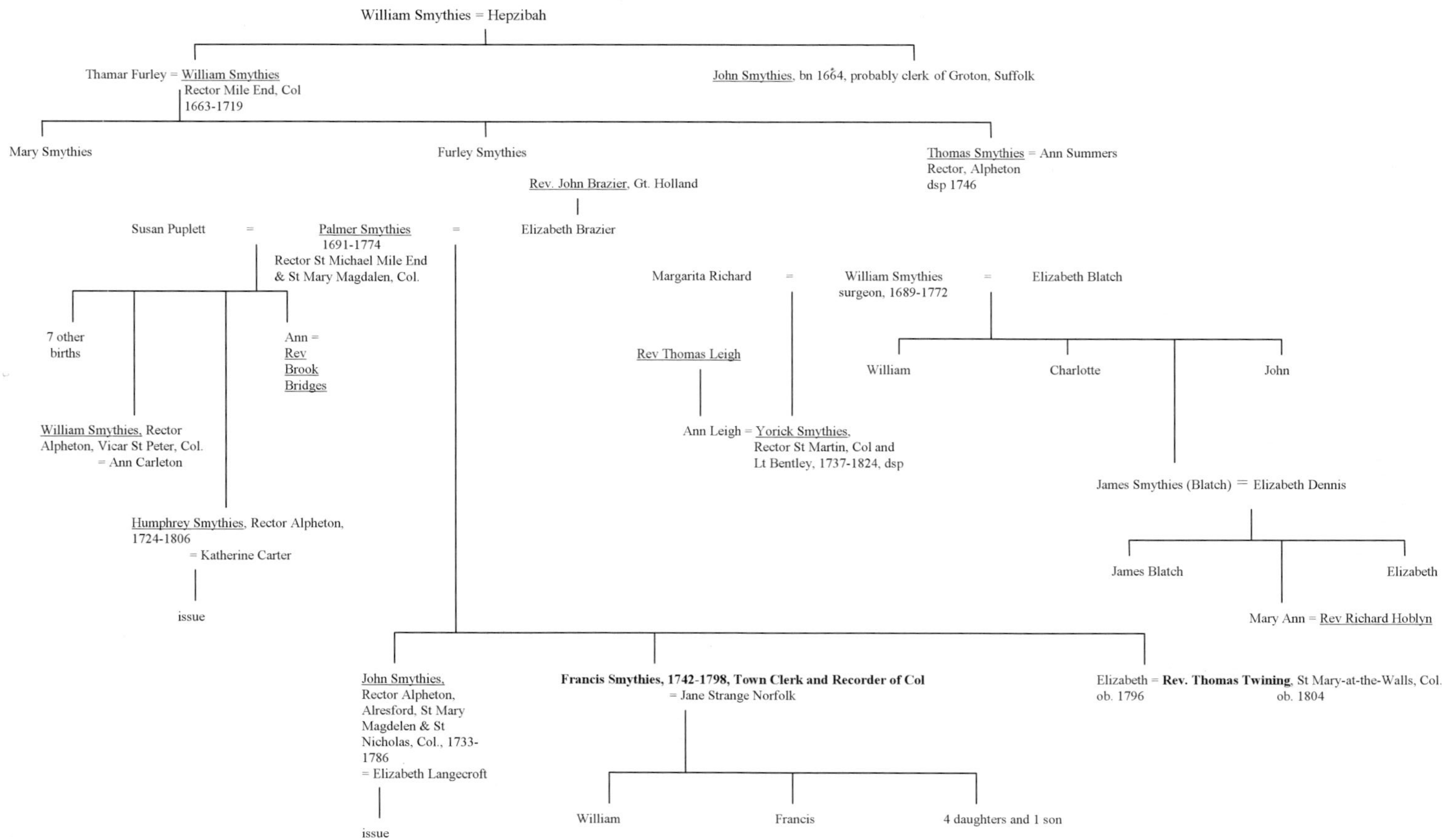

Figure 3.2 The Smythies family. Adapted from R. H. Smythies, Memorials of the Smythies family (London, 1912)

gossiped regularly about domestic servants and animals, who seem to have almost comparable identity status.[61] The letters were in part joint efforts since Elizabeth also often sent news, or added a postscript. In September 1764 she told about a hen who nested in the stable and provided only four chickens instead of the expected fourteen, about the funeral of a neighbour's 'disagreeable' child, about the exploits of the dog, Friday, the new kitten, the old cat Titty, the young servant Robert and the temperamental mare Fanny, who had put their chaise in a ditch. 'We din'd at Mr Boys's the other day; Fanny was very naughty indeed ... Robert did not open the gate quite as far as she cou'd have wish'd; it put her in such a passion ...'[62] The household family of the Twinings is written here to include animals and servants as well as the married couple. The funeral of the 'disagreeable' (probably disabled) child is an odd, jarring intrusion into this happy catalogue even though Elizabeth emphasised the humour of her husband walking in procession with this 'hat bands flying'. It might indicate the something that was missing from the Twinings' household. They never did have any children.[63]

As well as keeping up with intellectual and professional friends such as Dr Samuel Parr and Charles Burney, Twining's principal correspondents were family ones. He wrote often to his brother Dan (until he died in his teens in the early 1770s) and to his half-brother Richard Twining who was the head of the London business. Thomas Twining discussed scholarly and political matters with his intellectual friends, who also included the All Saints rector, Dr Nathaniel Forster. Letters to Richard include detailed consultation and advice over the publication of Thomas Twining's translation of Aristotle's *Poetics*. But with all his correspondents he chats informally, exchanges gossip about mutual friends, sends local news and talks about family matters both cheerful and worrying. His letters make plain the importance of family and domestic life to the social identity of a professional man, who clearly also received reciprocal news from other professional men. Twining certainly selected material depending on the recipient of a letter, but family (his own and other people's) was always an integral part of his subject matter. Consequently Twining's letters reveal the meaning and the operation of family for himself and for his social networks.

Richard and Daniel Twining were also charged with numerous domestic shopping commissions, particularly in the 1770s when the newly married Twinings were setting up home. As historians of consumption have found, shopping for domestic items was shared by men and women.[64] Thomas Twining was affluent enough to maintain a

---

61 Walker, *Thomas Twining*, letter 14, p. 55.

62 Richard Boys was Rector of West Bergholt. Walker, *Thomas Twining*, letter 13, 28 September 1764 to Daniel Twining.

63 R.H. Smythies, *Memorials of the Smythies family* (London, 1912).

64 Walker, *Thomas Twining*, letters 7, 8 and 9 to Daniel Twining of 9 and 27 December 1764 and 8 January 1765. The Twinings had married on 3 January. Letter 7 sends commissions for the tuning and mending of his harpsichord, letter 8 asks for dispatch of green and bohea tea and coffee (some of 12 — 14 shillings and some 'the cheapest, for servants') as well as a 'piece of very good worsted for breeches — 9 or 10/- the whole, to be sent by Unwin's wagon on Thursday'. James Unwin, carrier, JBB BD/895. M. Finn, 'Men's things: masculine possession in the consumer revolution', *Social History*, 25 (2000), pp. 133–55; A. Vickery, *The gentleman's daughter: women's lives in Georgian England* (New Haven and London, 1998), pp. 164–7.

comfortable household with several servants, but despite secure inherited capital he was not wealthy and seems to have rather disliked the process of extracting his tithes from curmudgeonly Essex farmers. Richard Twining was an important source of advice on matters of business, also advancing funds to ease the cash flow of the Thomas Twining household. Twining wrote in 1798:

> Then again, these plaguey money matters vex me. I wish it were half as difficult to get the money out of my purse, as it is. What an unthinking fool was I to tell you that £20 would hold me to the 6th Nov. ... You must help me out again in what way you please.[65]

Affection and compliments were regularly extended between close kin and friends ('... loves to Mother' or 'Yr Sister's love') cementing affective networks which oiled the wheels of social life as well as providing vital material and social support when called upon. The Thomas Twinings and the Mills leapt into concerted (but apparently ineffective) action when Thomas Clarke (Hester Mills' brother-in-law) was imprisoned in Newgate for debt. Hester Mills was Twining's key source of help over the period when his wife grew ever more ill and after her death in 1796. Two letters to Richard also detail the marital difficulties of Thomas' friends the Tindalls when rocky emotional relations between husband and wife were marked by jealousy and stubbornness. This, combined with the hostility of patrons of the husband's clerical living and his mastership of Bottesdale School, forced a separation when Tindall left his employment. The Tindalls are a clear example of how emotional instability could lead to direct material losses. Twining and other Colchester friends took on the role of mediators, and he described the emotionally fraught scenes that ensued.[66] Poor health, anxiety, worry, pain and grief have their part in this correspondence as much as the affectionate joy in everyday family life. Thomas Twining is an example of an eighteenth-century Colcestrian whose emotional as well as social and material investment in his family was deep and extensive.

If this chapter's opening example of Isaac Slythe resists such enquiries, that of Thomas Twining provides fuller answers about the importance of both his household family and his extended kinship networks. Other local examples, notably that of Revd Nathaniel Forster of All Saints, Twining's close friend and colleague, extend this view of family life further into the educated, professional middling sort at least, and while it cannot automatically be generalised across the middling sort, there were some

---

65 Walker, *Thomas Twining*, letter 216, p. 524, 10 October 1798 to Richard Twining. Letter continues 'I assure you this wanting money perpetually is so new a thing that it is no small worry to me. I know I am not actually poor; but really I have the present feel of poverty, & the inconveniences of it. I don't like to be forced even to imagine the misery of being in distressed circumstances. You must help me out again in what way you please. I don't wish to cut deeper into my balance with you than is necessary, as my Notley tithe day is so near, & my tithes here will soon come dropping in by degrees. (I have no *day* here; people call & pay when they please) ... £30 or £40 would not do. I wish you would put me in a way to get money. I would do anything however mean or rascally'. I should be a perfect miser, were it not that I am full as eager (& a little more) to spend as to get. Letter 217, p. 525 to Richard Twining, November 1798 reports that he netted £90 on his Notley tithes after he had paid the curate and for repairs, for the dinner and other expenses of the day.'... I do not on the strength of it mean to loosen the reins of my economy.'

66 Walker, *Thomas Twining*, letter 138, to Richard Twining, 14 November, 1790, pp. 363–4; *Ibid.*, letter 139, to Richard Twining, 3 January 1791, p. 365.

Colchester middling families who were sufficiently well documented over generations to reconstruct comparable patterns.

The Shillitos: stability and change

Although diversity, instability and movement characterised the eighteenth-century urban middling sort as a whole, as Chapter 1 has argued, the Colchester middling sort included a significant minority of families who persisted in the town across decades and generations. The Shillito family of All Saints parish were one such example. Because the Shillitos were given to stability rather than migration, there exists a dense collection of traces in the historical record which indicate at least some of the interpersonal and social dynamics of the household family as well as showing the effects of longer term social and economic change on one particular kinship group. The family achieved this stability not least because of the leverage they were able to exercise in local patronage networks. The need and preference among affluent figures from Colchester's 'big bourgeoisie' to consolidate a specifically urban power base produced a micro-cultural geography in this small town-centre parish that encouraged the persistence of specific middling trading households. The Shillitos provide a good example of how a middling family could ride out the contraction in the bay trade.

At first sight the Shillitos are a model example of success through stability. From the late seventeenth century five generations of Shillitos lived in Colchester, at least four resident in the same house in All Saints. This was one of the row of houses built along the line of the old castle bailey. These small, narrow, two-storey houses fronted the High Street and backed onto the castle. The first Shillito recorded in the town was Richard Shellito, common councillor on the corporation in 1635. Subsequently several seventeenth-century Shillitos traded as blacksmiths. Ephraim Shillito I moved into the then profitable bay trade. He took his borough freedom in 1700, as a cardmaker. His wife Elizabeth was sister to William Seaber, the borough High Constable, which linked the Shillitos to those who officered the corporation. Shillito held minor corporation office and was a frequent juryman in borough sessions. Within his own parish, he was churchwarden between 1737 and 1740, and witnessed several wills for neighbours, also receiving a £l0 legacy in the will of another.[67] All Saints was a small but mixed parish, which contained a population of middling trading and professional families alongside the mansions of some of the town's leaders, in particular Charles Gray at

67 Where not otherwise cited, the material on the Shillitos is drawn from J. Bensusan Butt, *Charles Shillito, Oliver Goldsmith* (Colchester, 1944). Colchester Borough Assembly Book, ERO D/B 5 Gb3, 1620–47; Oath Book, ERO D/B 5 R1, freeburgess admissions index, 1727; marriage licence with Elizabeth Seaber of or at Berechurch, ERO D/ABL 1727. For William Seaber see Chapter 6. Borough Assembly Book, 1712–41, ERO D/B 5 Gb7, entries for 2 September 1734, 1 September 1735, 5 September 1737, 4 September 1738, 2 October 1739, 1 September 1740. Borough Sessions Book 1734–68, ERO D/B 5 Sb5/3, Sessions of Easter 1736, Easter and Michaelmas 1737, Michaelmas 1738, Midsummer and Michaelmas 1739, Epiphany 1740, Epiphany 1741. Notes of wills; JBB archive ERO Acc 905, ms notebooks, Boxes 13 and 14: Joseph Duffield (ERO D/ACR 13/8, proved 1717), Hannah Rous (ERO D/ACR 14/222, proved 1728), Richard Winsley (NA PROB 11/664, proved 29 March 1734), Mrs Mary Rush (NA PROB 11/720, proved 6 August 1742). Will of Elizabeth Sumers widow, All Saints, ERO D/ACR 15/115 proved 1742. Will Peter Alvis, n. 29 above.

the Hollytrees, George Wegg at East Hill House and the All Saints rector, Dr Nathaniel Forster.[68] All Saints tradesmen supplied more corporation office holders than the size of the parish would predict and became readily incorporated into the patronage networks of Gray and Wegg.[69] In 1744 Ephraim Shillito became Master of the House of Correction, which was located in the castle just behind the family house. This office was handed down in the family first from father to son (to Ephraim Shillito jnr in 1757) and later from uncle to nephew (to John Smith in 1775).[70] It is likely that this office was a family affair in other senses. The inmates of the House of Correction doubtless generated duties carried out by the Master's wife and family.[71] Later, John Smith's wife, Elizabeth (and after her, her daughter Mary) looked after both the gaol and the book club library which was housed in the castle.[72]

The second generation of Shillitos in the High Street premises (Ephraim Shillito II, his wife Elizabeth and their children) thus inherited a legacy of trade, property and office holding.[73] After a few years living and working in south London when single and then as a young married couple (although they married in London both bride and groom were Colcestrian by birth) the younger Shillitos returned to Colchester in 1751 when their second child was born and apparently at the point where Ephraim Shillito I retired from trade.[74] When his father was 'old and infirm' Ephraim II also took over the House of Correction. He was named Assistant in the new Borough Charter of 1763 and like his father was incorporated into All Saints patronage networks. He received a mourning ring in the will of George Wegg snr from East Hill House. Charles Gray, his

68 J. Bensusan Butt, *All Saints' Colchester in the eighteenth century* (Colchester, privately printed, 1989).

69 S. D'Cruze, *The middling sort*, p. 117.

70 County Order Book, ERO Q/SO 8, 2 October 1744; *Ibid.*, 15 July 1746, Beetles and Blocks ordered for House of Correction, Shillito to set prisoners to work beating Hemp; Q/SO 10, 19 April 1757 'old and infirm' was succeeded by son Ephraim; Q/SO 12, 3 October 1775, salary £7 10s a quarter. For Neild's report on the Gaol see *Gentleman's Magazine* II, 1804, p. 705. Smith was the son of Elizabeth Shillito (née Parsley)'s sister. The House of Correction job remained in the Smith family until the death of William Parsley Smith in 1837.

71 County Order Book Q/SO 9, 14 January 1752 'Mrs Shillito to show cause why she left the Court'; in the next generation cf ERO D/P 245, St Leonards' overseers correspondence, Ephraim Shillito to Jonathan Tabor re poor woman in the Castle Gaol to whom he claimed to be 'doctor and nurse', see Chapter 8 below.

72 She died on 15 January 1802, aged 56. Her daughter (died 4 December 1852) continued these duties for thirty-seven years, as her epitaph (All Saints) records. JBB BD/1026, John Smith, cardmaker.

73 Ephraim Shillito II, baptised All Saints 9 December 1727, married by licence at St Mary Magdalen Bermondsey, 3 June 1748, to Elizabeth Parsley. He was then resident at St Thomas Southwark. Their first child Elizabeth baptised St Nicholas, Colchester, 26 November 1748, born 16 November 1748 — a seven month baby. Took an apprentice, Samuel, son of Ralph Newton to Ephraim Shillito, St Olaves Southwark, 1749, £11 11s. Board of Stamps, Apprenticeship Books, NA IR1, 18/217. Newton was transferred in 1750 (NA IR1 51/76) to Philip Sansom cardmaker of All Saints to complete his time. Shillito was trading in Colchester December 1751, at 96 High Street, four doors west of Castle Inn, rated 5 from 1754. J. Bensusan Butt, *Charles Shillito*, pp. 32–5.

74 Ephraim III was baptised at All Saints on 15 October 1751. Ephraim II began to attend All Saints vestry meetings from this point in place of his father. J. Bensusan Butt, *Charles Shillito*, pp. 32–5.

MP and landlord, supplied a loan for the extension of the family premises. Other affluent neighbours including Revd Forster put up the £500 guarantee to secure Shillito the agency for selling Sun Insurance from 1776, bay trade reverses having apparently damaged the cardmaking business. At this point his nephew John Smith took over the mastership of the House of Correction and the (presumably reduced) cardmaking concern.[75] The inclusion of Elizabeth Shillito's name in the borough records with her husband's when they took an apprentice, and the fact that she was sole legatee (apart from two mourning rings) in his will of 1791 indicate the extent of the partnership between the couple in managing both trade and property.[76] They had ten children in all, three of whom (Elizabeth, Ephraim III and Charles) survived into adulthood. The small house in All Saints must have been crammed full in the 1750s and early 1760s, containing grandparents, parents and children, as well as a couple of apprentices. It provided the base for the cardmaking business, the labour of office-holding, the rearing of a sizeable family including several infant deaths as well as the care of the older generation. Repeated infant mortality was yet another of the psychological pains of family life.

The next generation of Shillitos was confronted by changing social and economic opportunities as bay trade contraction and market sector growth accelerated. Elizabeth Shillito (the daughter) became a milliner, working at first as assistant to Susannah Gibbs, the wife of bookseller Samuel Gibbs, further up the High Street.[77] Someone has written on the title-page of a book[78] in the Castle Library:

Sam x x x Gibbs

Eliz. Shillito

The Shillito family had access to the castle, of course. Whether this was malicious or just mischievous, it may have indicated otherwise unrevealed tensions in the Gibbs trading household. After Susannah Gibbs died in 1772, Elizabeth set up trade on her own account from the Shillito family premises, which managed to accommodate her genteel wares alongside the cardmaking business; yet another level of spatial heterogeneity in the household. We cannot know how far she achieved the genteel, quasi-domestic setting for her wares that were fashionable for shops in the luxury trades. She advertised that she had '... just returned from LONDON with a fresh Assortment of MILLENERY HABERDASHERY & LINNEN-DRAPERY goods, with which ... (customers) ... may depend upon being served upon the most reasonable Terms. She also sells Smiths Lavender and Hungary Water, Eau de Luce, Essence of Bergamot, Almond Paste, Italian and Windsor Soap, Washballs and Hair Powder.'[79]

---

75 JBB BD/1133 Ephraim Shillito II, *BD*/768 Ephraim Shillito III.

76 Will NA Prob 11/1205, proved 5 May 1791.

77 JBB BD/980 Samuel Gibbs.

78 The book is Dr William King, *Discourse on the inventions of men in the service of God* (London, 1694).

79 *IpsJ* 8 May 1773. See also 29 February 1772 her first advertisement as 'assistant to the late Mrs Gibbs', having now set up 'next Mr Hedges, All Saints' (the Shillito family premises) with 'a stock of millinery &c' including 'Best Lavender and Hungary waters ... (and) ... Green and Bohea Tea'. H. Berry, 'Polite consumption: shopping in eighteenth-century England', *Transactions of the Royal Historical Society* 6th Series, 12 (2002), pp. 375–94.

She married James Dunthorne, the artist, in 1779. Dunthorne was the son of a Colchester portrait and coach painter (also James).[80] Although named in some contemporary sources as the 'Colchester Hogarth', career success eluded him. His art and career are explored further in Chapter 5. Dunthorne ran a print shop in Colchester High Street for a living. Elizabeth continued her milliner's and perfumer's business throughout their marriage until her death in 1807 as well as servicing the needs of a growing family. Elizabeth Dunthorne can be celebrated as an independent businesswoman, but continued the perfumer's shop because of material insecurity as much as for other reasons. Dunthorne died after a 'long affliction' in October 1794.[81]

Morbidity, artistic interests and only partly successful attempts to achieve social mobility through patronage also characterised the life course of Elizabeth's brother, Charles Shillito. He was working in the cardmaking business when, as a teenager (1778) he appeared before borough sessions for pulling the nose of a local surgeon. Shortly after this, Shillito moved away from Colchester and became a lieutenant of marines. He obtained this position through the All Saints rector, Nathaniel Forster, who applied through his friend Jeremy Bentham jnr. Shillito's naval career was cut short; he saw active service once in 1781 and thereafter retired on half pay due to ill health. He was married in Bath to Susannah Griffin, another Colcestrian. They had seven children over the next twelve years.[82]

The Shillitos had been long-standing Whigs, but Charles supported the Tories (Chapter 6). He was secretary to the Tory Constitutional Club in 1788–90. He was also a minor poet and playwright. An early elegiac poem of 1779 was not well received, and though two later plays of 1786 and 1789 were presented in Colchester and elsewhere in East Anglia as benefits for the Colchester Sunday Schools, they failed to please the all important London audience. Local patrons again intervened when Shillito's navy half pay was withdrawn in 1787. They secured him the mastership of the Church of England Charity School in All Saints, and he kept his family by teaching the charity children. That year he published *The Country Bookclub*, a poem modelled on Goldsmith's *Deserted Village*. Two other works were followed on 27 December 1792 by *God Save the Queen — a new song*, a product of his Tory patriotism.[83] From 1790 Charles Shillito also operated the Sun Insurance agency. He was to come to a sticky end; his decomposing body was found hanging in woods near Chelmsford in 1794 and the inquest brought in a verdict of suicide and lunacy. His widow continued

---

80 Judy Crosby Ivy, 'Dunthorne, John (bap. 1770, d. 1844) *Oxford Dictionary of National Biography* (Oxford, 2004), www.oxford.dnb.com/view/article/8287, accessed 19 March 2007. W.G. Benham, 'The Dunthornes of Colchester', *Essex Review*, 10 (1901), pp. 27–35, Chapter 5 below.

81 All Saints Registers D/P 200, 7 December 1779; Walker, *Thomas Twining*, Thomas Twining to Charles Burney, 12 November 1784, letter 89, pp. 265-6, also letter 90 Burney 30 December 1784, p. 268 sends, 'Thanks as to the Painter &c.' For Elizabeth Shillito, see *Holden's Directory*, 1805. Her death, *IpsJ* 21 March 1807.

82 Nathaniel Forster's correspondence is British Library, Add. Mss. 11277.

83 *IpsJ* 10 April 1790, 8 May 1790, 12 June 1790; Charles Shillito, *The sea fight, an elegiac poem from Henry to Laura founded on original correspondence between the parties in the year 1759. Written at sea* (London, 1779); *The country book club* (London, 1788); *The man of enterprise, a farce in two acts and prose* (Colchester, 1789); *God save the queen, a new song by Mr Shillito* (Colchester, dated 1761 in British Library Catalogue but unlikely given Shillito's age). Records of Colchester Charity School, ERO T/A 613, Acc 905, Box 6 and Box 12, ms notebook of September 1967.

in Colchester until 1807 (perhaps significantly the year her sister-in-law died) leaving the children to the care of friends and relations.[84]

The eldest sibling, Ephraim Shillito III had been apprenticed not into the bay trade, but to an Ipswich baker.[85] Returning to Colchester, he became a wine merchant in the 1780s, married the daughter of another Colchester wine merchant and took over the insurance agency from his father. He and his wife Kitty left Colchester for London after he had become bankrupt in 1796. He seems to have found employment with the East India Company. His wife's property at least seems to have survived the bankruptcy, since she distributed an estate of over £250 in her will.[86]

The family story of the eighteenth-century Shillitos speaks to the personal and familial consequences of broader currents of change. It seems that the closely entwined working and domestic lives of the first two eighteenth-century Shillito generations, with the overlaps between trade and office, home and parish, sociality and patronage, made those households more secure than their successors who were both pushed and pulled by wider social forces while still retaining the middling trading household family form. The decline of the bay trade and doubtless the shift in patronage networks in Colchester from the 1780s (see Chapter 6) prompted the third generation to diversify their occupations, leaving the cardmaking business and the House of Correction to their cousin John Smith. Such diversification carried risks, particularly in the economically volatile 1790s. Both James Dunthorne and Charles Shillito tried to establish careers in the arts when later eighteenth-century fashions for sensibility coincided with the increasing commoditisation of culture in fast-developing markets (Chapter 5). However, neither of these were a Tom Gainsborough and neither managed to break out of the limitations of the provincial market, though both were helped financially by local patronage. Although Ephraim Shillito III had no artistic pretensions his move into the drink trade also led to financial failure. Both Dunthorne and Charles Shillito came to rather sad ends. There were doubtless costs both material and emotional in such failures for families as well as individuals.

---

84 *IpsJ* 21 June 1794. A son, George, raised by uncle William Borrows, corkcutter, left for London and died a 'gent' in 1845. One son was a doctor. Another went into the marines and married a General's daughter. One daughter remained an independently maintained spinster and another married a farmer. J. Bensusan Butt, *Charles Shillito*, p. 38.

85 Apprenticed to Robert Cole, Ipswich baker, for £10 in 1766. (NA IR1 Apprenticeship Indexes, 55/207).

86 *IpsJ* 19 February 1785, Shillito in partnership with attorney William Suddell set up as brandy merchants taking the stock and premises of Thomas Dikes in St Nicholas. *IpsJ* 19 August 1786 Suddell left the partnership. From 1787 Shillito occupied premises at 56 High Street, rated 4. In 1788 he stood surety for James Green at the Seahorse (All Saints) and John Smith, innkeeper, at the Mitre (St James) (Alehouse Recognisances). That same year he headed the subscription list for Carter's *Siege of Colchester* and later also subscribed to John Fenno's *History of Colchester.* He was agent for Sun Fire Office in 1790. *Chelmsford Chronicle,* (hereafter *ChCh* 1 October 1790), 24 December 1790. In 1791 Shillito married Kitty Rondeau of St Giles, *IpsJ* 23 July 1791. For his bankruptcy, *IpsJ* 30 April. 14 May and 2 July 1796. Voted as 'gent' of Kennington Surrey in the 1812 borough election. He died at Poplar on 28 December 1822 aged 71, monument All Saints, Poplar. He was buried at the East India Company's burial ground there. His will, NA PROB 11 1661/493, proved 10 September 1822, left all to his wife. Kitty died on 28 July 1824 aged 57. Will Kitty Shillito, NA PROB 11 1689/490, 1824.

Conclusion

There were therefore key correspondences between middling family forms and functions across eighteenth-century urban society. The key distinctiveness of the material from Colchester is to demonstrate how the middling family adapted to economic change and the contraction of the town's key industry; bankruptcy or curtailed, uncertain incomes have been a recurrent theme across the different middling families discussed. For the range of the Colchester middling sort, from the more affluent, geographically mobile, non-conformist Slythes with which this chapter opened, to the small-trading, stable, Anglican Shillitos, the household family underpinned material welfare as well as social identity. The middling household was characterised by distinctive patterns of domestic consumption and in its less affluent reaches, heterogenous uses of household space. The wider slice of the middling sort that becomes visible from a survey of local wills confirms these key juxtapositions, as well as the ways that bequests carefully delineated wider kinship and friendship networks and marked the boundaries between family in this wider sense and the core household. Such boundaries also intersected with those between family, neighbourhood, religious congregation and wider society. These social, cultural (and psychological) force-fields were certainly gendered but were far more nuanced than contemporary prescriptive literature advocating separate spheres would have liked.

Family was also a crucial locus of intimacy, and personal sources on the best recorded households demonstrate the level of affective investment the middling family generated. Both the Taylors and the Twinings left sources which show family intimacy in a very positive light, though there are also traces of the pains and costs of this close correlation of affective, social and material interests which are also evident in other studies.[87] Furthermore, there is sufficient evidence of violence against both wives and servants to mitigate the more positive picture obtained from the Taylors and the Twinings. Chapter 8 will develop the discussion of instances where such pains included the infliction of physical violence, but even within the inevitably tangential sources we have on the Slythes, the Shillitos and in some wills, the tensions and difficulties of the middling family form in a shifting economy are evident. The interrelationship of materiality, social relations and affect in middling culture raised the emotional and personal stakes in business and exchange which were already high because of the small-scale nature of middling trade and professions and the ubiquity of extended credit. Authority within the family might compel individuals to subsume their personal interests into family ones and might bear more heavily on women than men. However, authority was always negotiated across relationships of affect, with attendant psychological benefits and costs. If family, primarily in its household meaning and secondarily in terms of extended kin networks was a crucial first line of defence against social and economic uncertainty, then patronage and one's 'friends'

87 J. Bailey, '"I dye [sic] by inches": Locating wife beating in the concept of a privatization of marriage and violence in eighteenth-century England', *Social History*, 31 (2006), pp. 273 et seq; E. Foyster, *Marital violence: an English family history, 1660–1857* (Cambridge, 2005).

could be almost as important. I underlined the significance of patronage to the Shillitos. Friends were more socially and economically significant than mere casual acquaintance and will form a substantive part of our discussion of middling trade, business and professional life in the following chapter.

Chapter 4

Credit and exchange

Friends and the public

If family formed the core of middling sort identity, being the locus of individuals' social, material and economic investment, then the next layer of middling society comprised those whom one could count as one's friends. In 1773, when Elizabeth Shillito (of the All Saints family discussed in the previous chapter) began her millinery and perfumery business, she advertised in the local paper and begged 'leave to thank her *friends* for their past favours and ... (acquainted) ... them and the *public*, that she is just returned from LONDON with a fresh assortment of Millenery Haberdashery and Linnen Drapery goods.' (my emphasis). The distinction between one's friends and the public is common in eighteenth-century Colchester sources. It was made in a very different context by attorney William Mayhew in 1749. Mayhew wanted the assistance of the borough MP to regain the town's Charter, then suspended. (Chapter 7) He wrote on behalf of the 'poor Burgesses of Colchester' who had applied to him, Mayhew, 'as one of ... (the MP's) ... Friends'. Much of the recent work on the eighteenth-century middling sort emphasises the importance of credit to middling lifestyles and argues that the social dimensions of maintaining and enhancing credit were fundamentally enmeshed with the financial ones. Relations of patronage and deference were also often channels of credit and obligation. Friends might well be creditors, but they might equally well be debtors. So, who were your friends? Milliner Elizabeth Shillito's were no doubt her chief and most affluent customers. In the previous chapter, the role of patronage networks was evident in the history of several members of the Shillito family. Your friends were those who supported or advanced your social and material credit. It was to your friends you would apply for a pension, a pardon or a loan. Friends would act as executor, trustee or witness to a will. They would put up a recognisance for your court appearance. They would witness your marriage. They might apply on your behalf to even more prestigious friends of their own. They were your landlord, your employer, the most affluent member of your parish vestry, the neighbourhood innkeeper or the local cleric. Across this wide spectrum of relationships both patronage and something nearer approaching reciprocity was involved.

When Hannah Hopkins, the widow of a prosperous mariner and ship owner made her will, she appointed as executors her brother and John Bartholomew, a merchant at the port, a friend and neighbour, clearly associated with her husband in his trade and earlier the executor of his will. Bartholomew had first appeared in Colchester as master of the sloop *Ceres*. He had a house near the Hythe in the 1730s and had married Hannah Pamplin, which had allied him to a successful middling family – the owners of the Fleece, a large inn in the town centre. They had two sons. He was an active trader and used the local courts to enforce his debtors to pay. At about the time of his wife's death in 1739 the *Ceres* was sold and Bartholomew seems to have remained in St Leonards and developed his merchant and ship-owning activities. By the later 1740s he was selling marble and portland stone and employed a skilled mason from London. He was a regular attender at St Leonards vestry and acted as overseer (Chapter 8). When, in 1740, a ring of timber thieves was discovered in the neighbourhood, they were taken to his house by the constable to be examined, apparently before the justice was informed. Again in 1760, he took a leading role in examining and apprehending small-time crooks embezzling sugar, a cargo on the Colchester to London pacquet, on which they sailed. In 1758 he appeared at petty sessions with a vagrant whom he had apprehended late the previous night. He maintained strong connections with the town's sea-going interest at the Hythe. He received £50 in the will of a spinster relation Elizabeth Freeman. As well as acting as executor for Hannah Hopkins and her husband, he obtained the administration of a debtor's estate worth £100 in 1742. In 1746 he stood bond for the administration of another seaman's estate, settled another in 1751, and that of a bricklayer in the small nearby port of Wivenhoe in 1753. He also maintained contacts with the wider middling sort in the town, standing bond for the administration of yet another estate and acting as agent for the sale of a farm in St Giles parish, both in 1748. In 1757 he acted as one of the assignees in the substantial bankruptcy of grocer and distiller, Samuel Todd (see below). If one needed a 'friend' in St Leonards, John Bartholomew clearly had influence at his disposal and can be seen to have deployed it.[1]

Peter Cresswell was a somewhat less substantial Colcestrian, but had similar public interests. He was a victualler and a weaver, busy enough to take on an apprentice. He held corporation office as a driver for the common lands in 1738, 1739 and 1740 and was a petty juror at borough sessions of Epiphany 1741. He was no stranger to the court, standing recognisance for his wife Sarah when she was fined for an assault in 1736, later for £20 for one David Rayner, who was being indicted on a bastardy order, and once again for £10 for weaver John Delight to answer for a grain riot. He voted Tory in the 1730s and 40s but by the 1754 election supported Whig candidate Isaac Martin Rebow and was recompensed with a new loom for his assistance to the campaign. Cresswell was at the outside fringes of the governing group in the borough. His alehouse and connections in the baytrade must have widened his social contacts, and although not of the most genteel he did have some influence in local society. He was sought out as a recognisance on more than one occasion and was later an active agent in an election.[2]

---

1 Will Hannah Hopkins ERO D/ACR 15/313, 1749; will Thomas Hopkins ERO D/ABW 95, 1747; deeds of the Fleece inn, ERO, Acc 47, CPL 638; will Hannah Bartholomew, wife of John, made 1736, proved 1739 ERO D/ABR 22/233; will Elizabeth Freeman, ERO D/ACR 15/246, made 1746, proved 1747. Monday Court Book 30 October 1738 for Bartholomew's prosecution for debt of Charles Walker; similarly, Monday Court Book 13 October 1740, prosecution of Thomas Webb. Sale of the *Ceres* and later expansion of business activities: *Colchester Journal* (hereafter *ColJ*) 3 February 1739; *IpsJ* 8 August and 12 December 1747, 11 June and 13 August 1748, 30 November 1754, for sale of the sloop *Friends Goodwill*. Borough Sessions Roll ERO D/B 5 Sr200, 1740, examination John Till the younger; Lexden and Winstree Petty Sessions ERO P/LWR1, 8 December 1758, ERO P/LWR4 2 January 1760. Administrations of estates: ERO D/ACWb51 Joseph Gould, 1742; D/ABWb157 James Cork, 1746; D/ABWb158 Peter Creffield, 1748; re Samuel Todd, *IpsJ* 29 January 1757. For other estates settled, see: *IpsJ* 27 April 1751, re Archer Allen, mariner; *IpsJ* 3 March 1753 re Stephen Barker, bricklayer Wivenhoe. Borough Sessions Book, D/B 5 Sb5/3, Easter 1736, Bartholomew prosecuted for six yards unkempt pavement at Hythe.

2 Borough Sessions Book, ERO D/B 5 Sb5/3, Easter 1738, took Joseph Lord apprentice; Michaelmas 1738, his apprentice Joseph Lord discharged as incapable; Epiphany 1741, petty

Each of these three examples, Elizabeth Shillito, John Bartholemew and Peter Cresswell, were involved in networks of (social and financial) credit. Your friends, ultimately, were those who established your credit. At this period credit was vital for all transactions by way of trade or even for household consumption. Specie was scarce in the eighteenth-century economy. Financial institutions were few and for the most part involved the London money market and finance for metropolitan and overseas trade. Provincial banking developed only from the last few years of the century. The national debt was by the middle of the century providing a safe, long-term, if low yielding investment. Annuities and mortgages were much-used financial devices which enabled a degree of security, but the vast majority of buying and selling depended on unsecured personal credit. Bills of exchange or promissory notes facilitated the circulation of credit (such paper could be discounted or proffered in settlement of a debt) but themselves also finally depended on personal credit. Credit was ubiquitous; retail as well as wholesale customers expected to buy on credit. This was not simply the privilege of elites; wage earners were paid at long intervals and needed credit to shop for day-to-day items. Tradespeople needed credit from suppliers. Merchants worked with long and often uncertain lines of credit to overseas customers and agents. Manufacturers, such as Colchester baymakers, worked with slowly circulating capital, much of their business resources being tied up in stocks of raw materials and finished goods. They supplied credit both up and down the chain of production and marketing.[3]

It was pretty much impossible to engage in any kind of economic activity without incurring debt and extending credit. Almost all transactions, therefore, were based on

---

2 *cont.*

juror; recognisances in Midsummer 1736 Sarah Cresswell for assault of John Mills, Easter 1737 David Rayner bastardy, Midsummer 1740 John Delight for riot. Assembly Book ERO D/B 5 Gb 7 and Gb 8, 24 July 1738, 23 July 1739, 28 July 1740; See also Poll Book 1735, 1741. For 1754 election see Rebow Papers, ERO, Box 2, T/A 491/1, and Chapter 7 below.

3 Of the growing literature on credit in its wider sense, key recent texts are C. Muldrew, *The economy of obligation: the culture of credit and social relations in early modern England* (Basingstoke, 1998); M.C. Finn, *The character of credit: personal debt in English culture, 1740–1914* (Cambridge, 2003); important earlier studies include B.L. Anderson, 'Money and the structure of credit in the eighteenth century', *Business History*, 12 (1970), pp. 87–110; B.A. Holderness, 'Credit in a rural community, 1660–1800', *Midland History*, 3 (1975), pp. 94–116; B.A. Holderness, 'Credit in English rural society before the nineteenth century', *Agricultural History Review*, 24 (1976) pp. 89–92; on the shortage of specie, J. Styles, '"Our traitorous moneymakers": the Yorkshire coiners and the law, 1760–83', in J. Brewer and J. Styles (eds.), *An ungovernable people; the English and their law in the seventeenth and eighteenth centuries* (New Brunswick, 1980), pp. 172–249; C. Muldrew, '"Hard food for Midas": cash and its social value in early modern England', *Past and Present* (2001), pp. 78–120; on credit and business more specifically, see e.g. J. Smail, *Merchants, markets and manufacture; the English wool textile industry in the eighteenth century* (Basingstoke, 1999); J. Smail, 'The culture of credit in eighteenth-century commerce: the English textile industry', *Enterprise and society* 4 (2003), pp. 299–325; J. Smail, 'Credit, risk, and honor in eighteenth-century commerce', *Journal of British Studies*, 44 (2005), pp. 439–56; J. Hoppit, 'Attitudes to credit in Britain, 1680–1790', *Historical Journal*, 33 (1990), pp. 305–22; P. Spufford, 'Rural credit in 17th-century England', *Annales-Histoire Sciences Sociales*, 49 (1994), pp. 1359–73. On banking the classic text remains L.S. Presnell, *Country banking in the industrial revolution* (Oxford, 1956).

an assessment of financial risk predicated on judgements about the (personal) trustworthiness of the debtor. Within these ongoing credit networks, debtors and creditors would only periodically 'reckon' the balance between them and settle in cash. Hence social credit and financial credit were mutually constituted. The value of commodities involved more than their monetary price and was implicated in other kinds of cultural values. Wealth, argues Muldrew, existed in the form of household credit:

> For the middling sort, especially, who depended on the market for their livelihood, wealth was not so much a state of ownership or inclusion in a privileged group, as a continual process of ethical judgement about credit ... a reputation for honesty, trustworthiness and good neighbourliness became an attribute of wealth, enabling someone to do more business.[4]

For many of the eighteenth-century Colchester middling sort, reputation (of individuals and their households) also called for some kind of participation in (minor) public office or other associational activity (in locations as diverse as a non-conformist chapel or a freemasons' lodge). Such activity required a certain benchmark of material substance, but also accrued social and cultural capital, demonstrating creditworthiness in all its aspects. There was a complex knot of significance in the Monday Court description of a witness as 'a person well known and worthy of good credit'.[5] Furthermore, as Joanna Bailey has argued, household reputation and the stability of social and emotional relationships had a direct effect on both social and monetary credit.[6] Chapter 3 has indicated some of the problems for credit maintenance caused by household emotional conflict. Household credit was never simple to maintain. As Margot Finn points out, it was a perpetual, confusing but vital business involving '... formal and informal loans, gifts of money and of goods, begging, borrowing, cadging ... Extended credit relations fundamentally shaped social and cultural life, and were in turn animated by social and cultural norms throughout this period.'[7]

This chapter looks at the business of credit and exchange in eighteenth-century Colchester, and the role of friends in facilitating this, through a series of topics. Firstly, credit networks and their relationship to patronage will be discussed through the accounts of Charles Gray, the mid-century Colchester MP. Secondly the discussion of Colchester wills begun in Chapter 3 is extended to review the role of friends as executors in managing family property. Thirdly, a series of mortgages will be examined, both in their role as providing credit and a source of investment and in

---

4 C. Muldrew,'Midas', pp. 81, 84, 98.

5 Monday Court Book. 23 February 1741, James Deane, carpenter,'being a person well known and worthy of good credit' swore on the Bible he was 'present today when Thomas Bumpsted of Boxford surgeon, brother of Benjamin Bumpsted of Bengal deceased signed Letter of Attorney for Thomas Bumpsted and Capt. Charles Raymond of the ship *Wager* to collect goods and chattels of said Benjamin Bumpsted deceased'.

6 J. Bailey, *Unquiet lives: marriage and marriage breakdown in England, 1660–1800* (Cambridge, 2003), pp. 30, 62; C. Muldrew, '"A mutual assent of her mind"? women, debt, litigation and contract in early modern England', *History Workshop Journal* (2003), pp. 47–71, p. 64.

7 Finn, *The character of credit*, p. 2.

terms of the credit networks that were operating. The rest of the chapter will examine credit at the point of its collapse, by discussing bankruptcy and business failure. Both patterns of bankruptcy and the provision of credit and capital through mortgages were subject to nationwide financial trends and the growth of wider money markets. In the post-Napoleonic period, grocer and hemp manufacturer James Lovett juggled local, metropolitan and national credit networks.

Friends, patrons and money

The Colchester MP, attorney Charles Gray lived in the town centre next to the castle. He had a busy career in local government and administration, and was an important local patron and the nodal point for several overlapping credit networks. Gray was a county JP and a commissioner for the Hythe Navigation. He was steward to two manor courts and for several landed estates and was Lord of Tendring Hundred. He was involved in the administration of local turnpikes and his accounts show payments of £80 for the repairs of a bridge (probably North Bridge) in 1772. In 1760 Gray had paid for the design and erection of the Obelisk erected by the Turnpike trustees at the lower end of Colchester High Street. Gray's accounts show him acting as banker for local government by funding the turnpikes as well as how bonds and bills issued by middling individuals passed through his hands. For example in 1729 he recorded 'To Mr Edwards bond £55' and 'allowance for Edwards bad debt, £46'. He was a trustee for the Charity School near All Saints Church and twice loaned the schoolmaster money to pay apprenticeship fees for his sons.[8] Gray also acted as one of the trustees for the insolvent clergyman Charles Lind.[9] By accepting payment in bills instead of specie, by investing in mortgages and loans, by mixing his own funds with parish, turnpike and other local government ventures, Gray (and individuals like him) were important solvents for local economic exchange.

As Chapter 2 discussed, Gray improved and extended his property in Colchester. His accounts record numerous dealings between himself and his local man of business, the architect, James Deane. 'Mr James Deane and his mother' received loans of £20 and £12 10s from Gray in the 1720s. Deane regularly paid the workmen and craftsmen who were labouring on the improvements Gray commissioned and was reimbursed only later. For general maintenance on the rented property Gray owned, Deane often employed and paid the workmen independently. In 1763, for example, Deane was paid £25 'in full of Mrs Simpson's'. However, on some occasions Deane was given cash to settle other tradesmen's bills. The same year, for 'work at Umfreville's £10 and B(yatt) Walker, carpenter £10', Deane was paid £20, to pass on £10 to Walker. The complex reckoning of accounts between Gray and Deane can be illustrated by this agreement of 1733:

8 JBB BD/423. Gray's accounts ERO D/DR B1 and B1A, diary ERO T28/24, D/Dre. Acc C15, Box 1.

9 BL Add Mss 33563, Bentham MS, re insolvency of Charles Lind, including accounts for 1760, power of attorney of 3 March, 1760, letter from Gray to Bentham of 4 August 1762.

> ... sold to Mr Dean 294 trees in the Wood at Hen. Turner's and 16 field timbers containing in all 70 load and 1/2 of timber for £130 out of which am to allow Mr Dean £64 towards his loss by Robt. Edwards and he is to pay me the remaining eighty four pounds in 3 months but I am to take in part of this Joseph Tod's Note for so much of the timber not exceeding 20 loads as he shall buy of Mr Dean.
>
> 28 May 1733
> Witness our hands
> Cha: Gray
> James Deane[10]

The role of the more affluent and respectable middling sort as bankers to their clients was not confined to Charles Gray. Other Colchester examples include Revd Thomas Twining who, probably given his own aversion to managing money, found himself rather embarrassed to be given 400 guineas to invest by an ex-servant of his, but accepted the charge and regularly rode over to pay out the interest.[11] Colchester gentleman, James Blatch, held the £100 savings of his servant Maria Lay. She distributed these in her will of 1799 which he witnessed. The will was made by attorney William Mason who was later to make Blatch's own will, so it can be inferred that her employer was also her banker and used his own legal advisor on her behalf.[12]

There is no source for Colchester equivalent to (say) the diary of Thomas Turner, grocer of East Hoathly, Sussex, where his extensive credit networks were laid out.[13] Given the research on other locations, however, the more dispersed references in Colchester sources can be interpreted as fragmented evidence of the complex and widespread credit networks now lost to view. Samuel Nockolds, High Street hatter, bought his wrapping paper from stationer Charles Darby who traded a few doors away.[14] The Creffield family household accounts of the 1740s show the minutiae of household expenditure. Their steward Richard King was repaid a large accumulation of small sums 'laid out' for the household: newspapers, letters, ale, travel, vegetables (four Red Cabages, 2s; turnaps and apols, 3d), meat and fish, mending clothes, everyday philanthropy ('laid out by my Mistress orders 2 pence for a porman'), a chimney sweep and the many other petty expenses that kept a large household running. The circulation of credit is evidenced in the bundles of overwritten paper comprising bills, receipts and promissory notes. Monies owed to one person are offset against balances due from elsewhere. To cite just one such example of many,

---

10 ERO D/DR Bl, General Account Book A.

11 R.S. Walker (ed.), *A selection of Thomas Twining's letters 1734–1804: a record of a tranquil life* (Lewiston, 1991), letter 274 to Richard Twining, 17 February 1803, pp. 640–1; letter 283 to Richard Twining, 13 and 14 October 1803.

12 His servant was Maria Lay who had deposited her savings (some £100) in his hands. He witnessed her will on 7 June 1799, which distributed this among her relations. ERO D/ABR 29/246.

13 D. Vaisey (ed.), *The diary of Thomas Turner* (Oxford, 1985). N. Tadmor, *Family and friends in eighteenth-century England: household, kinship, and patronage* (Cambridge, 2001) pp. 25–35; M. Finn, 'Men's things: masculine possession in the consumer revolution', *Social History*, 25 (2000), pp. 133–55.

14 ERO D/P 177/12/9, Samuel Nockold's workbook.

R. Hart's tailor's bill of 1742–3 (for mending and alterations as well as new clothes amounting to £6 10s 1d) was sent endorsed on the back to Creffield's lawyer, Samuel Wall who paid the bill not to Hart but to his partner, Charles Deboys.[15] At the turn of the century, the affluent Cock household of East Hill House were spending between £800 and £1,000 pounds a year. Taxes and rates and 'house bills' were the most sizeable items of expenditure (£196 and £114 respectively in 1799). They employed servants who cost them around £50 a year – less than they spent on travel (£87 in 1804), clothes (£97), their garden (£63) and charity and donations (£75). Although prestige purchases such as the Clementi pianoforte bought for £28 in 1807 came from farther afield, they purchased their clothes, books and most furniture and household items locally and attended assemblies, concerts and the Colchester theatre. They were also significant contributors to charity and welfare. As well as numbers of one-off donations of a couple of shillings to a 'poor man' or 'poor woman' they made regular donations to favoured charities including £50 to Kendall's charity in 1805, regular donations to the Colchester Lying-In Charity, an annual guinea to the Colchester Sunday Schools and had several regular pensioners. For example, Robert Wass, once waiter at the Red Lion, received a regular 2s 6d in his old age. Affluent households such as this were not only important customers to middling traders; their philanthropy contributed to the makeshift domestic economies of the poor and helped fund turn-of-the-century welfare.[16]

Friends and wills

Chapter 3 argued that will-making was a significant moment in the middling family life cycle, when family property was transferred for the best possible preservation of family interests. Wills marked and reinforced social connection by leaving legacies to friends and wider kin, perhaps particularly where bequests were left in kind. Their prime purpose, however, was to secure as far as possible the continuation of household and business. For the professional middling sort, it was a question of helping the next generation to comparative careers. Spouses and children were both the main dependents and the key interested parties. Chapter 3 noted an increasing formality in the devices will-makers used. A trust was set up in 19.1 per cent of Colchester wills proved in the archdeaconry courts between 1800 and 1829[17], compared to 5.7 per cent of the 1735–50 sample. The estate was sold up in 11.4 per cent of the pre-1750 sample and 16.9 per cent after 1800, leaving the provision for dependents to be made in cash or securities. Increasingly, widows and under-aged children (or the will-maker's next nearest kin where widows and children were not present) were surrounded by additional executors, trusts, or other mechanisms to better their chances in an increasingly complex economy. Looking specifically at husbands' wills (Table 4.1) growing use was made of life or widowhood interests in the estate for surviving wives (19 per cent provided life interests before 1750, rising to

15 ERO D/DRC F26. Creffield Family, receipts and bills 1740–48.

16 ERO D/DEt/F38; JBB BD/921 Robert Wass.

17 S. D'Cruze, *The middling sort in provincial England: politics and social relations in Colchester 1730–1800* (PhD thesis, Essex, 1990), pp. 46–56.

Table 4.1
Widows in husbands' wills

	1735–50	per cent	1780–99	per cent	1800–29	per cent
Provision for widows						
Sole absolute beneficiary	17	19.3	37	34.2	22	19.3
Major absolute beneficiary	31	35.2	9	8.3	9	7.9
Life interest most/all estate	19	21.6	20	18.5	40	35.1
Widowhood interest most/ all the estate			7	6.5	7	6.1
A major share/widows thirds	7	8.0	6	5.6	2	1.8
Cash provision	2	2.3	7	6.5	6	5.3
Provision, property/goods/cash	7	8.0	17	15.7	20	17.5
Minor remembrance	0	0	0	0	3	2.6
Household goods absolutely/ life interest in rest of estate	5	5.7	5	4.6	5	4.4
Total wills naming widows	88		108		114	
Executors in husband's will						
Wife sole executor	49	55.2	34	31.5	25	21.9
Wife + nuclear family	5	4.8	14	13.0	15	13.2
Wife + others	19	21.6	22	20.4	27	23.7
Total wills with widow executors	73		70		67	

Note: Samples are all Colchester locally proved wills for the specified dates where will-maker mentioned a widow.

35 per cent after 1800). Before 1750, 55.2 per cent of widows were named sole executor, decreasing to 21.9 per cent after 1800. Additional family members acting as executors increased from 4.8 per cent before 1750 to 13.2 per cent after 1800. Widows were sole or major absolute beneficiaries in 54.5 per cent of husbands' wills before 1750, and often only missed sole control of the estate through small remembrances to friends and wider kin, compared to 22 per cent after 1800. In no pre-1750 wills sampled was a widow's interest in the estate terminated on her remarriage. She was also less likely then to receive only limited provision from the estate.

Looking again at the wider sample of wills discussed in Chapter 3 (not only those where the will-maker is a man naming his widow), wills naming all executors from within the same surname set stayed a little above 35 per cent from 1735–50 to 1800–29 (Table 4.2). Executors living over 25 miles away, who have a small role at the end of the century, did not feature in the mid-century sample. Before 1750 a pairing of family with local friends as executors was more frequent. In the pre-1750 sample, 22.4 per cent made this arrangement compared to 17.5 per cent after 1800. Local friends acting alone as executors increased over time from 19.2 per cent of wills before 1750 to 25.4 per cent after 1800. Sometimes, of course, things did not work out. It took an action in chancery for the heirs of Thomas Harrison to extract the

18 J. Bensusan Butt, *When Gainsborough painted a Colchester attorney* (Colchester, privately printed, 1978), especially pp. 6–8.

Table 4.2
Executors

	1735/50	per cent	1780/99	per cent	1800/29	per cent
Wife Sole Executor	25	20	34	16.9	27	13.2
All Family	46	36.8	79	39.3	74	36.2
Family + Local Friends	28	22.4	36	17.9	36	17.6
Family + Distant Friends	0	0	5	2.5	5	2.5
All Local Friends	24	19.2	41	20.3	52	25.4
All Distant Friends	0	0	3	1.5	2	1
Local + Distant Friends	2	1.6	3	1.5	8	3.9

remaining balances of his property from the deceased estate of his executor the attorney William Mayhew (see below).[18]

As Alaistair Owen argues for the nineteenth century, such tendencies may have superficially decreased widows' absolute autonomy over the family property, but should be understood alongside the ongoing involvement that many widows (or older daughters) had in the family finances and contextualised within the wider range of welfare provision which wills were about, and which constrained both women and (albeit to a lesser extent) men in the interests of future family economic security.[19] Nevertheless, over time, the role of (mostly male) friends and kin in the administration of estates grew. Adult sons, sons-in-law, brothers, brothers-in-law, business partners, attorneys, neighbours, the mortgagor of the family property or a major trade debtor can all be found as trustees or executors. Friends substituted for adult male kin if such were not available but also often lent their expertise and in effect their credit to the continuing husbanding of family property.

Mortgages

Provincial banking in England was a development of the very late eighteenth and early nineteenth centuries.[20] Prior to this, the mortgage on property was an important vehicle for the investment of surplus funds, to raise capital for business, to pay legacies and annuities, for building improvement or other purposes. There were alternative secure longer-term investments, principally through the national debt. The market in securities, stocks and bonds was centred on the City of London. Government consols, East India or South Sea stocks were a major innovation of the late seventeenth and early eighteenth centuries. Although many small investors are recorded in and around the capital where the facilities of the Stock Exchange were accessible and attendance and financial information comparatively easy to obtain, the

19 A. Owens, 'Property, gender and the life course: inheritance and family welfare provision in early 19th-century England', *Social History*, 26 (2001), pp. 299–317; A. Owens, 'Inheritance and the life-cycle of family firms in the early industrial revolution', *Business History*, 44 (2002), p. 21; S. Nenadic, 'Middle rank consumers and domestic culture in Edinburgh and Glasgow, 1720–1840', *Past and Present*, 145 (1994), pp. 122–56.

20 Presnell, *Country banking*.

21 A.C. Carter, *Getting, spending and investment in early modern times: English public debt in the eighteenth century* (London, 1968), pp. 123–41.

market outside London was very limited and only larger investors were able to maintain London agents.[21]

Some affluent Colcestrians owned such paper securities (George Wegg held thousands of pounds in the Hudson Bay Company)[22] and others directed their executors to realise their estate and place the proceeds in government funds. Such individuals tend to be among the wealthiest in the town or to be gentry with country seats in the surrounding countryside. Even these investors were generally sufficiently prudent to spread the risk by investing widely in real estate as well as securities. When Richard Freshfield obtained a £250 mortgage on his brewery from Nathaniel Barnardiston (a Suffolk landed gentleman) in 1760, the latter expressly diverted capital from the funds to accommodate him.[23]

Three examples where the purpose of the borrowing is evident from the sources indicate the role of mortgage finance for the Colchester middling sort. Later in this chapter I will discuss the 1810 bankruptcy of Colchester grocer James Lovett. He had long been established in the High Street and had invested in real estate near his home and business in St Nicholas. He bought these properties for comparatively small sums and then took out mortgages to finance brick fronting, installing sash windows and other improvements. Mortgage finance allowed Lovett to improve his own premises originally bought for a few hundred pounds from a carpenter to a prestigious residence, shop and counting house, with a handsome frontage and accommodation for his mother next door, valued in 1810 at some £2,000.[24]

A little further up the High Street (No. 112) there was a small bakery, owned first by Thomas Fitch then by Thomas Chignell, which was under mortgage almost continuously from 1712 to 1775 for sums which increased from £30 to £200 as the property was periodically re-mortgaged. The first involvement of the Chignell family in the property was a mortgage of £60 from Elizabeth Chignell, spinster, to the then owner Thomas Fitch. She then lent £88 to her brother Thomas Chignell on mortgage once he had purchased the property from Fitch in 1744. When she married a farmer from nearby West Bergholt the mortgage was re-assigned to a Colchester grocer, Roger Munsey in 1749. When Fitch snr died in 1759, like other Colchester will-makers, he named his mortgagee, Roger Munsey, as his executor. The real estate seems to have provided capital to finance the bakery business that Fitch and Chignell ran. However the increasing sums under mortgage may indicate an over-extension of the Chignell's credit. Thomas Chignell snr died in 1759 and his son took over the business. Chignell jnr and his wife Mary sold their interest in 112 High Street in 1775, but he was in prison for debt by 1781.[25]

Elizabeth Godfrey was forced to mortgage her property at 30 High Street to finance her subsistence and pay back her late husband's (Thomas Smith's) debts. This mortgage was part of a complicated story which played out over two generations.

---

22 JBB BD/931.

23 ERO Acc 47. CPL 694.

24 Hollytrees Library MS.35; JBB notes on deeds of 108 High Street, 'Joslins', (previously Colchester Public Library 502, now lost) in ms notebook 73/7, ERO Acc 905, Box 17; G.O. Rickwood, 'Farewell to Joslin's', *Essex County Standard,* 17 January 1958, pp. 47–8, *Benham's guide to Colchester,* 1874 for contemporary illustration of the frontage.

25 *London Gazette,* 1 January 1781, p. 4, 4 September 1781, p. 8, 8 September, p. 8.

Elizabeth was the illegitimate child of Thomas Harrison. He had died in 1738 and her legacy of £500 fell under the substantial control of Harrison's executor, the attorney William Mayhew. Mayhew's influence was increased by successive debts owed him by Elizabeth's first husband Thomas Smith. Consequently, Mayhew acquired an interest in the property, by way of this mortgage, for their repayment in 1756. He later supplied £132 mortgage funds in 1781 and doubtless negotiated the two mortgages which were outstanding on the property in the interim.[26]

The deed drawn up in 1791 between Thomas and Mary Barns and Robert King (of nearby Little Bentley) to raise £600 on their brewery near Sheregate Steps illustrates a further use of the mortgage. The monies so raised are equal to the cash sum willed by Barns to his daughter Elizabeth Ann (who was also to receive total interest in his estate after her mother's death). Barns died the following day. Even though he may not have anticipated such a prompt demise (his signature on the deed shows no sign of illness) the mortgage was evidently to release cash from the family property to provide for his daughter without disturbing his wife's life interest in the remainder of his real estate.[27] Taken together, these three examples from the mid- and late eighteenth century indicate the range of uses of mortgage finance. They all involve trade and credit. Equally they all demonstrate the interlaced concerns of family and finance. The witnesses to Thomas Barns' will, for example, were his doctor (Robert Richardson Newell), his attorney (William Francis) and the man who was later to marry his daughter, silversmith James Thorn.

The growing numbers of provincial attorneys in the eighteenth century generally made their careers as 'men of business'. In a society and economy of growing complexity, conveyancing, will-making, property management and mortgage broking, as well as the holding of manorial and other local courts were far more profitable than litigation and formed the mainstay of most attorneys' portfolios. Some attorneys acted as bankers for favoured clients, as William Mayhew was doing for Elizabeth Godfrey. Frequently attorneys would act as brokers between those requiring funds and those seeking for an investment. The attorneys would bring lenders not only from the surrounding region but occasionally from London and farther afield into contact with local borrowers, evidencing the beginnings of a national finance market at least later in the century. Business contacts in the surrounding area and in the capital could be applied to match a suitable lender and borrower.[28] In Colchester, Benjamin Rolle, money scrivener, advertised in the *Ipswich Journal* of 6 May 1749 that:

> Any person wanting to buy or sell estates or to lend or borrow Money upon good securities may be assisted therein by applying to BENJAMIN ROLLE at his house in Colchester, and who constantly attends at the house of Mr. Joseph Dunningham ... the Three Crowns & Star ... where they may depend on Dispatch and Secrecy and that their Business will be transacted on reasonable terms. ... All letters sent post paid ... will be punctually answered and not otherwise.

---

26 Bensusan Butt, *When Gainsborough painted a Colchester attorney*, p. 7.

27 JBB BD/50, see also Chapter 8 below, n. 19; ERO Brewery Deeds, CPL 680.

28 M. Miles, 'The money market in the early industrial revolution; the evidence from West Riding attorneys, c.1750–1800', *Business history* 23 (1981), pp. 127–46; A.J. Schmidt, 'The country attorney in late eighteenth-century England: Benjamin Smith of Horbling', *Law and History Review*, 8 (1990), pp. 237–71. R. O'Day, *The professions in early modern England, 1450–1800: servants of the commonweal* (Harlow, 2000), pp. 162–78.

For the most part Rolle traded as a cooper.[29] The separate trade of money scrivener arguably diminished in importance later in the century as wider networks among attorneys developed. Colchester attorneys located and sometimes provided mortgage and other finance. William Francis, the attorney who witnessed Thomas Barns' will in 1791 took on the £600 mortgage for three months in 1801, until he located a new mortgagee. The Creffield household accounts discussed above show how lawyer Samuel Wall provided cash and credit. James Robjent, baymaker was bankrupted in 1772 for a debt of £300 he owed to Thomas Bayles, attorney. Peter Daniell, non-conformist attorney, was bankrupted in 1789, and gazetted as a money scrivener. The law of bankruptcy required that he be seen to trade on credit to avail himself of its provisions, however, it seems he was also securing mortgage finance.[30] Consequently, the mortgage, together with wills and trusts, was a legal device which enabled middling borrowers and lenders to manage property and credit in the long term. Its negotiation often involved friends but increasingly those friends included attorneys: specialist, professional men of business.

An investigation of the deeds of fifteen Colchester properties supplied information on forty-two separate mortgages on properties in Colchester town between 1712 and 1823.[31] The average amount and term of the mortgages was £261 for seven years. Almost half of them were transfers of an existing mortgage to a new mortgagee (eighteen transfers compared to twenty-two new mortgages – two unknown). The interest rate was found for twenty-three of the sample and was generally 5 per cent per year. Three mortgagees charged 3 per cent and two 4.5 per cent.[32] Although mortgage rates seem stable over time, the amounts mortgaged rose. Of forty-two mortgages, thirty-one were granted on property occupied by the mortgagor, though this group does include industrial premises such as merchants' yards or breweries. The mortgages were granted to Colchester traders, some merchants and widows. Fifteen properties account for forty-two mortgages, as some properties were constantly mortgaged and re-mortgaged. Only seven mortgages (one sixth) are the only one noted for that property. Two breweries have six mortgages apiece over forty-seven and eighty-four years respectively. The brewing trade required substantial investment in real estate and equipment and the mortgage freed up the power of capital otherwise locked in fixed assets.

Religious affiliation had some effect in matching mortgagors and mortgagees. Non-conformist Giles Nunn mortgaged several rentaries on North Hill to build a smart house; this deal has non-conformists as mortgagor, mortgagee, tenants and attorney (William Francis). Seven mortgages were granted where both parties were known to be non-conformist and five where both were Anglican. Seven have parties of different faiths. Therefore something like a quarter follow religious lines and something like a

---

29 JBB BD/707.

30 Brewery deeds at ERO Acc 47 CPL 680; *London Gazette* 22 November 1783, p. 8, 31 July 1784, p. 4, 10 September 1785, p. 4, 2 February 1790, p. 78; JBB BD/700 James Robjent.

31 The deeds included here are random survivals, some of them preserved in the Essex Record Office, others lent at various times by the current owners to Mr John Bensusan Butt and not on public deposit.

32 Rates accord with those cited by Schmidt, 'The country attorney'.

sixth clearly cross them. Religion was perhaps not the most important influence in making mortgages. However, for committed non-conformists such as Nunn (a perukemaker and full member of Lion Walk Independent congregation) it made a great deal of difference.[33]

Female mortgagors (sixteen of forty-two) are generally named together with their husbands, especially earlier in the century, or are widows. Women were a significant source of loan capital in general across the eighteenth and nineteenth centuries.[34] In this sample nine female mortgagees lent an average of £223 pounds. These tended to be women investing their legacies to gain an income, but some are clearly contributing capital to the business ventures of their kin.

Eleven mortgages on six properties had Colchester traders (excluding both merchants and professionals) as both mortgagor and mortgagee. These were comparatively small loans, £128 on average and without one larger sum of £420 the average over the remaining ten declines to £98. They tended on average to be in force longer than the whole sample which had a mean duration of seven years (median five years). The average duration for this group was ten years, accounted for by four examples of mortgages standing for between ten and twenty-nine years. Consequently something like a quarter of these forty-two mortgages were arrangements between local trading people who could watch each other's conduct as debtor and creditor. The low average amount testifies to the smaller-scale nature of much local business. The Lovett bankruptcy papers also demonstrate the high level of short-term credit in small amounts supplied by town traders either for goods or on notes and bills. These two kinds of debt were meshed into the complex network of credit among the town's trading community.

More than half the mortgages studied (including the eleven between traders) had both mortgagor and mortgagee resident in Colchester and were not part of a geographically widening market for mortgage funds. The average sum for these mortgages was £175, compared to a £261 average for the whole sample of forty-two. The latter figure is increased by one very large mortgage of £1,200 to John Thurstan, Hythe merchant, in 1791. Thurstan was in the coal trade with a yard at Hythe Bridge and a 40-ton sloop, the *Ceres*, shipping coal from the north. The mortgage was on his new built house on the site of the Old Rectory, Hythe Hill, and, given the risks inherent in the coal trade in the inflationary 1790s seems to have over-extended his credit. He went bankrupt in 1794.[35] Even with the Thurstan example removed, however, an average amount of £236, still about a third larger than the local trader/local trader average is obtained. Thurstan's creditor was of the gentry.

Sixteen mortgages, almost a third of the whole sample, were funds lent to Colchester mortgagors by rural mortgagees, mostly gentry, wealthy farmers and clergy. The mortgagors include a high percentage of brewers, a wealthy carpenter and a rich early nineteenth-century widow. The average amount here is £391 (reducing to

33 JBB BD/1195.

34 Schmidt, 'The country attorney'; J. Hoppit, *Risk and failure in English business, 1700–1800* (Cambridge, 1987), p. 150; A. Owens, 'Inheritance and the life-cycle of family firms', p. 21.

35 *IpsJ* 8 September 1787; *ChCh* 9 November 1787; *IpsJ* 5 July 1794. Mortgage at ERO D/Del/T316, mortgaged to Robert Knight, Bentley Hall, gent, 15 October 1791.

£337 without the Thurstan mortgage). The large difference in the size of town:town and town:country mortgages (£175:£391) make it quite likely that virtually two different markets were operating. Smaller-scale, rather longer-term finance came through the credit networks within Colchester itself while a more extensive network was beginning to spread nationwide for more sizeable loans.

The mortgage on real estate was a frequent financial device in Colchester and the local nature of much borrowing and lending made the mortgage one component of complex relationships of debt and credit among the middling sort. Above and beyond the local money market, rather larger financial dealings between people more widely separated geographically and occupationally were used to provide capital for more extensive ventures. At this level factors such as the larger mortgage amount, the comparatively shorter duration and the knowledge from other sources that mortgagees also placed their money in real estate and securities, meant that the mortgage was part of a wider money market where the relationship between mortgagee and mortgagor was one of credit, but not necessarily one of friendship. The attorneys who brokered the deal were more likely to have been positioned as the friends of either party. The mortgage, like all other forms of credit, was heavily embedded in social relations and the cultural meanings of any particular mortgage could be complex. Family and business concerns were central, and friends – including the attorney whose profession it was to act as one's friend in the eighteenth-century sense – were necessary to achieve the right financial outcome.

Small debts

Nationally, small debts could be pursued at growing numbers of local Courts of Requests; in Colchester they were brought before the Thursday Court. Individual creditors could also move 'against the body' of the debtor by having him or her committed to prison. At this time, imprisonment 'on mesne process' (that is until the case came to court) was for most a comparatively short-term measure. However, for some debtors, particularly those who were imprisoned for non-settlement after a court judgement, prison could be a longer-term measure.[36] There is now a growing literature on the imprisonment of debtors in the eighteenth and early nineteenth centuries.[37] Although some debtors with access to resources could live in some

---

36 I.P.H. Duffy, *Bankruptcy and insolvency in London during the industrial revolution* (London and New York, 1985), pp. 57–63.

37 P. Woodfine, 'Debtors, prisons, and petitions in eighteenth-century England', *Eighteenth-Century Life* 30 (2006), pp. 1–31; M.C. Finn, *The character of credit,* Chapter 4; N. Stirk, 'Arresting ambiguity: the shifting geographies of a London debtors' sanctuary in the eighteenth century', *Social History*, 25 (2000), pp. 316–29; J. Innes, 'The King's Bench prison in the later eighteenth century: law, authority and order in a London debtor's prison' in J. Brewer and J. Styles (eds.), *An Ungovernable People: the English and their law in the seventeenth and eighteenth centuries* (London, 1980), pp. 250–98. From an administrative perspective see V. Markham Lester, *Victorian insolvency: bankruptcy, imprisonment for debt, and company winding-up in nineteenth-century England* (Oxford, 1995) and critical review by M. Daunton, 'Victorian insolvency: bankruptcy, imprisonment for debt, and company winding-up in nineteenth-century England', *Journal of Modern History*, 70 (2), (1998), pp. 457–8.

comfort, especially those outside the walls in the so-called 'rules' of some of the London prisons, for many others the experience was far less pleasant. From an institutional point of view, the problems of overcrowding and the inefficient nature of the law made the debtors' prison a growing anomaly in a penal system, which by the early nineteenth century was increasingly expected to have some penitential purpose. Consequently periodic acts of parliament were passed to release imprisoned debtors.

The *London Gazette* notices of prisoners eligible for release under the act of 1761 name two Colchester individuals. There is a further one each in 1772 and 1774, three under the act of 1778, two in 1781, one in 1794 and two in 1797. For the most part these seem to be journeymen or artisans, though there are exceptions. Robert Mayhew and Joshua Purkiss were named as 'gent'. Bishop Camplin had come to Colchester in 1773, setting up in business at the top of the High Street. The family was of sufficient note for his daughter's marriage to be recorded in the local newspaper in 1776. His credit was running thin, however, and he was sued in the borough sessions for a debt of £3 16s 8 1/2d the following year. It is possible that this is the debt for which he was imprisoned,[38] but if so, it is unlikely to have been his only obligation. His old premises were empty in 1778 and Camplin does not reappear in Colchester sources after his imprisonment.[39] As mentioned above, Thomas Chignell, the baker, seems also to have over-extended his credit, but in the long term the business recovered. A Thomas Chignell was trading as a baker in St Botolph's Street in 1805 and the family continued there at least until the 1880s.[40] David Yeoman the linen draper seems to have recovered from his insolvency of 1772 in even shorter order; he took a shop at the smarter end of the High Street the following year where he traded until his death in 1782.[41] This albeit very partial list of eighteenth-century Colcestrians imprisoned for debt draws attention both to the possibility of imprisonment as a risk for middling and artisan debtors, and also to the variable outcomes possible for middling debtors who found themselves taken up. Both the variability of outcome and of the social embeddedness of insolvency and routes out of it are further illustrated for the larger Colchester debtors who became bankrupt.

---

38 Mesne process was possible for debts as little as 40/- in inferior courts until 1779. Duffy, *Bankruptcy*, p 63.

39 First advertised in Colchester having arrived from London, *IpsJ* 1 May 1773, Camplin seems to have leased a shop from the Winnock's Trustees, ERO D/Q 31/1/2. From 1775 also occupied a house and yard behind North Hill near the Wagon & Horses (Deeds of Bowling Green ERO D/DE T162). *ChCh* 14 June 1776, his daughter married a Mr Harris of Colchester. An affidavit of 3 March 1777, in ERO Borough Sessions File D/B 5 Sr255, 7 April 1777, notes a case against Camplin for a £3 16s 8 1/2d debt to James Taylor, carpenter. From 1777 the North Hill premises were vacant and Camplin seems to have left the town. JBB BD/136.

40 *Holden's Directory*, 1805. Thomas Chignell, son of Thomas and Mary baptised 20 June 1775; also Thomas Chignell son of Thomas and Mary Ann 13 February 1801, Lion Walk Independent Meeting baptism register, ERO D/NC 52/1/2; cf Census enumerators returns for 1841 lists a Thomas Chignell (40), baker of St Botolphs Street and family.

41 JBB BD/972. *IpsJ* 23 October 1773 had taken Mr Newton's shop opposite the Three Cups. This was 16 High Street (rated 18) where he remained till 1782, his widow staying in the house during 1783.

Bankruptcy

Bankruptcy offered a (not always satisfactory) resolution of insolvency and its problems for some debtors. The bankruptcy law in the eighteenth century was in theory available to all who dealt on credit with debts of over £100 to a single creditor (or more between multiple creditors). Following a statute of 1706 the law on bankruptcy was framed as a means for the dishonest insolvent to be punished, but (in theory) for the trader who failed because he was caught up in collapsing networks of credit to be enabled to resolve the difficulties of insolvency by distributing his or her property between creditors pro-rata. Bankruptcy law gave a good deal of power to creditors, for example the majority by number and value of them had to agree to when a debtor could receive a certificate of discharge and around 40 per cent of eighteenth-century bankrupts were never discharged. Bankruptcy proceedings were initiated once a debtor had committed a stipulated 'act of bankruptcy' – keeping house and refusing to see creditors, for example – by a creditor declaring the debt before the court of Chancery (striking a docket). Thereafter commissioners in bankruptcy examined the bankrupt to ascertain both assets and liabilities and at meetings of creditors, assignees were appointed to realise the estate and distribute the dividend between creditors. If a dividend of more than 6s 8d per pound was realisable and the bankrupt was co-operative, a certificate of discharge would in theory eventually be issued.[42]

There were two factors which reinforced the social embeddedness of bankruptcies in provincial towns such as Colchester. The overall regulation of bankruptcies was within the remit of the court of Chancery. In London there were lists of bankruptcy commissioners who held sittings in the (crowded and busy) Guildhall. Subsequent creditors' meetings were not necessarily heard before the same panel of commissioners. By contrast, in the provinces the commissioners were separately and locally appointed for each bankruptcy. In effect, commissioners were chosen by the attorney who sued out the commission of bankruptcy on behalf of a creditor.[43] The creditors' meetings were held locally, often in a room at one of the larger town inns. Rural bankruptcies used solicitors from nearby towns. Hence for the provincial urban bankrupt in a town such as Colchester the proceedings tended to be a highly visible affair.

There is some Colchester evidence of the dishonest bankrupt. Baymaker Benjamin Hall was bankrupted in 1795. He failed to satisfy the bankruptcy commissioners that he had given a sufficient account of his estate and eventually died in Newgate prison. The commissioners offered a 5 per cent reward for the discovery of any undisclosed property.[44] However, cases such as this are outweighed in the local sources by evidence of co-operative bankrupts who seem to be treated as unfortunate rather than culpable. Samuel Todd ran a distillery at Headgate as well as trading as a grocer,

42 For a more detailed discussion of the bankruptcy laws see J. Hoppit, *Risk and failure,* Chapter 3; Duffy, *Bankruptcy*, pp. 1–33.

43 Duffy, *Bankruptcy*, p. 17.

44 *IpsJ* 24 January 1795; J. Bensusan Butt, ms notebook, *Jul 65*, p. 14, ERO Acc. 905, Box 16.

Table 4.3
Colchester bankruptcies, 1752–99

Occupation	*1752–65*	*1770–84*	*1785–99*	*Total*
Law	0	1	0	1
Medical	0	1	0	1
Transport	0	0	1	1
Wood	0	0	1	1
Metal	1	0	1	2
General	0	1	3	4
Building	3	2	1	6
Inns	2	0	4	6
Baytrade	1	5	1	7
Food	1	1	5	7
Dress	1	4	4	9
Merchant/Industrial	2	2	7	11
Total	11	17	28	56

owning a large rented house in London Road and operating a brick kiln at Mile End. When he was bankrupted in 1757 the grocery and brick-making operations as well as the rented house were sold. However, he was enabled to continue the distillery business by means of £4,000 capital provided by subscription from local affluent farmers and tradesmen. The subscribers met every Monday at 4 pm to inspect the books and Todd was to pay 9 per cent per annum interest on the money.[45] Thomas Wilshire, one of the baymakers to be bankrupted in the financial crisis of 1772 (see below) was given a job as Collector of Customs through the patronage of MP Isaac Martin Rebow, who also gave up a claim to £168 interest on an outstanding loan for the benefit of the other creditors. By the time of Wilshire's death in 1788 he had fully recovered his finances and left a not inconsiderable estate.[46] When attorney Peter Daniell was bankrupted in 1783 his house and property were auctioned. However, the house was purchased by his next-door neighbour in Queen Street who rented it back to Daniell. His brother-in-law Timothy Walford seems also to have purchased the bulk of the estate and mortgaged it back to him. Certainly Daniell continued to practise successfully in the town, witnessing wills and administering other bankruptcies until his death in 1792.[47] In all these cases it was through the financial support of local friends, kin and patrons that Colchester 'men of credit' whose credit had unfortunately deserted them were enabled to rebuild their reputations and material prosperity.

To set these specific cases in context a search of the *London Gazette* was combined with information from the JBB database.[48] In all fifty-six bankruptcies of Colchester traders were identified between 1752 and 1799 (Table 4.3). The JBB

45 JBB BD/883; *IpsJ* 29 January 1757; ERO D/DJ 20/20, Deeds of Braiswick Farm, L/R 1767, Todd is among the occupants. This was the location of the Brick Kiln.

46 JBB BD/954.

47 JBB BD/224 and n. 27 above; obituary in *European Magazine*, 12 March 1792, *IpsJ* 17 March 1792 died 'in his 60th year'. He was buried at Lion Walk. National Archives RG 4/1508.

48 Online editions of the *London Gazette* were searched. These are available from 1752–1765 and 1770 onwards at www.gazettes-online.co.uk/.

database also shows a further two in 1740 and 1751, twelve from 1800 to 1809, and seven between 1810 and 1816.

Colchester bankruptcies largely follow the broad trend revealed in Hoppit's national survey; that is 'relatively low and steady' up to 1750 before 'rising steeply and continuously' in the second half of the century. The rate of increase accelerated from the 1770s, both nationally and locally.[49] Hoppit argues that higher rates of bankruptcy were intrinsic to eighteenth-century economic growth, because of the accompanying increase in risk as well as opportunity. He calculates a growth in the annual numbers of bankrupts across the century of 77 per cent adjusted for population growth, and an increase in real terms (adjusted for price increase and economic growth) from .21 per cent growth per annum between 1701–10 and 1756–65 and 2.64 per cent between 1756–65 and 1791–1800.[50] Sophisticated statistical analysis is inappropriate for the far smaller Colchester sample, but dividing the data into three periods (Table 4.3) there is an absolute increase from eleven bankruptcies in 1752–66 (average of .8 p.a.) to seventeen in 1770–84 (average 1.2 p.a.) and twenty-eight in 1785–99 (average 2 p.a.). Colchester's population grew by about 20 per cent over this period, (it was around 9,500 at mid-century and 11,081 in 1801), while the annual bankruptcy averages increased by 125 per cent.

Considering the Colchester bankruptcy figures in relation to the size of the business and trading population shows an even more pronounced rate of increase in the final decades of the century. *Bailey's British Directory* of 1784 lists 145 Colchester individuals, twenty of whom were lawyers, barristers or in the medical profession. Bankruptcy law confined itself to traders with debts over £100, so the Directory lists 125 individuals who might have become bankrupt. This is however a considerable understatement, since the JBB Biographical Dictionary gives information on in all 323 individuals who were trading in Colchester in the 1780s. *Holden's Directory* of 1805 lists 292 Colchester traders, less twenty-two in the medical and legal professions.[51] Compared to this the JBB Biographical Dictionary recognises 263 traders in the 1790s, though fewer in the 1800s. Despite the imperfections in the JBB database, therefore it seems to provide a reasonable recognition of the Colchester business population in the later decades of the eighteenth century. On the JBB figures therefore, bankruptcies amounted to 2.6 per cent of the extant business population in the 1750s, 1 per cent in the 1760s, 4 per cent in the 1770s, 3.1 per cent in the 1780s and a sharp rise to 9.9 per cent in the 1790s.

The mid-century focus of the JBB database means that it underestimates the size of the 1790s trading population, but even if the (adjusted) Holden's 1805 figure (270) was extrapolated back in time to the 1790s, this still reduces the percentage of bankruptcies only to 9.63 per cent. The lower figure for the 1760s can perhaps be associated with the temporary return of prosperity to the bay trade after the end of the Seven Years War in 1763 (no baytrade traders were bankrupted in the 1760s). The rise

---

49 Hoppit, *Risk and failure*, pp. 49–54.

50 *Ibid.*, pp. 46–7.

51 I have discounted apothecaries, since many provincial apothecaries were acting as general practitioners as well as shopkeepers, though have included chemists and druggists who seem in Colchester to be principally retailers.

Table 4.4
Bankruptcies per decade by occupational group

Category	*1750s*	*1760s*	*1770s*	*1780s*	*1790s*	*Total*
Law/Medical	0	0	0	2	0	2
Transport	0	0	0	0	1	1
Wood	0	0	0	0	1	1
Metal	0	1	0	0	1	2
General	0	0	0	2	2	4
Building	2	1	1	1	1	6
Inns	1	1	0	2	2	6
Baytrade	1	0	4	1	1	7
Food	1	0	1	2	3	7
Dress	1	0	4	0	4	9
Merchant/Industrial	*2	1	1	1	7	12
Total	8	4	11	11	23	57

*includes one 1751 bankruptcy not included in Table 4.3 above

in the 1770s included four baytrade bankruptcies in 1772 precipitated apparently by the financial crisis of that year. There were also three bankruptcies in 1773 (two Dress and one in the Food and Drink sector) which may well have occurred as the lines of failing credit from the 1772 crisis spread outward. Hoppit identifies such moments of financial insecurity as having greater and more direct effect on bankruptcy than either the quality of the harvest or the nascent business cycle. The 1772 crisis had a particular relevance for Colchester traders, since at its heart was the collapse of the Ayr Bank and its proprietor Alexander Fordyce. Fordyce had stood as the radical candidate for Colchester in the 1768 election (Chapter 6). However, financial instability seems to have been no respecter of political party; Fordyce supporters in 1768 were in fact under-represented in 1772–3 bankruptcies.[52]

Across the different occupational sectors in Colchester, the profile largely accords with the national picture, showing merchant activity and food and drink to have higher incidences of bankruptcy. Colchester figures do not follow the national ascendance of 'Textiles and Clothes' since this includes textile manufacturers in the north and west who had higher levels of failure.

The peak of bankruptcies in the 1790s is directly associated with the high inflation caused by the international wars originating with the French Revolution. The worst financial crises of these years were in 1793 and 1797. Three Colchester bankruptcies in 1793 were followed by four in 1794, five in 1795, one in 1796, three in 1797 and three in 1798. In this decade the capital-intensive trade of the Hythe merchants made them particularly vulnerable; six out of twenty-two traders were bankrupted. Comparatively speaking, innkeepers in a flourishing and comparatively low-capital entry trade seem superficially to have been better off. However, innkeepers were often defined as outside the bankruptcy laws, since they (so the law reasoned) provided services on demand rather than traded on credit. The high number of Colchester innkeepers in the JBB database for this decade also reflects the greater availability of primary sources such as land tax assessments and alehouse

52 Hoppit, *Risk and failure*, pp. 134–6, J. Hoppit, 'Financial crises in eighteenth-century England', *Economic History Review*, 2nd ser., 39 (1986), pp. 39–58; D'Cruze, *The middling sort*, p. 393.

recognisances, so over-state the growth in what was nevertheless a flourishing economic sector. By contrast the baytrade mustered only a single bankruptcy; that of William Argent. As argued in Chapter 1, the baytrade declined by concentration as well as contraction. The JBB database lists fifteen baymakers active for at least part of the 1790s, though some of these may have diversified into other activities or were living from rentier income. Hoppit identifies lower levels of bankruptcy with stagnating trades where risk avoidance is a key strategy for traders seeking to continue their businesses, which seems to be the case for the baytrade in 1790s Colchester.

The incidence of bankruptcy in Colchester therefore seems consonant with its economic status in the national economy; not at the forefront of growth but participating in the broader trends of rising incidence of bankruptcy towards the end of the century, highly sensitive to short-term financial fluctuations and more prone to bankruptcy in areas of economic growth (in particular the merchant activities around the Hythe). The concentration of local sources here also enable an examination of particular bankruptcies, the way they were managed, the networks of credit they reveal, the role of attorneys and the increasing draw of the London courts as well as the post-failure strategies of Colchester traders.

The social significance of bankruptcy of middling traders in Colchester needs to be gauged in its local context. Arguably in faster-growing and hence more volatile economic areas the higher occurrence of bankruptcy produced a greater familiarity with it as a potential outcome of trade. But in a far slower-growing town, the years of financial crisis when three or four hitherto respectable traders failed must have necessarily seemed alarming. Statistics and detailed studies such as Dickinson's and Hoppit's treat bankruptcy essentially as an individual experience. However, all bankrupt traders had families and kin. They also had networks of social connection and 'friends'. All these people, even if they did not directly lose money and hence jeopardise their own credit networks, were doubtless called upon socially and often economically to ameliorate the crisis.

The middling household comprised between four and seven people, so the seven bankruptcies of 1772–3 touched thirty to forty household members, as well as extended kin, in a population that had grown very little over the preceding decades.[53] The four bankrupts of 1772, for example, were all baymakers, so numerous weavers and their families as well as the households of the cardmakers, roughers and other middling textile trades would have been affected, not to mention the shopkeepers with whom these households traded, and others who were involved in the bankrupts' credit networks. If the middling sort comprised around 20 per cent of Colchester's population at the end of the century (say 2,000 people in all including small children), seven bankruptcies in two years must have had a wide reach among this social group. As the better-documented examples show, where bankruptcy could be seen as the outcome of misfortune rather than knavery, family, friends and patrons very often took on financial and social obligations, stretching their own credit to assist the bankrupt. As numbers of bankruptcies rose at the end of the century and where inflation was doubtless testing the credit of the middling community as a whole, bailing out bankrupted associates or kin must have been that much more difficult to achieve.

53 See Chapter 1 n. 17.

There is a discernible trend away from the local administration of Colchester bankruptcies. In the last two decades of the eighteenth century more bankruptcies were being heard in London at the Guildhall and indeed, more bankrupts from the surrounding countryside or smaller towns were having their hearings in Colchester. Whereas between 1752 and 1766 only three non-Colchester bankruptcies had their creditors' meetings in Colchester there were four such examples between 1770 and 1784 and fifteen in the last fifteen years of the century. No bankrupt Colchester traders had their cases examined in London before 1766; one did between 1770 and 1784 and eight from 1785 to 1799. It became more common for the attorneys organising the bankruptcy hearings to work in partnership with a London solicitor. No Colchester attorney named as organising a bankruptcy commission had a London partner before the 1770s. Two Colchester attorneys handled all three cases together with London partners between 1770 and 1784. The equivalent figures for 1785–66 were four Colchester attorneys handling seventeen bankruptcies with London partners. London attorneys without local partners handled one bankruptcy before 1785 and six thereafter. Town Clerk Francis Smythies handled two bankruptcies before 1784, early in his career and nine after 1785, six in partnership with London attorney Thomas Lowten. This partnership also figured in the copious litigation surrounding the borough corporation during the last two decades of the century.[54] William Francis, the non-conformist attorney already mentioned in this chapter handled one bankruptcy before 1785 and seven thereafter together with a London partner. These changes hint at two larger trends; firstly the greater intrusion of national markets and wider networks of credit in local economic affairs by the beginning of the nineteenth century, and secondly the importance of turn-of-the-century attorneys. London contacts and business were it seems the more important for the successful Colchester attorney by 1800.

James Lovett

James Lovett began trade as a grocer and linen draper at the Hythe in 1776 on borrowed capital of £500. He occupied sizeable property (rated £13) and was a regular attender at St Leonards vestry meetings. He married in 1777. In 1784 he moved to the High Street in St Nicholas (his wife's parish). He bought (the now) 108 High Street, acquiring the next-door property (no. 109) in 1799 for his mother.[55] He bought no. 108 for £600, borrowing two thirds of this. Around £2,000 was spent on improvements; the premises were 'repaired and re-edified' and new warehouses were added and the house re-fronted. No. 109 cost £500, £380 of this on mortgage, and a further £200 was spent to convert part of it into a counting house and repair the rest. Lovett traded apparently successfully for over twenty years. During the 1790s he must have felt confident of his position, encouraged no doubt by the economic inflation. He began to buy other local property as well as no. 109 High Street. Most of this was bought on mortgage, repaired and then rented out. However, the largest of these purchases, made in 1801, directly expanded Lovett's trading operations. He and his then partner,

54 JBB BD/811.

55 n. 22 above; *IpsJ* 23 June, 28 July 1810.

William Linton (a local auctioneer) spent £2,000 on property in nearby Helens Lane in which they set up a Hemp Manufactory. Linton had brought £6,000 into the partnership but the hemp factory entailed a further £1,000 mortgage. The business partnership with Linton ended a few years later, meaning the return of the capital. A second partnership with William Kendall brought in £2,500 capital but was dissolved in 1809. Lovett also had shares in two paquet boats.

By 1810, Lovett's credit was dangerously over-stretched. He had bad debts of £4,000. At his bankruptcy examination he explained his insolvency by the 'different nature of the trade since commencing therein'; not having sufficient capital and the cost of interest payments due to his 'relieving himself by Bills on Interest'. Bills of Exchange, while they facilitated trade, also extended chains of essentially unsecured credit throughout the business community. Nationally, the summer of 1810 began one of the periodic financial crises of the early industrial period. The overestimate of new market opportunities in South America provided an unwarranted economic stimulus at a time when both import and export markets were glutted. This was further boosted by the over-generous accommodation of bills by the Bank of England. Already in March five London merchants dealing in Baltic hemp failed. Hemp prices had been falling for months previously, something which must have affected Lovett's trade, though because the bankruptcy papers list trade creditors not debtors, it is not possible to recover the profile of Lovett's bad debts. The key bankruptcy which precipitated the wider 1810 crisis was that of Thomas Coles and sons, West India brokers and their bankers Brickwood and Co. on 6 July. Two of Lovett's creditors were London firms who failed later that year, and Richard Shaw, a Stoke on Trent merchant to whom Lovett owed some £600 was bankrupted in 1811.[56]

Lovett's total debt of some £16,000 has a heavy preponderance of borrowed capital (£9,030 5d plus £2,210 3s 7d held as executor) over trade debts (£4,924 11 2d). His trade debts in total were only around 20 per cent greater than the figure he estimated for bad debts. All the trade and finance debt was essentially unsecured. The largest finance creditors were William Kendall, Lovett's ex-partner (£1,367 on a bond), Thomas Cooper a wealthy farmer of Langenhoe (£2,066 on a bond guaranteed by Kendall) and Lovett's mother Hannah Peggs (£1,000 lent on mortgage on family lands in Tollesbury). Most of these unsecured creditors were Colchester tradesmen and local farmers whose notes and bills were part of the circulating trading capital of the town and its rural hinterland. The only London finance is provided by Philip Sansom (£359 10s 6d), a merchant born and brought up in Colchester.

Lovett's owed roughly equal amounts to town and country unsecured creditors, something over £4,000 from each location (see Table 4.5). With the bay trade much declined a substantial grocer had a good deal of trade in the countryside. The balance tips decisively in favour of the town, however, if the £2,210 to which Lovett had access as an executor are included. This came principally from the estate of Francis Snell[57] (died 1794), an affluent Colchester tailor with premises near Lovett's. Local connection and credit remained important into the nineteenth century. Lovett also

---

56 Duffy, *Bankruptcy*, pp. 182–3, 186–91. For Richard Shaw's bankruptcy, *London Gazette*, 14 July 1810, p.16, 18 September 1810, p.16, 20 October 1810, p. 16, 18 June 1811, p.16.

57 Francis Snell, JBB BD/813. His will is NA PROB 11/1240, proved 7 January 1794.

Table 4.5
James Lovett: debts proved

Funds borrowed	Colchester[1]	4374.11.0	
	London[2]	359.10.6	
	Country[3]	4295.18.11	
			9030.0.5
Goods bought	Colchester		
	23 creditors	499.2.6	
	London		
	32 creditors	2365.17½	
	Country		
	12 creditors	431.10.1	
	Other		
	12 creditors	1628.1.7	
			4924.11.2½
Monies held as executor	Francis Snell	2172.1.9	
	Geo Rusher	38.1.10	2210.3.7
Other	Rents on Bures property	11.10.0	
	Stonemason; St Nicholas Parish work	50.0.0	
	Due re share of paquets (St Peters Paquet and the Sally)	577.16.3	
	R. R. Newell; Doctors Bill	11.18.0	
			650.14.3
			£168150 8.5½

[1] includes £1367 16s 10d owed to William Kendall
[2] Phillip Sansom
[3] Essex and Suffolk

owed £577 for his share in two sailing paquets and (mixing private and local government monies) £50 for stonemason's work carried out for St Nicholas parish.

The bankruptcy papers also provide an idea of the geographical spread of his business, the kind of commodities traded in and the range and numbers of his trade creditors. Almost £5,000 worth of trade debts were declared during the bankruptcy from a total of seventy-nine creditors (Table 4.6).

In contrast to the finance creditors, by far the greatest amount of trade debts were incurred in London (£2,365 between thirty-two creditors, an average debt of £73 9s). Seventeen different trades were represented from grocers and drapers to a (washing) blue manufacturer. The largest sums owed were to tobacconists (£398 19s 9d) and to warehousemen (specialist wholesale suppliers – £386 12s 4d). Tea dealers were owed £363 3s 0d, general merchants £268 15s 9d, druggists £256 1s 3d and drapers £216 7s 6d. Lovett's main trade was to meet the demand for metropolitan goods in the provincial market.

Colchester items total £499 between twenty-three creditors (£22 average) and country items £431 between twelve creditors (£36 average). Both country and Colchester creditors are clearly far less important to the overall business than either London or Midlands and Northern England suppliers. Lovett's trading patterns show the importance of the capital and the fast-growing northern production centres as well as the progressive integration of the national market and the acceleration and direction

Table 4.6
James Lovett: trade creditors

LONDON TRADERS	
Tobacconists	£398.19.9
Warehousemen	386.12.4
Tea dealer	363.3.0
Merchant	268.15.9
Druggist	256.13
Drapers	216.7.6
Oilman	109.8.8
Cornfactor	92.3.2
Vinegar seller	59.5.6
Cheesemonger	55.3.0
Haberdashers	50.9.1
Wine merchant	46.13.6
Unspecified	24.2.8
Stationer	14.710
Coffee dealer	10.4.0
Brushmaker	5.13.½
Potter & Glass seller	5.7.0
Blue manufacturer	3.0.0
ESSEX & SUFFOLK TRADERS	
Papermakers, Melford & Gt. Baddow	79.16.0
Victualler, Ardleigh	79.4.0
Soapboiler, Nayland	64.13.4
Grocer, Diss	60.0.0
Butterfactor, Ipswich	59.4.0
Merchant, Ipswich	20.5.9
Cheesemonger, Ipswich	20.0.0
Potashmaker, Lt Baddow	19.14.8
Manufacturer, Stoke Holycross, Norfolk	12.12.9
Grocer & Draper, Nayland	64.13.4
Fustian weaver, Haverhill	5.16.0
COLCHESTER TRADERS	
Soap manufacturer	140.16.8
Grocer	113.5.1
Seedsmen	37.17.3
Plumber & Glazier	30.13.7
Freight charges	28.9.11
Baymaker	28.18.0
Ironmonger.	24.6.6
Wheelwright	22.19.0
Winemerchant/victualler	14.2.6
Chinaman/potter	9.1.11
Tea dealer	7.0.0
Draper	5.17.6
TRADERS FROM OTHER AREAS	
Stoke-on-Trent, Merchant	629.3.0
Textile Manufacturers, Leeds, Manchester, Norwich	455.17.8
Cheesefactors, Leics & Staffs.	261.12.6
Salt proprietor, Chester	131.0.0
Grocer, Hull	74.9.0
Shipchandler, Hull	33.11.9
Hosier, Newark	20.1.8

of economic change during early industrialisation.

Lovett owned fourteen properties, most of them in Colchester and purchased from the late 1790s when the wartime inflation and the town's expansion due to the garrison must have favoured such a business as Lovett's. As well as residential properties acquired on borrowed capital and renovated for rent, he owned a hemp factory in Helens Lane. Most of the mortgagors are from the Colchester region, though only one (David Dixon Lloyd, a neighbour and wine merchant who provided £300 by purchasing an annuity to allow Lovett to purchase a house in George Lane) is from the town itself. Of the £4,240 that Lovett declared as outstanding to mortgagees the only monies to be supplied from farther away were the £1,660 secured on 108 High Street, comprising £1,100 to Thomas Price, attorney of Worcester and £560 to a Mrs Nash of Kentish Town. Therefore over 60 per cent of Lovett's borrowing on property and almost all his short-term finance was derived from regional and local sources. The Hemp Factory was charged with a £1,000 mortgage to Mr. Benjamin Gilson of Halstead, Essex.

Lovett was overstretched in attempting to run the Hemp Factory as well as the Grocers and Drapers business after the partnership with William Linton ended in 1805, during a period of high inflation when he was also making other purchases of property. The new partnership with William Kendall supplied £2,000 but this seems to have been used for further expansion rather than consolidation, so that when that partnership ended in March 1809, Lovett found himself well out on a limb. However, James Lovett was by no means a reckless adventurer. The bankruptcy came after nearly 40 years of trading during which he built up a substantial business from an original £500 of borrowed capital. A decision to start a Hemp factory in 1801 was not unreasonable. Colchester was full of unemployed clothworkers. There was an identifiable market opportunity to sell sacking to a productive grain growing region from a location well south of the established centre of hemp weaving in Diss (Norfolk). Lovett's mistake, in the end, was to ride the inflationary boom during the French Wars rather too far and to underestimate the progressive economic instability and credit shortage which finally pulled the rug from under his feet during the financial crisis of 1810. His failure can be positioned against the wider workings of the market, the volatility of trade based so heavily on discounted paper, and a financial crisis of national scope. Nevertheless, his credit had important local dimensions in the town and surrounding rural area. It also had significant family underpinnings. Lovett's mother, Mrs Hannah Peggs, had lent him £1,000 by mortgaging family lands at Tollesbury. She was living in part of the property that was put up for auction in 1810. However, by being listed as an unsecured creditor, she presumably eventually received her dividend of 8/- in the £, in effect returning to the Lovett family some £400 in addition to the £113 balance that the commissioners allowed.

Conclusion

Although Colchester lacks sustained and detailed evidence to reconstruct the credit networks of particular middling businesses over time, exploration of a range of sources all show credit networks in operation. Friends, often together with adult kin, were important figures for any middling family's credit, both short and long term. At points friendship shaded into patronage; patronage was always negotiable and patrons had to support the credit of their clients to remain worthy of the name. Friendship, money and patronage formed one axis of middling credit which intersected with that of family and property. Family and household prosperity were the *raison d'etre* of husbanding (and if possible expanding) credit. There was an important local dimension to the circulation of social and financial credit, as much in the early 1800s as before 1750, though the nature of trade and the growth of national (and international) markets meant that friends might be located at a distance. Rather than seeing economic and market development as eroding or replacing local credit networks and the role of friends within the Colchester middling community, the picture seems to be one of increasing complexity in credit and exchange relations. Local attorneys made ever more work for themselves out of this trend. They could not only manage the formal legal devices and processes that were called for (conveyances, trusts, mortgages, wills, bankruptcies) but could also link local, regional and national and in effect were making a profession out of the business of 'friendship'. James Lovett's bankruptcy provides a detailed picture of the intersections of national and local aspects of middling credit at the end of our period and shows how wider financial trends, the dense local trading network and an experienced businessman's (under)estimate of risk in an inflationary and unstable economy, operated together to bring about his financial failure.

Chapter 5

Politeness and association

Improvements and genteel culture

Particularly after the 1730s Colchester acquired many trappings of contemporary genteel culture. The architectural renovations discussed in Chapter 2 were accompanied by other improvements to the urban infrastructure. By mid-century, lime trees had been planted beside new and elegant gravel walks around St Mary-at-the-Walls Church ('much resorted to by people of the best Fashion')[1] and in Sir Isaac's Walk along the top of the southern town wall. Colchester was to boast two bowling greens, a flower garden and by 1810 a botanical gardens.[2] Many new high-street shops appeared after the 1730s. Bow-fronted windows were illuminated at night to display their wares. Colchester's shops offered books and music, china ('Delft and glassware of all sorts')[3] and other domestic goods, clothing and millinery ('fans mounted and mended'),[4] furniture ('Whist and Buroe Tables Oblong and Oval'),[5] tea, sugar and other colonial goods. Visual art was on offer at James Dunthorne's print shop in the 1780s. Eighteenth-century retail practice was making shopping an increasingly comfortable and sociable practice.[6] From 1752 there was a sea water baths at Wivenhoe 'finished in a Genteel Manner for the Reception of Company'.[7]

Innkeepers promoted sporting events, and inns were key sites of both leisure and business. In the 1780s sailing matches pitted teams from the surrounding coastal villages and towns and were amplified by evening dinners and balls in Colchester's leading inns.[8] There was a race course on Mile End Heath in the second half of the century and John Ennifer, innkeeper at the Golden Lyon in Colchester High Street

---

1 P. Morant, *The history and antiquities of the most ancient town of Colchester* (Colchester, 1748), book 2, p. 4.

2 One bowling green was near St Marys Church (ERO D/DE T162); the other was part of the Three Crowns property in St Peters (ERO Acc C16, Free School trustees papers, Trunk 1, Box 2); *IpsJ* 24 February 1755 Old Three Crowns to be let 'to which belongs the only Bowling-Green in the town ...'; for the flower garden, *IpsJ* 10 April 1773, 22 April and 16 September 1775; re the botanical garden, G. Martin, *The Story of Colchester*, (Colchester, 1959), p. 87.

3 *IpsJ* 2 May 1761, Richard Hassells and John Keeling, chinamen, JBB BD/482.

4 *IpsJ* 8 October 1796, Mary Waynman, milliner, JBB BD/923.

5 *IpsJ* 12 October 1754, Clark Blyth, joiner, cabinet and chair maker, JBB BD/82.

6 H. Berry, 'Polite consumption: shopping in eighteenth-century England', *Transactions of the Royal Historical Society* 6th Series, Xii (2002), pp. 375–94.

7 Original proprietor Horatio Flack, JBB BD/311, later Thomas Tunmer, JBB BD/891. *IpsJ* 23 May 1752; W. Radcliffe, 'Thomas Tunmer and a forgotten spa', *The Practitioner*, 193 (1964), pp. 363–7.

8 *ChCh* 15 July 1785, 11 and 18 August 1786, 7 September 1787. *IpsJ* 15 August 1789, the gentlemen of the White Hart Club invited competitors to a race though this seems not to have come off.

advertised a pack of subscription fox hounds kept at Lexden in 1756.[9] Cock fighting was not infrequent in village inns and was a place where men of a wide social range could come together, though it was repeatedly forbidden by county magistrates.[10] Innkeepers invited scratch cricket teams to compete for the prizes they provided. Frequently these were items of men's attire; eleven wigs at the Ship, Alresford in 1766, eleven pairs of gloves worth 2s a pair in East Donyland the same year, eleven silk waistcoats at Wivenhoe or eleven half-guinea hats at the Cock and Pye on North Hill in 1770.[11] Like other such events, cricket matches were generally followed by a convivial dinner at the presiding inn. They linked masculinity, sociability and competition for the accoutrements of genteel self-presentation, with local particularism and the potential for a certain disorder. In 1777 a Stowmarket (Suffolk) team alleged that Colchester's supporters staged a 'disturbance' which 'prevented the Stowmarket gentlemen going in a second time' when they needed only another 24 notches (runs) to win. There were 44 guineas in prize money at stake.[12] The following year the team from the village of Nayland made a similar complaint throwing doubt on the decisions of Colchester's umpire. This was Enoch King (a pavior of St Botolphs), whom Colchester defended in verse in the following week's newspaper:

> But how could you dare upbraid our Umpire?
> Enoch King, we fear not his name
> The game knows so well, no one can excel
> In him we repose for the same.[13]

Nayland got its own back by publishing a not unpolished playlet in the following week's paper, satirising the Colchester team.[14]

The major eighteenth-century inns were those nearer the London road — the Three Cups and the White Hart at the top of the High Street or the King's Head in Head Street — which partially eclipsed the longer-established Red Lion, situated further down the High Street. Transport improvements encouraged the inn-keeping trade.[15] Monthly assemblies were held at the King's Head and later at the White Hart. There were Coffee Rooms at the White Hart and the Three Cups. Improvements at the major inns were legion. At one stage a full-sized organ was installed at the White Hart. Dining and political clubs, the medical society, the town's two Masonic lodges, much

---

9 *IpsJ* 8 May 1756, also 7 September and 21 December 1754. J. Cooper *et al.*, *The borough of Colchester* (Woodbridge, 1994), p. 174, also mentions horse races on Lexden Heath in 1785, a riding school in Angel Lane in 1792 and the East Essex Foxhounds est. 1798.

10 *IpsJ* 14 January 1758, 3 March 1764.

11 *IpsJ* 14 June and 26 July 1766, 11 August and 22 September 1770, 17 August 1771.

12 *IpsJ* 20 September 1777.

13 *ChCh* 21 August 1778; JBB BD/1202.

14 *ChCh* 7 August 1778; J. Bensusan Butt, *Benjamin Strutt, William Cole and James Fisin* (Colchester, privately printed, 1994), p. 22.

15 A.F.J. Brown, *Colchester in the eighteenth century* (Colchester, 1969), p. 16; J. Bensusan Butt,'Living in style in eighteenth-century Colchester, text of lecture given 22nd February', 1967; Chapter 1 above, n. 53.

local administration and the socialising associated with it took place at an inn. They were also the venues for occasional spectacles and curiosities. There were manifestations of popular scientific culture; lecturers, flower shows, fringe medicine or new inventions including a horseless carriage or Moore's Musical Clock. There were also more carnivalistic enjoyments including conjurers and 'surprising dancing bears'.[16]

Colchester had a lively literary, musical and theatrical life. The town boasted painters and artists, both amateur and professional, notably the James Dunthornes snr and jnr, discussed further below. The better off in Colchester, as elsewhere, were given to having their portraits painted, some by local artists and some by those of greater reputation including Gainsborough in his Ipswich period.[17] There was an appreciation of grand painting — or at least of its value as a curiosity. The Great family of apothecaries' collection of paintings were believed to be Van Dykes.[18] The Norwich Company of Comedians visited the town each season from the 1730s. They performed in the Moot Hall until 1764 when a theatre was built for them, by subscription. Musical concerts were not infrequent from the 1730s and 40s. Handel's *Messiah* was performed in 1759 and 1790. The town's musical circle of middling sort and town gentry met regularly at the home of lawyer George Wegg. Both the theatre and the music concert are discussed further below. The Castle Book Society was originally convened by Charles Gray who in 1749 refurbished a room in the castle to house the library left to the town in the sixteenth century by Archbishop Harsnett, hitherto neglected and stored in the grammar school. The society had thirty invited members, whose subscriptions (2 guineas per year in 1820) funded the purchase of books nominated annually by members which were read and discussed then sold the following year (the nominating member having first refusal for half the original purchase price). The permanent library was also enhanced by donations and legacies. It comprised religious, architectural, scientific, alchemical and other scholarly works. John Wesley donated Samuel Wesley's *Dissertations on the Book of Job* in April 1759. This serious-minded and long-lasting institution comprised only one segment of the literary interest in the town.[19]

---

16 ERO Acc 905, Box 2, 'IpsJ extracts; sports, luxuries &c'; J. Bensusan Butt, 'Living in style'; P. Elliott, 'The origins of the "creative class": provincial urban society, scientific culture and socio-political marginality in Britain in the eighteenth and nineteenth centuries', *Social History*, 28 (2003), pp. 361–87; *IpsJ* 28 April 1753 for the dancing bears; *IpsJ* 24 January 1767 for Herman Boaz conjuror; *IpsJ* 23 December 1786 for the French Hercules, strong man; *IpsJ* 25 October 1766 for two lions and a tyger.

17 J. Bensusan Butt, *When Gainsborough painted a Colchester attorney* (Colchester, privately printed, 1978); R.S. Walker (ed.), *A selection of Thomas Twining's letters 1734–1804: a record of a tranquil life* (Lewiston, 1991), letter 216, 10 October 1798, p. 524, Thomas Twining to Richard Twining, 'I owe poor Dunthorne for disfiguring my *human face divine…*' Twining later had his portrait painted by James Halls, see Figure 3.1.

18 See Chapter 1 n. 45.

19 ERO Acc C905 Box 2, 'Boggis IV' notes from original records including Minute Books, Book of Laws and Orders 1790–1813, Book of Clubs including Treasurers' Accounts from 1792; T. Cromwell, *The history and description of the ancient town and borough of Colchester*, two vols (Colchester, 1824), Vol. 2, pp. 344–5.

The William Keymers (father and son), printers and booksellers, ran a circulating library. A catalogue of 1797 lists 3,316 volumes. In 1791 terms were 16s a year, 5s a quarter, or 1d an evening per volume.[20] As the sources for this chapter underline, the local newspaper, *The Ipswich Journal*,[21] was a central means through which the availability of genteel commodities and properties, as well as the announcement and description of polite events was disseminated. Subscription lists for local publications demonstrate the willingness of middling sort as well as gentry readers to acquire a library. Despite Philip Morant's difficulties in recruiting sufficient subscribers for his two-volume history of the borough in 1748, later (cheaper) town histories borrowed much of his scholarship but attracted much better support from middling Colchester subscribers.[22] Among many other examples of local publications, Susan Smythies' novel *The Brothers* (1758) attracted thirty-five Colchester subscribers among an extended subscription list, over a quarter of whom came from Essex and Suffolk. She wrote three popular novels and was a member of the Colchester clerical family.[23] Clara Reeve was daughter of an Ipswich clergyman. One of her sisters ran a long-established millinery business in Colchester High Street and another married Charles Frederick Reinhold, the organist and musician (see further below). A writer of liberal politics, Clara Reeve lived for a time in Colchester and later in Ipswich. Her novel *A Champion of Virtue* re-published as *The English Baron* became a standard of the gothic genre. Her first publication *Original Poems on Several Occasions* (1769) included forty-nine Colcestrian subscribers from the town gentry and affluent middling sort.[24]

Literacy and numeracy have been noted as both useful and incipiently socially elevating skills in middling culture. Commercially provided education (especially for girls) often emphasised genteel as well as practical accomplishments, and Colchester acquired a good handful of such schools as well as commercial schools aimed at middling boys. At the Misses Lind's school, as well as English and Needlework, the 'other Accomplishments' on offer included 'Dancing 1/2gn Entrance Half a Guinea per Quarter; Writing and Arithmetic, 10 shillings per Quarter. Musick if required'.[25] Dancing and music masters gave lessons. The dancing pupils of Isaac Wood regularly demonstrated their prowess at a special ball (2s 6d at the door).[26]

Much cultural consumption was commercially provided and hence nominally available to anyone with the necessary cash (sometimes as little as the penny to borrow a volume from the circulating library or the three pence to attend the flower

---

20 Of many advertisements, see *IpsJ* 28 January 1786, or *IpsJ* 1 October 1791. ERO Acc 905, Box 16, notebook *Feb 64*, p. 21; Box 15, notebook *Bird 1*, p. 11. JBB BD/1016.

21 The *Chelmsford Chronicle* also covered the area, but on the whole had less Colchester news.

22 R. Sweet, *The writing of urban histories in eighteenth-century England* (Oxford, 1997), p. 272.

23 A. Sherbo, 'Smythies, Susan (b. 1720)', *Oxford Dictionary of National Biography* (Oxford, 2004) [www.oxford.dnb.com/view/article/72236, accessed 18 July 2007]; Subscribers list transcribed in ERO Acc 905, Box 2.

24 G. Kelly, 'Reeve, Clara (1729–1807)', *Oxford Dictionary of National Biography* (Oxford, 2004) [www.oxford.dnb.com/view/article/23292, accessed 18 July 2007]; Subscribers list transcribed in ERO Acc 905, Box 2.

25 *IpsJ* 29 October 1768; JBB BD/533.

26 *IpsJ* 2 October 1756; JBB BD/963.

gardens on a Sunday). Nevertheless those commercial proprietors who offered such genteel amusements were frequently careful to specify the demeanour they required in their patrons. Auricula Feasts (flower shows) were held each spring, often at the Castle Inn near North Bridge, combining friendly competition and sociability among the 'Sons of Flora' with the public display of the flowers. Henry Stow, fulling miller at Lexden Mill, was one of a number of local aficionados of ornamental plants. As well as auriculas, he turned his hand to tulips. In 1763, he advertised his annual display of blooms:

> Any Gentlemen or Ladies that are fond of the TULIP are very Welcome to feast their Eyes with such as are at Lexden Mill, near Colchester, Essex. The best Time for seeing the Tulip is about Eleven O'Clock in the Day. From their humble servant HENRY STOW.
> N.B. I would not be understood by this to give a general Invitation to all the meaner Sort of People; but only to such of them as love Flowers, can behave civilly, and come without Dogs.[27]

Stow's advertisement is precise about the nature of the gaze that he invites. He was a prosperous middling tradesman and addressed an audience far wider than the gentry or town elite. Nevertheless the pleasures he offered were very much those 'of the imagination' even more than of the senses. The meaner sort of people (or their dogs) were clearly not imagined as likely to appreciate the spectacle he placed on view. Historians explaining such social inclusions and exclusions within urban culture have often drawn on the heuristic concepts of politeness and association.

Politeness

Although they continue to debate its precise chronologies, characteristics and social reach, historians now broadly agree that politeness was a significant strand in eighteenth-century culture.[28] Politeness was not exclusively an urban phenomenon, though it was increasingly inscribed on urban culture. Although there is evidence in abundance of metropolitan politeness, provincial towns also seized upon politeness to mark their distinctive identities. Within towns, politeness was more than the exclusive

---

27 *IpsJ* 14 May 1763; JBB BD/838.

28 An excellent historiographic review of this now complex and extensive field is L.E. Klein, 'Politeness and the interpretation of the British eighteenth century', *Historical Journal*, 45 (2002), pp. 869–98. Texts defining key areas include: P. Langford, *A polite and commercial people: England, 1727–1783* (Oxford, 1989); P. Borsay, *The English urban renaissance: culture and society and the provincial town* (Oxford, 1989); J. Brewer and R. Porter (ed.), *Consumption and the world of goods*, (1993); J. Brewer, *The pleasures of the imagination: English culture in the eighteenth century* (London, 1997); P. Langford, *Englishness identified: manners and character 1650–1850* (Oxford, 2000). J. Tosh, 'English politeness: conduct, social rank and moral virtue, c.1400–1900', *Transactions of the Royal Historical Society*, 12 (2002), pp. 261–6 introduces a recent collection of conference proceedings. See also P. Carter, *Men and the emergence of polite society; Britain 1660–1800* (London and New York, 2001); A. Vickery, *The gentleman's daughter: women's lives in Georgian England* (New Haven and London, 1998); D. Wahrman, *Imagining the middle class: the political representation of class in Britain, c.1780–1840* (Cambridge, 1995); D. Wahrman, *The making of the modern self: identity and culture in eighteenth-century England* (New Haven and London, 2004); K. Wilson, *The sense of the people: politics, culture, and imperialism in England, 1715–1785* (New York, 1995).

province of urban elites and visiting landed gentry. The earlier restriction of polite culture to social sites accessible only by the manifestly 'chief inhabitants' of a provincial town such as Colchester was eroded, not least through the growth of the market during the second two thirds of the century. By the 1780s politeness was a cultural resource much used by the middling sort and respectable artisans. Langford suggests that by the end of the century even the labouring classes could display aspects of politeness.[29]

In practice, of course, different aspects of genteel culture were patronised by differentiated yet overlapping groups. The respected Quaker philanthropist, John Kendall (whose family were cabinetmakers and booksellers and thus provided some of the material trappings of genteel culture) disapproved of the theatre on religious grounds. On one notable occasion he succeeded in emptying Colchester's theatre by his eloquent persuasion.[30] Such differences in preference and interest were not infrequently inflected by religion and politics.

Much of the historical debate over what politeness consisted of has been occasioned by its complexity and multiple appropriations in eighteenth-century culture. It was an ideologically inflected characteristic of the nation, that 'polite and commercial people'.[31] Herman Boaz, the well-travelled conjurer (with his learned dog), aimed to be attractive to both polite and popular impulses, with a little patriotism thrown in. He aimed to 'present the curious with a more interesting spectacle' than available elsewhere in either Art or Nature. He continued,

> His amusements are chiefly calculated for the Genius of the British Nation, being rather more apt to raise the Mind than affect the Senses. The many new discoveries Mr Boaz has (by his close Application) made in that Art, he hopes will suit the Learned and Virtuosi in that Kind.[32]

He seems to have succeeded, and extended his booking for an extra week's performances at the King's Head assembly rooms.

The language of politeness was terminologically broad — contemporaries used it to describe literature, architecture and music (as well as conjuring). Eighteenth-century Colchester trade advertisements generally talked of material culture (things and places) as 'genteel' and this is a term I am using for such material underpinnings leaving 'polite' to refer more directly to social action and interaction. Politeness involved genteel material culture, bodily deportment and attachment to (or acquaintance with) certain ideas. While it negotiated differences of class, it was potentially more troubling to gender identities, in particular masculinity. Politeness

---

29 H. French, *The middle sort of people in provincial England, 1600-1750* (Oxford, 2007), p. 243; P. Langford, 'The uses of eighteenth-century politeness', *Transactions of the Royal Historical Society*, 12 (2002), pp. 311–31.

30 David J. Hall, 'Kendall, John (1726–1815)', *Oxford Dictionary of National Biography* (Oxford, 2004), http:www.oxford.dnb.com/view/article/15350, accessed 23 July 2006.

31 P. Langford, *A polite and commercial people*; K. Wilson, 'Citizenship, empire, and modernity in the English provinces, c.1720–1790', *Eighteenth-Century Studies*, 29 (1995), pp. 69–96.

32 See n. 16 above.

33 P. Carter, 'Men about town': representations of foppery and masculinity in early eighteenth-century urban society, in H. Barker and E. Chalus (eds.), *Gender in eighteenth-century England* (Harlow, 1997), pp. 31–57; P. Carter, *Men and the emergence of polite society*, p. 10, Chapter 4, especially p.145.

called for refined masculinities, the social association of men and women, and the rejection of rougher manly behaviour; it could shade into foppishness and effeminacy.[33] It existed materially, in the body and as a social imaginary; the point of polite conduct was to develop a polite personality.[34] As a descriptor of bodily deportment, self presentation, conversation and behaviour, politeness was a means of facilitating harmonious social interaction. Politeness was therefore the habitus of that other key facet of eighteenth century culture, the association of individuals in clubs, organisations or more informal groupings in such venues as theatres, coffee houses or socialising in a domestic setting (Chapter 2). The tenets of polite deportment were available to learn, and those that could deploy them acquired social ease. To this extent politeness was a means of levelling up, though the necessary self presentation and skills (beginning with literacy, numeracy, a respectable set of clothes and clean linen) required a certain material underpinning.

In short, as Klein puts it,

> ... politeness was an idiom with uses for a wide range of people, including some who were neither aristocratic nor landed nor middling. Of course, politeness was expressed differently by — and had different meanings for — different people in different circumstances, but it also often served as a medium facilitating interaction and access to shared experience. It served purposes of distinction and also of solidarity.[35]

In a provincial urban setting such solidarities could attach to locality as well as the differentiation of polite society from the 'meaner sort of people'. The aspects of eighteenth-century Colchester's urban culture explored further in the rest of this chapter were frequently expressed through idioms of politeness and were participated in (and often organised by) the middling sort.

Colchester Theatre

Urban culture was often also civic culture, either in the narrow sense of invoking the patronage and involvement of town institutions, in particular the corporation, or in the looser meaning of enhancing the dignity and distinctiveness of the town. Very often both these aspects were combined, for example in the combination of cultural (artistic, musical or associational) activity with philanthropic or humanitarian goals. Furthermore, as I have argued, urban culture more often than not intersected with commerce or private enterprise. Public finance was not available to fund cultural activities on any meaningful scale, so combinations of private subscription and commercial venture met the costs. Although gentry patronage was not infrequently sought to scaffold other funding for larger projects, and leaders of the town gentry deployed personal funds to underpin cultural activities, the role of the smaller subscriber or the middling business remained central to the town's cultural life. The cultural venture which perhaps best exemplifies this concatenation of politeness, civic patronage and commerce was Colchester's first purpose-built theatre which opened in 1764. The Norwich Company of Comedians were regular visitors to Colchester around

34 Carter, *Men and the emergence of polite society*, pp. 197–8.

35 Klein, 'Politeness and the interpretation of the British eighteenth century', p. 873.

36 Cooper *et al.*, *Colchester*, p. 174.

mid-century, performing in the major inns.[36] Theatrical audiences comprised a broad enough social spectrum to trouble the boundaries of politeness. In 1762, 'at the request of the Ladies and Gentlemen in general, who have often been disturbed by the rude Behaviour of Persons frequenting the Sixpenny Gallery, there will be no Sixpences taken in future'.[37]

Civic patronage actively repositioned the theatre as an ornament to the cultural life of the town. One of the first acts of the renewed corporation was to commission the building of a permanent theatre, to be located on corporation property immediately behind the Moot Hall.[38] Theatre audiences accessed the theatre through the Moot Hall itself. A formal agreement was made with the Norwich Company the following month giving a ninety-nine-year theatrical monopoly and specifying that the theatre to be built should include a special box for the mayor and his party, embellished with the borough arms.[39] Articles of Agreement for the building of the theatre were drawn up the following September between the architect Thomas Ivory of Ipswich and his son William, the Manager of the Norwich Company, Henry Crouse and the 'Proprietors and Subscribers'. These last were the then Colchester mayor, Thomas Clamtree, the deputy recorder William Mayhew jnr and eight other Colchester gentlemen, merchants and baymakers. These eight subscribers paid £50 apiece and received in return a silver entrance ticket and the promise of 2s 6d per night of the performing season or a minimum of £3 2s 6d a year.[40] The Norwich Company performed for an eight-week season each year in the 1760s and 70s, and after a few years' intermission and a complete refit of the by then dilapidated interior, from the mid-1780s. The repertoire was standard eighteenth-century repertory fare; Shakespeare, Sheridan, Farquhar, Cibber and other contemporary drama, combined with farce and 'interlude'.

The theatre opened on 29 October 1764 with *The Beaux Strategem*. As an added attraction, the Norwich Company had borrowed an actor from Drury Lane for the part of Scrub. The local newspaper's pre-announcement, two days before the opening, emphasised the intersections of taste, morals, cash and civic aggrandisement in this new cultural development.

> ... the erection of this Theatre not only manifests the Taste and Spirit of the town of Colchester but indicated a Continuance of its Favours; For, as of all moral Diversions the Drama has the Preference, so will it ever find Encouragement from Persons of the most refined Taste. And as the surest Method of securing Success is providing Entertainment worthy of the Design, we get Leave to assure the Public, that no Expence has been spar'd in ornamenting the Theatre.[41]

The social calibre of the audience was underlined in the following week's newspaper, which also managed to combine approbation of both tasteful simplicity and the luxuries necessary to customers' comfort:

> On Monday last the New Theatre was opened to a Polite Audience; the Neatness and

37 *IpsJ* 6 November 1762.

38 ERO D/B 5 Gb8, Colchester Borough Assembly Book 1 February 1764.

39 ERO Acc 905 Box 2, MS 'Typed Boggis Notes', p. 1a(2).

40 Five further Colchester tradesmen became silver-ticketed subscribers the following 2 November, ERO D/B 5 Gb8, Colchester Borough Assembly Book; JBB BD/164, Thomas Clamtree.

41 *IpsJ* 27 October 1764.

> Simplicity of the building, enriched with the Elegance and Taste of the Scenery and Fitting was received with universal Applause. The House is now compleatly finish'd, the Walls boarded and covered with Crimson Hangings and ev'ery Precaution taken to have it rendered warm and commodious, to those Ladies and Gentlemen who shall be pleased to give this publick-spirited Undertaking Encouragement.[42]

The implicit tensions between the claimed civic and moral virtues of the theatre and the pleasure and luxury of the audience experience were of course implicated in the thoroughly gendered contemporary debates about luxury, consumption and the ambiguous moral standing of the stage both as an art and a profession.[43] The Norwich Company used these widely circulated cultural references in the opening prologue, where a male and a female actor contended for the right to speak the first words on the new stage. 'Man' argues for the sense and manly virtue embodied in a male orator, and 'Woman' for Dame Fashion and the tastes of the female audience as the key to a theatre's success. Eventually sharing the prologue, the performers appealed respectively to the male and female audience; to manly vigour and reason and to female beauty and influence — both key auguries of the drama.

MAN Built for your Ease and Pleasure, Sirs, behold,
This Night, our little Stage its Scenes unfold.
Happy Yourselves, each Privilege restor'd[44]
Here, to the Muse, your fav'ring smiles afford:
Bid Genius flourish, and on Fancy's Wing
Mounted aloft, hear sweetest *Shakespear* sing!
Precepts from hence with ten-fold Vigour dart,
And seize thro' Eyes, and Ears, the captive Heart.
Be *Vice* abash'd then, and be *Virtue* bold;
Be Honour ever free, and never sold!
Protect the Stage on this determin'd Plan,
And prove that Reason is the Test of Man.
The Fair shall follow …

WOMAN … How, Sir! You exceed
Your Task! *The Fair shall follow* … no … the Fair shall lead.
Ladies assert your sov'reign Right to Sway;

---

42 *IpsJ* 3 November 1764, ERO Acc 905 Box 2, 'Typed Boggis Notes', p. 12.

43 Brewer, *The pleasures of the imagination,* Chapter 7; D. Wahrman, 'Percy's prologue: from gender play to gender panic in eighteenth-century England', *Past and Present,* 159 (1998), pp. 113–60; of recent work on gender and the eighteenth-century theatre, L. Freeman, *Character's theater: genre and identity on the eighteenth-century English stage* (Philadelphia, 2002); S.C. Harris, 'Clearing the stage: gender, class, and the freedom of the scenes in eighteenth-century Dublin', *Publications of the Modern Language Association of America,* 119 (2004), pp. 1264–84; M. Kobialka, 'Words and bodies: a discourse on male sexuality in late eighteenth-century English representational practices', *Theatre Research International* 28 (2003), pp. 1–19; on the luxury debates more generally, M. Berg and E. Eger (ed.), *Luxury in the eighteenth century, debates, desires and delectable goods* (Basingstoke, 2003) reviewed by L. Klein, 'Luxury in the eighteenth century: debates, desires and delectable goods', *History Workshop Journal,* 57 (2004), pp. 289–93.

44 A reference to the restoration of the borough charter the previous year.

And here despotick, bid your Slaves obey!
Let Beauty patronize the Stage's Cause,
And who shall venture to dispute its Laws?
With gracious smiles our new Design approve,
And frequent here, to our Assistance move.
Be but our House the Fav'rite of the Fair,
And let the Men forsake it ... if they dare.

The gendered rhetorical gesture of this prologue worked precisely because the theatre was one of the key sites of women's high visibility in eighteenth-century urban culture. These conventional gender gambits doubtless won their audience by their very familiarity and thereby glossed the underlying contradictions in the mixed high and low pleasures of the eighteenth-century stage, where tragedy and moral improvement was routinely paired with farce and comedy on the same bill. Such contradictions needed resolution particularly since the theatre was got up as an essay in civic virtue. Furthermore, by the allusion to Shakespeare the prologue attached itself (and the Colchester theatre) to English national identity. If politeness could be used to express towns' individual identities it was also part of an increasingly national culture — to be polite and provincial was therefore to be distinctive, sometimes limited, but not backward.[45]

If the theatre was a space which articulated gender difference (both on stage and in the audience) through women's presence rather than their absence, it was at the same time a civic space where aspects of Colchester's governance, philanthropy, religious and associational life were brought into cultural visibility. The mayor in his box emblazoned with the borough arms embodied the corporation's patronage. Regularly each season, particular performances were 'bespoke' by local charities and organisations as well as by the mayor. The local charity schools received a benefit night each season from the 1780s. The impetus for this seems to have arisen from the Anglican school trustees who with rather faint-hearted generosity passed on a third of the takings to the Presbyterian school.[46] The benefit performance for the schools in 1789 included the first performance of *The Man of Enterprise* written by local writer and the then master of the Blue Coat School, Charles Shillito (Chapter 3). When '*The Wonder* with, for the first time *Animal Magnetism*' were performed for the (Tory) King's Head Club the event produced 'an assemblage of beauty and elegance rarely to be seen in a provincial theatre; (the) greatest part of the pit was rail'd into boxes. The approbation of the performance is so great that every other species of amusement is relinquished for the theatre.'[47] The change in seating arrangements seems to indicate a more 'tonnish' audience than usual. In this case the financial benefit seemed to have flowed to the theatrical company rather than the other way.

The local Angel Lodge of freemasons subsidised performances for many years. They did more than this, in fact, and actively contributed to the spectacle. In 1788 it

---

45 Brewer, *Pleasures of the imagination,* pp. 495–8.

46 *IpsJ* 5 November 1785. The profits were £35 14s 6d. ERO T/A 613 and Acc 905, Box 6, report of Nathaniel Forster and committee on Charity School finances, 15 March 1780.

47 *IpsJ* 14 November 1788.

was *Hamlet* and the farce *Who's the Dupe*. As usual the masons met at their lodge (at the Angel Inn) and processed to the Theatre in full regalia in which 'the company of Visiting Brethren ... (was) ... esteemed a favour'. The play was proceeded by 'the Masonic Ode ... sung by Bro. Inchbald, Mr Johnson, Mr Townsend and Mr Fisher. During the performance of the Ode the Brethren present will appear upon the stage.'[48]

The masons were a longstanding part of the associational life of the town, and as such will be discussed more fully below. The relevant point at this stage in the discussion is the way in which the theatre (in conjunction with the processional space of the High Street) provided the location for the public inscription of masonry on the cultural identity of the town. Advertising a 1784 benefit for one of the actors, Mr Osborne, the newspaper announced that at the

End of the Play, the Stage,
by DESIRE of several LADIES
will be formed into
A FREE MASONS LODGE
By the most Honourable, Antient, Free and Accepted Masons of the Angel Lodge
Wherein will be Sung
An ODE to MASONRY
An Epilogue in the Character of a Free-Mason's wife by Mrs MEZIERE
And an Epilogue on the sublime art of MASONRY by Brother TAYLOR of this Town
To which will be added the Comic Opera call'd
The PADLOCK

Consequently, the theatre was the place where the masculinity of the lodge, normatively veiled in secrecy, was both displayed before a (desiring) female audience and interrogated by a female character. The theatre's first prologue had underlined that desire (characterised as female) was a key mover in realising polite culture through theatrical performance. Under the aegis of corporation patronage, Colchester's eighteenth-century theatre was a sufficiently genteel space, and the habitus[49] of its audience sufficiently polite without any sixpenny gallery, for the gendering of the town's associational life to be celebrated without troubling the hierarchies and exclusions which underpinned it.

Colchester Theatre was a regular high spot of wintertime leisure. A new theatre, which similarly combined corporation influence (its prime mover was the then borough chamberlain, Benjamin Strutt) and private finance from local subscribers, was built in Queen Street in 1812 and continued the traditions of high drama (it opened with *Cymbeline*), masonic patronage, and civic high(ish)-mindedness.[50]

---

48 *Ibid*. They were already bespeaking plays in 1761 including procession and masonic odes on stage. For example *Love for Love* on *IpsJ* 21 November 1761.

49 P. Bourdieu, *Outline of a theory of practice*, R.T. Nice (ed.) (Cambridge, 1977).

50 ERO Acc 905, Box 2, MS *Colchester Theatre;* Cromwell, *Colchester*, Vol. 2, pp. 340–1.

Association

The spatial contexts for politeness in Colchester were the ordered interior and exterior terrains produced by the urban renaissance. Chapter 2 has considered both domestic interiors and the architectural transformations in the urban landscape. This chapter has emphasised how inns provided (commercial) venues for many aspects of genteel business and leisure. It has explored the theatre as a space in which polite cultural production celebrated gender difference as symbolic of a properly ordered society and was inflected with a civic consciousness. Taken together these moves signalled a provincial urban identity that emphasised local distinctiveness, national identity and social inclusiveness, glossing the power differentials by class, race and gender which shaped social practice and thus made polite culture possible. Colchester sources provide very ambiguous evidence for the development of a public sphere in Habermas' sense. Habermas argued that the (French) eighteenth-century coffee house in particular provided places where the free association of individuals and the discussion of political and intellectual matters could take place. Theoretically Habermas' unitary public sphere was the cultural space where public opinion was formed and as such was bourgeois, masculine and part of the making of modernity. While Habermas' public sphere differentiated itself from the private, it was distinct from other kinds of activity that can also be designated as public or as taking place in public; the whole world of commerce for example since business and trade served essentially private interests of profit accumulation. Habermas' concept is not therefore the same as that adopted by women's historians who shaped arguments about the separation of, and the reconfiguration of the gendering of, public and private spheres — a proposition which current work on eighteenth-century gender history is actively re-thinking. A number of historians have sought to extend the basis of Habermas' thinking by positing multiple public spheres of political association which could be differentiated by both class and gender.[51] Such formulations much better express the grain and the texture of historical change, though in so doing leave behind something of Habermas' original theoretical argument.

Mah points out that Habermas also distinguished the public sphere from the 'representative publicness' characteristic of pre-modernity, 'itself capable of social criticism and contestation', but 'based around people's different kinds of corporate identity'.[52] In other words, the kinds of public and political articulations based around the notions of rights and privileges which were core to eighteenth-century Colchester's political life (Chapters 6 and 7). Those taking coffee at the Three Cups on 9 December 1774 included both Francis Smythies, town clerk and at that period associated with the pro-establishment Compromise Party, and three of his kin (James Blatch, William Smythies, Humphrey Carleton) but also William Seaber the anti-compromise and potentially radical political manager. Colchester's inns were politically

---

51 J. Habermas, *The structural transformation of the public sphere*, trans. T. Burger and F. Lawrence (Cambridge, MA, 1989); C. Calhoun (ed.), *Habermas and the public sphere* (Cambridge, MA, 1992); H. Mah, 'Phantasies of the public sphere: rethinking the Habermas of historians', *Journal of Modern History*, 72 (2000), pp. 153–82, p. 158. See Chapter 3, n. 3 above.

52 Mah, 'Phantasies', p. 165.

partisan; the Hand in Hand Club was convened in the interests of the radical candidate George Tierney in the 1788 and 1790 elections.[53] It met at the Red Lion and charged members 3s 6d per meeting where campaign business was followed by dinner. The Constitutional Club in the Tory interest met at the White Hart and charged 5s. These were not organisations intended for the labouring poor; they combined political interest with polite sociability. At the Hand in Hand, after some rapidly accomplished business,

> ... the remainder of the day was devoted to conviviality, no circumstance arising to interrupt that general harmony which has so invariably distinguished this respectable Club from its first institution.[54]

It was perhaps no coincidence that the longstanding innkeepers of the Red Lion, James and Ann Triggs, left the inn shortly after Tierney's election defeat in 1790 and furthermore that they found work through members of the local opposition party.[55] Local Colchester sources therefore provide much evidence of associational activity taking place in different degrees or kinds of publics – all of them sites where polite masculinities and femininities were being forged[56] – but are much more ambiguous about a public sphere.

Colchester's associational life was broad and varied. In most towns, the second half of the century saw a proliferation of clubs and organisations. Their membership was socially broad but the male middling sort formed the majority of members.[57] Family remained an important determinant of social connection. Religious affiliation, especially the division between Anglicans and protestant non-conformists, was another important influence in the selection of social contacts. While it would be over-stretching an already elastic definition to argue that mid-eighteenth-century Colchester non-conformity had become polite, its theological disputations and its religious emotionality were contained. Overall non-conformity's comparative religious quietism, its sociality and its recognisable institutional presence helping shape the patterning of

---

53 J. Money, 'Taverns, coffee houses and clubs; local politics and popular articulacy in the Birmingham area in the age of the American Revolution', *Historical Journal*, 14 (1971), pp. 15–47; P. Clark, *British clubs and societies, 1580–1800: the origins of an associational world* (Oxford, 2000). These were the people assembled in the Three Cups coffee rooms when attacked by Samuel Wall, attorney in a fit of insanity. See Chapter 8, note 27 below. JBB BD/811 Francis Smythies, BD/149 Humphrey Carleton; BD/809 William Smythies; BD/75 James Blatch; BD/753 William Seaber.

54 *IpsJ* 1 March 1790.

55 JBB BD/888, James and Ann Triggs. They kept the Red Lion (rated at £50) between 1775 and 1790. They left the inn only a few months after the defeat of the radical Tierney. *IpsJ* 2 March 1793 public apology by woolcomber John Green for slandering Triggs. Triggs then worked for Benjamin Hall, and later Philip Havens (both baymakers). Havens left him a legacy in his will. By 1798 the Triggs' lived on St. Johns Green (*IpsJ* 21 December 1798). Ann died on 11 September 1804 aged 71 and was buried at Stockwell Independent Chapel. James Triggs died in 1812. See also Chapter 1 above, n. 72.

56 Carter, *Men and the emergence of polite society*, pp. 44–5.

57 Clark, *British clubs*, pp. 95, 217.

social and political association in the town, does bear comparison with the socially facilitating aspects of polite association.

Masons

John Money outlines the growth of freemasonry in eighteenth century towns in the third quarter of the eighteenth century and indicates the flexible political utility and the growing respectability of the craft as a component of urban culture. Masonry offered a 'new form of corporate civic Christianity which offered surrogate forms of ritual well suited to a commercial society'.[58] Masonry was, of course, a masculine, Anglican and largely middling associational form. Colchester's non-conformists did not join its Masonic lodges. Colchester's first lodge opened in 1735, moving from the Three Cups to the Angel Inn in 1752. Its founder members were six tradesmen; a tallowchandler, a carpenter, a bricklayer, an apothecary, a butcher and a weaver. The lodge met fortnightly over the next four decades but remained very much a minority interest for some time.[59] There were only seven members in 1750 and it appears that some thought was given to winding up the lodge. Nevertheless this small group remained energetic enough to commission performances at the local theatre and take some share in public civic ritual. In line with the national chronology of expansion, Colchester masonry was revitalised, not least it seems because of the growing interest of a wider number of middling individuals and one man in particular; Thomas Boggis the prosperous baymaker and sometime mayor, who had renovated the High Street mansion now known as the Minories (Chapter 2). Boggis was first master of Angel Lodge and in 1776 was instrumental in the founding of a second local lodge — the Lodge of Unity. Essex became a separate Masonic Province in 1776 and the new provincial grand master, Thomas Dunckerly, appointed Boggis as his deputy. Thus Colchester housed two of the six Masonic lodges in Essex in 1786.[60] The Lodge of Unity, meeting at the Red Lion, attracted distinctly more prosperous members than Angel Lodge although social inclusiveness was served by the membership of Boggis' servant, James Brooker and the Red Lion landlord, James Triggs. Several better-off Angel Lodge members transferred including George Reynolds, innkeeper of the White Hart and Colin Hossack, surgeon. Other merchants, clergy, town and country gentry also joined. The Whig/radical political club would later meet at the Red Lion. In the mid-1780s, Colchester political groupings reconfigured after the ending of the longstanding Whig/Tory political compromise, and the Lodge of Unity membership united Tories Edmund Affleck (borough MP) and Boggis in brotherhood with Whig Nicholas Corsellis of Wivenhoe and Samuel Tyssen, Esq of Kelvedon.[61] Compared to

---

58 J. Money, 'Freemasonry and the fabric of loyalism in Hanoverian England', in E. Hellmuth (ed.), *The transformation of political culture: England and Germany in the later eighteenth century* (Oxford, 1990), pp. 235–74, p. 269.

59 Where not otherwise referenced the details on Angel Lodge come from Pat Clayton, *Angel Lodge No. 51, Colchester: 250th Anniversary Celebration 12th December 1985*, unpaginated, copy in ERO Acc. 905 Box 9.

60 A Hewitt, Librarian, Freemason's Hall to JBB 8 February 1972, copy in author's possession.

61 *Ibid.* enclosures giving lodge membership lists.

the seven members in 1750, the Angel Lodge could muster a procession of 25 to march to the theatre for a play in celebration of the Peace of Versailles in 1783. That year there were even plans to establish a third local lodge.[62]

Money describes a decline in masonry, particularly in its older, southern centres towards the end of the century. In Colchester the death of Thomas Boggis in 1790 rapidly put paid to the Lodge of Unity though Angel Lodge survived over the subsequent centuries. Boggis' role was central. In 1791 Angel Lodge had to ask the provincial grand master to request Boggis' executors to return the lodge records. Angel Lodge was in sufficiently good heart to endow an educational charity for the sons of members in 1793 and to thoroughly refurbish its room at the Angel Inn in 1809. The less socially prestigious Angel Lodge displayed more staying power than the Lodge of Unity. By the end of the century its membership, and that of a third lodge, the Devon Lodge, included many soldiers.[63] Angel Lodge was also the more visible aspect of Colchester masonry through its public processions and exhibitions at the local theatre. The craft apparently answered needs and desires of the Colchester middling, Anglican tradesman more than the gentleman or the professional, who were likely to have other opportunities for association and self expression.

I have already reviewed the ways that masonry contributed to the polite pleasures assembled in Colchester Theatre, where the commissioning desires of a female audience were gratified by the lodge's display of harmonious (moral, Christian, middling) masculinity on stage. In 1777 ladies were also invited to a breakfast that preceded a Masonic sermon at St Peters.[64] Female approbation seems to have been important for the public face of masonry. Women could not be lodge members, but they were incorporated into the moral and associational project of the craft.

Colchester Medical Society

There is an established literature about the emergence of a masculine medical profession at this period. Until the later nineteenth century the comparative insecurities of modernising scientific medicine were in no small part combated through an energetic exclusion of women from practice.[65] The Colchester Medical Society was the first English provincial medical society and the second oldest in England, only a year younger than the London Medical Society. It was founded in 1774 by seven Colchester (mostly young) surgeon apothecaries. Robert Richardson Newell, a Scottish trained apothecary aged only 24 at the time, is generally given credit for its

62 *IpsJ* 21 December 1787.

63 Clayton, *The Angel Lodge*; *IpsJ* 12 January 1793; Cooper *et al.*, *Colchester*, p. 174.

64 *IpsJ* 28 June 1777.

65 Of an extensive if uneven literature, see for example, J. Donnison, *Midwives and medical men: a history of the struggle for the control of childbirth* (London, 1988); D. Porter and R. Porter (eds), *Patient's progress: doctors and doctoring in eighteenth-century England* (Oxford, 1989). For the practice of midwifery and the idea of a public sphere, L.F. Cody, 'The politics of reproduction: from midwives' alternative public sphere to the public spectacle of man-midwifery', *Eighteenth-Century Studies*, 32 (1999), pp. 477–95. For the marginality of the professional scientific community, P. Elliott, 'The origins of the "creative class" pp. 361–87.

inception. He was secretary until his death in 1814.[66] The society attracted members throughout Essex and Suffolk and formed a medical library. In its early years it met at the White Hart combination room.[67]

The Medical Register for 1779 praised to the Society, which had then increased to nineteen members. The Society bid fair to 'not only to improve and extend the knowledge of medicine, and to diffuse an useful spirit of inquiry; but likewise to promote a state of harmony amongst Medical practitioners, which we have observed, and a worthy correspondent at Colchester joins with us in lamenting, is but too frequently interrupted in country towns'. It was, however, regretted that the Society 'does not include all the Practitioners at Colchester, by whom the institution deserves particularly to be encouraged, as tending to collect useful observations on the prevailing diseases of that town, and neighbourhood'. This was a modernising, professional society of more democratic style than the Castle Book Club. Comparable to Kathleen Wilson's depiction of the Dispensary Movement, at its monthly meetings the chair was taken by each member in rotation.[68] The existence of some professional rivalry seems indicated by the foundation of the Essex and Suffolk Medical Society in 1788, though this venture seems not to have survived for more than a few months.[69]

In 1775 the Colchester Medical Society had published a booklet on the resuscitation of the drowning. It used the Humane Society's recommended equipment – a 'fumigator, which was a small pair of bellows and a tube, by which means they blew tobacco smoke into the rectum' by which R. R. Newell resuscitated his maid who had fallen down a well. Apparently, the following day she 'complained of a great sense of weight and fullness in the intestines, and I therefore gave her a gentle purge, which produced good effects'.[70] It would probably be gratuitous to pause too long on the potential sexual allusions of such a disposition of bodies and knowledge.[71] These were, nevertheless, semi-experimental methods at the forefront of (masculine) enlightened science. The Medical Society also advertised other successes such as the recovery of a young child cut for the stone 'by some of the gentlemen of the medical society.'[72] These were no quacks, but gentlemen

---

66 JBB BD/613 for R.R. Newell. For the other members see JBB BD/453 Colin Hossack MD, BD/536 Jordan Harris Lisle, BD/233 Cater Day, BD/825 Joseph Stapleton MD, BD/830 Robert Sterling FRS, BD/885 Henry Topping MA.

67 Bensusan Butt, *Benjamin Strutt*, p. 20 letter from Philip Gretton 20 August 1779.

68 Material lent to JBB by Dr Douglas Clendon enclosing letter to Clendon from Librarian, Royal Society of Medicine, 21 December 1950; J. Penfold, Brochure for Colchester Medical Society exhibition at the Minories, 1974, all ERO Acc 905, Box 5; K. Wilson, 'Citizenship, empire, and modernity in the English provinces, c.1720–1790', *Eighteenth-Century Studies*, 29 (1995), pp. 69–96; K. Wilson, *The sense of the people: politics, culture, and imperialism in England, 1715–1785* (New York, 1995), pp. 60–82; A. Wilson, 'Conflict, consensus and charity: politics and the provincial voluntary hospitals in the eighteenth century', *English Historical Review* (1996), pp. 599–619.

69 For the Essex and Suffolk Medical Society, *IpsJ* 26 January and 23 February 1788.

70 W. Radcliffe, 'The Colchester medical society, 1774', *Medical History*, 20 (1976), pp. 394–401, here pp. 396–7.

71 M. Poovey, *Uneven developments: the ideological work of gender in mid-Victorian England* (London, 1989).

professionals.

The society linked Colchester practitioners into wider national professional networks. In 1786 J. Coakley Lettsom, the prison reformer, supporter of smallpox vaccination, and founder of the London Medical Society was elected a member of the Colchester society. The Medical Society was a concerted effort to blend practice and science as well as to raise professional credentials and was at the forefront of early efforts at modernisation within medicine. It was an example of later eighteenth century organisations whose objectives combined association among members with reforming or philanthropic objectives, thus extending and refining projects of governance of the urban poor. In Colchester, in the field of health it was soon joined by the Lying In Charity (1796), the Essex Dispensary (1798) and the Colchester and Essex Hospital (1820).[73]

Social networks, sensibilities and artistic careers

Castle Book Society members included clergymen, town gentry and the more prosperous tradesmen and professionals. Sermons and other religious writing far outweighed the amount of other local publications.[74] There was an unsurprising overlap between the Book Society and those involved in the musical circle, in particular through George Wegg, Thomas Twining and Revd Yorick Smythies of St Martins. Colchester's scholars were hooked into far wider networks of the erudite and philanthropic. The All Saints Rector, Nathaniel Forster, wrote on economics as well as theology and was a friend to Jeremy Bentham. Historian Philip Morant was of course a clergyman. Revd Thomas Twining was both a classical scholar and an accomplished amateur musician and musicologist, in regular correspondence with Charles Burney. Charles Gray and George Wegg were members of Jonas Hanway's Marine Society. Book Club member and leading baymaker Michael Hills was married to the sister of both Robert Dingley, Hanway's associate, architect and merchant, and of the inventor Charles Dingley.[75]

The rising generation of literary, artistic and musically interested Colcestrians in the 1780s included Benjamin Strutt, then a lawyer's clerk. Strutt, who became the

---

72 *IpsJ* 31 May 1783.

73 Clark, *British clubs*, p. 95; compare S. Lloyd, 'Pleasing spectacles and elegant dinners: conviviality, benevolence and charity anniversaries in eighteenth-century London', *Journal of British Studies*, 41 (2002), pp. 23–57; Cromwell, *Colchester*, Vol. 2, pp. 307–10, 343–4; C. Joscelyne, *Medical practice and medical theory: smallpox in Britain during the long eighteenth century* (PhD thesis, Essex, 1990), pp. 287–9; Radcliffe, 'The Colchester medical society'; J. Penfold, *The history of Essex County Hospital, Colchester, 1820–1948* (Colchester, 1984).

74 Of the 202 titles published in or concerning Colchester listed on the Eighteenth Century Short Title Catalogue, 122 are sermons or other religious matter. J. Gregory, 'Christianity and culture: religion the arts and the sciences in England 1660–1800' in J. Black (ed.), *Culture and society in Britain, 1660–1800* (Manchester, 1997), pp. 102–23.

75 R.D. Sheldon, 'Forster Nathaniel (1726–1790)', *Oxford Dictionary of National Biography* (Oxford, 2004), www.oxford.dnb.com/view/article/9914, accessed 4 August 2007; J. Bentham, *Correspondence of Jeremy Bentham*, ed. I. Christie (London, 1968); R.S. Walker (ed.), *A selection of Thomas Twining's letters 1734–1804: A record of a tranquil life* (Lewiston, 1991); J.H. Appleby,

borough chamberlain, town historian, minor artist and political man of business in the following decades, (Chapter 9) maintained a lively correspondence with a circle of youthful friends. Some of it is more or less incomprehensibly in the style of *Ossian*:

> Does he remember his friends in Colona – the Chief of the Iron Arms, with Unworn's son was there – Malvina of Harps raised the Song – she spoke of Cruther healer of wounds – they gave their sighs to the gale ... their wailings broke through the surrounding gloom.[76]

Other letters discuss philosophy or Strutt's ambitions to improve his painting 'I must and will be two degrees above Sir Joshua – it is necessary to attempt things impossible that we may do those which are wonderful.'[77] This group included Clara Reeve the author, James Dunthorne jnr the artist, Jacob Pattison the able young apothecary unfortunately stabbed by the irate draper Robert Kendall and Philip Gretton, later an august member of both the Medical and the Castle Book Societies. Almost twenty years later, the authors and engravers Jane and Ann Taylor were part of a similar literary circle of young people, now including Benjamin Strutt's young adult offspring.[78]

Colchester individuals whose scholarly, literary, artistic or philanthropic interests positioned them within wider social networks (in the county and the metropolis), variously used the mail, the horse and the post-coach to inhabit more expansive cultural landscapes. They do not seem to have entered such networks in the subordinated way that French records for 'ingenious and learned' men from smaller Essex towns early in the century.[79] Rather than seeking a Habermasian public sphere 'in' Colchester, the interaction and exchange of ideas between such networks within the virtual cultural spaces delineated by the (then) modern communications technologies perhaps indicate Colchester's contribution to a geographically more diffuse public intellectual sphere.

Using as a starting point the discovery of three books of musical parts originally from the library of George Wegg of East Hill House (died 1774), Peter Holman has reconstructed much detail of the musical 'concert' who regularly met there from the 1750s, probably until the early nineteenth century when the house was occupied firstly by Wegg's widow and secondly by his great-niece Susan and her husband, doctor Horatio Cock. As well as Wegg, this group included a number of individuals

---

75 *Cont.*

'Robert Dingley FRS 1710–1781, merchant, architect and pioneering philanthropist', *Notes and Records of the Royal Society of London*, 45 (1991), pp. 139–54; J.H. Appleby, 'Mills models and magdalens – the Dingley brothers and the society of arts', *Royal Society of Arts Journal*, cxl, no 5427 (1995), pp. 267–73; ERO Acc 905, Box 10, envelope 'R.D. Mackintosh', correspondence with Harold Jowitt re portrait of Elizabeth Dingley, and Box 4, correspondence with Colonel Boggis re portrait of Frances Boggis née Hills.

76 Benjamin Strutt to Jacob Pattison, 3 June 1778, Bensusan Butt, *Benjamin Strutt*, p. 18.

77 *Ibid.*, p. 19.

78 J Gilbert (ed.), *The autobiography and other memorials of Mrs Gilbert*, 2nd edn (London, 1876); L. Davidoff and C. Hall, *Family fortunes, men and women of the English middle class, 1780–1850* (London, 1987), p. 65.

79 H. French, 'Ingenious & learned gentlemen' – social perceptions and self-fashioning among parish elites in Essex, 1680–1740', *Social History*, 25 (2000), pp. 44–66.

already discussed here, in particular the Revd Thomas Twining (an accomplished amateur fiddle player to whom Wegg left a large section of his music library) and James Dunthorne jnr the artist. Revd Richard Daniel, rector of Mistley but resident in Angel Lane, was left Wegg's cremona fiddle and 'all my concerto music'. Holman finds the Colchester music group unusual in several respects. Firstly they differed from the common pattern of having professional leadership and staging regular public concerts (with the more challenging parts taken by the professionals). This activity depended not on a single enthusiast, such as John Marsh in Salisbury, but by a circle of talented amateurs who were part of a regional network of professional and amateur musicians and composers.[80]

Colchester was the base for a succession of professional musicians and composers across the century who led the public performances that occurred. Joseph Gibbs, the organist, was born in Colchester (1698) and lived there while he was organist at Dedham. He later moved to Ipswich while he was organist at St Mary le Tower (1748). Frederick Charles Reinhold (pupil of William Savage, choirmaster at St. Pauls Cathedral) became organist at St Peters Church in 1760 until he moved to London.[81] James Fisin, Reinhold's pupil was the 'leader of the band' on many occasions during his years in Colchester. Apart from a period in London in the 1780s and a few years in Chester (1801–1804) he remained in Colchester attaining a hoary old age. He was a minor composer, and conducted a number of public concerts; perhaps most notably the 1790 performances of the *Messiah* and other oratorio with the internationally famous soprano Nancy Storace, and Thomas Twining playing in the band. Fisin's compositions included an *Ode to Charity* for the use of the Sunday Schools and a march for the Loyal Colchester Volunteers.[82]

While good amateur players seem to have participated in the band for public concerts in Colchester as elsewhere, for the most part the amateur music-making took place in the (prestigious) domestic environment of East Hill House. There were some partial exceptions – for example the series of ten subscription concerts put on for the benefit of the artist James Dunthorne jnr. These concerts were undertaken at a period when there was no resident leading professional musician in Colchester (Fisin was then in London) and the audience of subscribers was necessarily a far narrower public than for professional concerts. This was a sufficiently polite milieu for Nathaniel Forster's teenage daughter Catherine to perform a series of 'Bach Concertos'.[83] Hence the musical concert occupied an interestingly liminal space between public and private; between performance and the imaginative pleasures of musical exploration, knowledge and study. There is some comparison between this kind of event and the

---

80 Brewer, *The pleasures of the imagination,* chapter 14; W. Weber, 'The fabric of daily life and the autobiography of John Marsh', *Huntingdon Library Quarterly,* 59 (1997), pp. 145–69; P. Holman, 'The Colchester partbooks', *Early Music,* 28 (2000), pp. 577–95; JBB BD/931 for George Wegg; for the Cock's household accounts see Chapter 4.

81 *IpsJ* 22 November 1760; Holman, 'Colchester partbooks', p. 582.

82 Bensusan Butt, *Benjamin Strutt,* pp. 39–55.

83 Holman, 'Colchester partbooks' presumes these were J.C. Bach's *Six Concerti pour le clavecin,* op. 1, which are in Set 1 of the Colchester partbooks. Nathaniel Forster to Peter Forster, 1 March 1782, BL Add Mss 11277.

series of scientific lectures that independent minister Isaac Taylor later gave to his friends and neighbours for small fees (see Chapter 3). Twining specifically made the distinction between these and 'public' performance, joining in these concerts while having given up performing 'in public'.[84] One of Dunthorne's watercolours, *A Musical Entertainment*, depicts the concert assembled in an affluent domestic setting with a small audience (male and female), most of them attentive but one or two deep in conversation. A male string quartet accompanies a woman (identified as Miss Marshall the accomplished keyboard player from Ipswich) playing the harpsichord. A young girl (Catherine Forster?) plays a glockenspiel.[85]

The group was musically ambitious, performing older and contemporary works, including some requiring wind and brass players. Such works were less commonly undertaken by amateur groups and Holman thinks it likely that such parts were taken by band musicians from the East Essex Militia whose Colonel Isaac Martin Rebow was Colchester MP.[86] Holman also remarks on the unusually high number of amateur composers in eighteenth-century north-east Essex and south Suffolk, including Twining himself, the Revd William Jones of Nayland and John Carr a grocer in the small village of Boxford and father of the Colchester grocer Samuel Carr. As subscribers' lists for their published music shows, the geographies of the musically inclined extended outside the town, firstly into regional and thence into metropolitan networks. Rather than being a paler imitation of London or musical circles in larger provincial centres, the Colchester concert was distinctive in several ways. Very much of the town and involving Colchester middling individuals, the musical circle nevertheless extended into geographically wider cultural life through its connections and subscriptions. It assembled in domestic space as well as undertaking semi-public performance by accomplished amateurs. It had a life greater than the patronage of Wegg and the East Hill House family, though it was the cultural and material consumption of that family which provided the necessary space, music and harpsichord. Wegg in fact, said Twining, eventually lost his taste for music.

> Our concert at Colchester still goes on. ... (Twining wrote in 1773) ... The best joke is that Music ... tires Mr. Wegg to death, & I believe he wd. Give anything to get rid of his concert if he knew how, without giving up his consistency, or his connoisseurship. Is there not humour in the idea of a Man's buying a harpsichord, books, apparatus, & being at a great expence, in order to be regularly plagued once a fortnight with a concert which he can't stop.[87]

Over the second half of the century, demographic and economic growth increased the numbers of those accessing polite culture and growing retail markets disseminated its commoditised accoutrements, from clothes and domestic things to conduct literature. Politeness became a means of social exclusion of those who could not or did not play

---

84 Holman, 'Colchester partbooks', p. 589 quoting Twining to Charles Burney of 5 May 1782. Twining did in fact play in the public performance of the *Messiah* in 1790. Walker (ed.), *Thomas Twining*, p. 359.

85 *A musical entertainment* is viewable at www.bridgeman.fr/, Image number DEC 84530, wrongly attributed to John Dunthorne the younger.

86 Holman,'Colchester partbooks', pp. 591–2.

87 Twining to Revd Charles Jenner of Claybrook, 13 August 1777, quoted by Holman,'Colchester partbooks', p. 585.

by the rules. At the same time, a cultural reaction to its arguably empty and formalised codes set in. Later eighteenth-century cultures of sensibility valorised natural feeling and the expression of the (apparently authentic) self, setting out the stall (as some historians have argued) for the later cultural ascendancy of modern subjectivities.[88] Literary and artistic romanticism, the rediscovery of the picturesque in rural scenes not least through the growth of travel and tourism, changes in fashionable dress and appearance can all be loosely associated with the trope of sensibility. The greater evangelical energies, among both non-conformists and the St Peters Anglicans later in the century were also chronologically coincident with the greater emphasis on emotional authenticity in the shaping of secular sensibility.[89] I shall conclude this chapter by examining the effects of such trends on two particular life histories, those of the James Dunthornes (father and son). Something of a generational cultural shift from politeness to sensibility is evident in the careers of these two Colchester artists, as well as the opportunities and limitations that a provincial urban context lent to their careers.

James Dunthorne snr was born in 1730, the son of John, a Baptist minister. He was apprenticed to Joshua Kirby, 'limner etc.' of Ipswich in 1745. Kirby was a long-time friend of the artist Thomas Gainsborough. Returning to Colchester from his apprenticeship, James Dunthorne married Elizabeth Hubbard in 1752. For a while at least the couple were associated with the Lion Walk Congregational congregation, where they baptised several of their children.[90] Dunthorne traded from a succession of shops in Colchester High Street.[91] He undertook decorative painting and drawing, for example selling the print of a newly discovered Roman mosaic pavement (price 1s 6d coloured).[92] Something of his range of skills is perhaps indicated in that an ex-apprentice later traded as a painter and glazier.[93] For a short while he worked in partnership with William Cole the non-conformist land surveyor (and composer).[94] He

---

88 G.J Barker-Benfield, *The culture of sensibility: sex and society in eighteenth-century Britain* (Chicago, 1992); Klein, 'Politeness and the interpretation of the British eighteenth century'; Brewer, *The pleasures of the imagination*, Chapter 15 and conclusion.

89 L. Davidoff and C. Hall, *Family fortunes*, pp. 78–99; P. Carter, *Men and the emergence of polite society*, p. 44.

90 L. Spurrier, *The memorials of the Baptist church, Colchester* (Colchester, 1889); James was apprenticed as the son of John for £25, NA IR1 17/151. JBB BD/1185, he married Elizabeth Hubbard at St James, 3 October 1752. (She was buried at St Nicholas, 8 September 1812.) Several of his children baptised at Lion Walk in 1760 do not include James Dunthorne jnr. Both Dunthornes are mentioned briefly in J. Crosby Ivy, 'Dunthorne, John (baptised 1790 d. 1844)', *Oxford Dictionary of National Biography* (Oxford, 2004), www.oxford.dnb.com/view/article/8297, accessed 8 August 2007, which distinguishes them from the John Dunthornes, father and son, of Dedham.

91 Dunthorne occupied premises in Pelham's Lane, St Runwalds, rated 8 between 1754 and 1788; in 1770 he was rated 10. *IpsJ* 20 August 1768, his premises 'near the Buttermarket' were taken by John Brock, saddler. G.O. Rickword also identifies his premises in late life as 104 High Street, on the boundary of St Nicholas with All Saints, *ex inf.* Bruce Neville.

92 In 1760 was paid £1 17s by All Saints churchwardens, ERO D/P 200/5/1, as part of expenses incurred to mark the death of George II; re mosaic pavement *IpsJ* 10 September 1763.

93 Borough Petty Sessions, ERO P/CoR, 8 August 1779, settlement examination of James Ratcliff glazier and painter. cf Dunthorne's advertisement for an apprentice *IpsJ* 3 July 1762.

undertook decoration for the new chapel built at Lion Walk in the 1760s, may have undertaken coach painting, designed the brass stamp for the Castle Book Society and painted the King's Arms for the corporation. After his death, a sale of his 'Relics' included 'inimitable Deceptions in Oil-Colour' (presumably *trompe-l'oeil*)[95]

Dunthorne snr did undertake portraits, but of no outstanding artistic merit. A sketch of him in E.P. Strutt's sketchbook depicts a rounded and rather unctuous character and is captioned 'Let me take your portrait, dear.' Thomas Twining was deprecating about the portrait Dunthorne painted of him:

> My sister wished for my picture: I said she should have this if she thought there was likeness enough to make it at all worth her acceptance ... One thing I can say of my Dunthorne; that every body knows it immediately. But that may be true of a bad picture.[96]

Socially, Dunthorne was well enough connected in Colchester to be left a guinea mourning ring by George Wegg.[97] He died late in 1815 aged 85, 'a celebrated painter much respected'.[98] There appears to be a little hyperbole in the newspaper obituary; doubtless a 'much-respected' tradesman among his middling provincial contemporaries, Dunthorne snr was perhaps not much celebrated as a painter, in the sense of the painter as artist.

James Dunthorne junior did, however, have clear aspirations towards an artistic career. A little of his biography was introduced in Chapter 3, since his marriage in 1779 to Elizabeth Shillito connected him to the All Saints family. Elizabeth's brother was the sometime naval officer, schoolmaster, minor poet and author, Charles Shillito whose limited success as an author mirrors Dunthorne's only partly fulfilled ambitions as a painter. Dunthorne had artistic ability, but was unable to convert this into a properly remunerative career. Above all he was unable to establish much of a reputation in London although a number of his designs were engraved by Rowlandson and he regularly exhibited at the Royal Academy between 1783 and 1792. He made a living chiefly through keeping a print shop at the more fashionable uphill end of Colchester High Street. His forte at this period were pictures of fashionable Colchester social events, including *The card party, A musical entertainment* and *The tea room at a Colchester ball.* These included pen sketches of local residents, for example in *The*

---

94 *IpsJ* 3 September 1766; 'N.B. Perspective views of particular places will be inserted at the Head of the Plans if desired'. S. Mason, *Essex on the map* (Chelmsford, 1990), p.112 ff., finds no evidence that this partnership lasted. Only a map and drawing of Copford Place (1810) is signed by both men.

95 Between 1765 and 1767 he was paid £9 15s 6d for work at Octagon Chapel, Lion Walk, then being built, ERO D/NC 52/5/2. In *IpsJ* 28 March 1767 he advertised a coach for sale (perhaps painted by himself). He made the brass stamp design for Castle Book Society in 1794 (n. 19 above) and in 1796 was paid 12 guineas by the Corporation 'for ... (painting) ... the King's Arms', Borough Chamberlain's Account Book, ERO D/B 5 Aa2/1, 23 September 1796; *Colchester Gazette,* 14 August 1816.

96 n. 17 above.

97 NA PROB 11/1035, proved 17 September 1777.

98 *IpsJ* 30 December 1815. He was buried St Nicholas 'from St Mary's' aged 85, 1 January 1816. His will is at ERO 679 CR 19, 1816. See W.G. Benham, 'The Dunthornes of Colchester', *Essex Review,* 10 (1901), pp. 27–35, here p. 29 for sketch portrait by E.P. Strutt.

Figure 5.1 James Dunthorne, *The tea room at a Colchester ball*, watercolour, *c.* 1784. Reproduced by kind permission of Colchester and Ipswich Museums Service

card party, set in the assembly rooms of the White Hart, Miss Mary Keeling (later Mrs George Round), Dr Moses Griffiths, Mrs Whaley the White Hart proprietor's wife and his partner, Peter Desbrosses the wine merchant, have been identified.[99] In each of these three companion images the composition centres on a young, attractive female figure, but also includes numerous genteel, middling women of all ages, all fully engaged in socialising along with men. Dunthorne's conversation pieces underline the high visibility of women in Colchester polite society as well as the importance of domestic or quasi-domestic interiors as the locus for polite social association.

Dunthorne designed the frontispiece to Charles Shillito's *A country book club* (1788). Although disparaging about Shillito's poem the *Monthly review* thought the frontispiece (etched by Rowlandson) 'not destitute of humour'.[100] Dunthorne also selected some more melancholy subjects including *Death preaches to a careless audience* (1785). *Ague and fever* and *The hypochondriac* (1788) are medical studies which are captioned:

> This Mind distemper'd – say what potent charm
> Can Fancy's spectre – breeding rage disarm?
> Physic's prescriptive art assaults in vain
> The dreadful phantoms floating 'cross the brain!
> Until with Esculapian skill the sage M.D.
> Finds out at length by self-taught palmistry
> The hopeless case – in the reluctant fee:
> Then, not in torture such a wretch to keep
> One pitying bolus lays him sound asleep.

Dunthorne's view of the medical practitioner was hardly as sanguine as that promulgated by the Medical Society. Although the verse does not specify how terminal was the sleep that Dunthorne advocates, his own subsequent 'long affliction' may be prefigured here.

Earlier he was outgoing enough to send up a six-foot air balloon from the castle which travelled as far as Purleigh near Maldon.[101] He was a violin player as well as an artist, and was part of the musical concert. As such he came to the notice of the Rector of All Saints, Dr Nathaniel Forster and Revd Thomas Twining. On 1 March 1782, Forster wrote to his cousin Peter Forster, rector of Hedenham, Norfolk, to describe how ten concerts had been arranged for Dunthorne's benefit with thirty subscribers at half a guinea. 'Two acts in each concert, five pieces in each ancient and modern. The performers are Twining, Hankey, Jones, Smith and Brockwell, divines, with young Dunthorne and 5 others. Vast collection of music. Twining always enchanting. All Jones' young men are subscribers.'[102] Revd William Jones, perpetual curate of nearby Nayland was another musical enthusiast and author. In 1784 Dunthorne subscribed to Jones' *Art of music* and may have engraved the scores.[103]

---

99 No. 12 High Street, *ex. inf.* Bruce Neville; W.G. Benham,'The Dunthornes'.

100 J. Bensusan Butt, *Charles Shillito, Oliver Goldsmith* (Colchester, privately printed, 1994), p. 23–4.

101 *IpsJ* 3 and 10 January 1783.

102 Nathaniel Forster to Peter Forster, 1 March 1782, BL Add Mss 11277.

Also in 1784, on 12 November, Twining wrote to the musicologist Charles Burney about Dunthorne:

> 'I want your opinion and advice about a young man of this place who is interesting to me. He is a painter, a sensible. modest, quiet man – I won't say he has a genius for his profession; that is a word that is not to be prodigally bestowed: but has talents; seems (so far as I am able to judge) to draw correctly, and has really considerable ingenuity in the invention of subjects of the ludicrous kind, some of which were in the two last years' (Royal Academy) exhibitions. ... He is a married man; his wife is a milliner, but her business has not answered, and his cannot in such a place as this; he has a few scholars, sells prints, and now and then paints a Portrait: but all this is scarcely bread and cheese, and moreover, he is here out of the way of improvement. He wishes much to be *établi* in London if he cou'd get employment there as a drawing Master ... if it should perchance be in your power to suggest anything, you will give me great pleasure. At the same time, I am aware of difficulties: I know (at least I am told so) that London is overstocked with artists and ingenious men who want employment.

Twining continues that he would be personally sorry if Dunthorne left Colchester.

> He has true Musical feelings, and relishes Em. Bach, Haydn &c., tho' as a fiddler he is shambling and incorrect. He loves humour, and has that modest quietness, and unpushingness (a pretty vocable!) about him, that never did anything but harm to its possessors since the world stood.[104]

There were, however, potentially other opinions as to Dunthorne's character. Benjamin Strutt, himself an artist and antiquarian, was jocularly unflattering about several friends and contemporaries including Dunthorne whom he said was 'a Mimic' and 'faithless and insincere'.[105] H.D. Bland, whose rather malicious *Anecdotes* survive in manuscript, is even more damning.

> James Dunthorne, limner and musician, was on excellent terms with himself. He was insufferably vain and self-conceited. He was playing at a concert where he thought himself the first fiddle, and honest Joe Manning ... (apparently the only professional musician in the group) ... was stationed at the same music stand, which gave great umbrage to Dunthorne, and he contemptuously desired Joe to stand farther off, at the same time saying that men of his talent could not well brook the encroachment of their inferiors. Joe felt nettled at the observation, and retorted aloud 'you an artist, Jim? A pretty artist surely as, clever a fellow as you think yourself, you are not artist enough to – without —ing' which raised a laugh at Dunthorne's expense.[106]

Bland was not likely to have been a direct witness and was probably relating a story heard second- or third-hand or fitting the crude joke to a plausible candidate. Manning's comment was hardly an example of polite repartee, but it did challenge both Dunthorne's refinement and his masculinity. However, perhaps what Twining read as 'unpushingness' might also be perceived as unfounded artistic pretension. Dunthorne was clearly ailing in the 1790s and a further benefit concert was held for

103 JBB BD/1110.

104 Walker (ed.), *Thomas Twining*, letter 89 to Charles Burney, 12 November 1784, pp. 265–6 and letter 90 to Burney, 30 December 1784, p. 268.

105 Bensusan Butt, *Charles Shillito*, pp. 14–38.

106 MS *Bland's Anecdotes*, ERO Acc 905, Box 2, p. 83.

him on 30 July 1793, his wife publishing her gratitude to supporters after the event. His 'Drawings, Prints, Music etc.' were sold on 16 August 1794 so the family's financial difficulties seem to have been acute. He succumbed to a 'long affliction' soon after and was buried at St Nicholas on 11 October 1794.[107]

James Dunthorne junior adopted a different artistic persona than did his father, who painted coaches as well as portraits and took work engraving maps and surveys. Thomas Twining's assessment seems accurate. As a 'limner' of talent if not of genius, Dunthorne found it difficult to make his way without breaking into the London market and seems reluctant to take up coach painting like his father. Whether or not Dunthorne amounted to a 'Colchester Hogarth' his history exemplifies not only the opportunities but also the vicissitudes of the career of a minor artist in a Georgian provincial town.[108] His artistic legacy, if nothing else, provides the historian with rare visualisations of the polite society of eighteenth-century Colchester. By contrast, as Chapter 9 will suggest, his contemporary Benjamin Strutt combined literary and artistic sensibilities with a lawyer's training and the organisational abilities of a man of business to build a career rooted in both amateur literary and artistic talent and local particularism.

Conclusion

I have argued for the central role of the middling sort in shaping an urban provincial culture characterised by a combination of politeness and association. Commercial activity produced much polite culture, both in terms of social activity and its material accoutrements. This was intermeshed with civic and philanthropic impulses, which offered patronage rather than hard cash. Women have been argued here and elsewhere as active participants in urban culture, and by using the local theatre as an example the celebration of gender difference alongside social inclusiveness seems to have served to gloss contradictions – between taste and luxury, between desire and discernment, and around the fuzzy boundaries of what (or more particularly whom) could be deemed polite in an economy where so many genteel commodities and polite amusements could be acquired on the open market. Historians have argued that cultures of sensibility which prioritised emotional authenticity over the rules and skills of polite social interaction shifted the cultural ground towards the end of the century. Nevertheless, sensibility was a cultural reaction to politeness framed from within polite cultural arenas. From the point of view of the middling sort of a provincial town such as Colchester, in the latter decades of the century politeness and sensibility in varied combination were an attractive and accessible composite cultural idiom through which they could express their social place in urban society.

---

107 Chapter 3 above, n. 69.

108 *DNB*, entry for John Dunthorne, senior and junior refers to James Dunthorne junior as 'the Colchester Hogarth' see note 90 above. Re the importance of London for an artistic career see Brewer, *The pleasures of the imagination*, Chapter 7; for London-centred spatial politics of the art market, R. Dias, 'A world of pictures: Pall Mall and the topography of display 1780–99' in M. Ogborn and C.W.J. Withers (eds.), *Georgian geographers: essays on space, place and landscape in the eighteenth century* (Manchester, 2004), pp. 92–113.

Chapter 6

Chief priests, lawyers and tradesmen

Introduction

The governance of eighteenth-century towns required the active participation of the urban middling sort. Without a salaried professional bureaucracy, the administration of policing, social welfare, the maintenance and improvement of the urban infrastructure and other matters such as some educational provision were delivered through a variety of institutions all of which depended on office-holders drawn from the middling sort. Different towns drew on variable levels of gentry patronage, sometimes approaching but never effectively achieving dominance. Without the surplus labour of numerous middling individuals the superficially muddled array of institutions which handled local administration would have failed. Towns were run by various combinations of borough corporations, improvement commissioners, manorial courts, parish vestries, quarter and petty sessions (borough or county) local charities and endowments. Improvement commissioners, set up by act of parliament, tackled large public works such as paving, lighting, turnpikes or canals. Private citizens also banded together to raise subscriptions to provide social amenities such as Colchester theatre. Private charity administered by trustees also assisted in welfare. Educational initiatives were by private bequest, or by courtesy of market forces. Common features of eighteenth-century local government, such as multiple office-holding, the mix of office with business, politics and social association, as well as the fact that many of these institutions had been formed in (and for) an earlier age, led historians to perceive corruption and inefficiency. This view has now been substantially revised, however, by a greater scholarly attention to the processes rather than the structures of local administration and a better appreciation of the creativity with which the (sometimes creaking) institutions of eighteenth-century town governance were employed.[1]

Governance entails systems, ideologies and institutions but also individuals. Historically, it is experienced from two directions – by those who were involved in its implementation and by those who were subjected to its everyday exercise of capillary power. Middling individuals were prosecuted for nuisances, debt or assault and if they moved parish could be examined as to their settlement. However, far greater numbers of the working classes and the poor were policed by the processes of governance.

---

1 J. Innes and N. Rogers, 'Politics and government', Chapter 16 in P. Clark *et al.* (eds.), *The Cambridge urban history of Britain* (Cambridge, 2000); R. Sweet, *The English town 1680–1840: government, society and culture* (London, 1999), Chapter 2. Compare J.M. Triffit, *Politics and the urban community; parliamentary boroughs in the south west of England 1710–1730* (DPhil thesis, Oxford, 1985); J. Barry, 'Bourgeois collectivism? Urban association and the middling sort' in J. Barry and C. Brooks (eds.), *The middling sort of people* (London, 1994), pp. 18–40; A.T. Patterson, *A history of Southampton* (Southampton, 1966); E.A. Goodwyn, *A century of a Suffolk town: Beccles 1760–1860, part 1, 1760–1815* (Ipswich, 1965); F. Hill, *Georgian Lincoln* (Cambridge, 1966); A.F. Bottomley, *A short history of the borough of Southwold* (Southwold, 1974).

This, together with the preponderance of the middling sort among the greater and lesser officers of corporation, commission, trust and vestry forged a significant divide across town society. On one side of this line, respectable, rate-paying, middling households included office-holding along with business and family concerns among the spectrum of their activities. Although women were local rate-payers, in Colchester they did not hold office. Even so there are indications that women of such households were involved informally in the everyday processes of governance. On the other side of the line, the familiarity of both women and men with local governance was of a different nature. The artisan and labouring population of the town certainly treated local governance as a resource to secure (valuable and saleable) rights to borough votes, to obtain redress for interpersonal violence or other grievance and to access welfare and poor law relief.[2] Nevertheless, they did not hold office, their greater material insecurity and the limited domestic space they could control, the comparative fragility of their credit, as well as the ways that popular culture was often given to bumptious articulation out of doors, positioned Colchester's working and artisan classes as the main objects of governance, as Chapter 8 will explore.

The corporation

Colchester had seen a number of renewals and amendments to its charter over the centuries. That in force in the early eighteenth century dated from 1693, but its provisions followed those of a 1635 charter. The eighteenth-century corporation was composed of a mayor, twelve aldermen, eighteen assistants and eighteen common councilmen. These officers were appointed for life and were chosen by a two-stage process. Free-burgesses who were Colchester rate-payers nominated two candidates, of which the remaining corporation members selected one. Only common councillors were eligible to be appointed assistant; only assistants could be appointed aldermen and only aldermen could be appointed mayor. The mayor was chosen annually. There was also a recorder (charged with giving legal advice) and a high steward whose office was largely honorific. Recorders often appointed a deputy and a town clerk. The two-stage election process was also used to choose head men (sic) for each of the four wards. These four then chose five other burgesses apiece and this electoral college of twenty-four burgesses elected other borough officials (claviers, the chamberlain, treasurers of the common lands, the coroner, and two JPs from among the aldermen). The mayor, his deputy, the mayor for the previous year, the recorder and his deputy were also justices of the peace, and a good deal of the labour of borough administration was taken on by the justices together with the recorder, chamberlain and town clerk.

There were around 1,500 free burgesses, who normally gained their freedom either by descent (inherited from their father or grandfather) or through apprenticeship (inherited from their master). Family and trade determined a man's qualification as a burgess. No women were eligible. Honorary burgesses could be created with the

2 B. Lemire, *The business of everyday life: gender, practice and social politics in England, c.1600–1900* (Manchester, 2006), pp. 16–55; K. Wrightson, *Earthly necessities: economic lives in early modern Britain* (New Haven, CT, 2000).

consent of all the existing burgesses 'in Common Floor assembled'. This was a route by which sufficiently interested and affluent individuals could be admitted, usually because they were willing to take on the (expensive) office of mayor. Individuals wanting to trade in Colchester could buy their freedom to avoid paying foreign fines (though the corporation ceased trying to collect these after 1763). The possibility of creating honorary burgesses also opened the way for mayors, who wanted additional funds or to affect the party balance on the corporation, to admit new burgesses *en masse* sometimes for cash. And since the consent of the free burgesses was always disputable such creations were inevitably controversial. During a period of particularly intense party conflict in the late 1730s the legitimacy of many such burgess creations was challenged at law. The aldermen were found not to have been properly elected and consequently the charter lapsed for twenty-one years from 1742.

If Colchester Borough shared the oligarchic tendencies of many other eighteenth-century corporations, this had the advantage of filling the upper echelons of local government with men who sought and could afford to take on the not insignificant amount of labour and expense involved. Furthermore, such public service was a highly political matter. Local party struggles were conducted along two intersecting axes; the parliamentary representation and control of local government. The corporation's complex election procedures helped dominant parties to monopolise senior office. If the free burgesses nominated candidates of the 'out' party, the corporation members could simply not select them. The ranks of the common councillors often included members of the opposition party whose promotions had been blocked. Nevertheless, the element of resident freeburgess participation meant there was a need to husband political interests and that there was always the risk of riot if the oligarchy was too heavy-handed in getting its party elected.

The mayor, town clerk and recorder held Monday (for freemen) and Thursday courts (for other inhabitants). By the 1730s Thursday court dealt mainly with debt recovery. Cases were presented and administered by four appointed attorneys. These courts also registered property transfers and indentures of apprenticeship. Burgesses were sworn to their freedoms at Monday and Thursday courts as well as at assemblies, so the queues were long in the run-up to election time. There were quarter and petty sessions and an admiralty court to administer the fisheries. When the charter was in abeyance business was handled by county justices. Although petty sessions were still held locally, Colcestrians in search of justice had often to attend the county quarter sessions at Chelmsford, with a consequent reduction in the number of cases brought.[3]

The range of matters that regularly came before borough quarter sessions was wide. As well as criminal cases (usually assault and petty theft), rating appeals and indictments for nuisances, badly kept pavements, unlicensed alehouses, disorderly houses, harbouring vagrants, registering changes or terminations of apprenticeships, swearing oaths under the Test and Corporation Acts, illegal Sunday trading and weights and measures offences all formed part of the regular matter of the sessions. 'Employing illegal helps', pursuing an unapprenticed trade and forestalling the market also appear, though Colchester juries were reluctant to bring a guilty verdict in such

3 J. Cooper *et al.*, *The borough of Colchester* (Woodbridge, 1994), p. 161.

cases.[4] The sessions generally sat for three or four days each quarter and were administered by the mayor, recorder and their three fellow aldermen JPs. A grand jury and a petty jury (or law inquest) were convened of larger and smaller middling ratepayers respectively.[5] As well as the business of considering indictments, these juries investigated public nuisances and encroachments. Petty jury presentments were signed by all jurors who processed around the town seeking out 'siller dores' left open, noisy 'Ingine Loombs' and other nuisances.[6] Where criminal cases were to be tried a fresh jury consisting of some but not all grand or petty jurors was drawn up on each occasion.

Seventeenth-century Colchester had not been noted for its private charity.[7] Since 1698, the borough had also administered poor relief, both out relief and in a central workhouse. The mayor and aldermen were assisted in this task by a workhouse governor, deputy governor and treasurer, twelve assistant governors and forty-eight guardians elected in complex rotation by rate-paying burgesses. On the basis of seventeenth-century experience, the workhouse was expected to fund itself through the inmates' work. Children, the elderly and infirm were set to carding and spinning. Eighteenth-century bay trade reverses made this exercise less viable, though from a Tory perspective, MP Charles Gray could still argue that this use of the labour of the poor could revive the flagging woollen industry. The workhouse corporation did not, however, long survive the suspension of the charter and was not revived with the new charter of 1763, according to historian Morant, a victim of the conflict between parties.[8]

---

4 ERO D/B 5 Sr178 Sessions Roll Epiphany 1734/5, Esther Osborne, Abraham Choping found guilty of employing illegal helps, fined 40/- respited to 5/- and payment of fees, was the only case proved for this offence between 1735 and the suspension of the borough sessions in 1742; D/B 5 Sr180 Midsummer 1735, Charles Saunders and John Garritt indictment for their illegally following the trade of a taylor discharged; D/B 5 Sr181 Michaelmas 1735, Licence for presbytarian preachers at the chapel in St Botolphs attached to Winsley's almshouses; D/B 5 Sr182 Epiphany 1736, John Rootsey, oil miller and Baptist minister won an appeal that he was over-rated for a newly erected windmill in St Giles (rates reduced to £5); D/B 5 Sr183 Easter 1736, Matthew Graves presented for forestalling the market in butter, no indictment; D/B 5 Sr186 Easter 1737, William Weller, innholder and John Musset, mason, bound on joint £20 recognisance to prosecute Henry Nugent, mariner for stealing a linen gown.

5 P.J.R. King, *Crime, law and society in Essex, 1740–1820* (PhD thesis, Cambridge, 1984), pp. 313–15 finds that the 'petty jurors of late eighteenth-century Essex were predominantly middling men – farmers, tradesmen and artisans' whereas grand jurors were drawn from the gentry and large commercial groups (victuallers, millers, clothiers and maltsters). Colchester Borough Sessions juries seem to have been slightly less affluent overall.

6 ERO D/B 5 Sr187 Borough Sessions Roll, Law Inquest Presentment, Midsummer 1737, Chapter 2 above note 78; D/B 5 Sr191 Midsummer 1738 Richard Belgrade presented for 'Sello Dores Lying Open', D/B 5 Sr192 Michaelmas 1738 John Crosby for 'blocking heyway with his waggon' and Mr Whaley 'for dungel'.

7 N. Goose, 'The rise and decline of philanthropy in early modern Colchester: the unacceptable face of mercantilism?', *Social History,* 31 (2006), pp. 469–87.

8 There were twelve guardians and three Assistant Governors from each ward. Elections by the 'inhabitants' of the town (rate-paying burgesses) took place at an assembly biennially when 6 guardians per ward retired, six continued in office a further two years and six fresh guardians

The borough institutions gave scope for an official role for some 280 or so individuals in any year, counting grand and petty sessions jurors and constables: that is, about a third of the resident burgesses. However, if duplications of office are taken into account, this number can be reduced to an estimate of 180–200 people. Even this reduced figure comprises around a quarter of resident burgesses, over 6 per cent of the adult male population and something like 10 per cent of the town's middling sort. Despite the civil disabilities they suffered in eighteenth-century England, non-conformists were represented on Colchester corporation roughly in proportion to their presence in the population. The corporation of the late 1730s contained 23 per cent dissenters, and the new corporation named in the charter of 1763 had 27 per cent non-conformists.[9] Furthermore, if the processes of governance are understood to extend outside the corporation, including not only the improvement commissioners but local trusts and charities as well as parish administration, holding some sort of office was a sufficiently widespread experience to be characteristic of the adult male middling sort and formed a component of middling masculinity already established in mid-seventeenth-century Colchester.[10]

Commissioners and trustees

Colchester corporation held fishery rights over the River Colne (though the precise geographical extent of the fisheries was recurrently disputed). From the late seventeenth century, there had also been commissioners to improve the navigation of the river. These earlier eighteenth-century commissioners had a strong representation from local gentry, but key roles were reserved for the borough mayor and other senior officials. When the borough charter was lost in 1742, the navigation commission fell into abeyance until a separate act of 1750 vested the collection of channel dues to a revived body of commissioners including the magistrates of the eastern division and left the matter of fisheries administration and paving offences to parish surveyors. The state of the paving was a loud lament in Morant's 1748 borough history and neglect of

---

8 *cont.*

were elected. Corporate poor relief had begun in 1621 with the amalgamation of local charitable bequests, with the workhouse established in 1698. G. Martin, *The story of Colchester* (Colchester, 1959), pp. 55, 75; Cooper *et al.*, *Colchester*, p. 158; C. Gray, *Considerations of several proposals lately made for the better maintenance of the poor* (London, 1751); P. Morant, *The history and antiquities of the most ancient town of Colchester* (Colchester, 1748), book 2, p. 20.

9 These statistics were obtained by correlating listings of members of the corporation in the borough Assembly Book for 1733–37, ERO D/B 5 Gb 7, inclusive and in the new charter of 1763 with a listing of names collated from all available Colchester non-conformist sources for the period, S. D'Cruze, *"Our times in God's hands", religion and the eighteenth-century middling sort, a study of Colchester,* studies in Essex history (Chelmsford, 1990), p. 94, n. 35. Compare Barry, 'Bourgeoise collectivism', for Bristol where dissenters sat on the corporation and J.R. Smith, *The borough of Maldon 1688–1768; a study in English urban history* (MPhil thesis, Leicester, 1981), especially pp. 64, 96, 73, for Maldon, where they did not.

10 R. Deane Smith, *The middling sort and the politics of social reformation, Colchester 1570–1640* (New York, 2004), pp. 59–62. Compare A. Borsay, 'A middle class in the making; the negotiation of power and status at Bath's early Georgian general infirmary', *Social History*, 5 (1999), pp. 269–86.

the (valuable) fisheries was one of the complaints of the campaign to regain the charter over the succeeding decade.[11] Sadly, the Commission's minutes and other records do not survive, so there are few insights into to their operation. In 1780 moves were made to fund town improvements through the collection of a rate as well as channel dues. The Commission was the most suitable body to tackle paving and lighting not least since the new (1763) corporation remained liable for debts inherited from its predecessor. Like most matters of local administration this issue had a decidedly political edge. Revd Nathaniel Forster put forward proposals, but as he wrote to the then Whig MP, Sir Robert Smyth, to little avail:

> I have done with them. Finding that no good was to be done, that Frank (Smythies, the Town Clerk) was sure to carry his point, that scarce a gentleman attended and that the rest were to a man either devoted to, or duped by him, I have taken the magnanimous resolution of seceding. Nor do I ever intend to get another head ach (sic) at a meeting of the Commissioners of Channel duties. Honest Frank and his reverend master gained yesterday, as I hear, an easy victory.[12]

An attorney and son of a local clergyman Smythies ended his career (died 1798) at the most affluent reaches of the middling sort. A big, handsome man, he was capable, shrewd, power-hungry and violent.[13] By the mid-1780s he had the borough corporation by its collar. Forster's complaint in 1780 underlines how far the middling corporation officers remained imbricated in the politics of the (arguably) more progressive commissioners. The Act of 1780 gave new energy to the Commissioners which included non-conformist Hythe merchants, such as the Tabor family who did not sit on the corporation. The overlap in personnel between the corporation and other institutions extended to such superficially peripheral and ostensibly private bodies as school or charity trustees. The Blue Coat (Anglican) Charity School in All Saints, for example, was by 1780 sufficiently under-funded to close the school to girls. The trustees included Charles Gray, Smythies and Forster. It was Nathaniel Forster (among others) who recommended increasing the funds through annual charity sermons and benefit nights at the local theatre. The charity sermons in particular which included a published sermon, a procession of the children and a formal tea in the castle bailey became a regular moment where philanthropy and patronage were visibly celebrated. The Charity School may have been small beer in terms of prestige and income, but it was nevertheless fully incorporated into projects of governance, sharing trustees with more prestigious institutions, providing an opportunity for patronage in the appointment of the schoolmaster (including the author Charles Shillito), and preserving the rights of a few poorer burgesses to have their sons educated, clothed and apprenticed.[14]

---

11 W. Page and H. Round (eds.), *Victoria county history of Essex,* Vol. 2 (London, 1907), pp. 432–3.

12 ERO D/Dfg/21, Nathaniel Forster to Sir Robert Smyth, April 1780; D/Dfg/F4, Smyth family correspondence including a copy of the 1780 Navigation Bill.

13 J. Bensusan Butt, *Charles Shillito, Oliver Goldsmith* (Colchester, privately printed, 1994), p. 37 quoting Henry Crabb Robinson.

14 JBB MS, *Channel Acts and Bay Trade* in author's possession; ERO T/A 613, Blue Coat Charity School Records 1710–1780. See also L.C. Sier, 'The Blue Coat School, Colchester', *Essex Review,* xlix (1940), pp. 125–33; Charity School benefits at the theatre include *IpsJ* 22 October 1785, 12 November 1789; ERO Acc 905, Box 6, MS *Colchester Theatre;* Morant, *Colchester,* book 3, p. 191.

Public and private: institutions, officers and finance

A common strand of eighteenth-century opinion conceptualised the capacity for political action as the exercise of proprietorial rights and the role of institutions (such as corporations) as administering assets for the benefit of their members (burgesses). Borough corporations were in this sense private organisations, in contrast to the county justices or the improvement commissioners who were direct appointees of the state. Trustees of charities, similarly to the trustees and executors of individual wills, were also administering private property and exercised rights over that property. Beneficiaries of such trusts also held attenuated rights to the benefits so produced. The rights of each person or institution blocked out a little area on the social and political map where theoretically no other writ could run.[15] The Jacobite, William Oldisworth made the point when arguing against the disestablishment of the church, a measure, he threatened that would reduce the church to an 'outhouse' on a par with the many existing 'little supremacies' which claimed legal autonomy. He argued,

> Have not the Lord Mayor, the Lords and Commons, nay every Society and Club their particular Powers which they claim as Rights unalterable, and Independent of all others?[16]

The universalising discourse of rights concealed its gendered nature, though women also participated in civic life.[17] At law men had a greater autonomy over property in general; rights were not only proprietorial, they were gendered. Neither was this simply a matter of petty politics. The ability to exercise such rights was held to be the defining characteristic of national manly political virtue. Martin McCormack argues that independence (the ability to freely exercise rights) was the key capacity of political subjects. Political virtue was an attribute of manliness, to the extent that '... politics and masculinity were inseparable in this period: manliness was important in political situations, but politics was also central to the business of being a man'.[18] Women could not become free burgesses.[19] Nevertheless women could and did hold property

---

15 K. Wilson, *The sense of the people: politics, culture, and imperialism in England, 1715–1785* (New York, 1995); J. Innes and N. Rogers,'Politics and government', Chapter 6 in P. Clark *et al.* (ed.), *The Cambridge urban history of Britain* (Cambridge, 2000); earlier explorations include J.G.A. Pocock,'The varieties of whiggism from exclusion to reform: a history of ideology and discourse', in J.G.A. Pocock, *Virtue, commerce, and history: essays on political thought and history, chiefly in the eighteenth century* (Cambridge, 1985); H.T. Dickinson, *Liberty and property: political ideology in eighteenth-century Britain* (London, 1977); J.A.W. Gunn, *Beyond liberty and property; the progress of self-recognition in eighteenth-century political thought* (Kingston, Ontario, 1983).

16 W Oldisworth, *A Dialogue between Timothy & Philarkeus*, 2nd edn (London, 1709), pp. 181, 186, quoted in J.A.W. Gunn, *Beyond liberty*, p. 49.

17 H. Smith, *All men and both sexes; gender, politics and the false universal in England, 1640–1832* (University Park PA, 2002); R. Sweet,'Women and civic life in eighteenth-century England', in R. Sweet and P. Lane (eds.), *On the town: women and urban life in eighteenth-century England* (Aldershot, 2003), pp. 21–42.

18 M. McCormack, *The independent man: citizenship and gender politics in Georgian England* (Manchester, 2005), p. 33; K. Wilson, *The island race: Englishness, empire and gender in the eighteenth century* (London, 2003), p. 37.

19 In the borough of Maldon, although women could not be burgesses, daughters of burgesses did pass the right on to their sons; Smith, *Maldon*.

and exercised the rights associated with that ownership, for example as bond-holders for local charities.[20] Rights in this sense were incommensurable; the exercise of one right might well bar the exercise of another. In a 1753 political dispute which pitted one set of rights against another, the burgesses' rights to graze cattle on the 'half year' lands led to a riot when the calendar change of 1752 delayed the due date for ten days. Apparently the only landowner who kept her land enclosed and denied them entry was Elizabeth Selly. Her emphatic exercise of her property rights made a distinctly political point. She was a lifelong Colchester resident, a 'considerable brewer' and a woman who managed her business and property.[21]

Rights were therefore specific, utile, valuable and often in some measure alienable (a vote could be traded for cash). They accrued to (autonomous and therefore more often masculine) individuals and also to institutions. Local politics recurrently traded in a rhetoric of rights and the defence of such little supremacies and in so doing acted as an arena for the making and re-making of middling masculinities in both more and less polite manifestations. Furthermore, the process of local government frequently complicated these rhetorics, since multiple office holding and the combination of administrative business with profession, trade, family and other kinds of social connection meant that the field of governance extended across institutional barriers. Having an eye to the social embeddedness of some of the cash flows involved points up the complexities of the process.

In Colchester, as in many other eighteenth-century towns, the corporation lacked the finances to fund all of its activities. In the first third of the century its income of around £500 from rents on property, tolls and fines generally covered routine expenses. However, the costs of repeated litigation led to a growing accumulation of debt across the century which the corporation sought to manage by borrowing and mortgaging its assets. The litigation arose out of the conflicts of local politics. As indicated above, majority parties pushed the uses of their authority up to and beyond legitimacy in such matters as mass creations of free burgesses or extracting fines from 'foreign' traders and the law provided the means for the minority party or other groups who felt their rights had been abrogated to seek redress. Litigation was therefore the continuation of politics by other means. Contemporary and subsequent commentators have made cogent comments about corruption. However, local political struggles formed, as I will argue in the following chapters, the conditions of possibility within which local administration could be achieved. Without the kind of controlling landed interest present in some other boroughs, the hard-fought political struggles between conflicting middling interest groups over the structures of Colchester's administration were pretty much inevitable, if costly and undignified. The resultant financial pressures nevertheless affected the processes and financing of governance.

The corporation's chief assets (the fisheries, the waterbailiffship which administered the port, the markets and trade halls and various real estate, in particular 1,000 acres of agricultural land in Mile End) were repeatedly mortgaged or leased out. Daniel Defoe took the original ninety-nine-year lease of the Mile End (Severalls)

20 Bonds of Winsley's Charity, ERO D/Q 30/4/8.

21 Phillip Morant to Hardwicke, ERO D/Y/2/2, 19 October 1753; JBB BD/759 for Elizabeth Selly.

estates in 1720 for two payments of £500 and £120 a year. By the time the charter lapsed in 1742 the corporation had debts of over £3,000. There was a certain advantage in this situation while the charter was in abeyance, since the interests of mortgagees and lessees meant that the properties involved were administered and eventually returned to the new corporation (often to be used as collateral for later loans). This financial situation also led to complex and overlapping interests in corporation assets. By the 1740s City of London alderman, Walter Bernard held the mortgages of both the Severalls estate and the waterbailiffship with associated properties at the Hythe. After the Hythe tenant had gone bankrupt (1745) Bernard granted a 14-year lease to non-conformist merchant Jonathan Tabor. Under the terms of this lease Tabor occupied the property but also in effect acted as waterbailiff, collecting tolls, respecting the rights of burgesses and undertaking to defend Bernard's rights at law if necessary. Through his lease, Tabor thus acquired rights over (corporation) property but also the rights and obligations of (quasi-) office. The Tabor family were still in occupation of the Hythe property when Robert Tabor (son of Jonathan) became a commissioner under the 1780 improvement act, acquiring *de jure* as well as *de facto* office, but remaining outside the corporation.[22]

Meanwhile, rents due to Bernard on the Severalls Estate were paid by tenants to his agents. Successively these were attorneys William Mayhew senior and junior and then Francis Smythies, all of them deeply involved in local politics and holders of senior borough office. The last was the very town clerk who proved so successful in getting his measures through on the harbour commissioners. William Mayhew snr (died 1764) was a central figure in the campaign to regain the borough charter, when he managed a sizeable political interest in the name of burgess's rights. Rights that he also indirectly defended by assiduously evicting squatters from Kingswood Heath on the Severalls' land. Mayhew jnr (died 1787) was named deputy recorder in the new charter and later high steward. Although the Severalls property was alienated, borough officials were the ones managing its income. When the corporation was in operation, its highly convoluted system of accounting led to the mixing of official finances with the professional and business income of its officials. A chamberlain collected the smaller rents but legitimately retained commission of 1s in the pound. The mayor collected the income from the oyster fisheries and deducted expenses before (sometimes after some years) he paid the balance over to the town clerk.[23] Such practices were not necessarily aberrant in an era when the government paymaster was given £10,000 on appointment and expected to profit from the office.[24] The Mayhews and Francis Smythies also severally defended chancery cases where the not unusual practice of amalgamating clients' assets acquired through their professional business with their own became (let us say) over-extended. Smythies jeopardised his credit and his political capital by evading settling accounts with local

---

22 Cooper *et al.*, *Colchester*, pp. 163–4; JBB MS, *Channel Acts and Bay Trade*.

23 Cooper *et al.*, *Colchester*, p. 165.

24 J.H. Plumb, *Chatham* (London, 1953); J.H. Plumb, *Walpole*, two vols (London, 1956) for Pitt the Elder who refused to profit from the office; R. Thorne, 'Rigby, Richard (1772–1788)', *Oxford Dictionary of National Biography* (Oxford, 2004) www.oxford.dnb.com/view/article/23647, accessed 20 October 2007, for Richard Rigby, whose eventual settling of these accounts marked his retirement from politics.

gentleman Nicholas Corsellis over a shared farm of the Stamp Duty.[25] The business of local government was handled by men of business alongside all their other business. Office was in this sense another asset conveying rights to benefit. In Bourdieu's terminology, office, trade, profession, household and family were each fields where social, cultural and material capital intersected.[26] Local government was therefore a means of extending middling credit (social and financial). It also bound the middling sort into structures of authority as well as giving them plenty of (often otherwise thankless) chores to do.

This last effect can be seen at work at the farther reaches of local government, where cash flows could be equally convoluted. Several petty sessions examinations show poor rates to have been collected from tenants by landlords or landladies along with the rent. Baymaker Isaac Boggis deducted parish rates from the wages he paid. The churchwarden's wife in St Runwald seems to have collected rates.[27] Appointments of masters of parish workhouses or the House of Correction clearly assumed that wives as well as husbands would share the duties. Some of the chores of (male) officials fell into the remit of women's household responsibilities.[28] Governance was a politicised process that did the work of making and re-making power differentials between those who governed and those who were governed, though petty officials in particular were always liable to challenge. It permeated contiguous if heterogeneous structures, from the corporation and the improvement commission, via trusts, charities and parishes to neighbourhoods and households. Among those who were connected into the processes of town government, even informally, its little institutional supremacies were, when viewed in close focus, very porous both in terms of the personnel who fulfilled the functions of governance and of the cash flows that paid for it. A good percentage of the middling sort had roles to play, either officially or quasi-officially. Such roles made a difference to the subject positions individuals could occupy and to the ways that they could imagine the town and their place within it.

---

25 The venture realised at least £5,000 by 1795, though Corsellis was denied his share and the matter ended in Chancery, apparently in Smythies' favour. ERO D/DHt E24; Walker (ed.), *Thomas Twining*, letter 129, T. Twining to R. Twining, 16 April 1790, p. 345.

26 P. Bourdieu, *Outline of a theory of practice*, R.T. Nice (ed.) (Cambridge, 1977).

27 For the woman collecting churchwarden's rates see ERO P/COR/1 12 August 1749, Examination of William Goulding, who had not recently paid rates or taxes, 'though he heard his late wife, formerly the widow of William Bull, declare that soon after her marriage to him she paid to the *wife* of Joseph Wheeley, one of the churchwardens of St Runwald, 2d for churchwarden's rates' (my emphasis).

28 ERO P/CoR 10b, 8 June 1784, examination of Sarah Gardner, governess of the St Leonards workhouse; P/CoR 4, 31 January 1774, examination of Peter and Mary Mavis, keepers of St Mary-at-the-Walls parish workhouse; Chapter 3 above n. 58 for the contribution of the women of the Shillito and Smith families to the duties of office-holding.

Impolitics[29]

I have argued that town governance was a political matter which intersected with the politics of parliamentary elections. I shall discuss local politics in closer detail through the three case studies which comprise the following chapter. The remainder of this chapter will trace the intersections of governance and parliamentary elections across an overview of eighteenth-century borough politics. A number of factors (not least the unwieldiness and contentiousness of the borough itself) prevented external landed interests from exercising any significant political control in Colchester. [30] The Civil War and its aftermath had (one way or another) loosened the grip of resident gentry such as the Lucas' and the Grimstons. Lord Hardwicke had acquired the residue of some of the Lucas property, but aside from the interest of a landowner had bigger fish to fry elsewhere. Similarly Richard Rigby of Mistley Hall (sometime Forces Paymaster) and the aristocratic parson/journalist Revd Bate Dudley contented themselves with occasional and fairly indecisive forays into Colchester affairs.[31] Eighteenth-century governments were not, of course, uninterested in Colchester elections and in 1741 gave the outcome a hefty push. They were, however, one of a number of players and never exercised a controlling interest.

In the later seventeenth century local gentry had played a leading role in borough politics. In the 1700s East India money found its way into local politics through a couple of parliamentary candidates, but overall the close attention to the borough by families whose social mobility and elevation to the (town) gentry had come through the bay trade meant that in the early eighteenth century the families of Creffield, Tayspill and Rebow (all Colchester residents) led the parties which contested local politics. The Rebows and their relations by marriage the Martins and the Prices provided leadership and patronage for the local Whigs. Although the Tayspill and later the Creffield names died out by the 1730s, their money and the political leadership it brought were handed on. Charles Gray acquired much of his fortune and his place in local Tory politics to a marriage with a Creffield widow.[32] Sir Isaac Rebow, Whig leader early in the century, had made his money in the cloth trade and was resident in Head Street. By the 1760s his descendant Isaac Martin Rebow had moved to his Wivenhoe mansion, relinquished any direct involvement in trade and interested himself chiefly in his position as a Colonel in the Essex militia. Both Tory Gray and his close friend and relative by marriage George Wegg were lawyers; 'typical of the new elite of professional men which was gradually developing in the town'.[33] These political

29 Walker, *Thomas Twining*, Thomas Twining to Richard Twining, 14 December 1788, 'The brief history of Colchester politics (read Impolitics) is this …'

30 S. D'Cruze, *The middling sort in provincial England: politics and social relations in Colchester 1730–1800* (PhD thesis, Essex, 1990), Chapter 2.

31 R. Thorne, 'Rigby Richard (1722–1788)', H. Barker, 'Dudley, Sir Henry Bate baronet (1745–1824)', www.oxford.dnb.com/view/article/ 8152, accessed 20 October 2007.

32 Martin, *Colchester*, pp. 71–3.

leaders owed their position in Colchester politics to husbanding their interests in the borough and maintaining wider political and patronage networks that spread throughout the middling sort to the artisan free burgesses. Therefore, although some local landed gentry figured significantly in Colchester (Sir Robert Smyth of Berechurch sat as MP in the 1780s, and the Earl of Rochford from St Osyth served as High Steward from 1763) they were far from exercising control and there was plenty of scope for middling merchants, tradesmen and professionals to hold office and join the skirmish for influence, status, financial advantage and even for the better governance of the town.

The War of the Spanish Succession (1702–13) had damaged the bay trade, closing overseas markets for Colchester cloth. Serious riots and labour disputes had followed in 1715 as baymakers attempted to restrict entry into the trade. A Whig majority on the corporation struggled to keep control by selling borough freedoms to potential supporters in 1711 and 1713.[34] Trade fluctuations in the 1720s caused bankruptcies and the Dutch baymakers gave up control of the bay hall in 1728; at the same time town Tories managed to seize control of the corporation which became dominated by six Tory aldermen who were energetic in attending courts, committees and assemblies and disposing of the borough's business. Nationally, this was a period when the Tory Party was excluded from power and held in deep suspicion because of its (actual and putative) associations with Jacobitism. The Walpole administration was by this time in difficulties over its unpopular excise scheme. Colchester corporation joined the many middling sort nationwide who vociferously opposed the excise as eroding their freeborn right to trade.[35] The Tory-controlled corporation obtained a like-minded MP in a 1735 by-election but collapsed ignominiously over the following general election in 1741. In the preceding struggle for a majority, Whig alderman George Gray was tried for sodomy in an attempt to eject him from the corporation (Chapter 7). Over the preceding decades both Whigs and Tories had sold borough freedoms and created honorary freeburgesses both to provide some much-needed finance and to bolster majorities in corporation and parliamentary elections. At law the Whigs contested the validity of honorary freeburgesses, and the integrity of Tory aldermen's credentials through invalid election. They secured a corporation majority which they used to railroad the election of two Whig candidates in 1741.

Popular disturbance and economic hardship also raised the political temperature. With the onset of war in earnest in 1740,[36] prospects for the bay trade declined. Weavers (paid by the piece) and baymakers felt the pinch. The winter of 1740 was almost the most severe of the century. Colchester and the surrounding region saw grain riots. The magistrates tried exhortation, coercion and initiatives to relieve hardship, including a petition to the Secretary of State. Renton argues that the idea of

---

33 For Rebow's involvement in the Essex militia see ERO L/V 4/2–10; D. Stephenson, *The book of Colchester, a portrait of a town* (Buckingham, 1978), p. 90.

34 Cooper *et al.*, *Colchester*, p. 111.

35 P. Langford, *The excise crisis society and politics in the age of Walpole* (Oxford, 1975), ERO D/B 5 Gb7 Assembly Book, 1 September 1740.

36 The War of Jenkin's Ear (1739), fought at sea, evolved into the full-blown sea and land War of the Austrian Succession (1739–48).

a moral economy and the right to food at fair prices could be shared between the poor and the provincial middling sort.[37] Army enlistment may well have mopped up some of the male unemployment, but it left wives and children dependent on the parish. Colchester's strategic position on the east coast meant yet another administrative headache for the corporation, as a substantial military encampment was set up on Lexden Heath in summer 1740, with attendant problems of provisioning and public order. The ruthless machinations at the 1741 poll are too convoluted to be retold here.[38] Suffice it to say that even by eighteenth-century standards the 1741 Colchester election was hardly 'free and fair'. The struggling Walpole administration supplied local Whigs with secret service funds.[39] The Tory candidates Charles Gray and Samuel Saville (a rural minor gentleman seated some 15 miles away) both had Jacobite leanings and would have necessarily been objectionable to the government.[40] The Whigs won a pyrrhic victory, since the following year they lost the borough charter, when the whole aldermen's bench was adjudged incorrectly elected. They also lost the parliamentary representation on petition. At this period voting behaviour shows an unambiguous party divide. Only very few voters changed party between the 1734, 1735 and 1741 elections. By comparison, from 1768 there was a frequent tendency to vote one Whig:one Tory, even in the politically inflammatory 1790s.[41]

Through the 1740s and 1750s the chief issue in Colchester politics was the regaining of the charter. With the Tory party proscribed, in effect this meant securing at least one Whig MP willing to go to the trouble and expense. Successive Whig members proved reluctant, despite the energetic campaigning, bullying and flattery of Colchester interests organised by middling political managers and based on freeman's clubs. The Charter Club led by attorney William Mayhew and its extensive appeal to a politics of rights will be considered in Chapter 7. The charter was regained only after a new Whig MP, Isaac Martin Rebow was persuaded to compromise with the Tory

---

37 S. Renton, 'The moral economy of the English middling sort in the eighteenth century, the case of Norwich in 1766 and 1767', in A. Randall and A. Charlesworth (eds.), *Markets, market culture and popular protest in eighteenth-century Britain and Ireland* (London, 1996), pp. 115–36.

38 D'Cruze, *The middling sort*, pp. 330–2.

39 R. Romney Sedgwick, *The history of parliament: the house of commons, 1715–1754* (London, 1971), Vol. 1, pp. 241–2, Vol. 2, p. 307. Whig John Olmius, Walpole supporter and later Colchester MP, gave evidence to the parliamentary committee investigating Walpole's alleged misconduct after his resignation, particularly mentioned Weymouth and Essex as examples of Walpole's 'notorious attacks upon the freedom of elections'. L. Namier and J. Brooke, *The history of parliament: the house of commons 1754–1790* (London, 1964), Vol. 3, p. 226.

40 Saville was seated at Stisted some 25 miles away. He was among those notified to the French Government as reliable Jacobites in 1743. R. Romney Sedgwick, *The history of parliament*, Vol. 2, p. 409, for Charles Gray, Vol. 2, pp. 81–2. There is evidence that both the Tories had Jacobite leanings and were implicated in plans in 1743 and 1744, for a French landing at Maldon. A.N. Newman, 'Leicester house politics 1750–60', *Camden Miscellany*, 23 (1969), pp. 85–229, pp. 181–2. In Gray's papers ERO D/DRb Z1-3 includes memorandum book with note of Jacobite toasts. See also ERO D/DRc F17; Gray to Peter Creffield, 30th March 1742: 'We had ye good fortune to carry 15 of ye 21 on ye Secret Committee, and things seem to bear a much better aspect now than they did some days ago …'

41 D'Cruze, *The middling sort*, Chapter 8.

Charles Gray to secure the charter in return for an uncontested election in 1761. The new Charter was obtained in 1763 and Colchester entered on two decades of political Compromise when the mayoralty alternated annually between Whigs and Tories and political opposition became focused on anti-Compromise interests worked up independently by middling political managers. Such interests generally purported to defend the burgesses' rights and liberties. Historians of eighteenth-century political culture are showing how wars or political crises which threatened national identity were expressed through anxieties over gender. Luxury was the national malaise which produced masculine effeminacy and female boldness. Restabilisation called for reinforcement of the normative gender order and the virtuous manly exercise of rights and liberties.[42] While talk of rights and liberties were mostly the oppositional discourse of popular Toryism up to mid-century, with the recuperation and renovation of Tory politics with the ascension of George III, and the early radical stirrings around the Wilkite movement in the 1760s, Colchester too saw a shift in the uses of 'rights' arguments.[43] Rights and radicalism were appropriated to the power struggles defined by the local political situation. Rights were the talk of anti-Compromise political interests in the borough in the 1760s but from the later 1770s the discourse was debated between oppositional groups (often dissenting) and the populism of a renovated corporation party.

The themes of political partisanship imbricated with social connection and the workings of credit, of politics as important to middling identities (especially masculine ones), and of proprietorial rights as informing oppositional political discourse can be traced through to the Napoleonic period. National politics over this period saw the loss of the American colonies and the subsequent post-war recovery accompanying the successes of the ministries of the Younger Pitt. In Colchester it looked like the return of prosperity for the bay trade and was celebrated with processions and illuminations. The 1783 East India Bill whose defeat brought Pitt to power and the 1788 Regency Crisis opened up questions of the constitution of the state and the legitimacy of power. The question of reform of the parliamentary franchise exercised both establishment Whigs and a developing reform movement. By the French revolution (1789) gentlemanly agitations for moderate reform were accompanied by a popular radical movement which took in a social range from the urban middling sort excluded from voting by the eccentricities of the unreformed borough franchises to artisan and other working people's commitment to a universal adult (and not always only male) franchise.

Within this changing national political landscape, three phenomena in particular are indicative of shifts in Colchester politics. Firstly the more frequent appearance of parliamentary candidates with little or no previous connection to Colchester but with

---

42 K. Harvey, review of *The independent man: citizenship and gender politics in Georgian England,* Matthew McCormack (review no. 530), www.history.ac.uk/reviews/paper/harvey.html, accessed 14 November 2007, and McCormack's response; D. Wahrman, 'Percy's prologue: from gender play to gender panic in eighteenth-century England', *Past and Present,* 159 (1998), pp. 113–60; K. Wilson, *The island race: Englishness, empire and gender in the eighteenth century* (London, 2003); P. Carter, *Men and the emergence of polite society; Britain 1660–1800* (Harlow, 1997).

43 McCormack, *The independent man,* Chapter 4.

Table 6.1

Colchester, London and Country voters, 1741–1831

Election	London voters	Country voters	Colchester voters
1741	59	402	1100
1747	75	420	845
1768	190	573	824
1780	50	280	351
April 1784	58	370	491
July 1784	170	428	463
1788	227	525	528
1790	7	300	430
1796	20	300	428
1806	198	587	359
1807	38	437	412
1812	296	702	408
Feb 1818	19	103	334
June 1818	98	299	381
1820	330	605	448
1830	329	459	450
1831	318	487	304

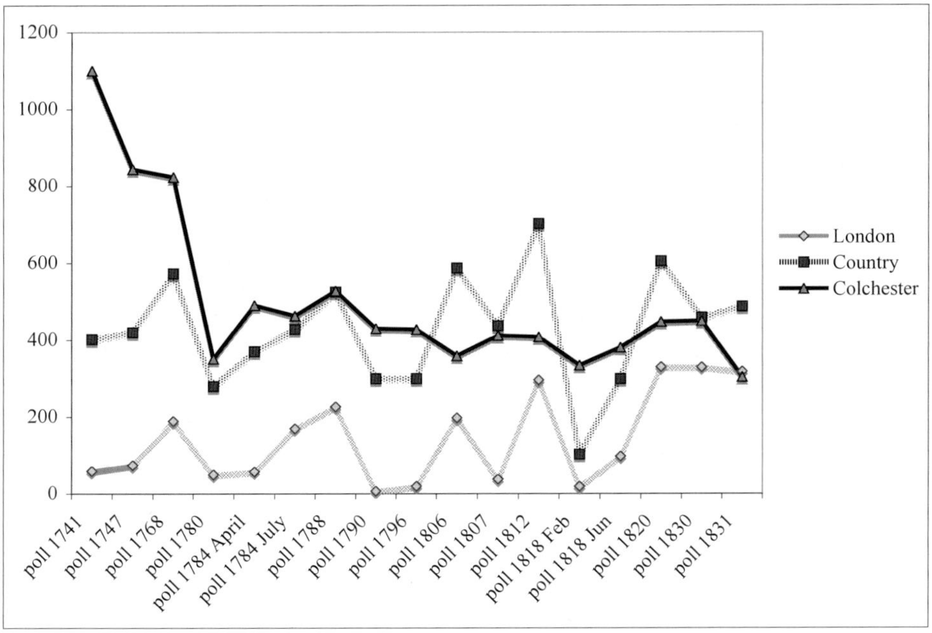

very well-lined pockets. The first outsider of this series in 1768, banker Alexander Fordyce, was seen off by the Compromise, but it was a close-run thing. The Compromise came near breaking. Mrs Ennew, the wife of Rebow's man of business Samuel Ennew, was said to have promised the post boy a pair of leather breeches not to vote for Gray.[44] As the Compromise ended due to mortality and retirement middling political managers struggled to re-shape and lead political party in the town, generating

44 ERO D/DRg4/35–61, Wegg to Gray, 5 and 6 March 1769.

interests sufficient to attract outsider candidates, and gain control of borough institutions. Secondly a decreasing proportion of the electorate was Colchester-resident. Outvoters, in particular London voters, were less well enmeshed in the quotidian workings of local politics. They were arguably more likely to vote either in accord with their views on national politics or (perhaps more probable) the size of the candidate's payment. As Table 6.1 illustrates, whereas Colchester freemen comprised 63 per cent of the borough electorate in 1747, this percentage had dropped to 41 per cent in 1790. From the middling political manager's point of view, London and Country outvoters could be secured fairly speedily (but perhaps rather less securely) once the candidates' guineas were in the campaign coffers. Lastly, although non-conformity had long been associated with Whiggishness, because the civil disabilities of dissenters became a significant argument in the growing franchise reform campaigns the politicisation of non-conformists across the country was heightened. Colchester dissenters, the middling group at the centre of opposition politics, became pitched against a corporation party led by the town clerk Frank Smythies which espoused Pittite Tory patriotism, not only in parliamentary elections but across the landscape of local politics.

The Smythies corporation party arose out of the manoeuvrings that succeeded the Compromise and captured the borough despite the election of local landed (Whig/radical) gentleman Sir Robert Smyth in 1780 and the muscle of Sir Richard Rigby, from Mistley Hall weighing in for the government in a by-election in 1781. In August 1785 a group of middling tradesmen mounted a takeover of the corporation by creating seven of their number new aldermen from scratch in one day to achieve a controlling majority on the bench. A pro-Smyth newspaper item castigates these creations as an insult to the absent 'Sir R... S...' and his party and decries the usurpers as of low social standing. This is the first point at which the two parties are clearly described and the two leaders, Smyth and Smythies are distinguished.[45] For three years from 1787 Smythies also held the office of borough recorder, much to the offence of the local political establishment, who thought the office above his station and contravening the wishes of the previous recorder, William Mayhew jnr, who had nominated another successor.

1788–90 was a critical period in borough politics, which reflected national issues including the Regency Crisis and the response to the French Revolution. In Colchester the corporation and opposition parties were locked in struggle. July 1788 saw the corporation party triumph by main force over the elections of the treasurers of the borough common lands. Though the treasurers were comparatively minor officials, the issue of the burgesses' grazing rights on the Half Year Lands were a recurring grievance – it had caused riots during the 1750s when the charter was suspended. In

45 ERO D/B 5 Gb8 Assembly Book 29 August and 10 September 1785; *IpsJ* 3 September 1785. The aldermen created were Phillip Affleck, brother and agent to the Tory MP; Samuel Tyssen, an outsider candidate put up by the Potter faction in the July 1784 election to allow a petition (for which see *IpsJ* 26 February 1785); Edmund Lilley, baymaker, William Argent, baymaker, Edward Capstack, currier, William Swinborne, tanner, Bezaliel Angier, baymaker. The remaining Whig aldermen were Sir Robert Smyth, the dying Phillip Sansom, a cardmaker and Stephen Betts, tinman, a principled radical who persevered in a minority of one into the 1790s.

order to get the right men in riotous disorders were caused. Opposition burgesses were barred from voting and Smythies; 'so far forgot his dignity as to jump off the bench and seize one or more of them by the collar'. For Smythies the performative shaping of political masculinity was recurrently marked by physical violence. He convened a petty sessions on the spot and the rioters were summarily dispatched. According to one protester, Smythies 'Deserved hanging far more than Dr Dodd did'.[46]

At a by-election the following November the Colchester opposition introduced the radical George Tierney while the corporation party backed George Jackson, a candidate 'in the Government interest'.[47] In a thoroughly disreputable election, the 'Saucy Clerk' Smythies and the mayor admitted numerous freeburgesses to swing the voting while polling was in progress, and closed the poll peremptorily when the votes were 640 apiece. Tierney won the seat on petition, though lost in the general election of 1790 when the evangelical Pittite Tory, Robert Thornton managed to split the opposition vote. The Thorntons had previously bought the living of St Peters and installed the evangelical Revd Robert Storry.[48]

Political opinion and political party were not confined to the free burgesses. Revd Thomas Twining, highly partisan on behalf of his brother-in-law Smythies, was delightfully catty about Thornton. Thornton was a member of the evangelical 'Clapham sect' or as Revd Twining acidly put it 'of the Saint Party', continuing:

> He was very drunk here, &, formerly, I am told upon his Ipswich canvas, & is a man very subject to be drunk: not that this at all derogates from his saintship: O no – they sin, that grace may abound ...[49]

Middling sort merchants, bankers and the 'Methodistical', Robert Storry were involved in the wheeling and dealing. Banker C.A. Crickett the high steward was sympathetic to the corporation party. He seems to have been connected with the issue of Smythies' 'vile non-settlement of accounts' which he owed Revd Nicholas Corsellis from Wivenhoe, over a farm of the Stamp Duty. Crickett and Corsellis, who in 1785 had both opposed the corporation, went so far as to fight a duel on Lexden Heath in July 1789.[50] Corsellis had switched his support from Thornton to Tierney. The pro-Thornton dissenting party were also 'highly incensed'. They planned to discredit Crickett's bank by making large withdrawals and refusing his bank notes. Revd Robert Storry had apparently been discussing the matter with Ipswich banker Mills. Charles

---

46 Colchester Public Library, Rebow Scrapbook, 29 July 1788. ERO D/B 5 Gb8 Assembly Book 29 July 1788, P CoR 12 examinations for 28 July 1788; McCormack. *The independent man*, p. 49.

47 Namier and Brooke, *The house of parliament 1754–1790*, Vol. 2, p. 668.

48 Namier and Brooke, *The history of parliament*, Vol. 3, pp. 524–5; R. G. Thorne, *The history of parliament*, Vol. 2, pp. 158–60; L. Davidoff and C. Hall, *Family fortunes, men and women of the English middle class, 1780–1850* (London, 1987), p. 83.

49 Walker (ed.), *Thomas Twining*, letter 326, Thomas Twining to Richard Twining, 27 March 1790, pp. 340–1.

50 *IpsJ* 4 July 1789. Corsellis voted for the outsider Samuel Tyssen in 1784. ERO Acc. 905, MS *Boggis II*.

Whaley, Crickett's partner in Colchester was also thinking of joining Mills.[51]

Neither was this behind the scenes politicking a strictly male affair. In 1768 Mrs Samuel Ennew had distributed breeches in the Tory cause. In 1788 Mrs Jane Smythies had clear political opinions. She disapproved of Revd Henry Bate Dudley of Bradwell who had opposed Smythies' bid for the Colchester recordership, condemning his 'Foxity attachment'. A contemporary political broadsheet describes in biblical parody how Frank was controlled by two women in his house. One, his 'helpmeet', was 'well skilled in cunning and learning, and the hand-writing of any man could well adopt'. She planned to advance his interests by forging a letter and had done so in the past on his behalf. Although the specific allegation is unsubstantiated, the satire could have no bite unless the portrait of Jane Smythies as a backstage political manager was recognisable to contemporaries.[52]

By the 1790s the two town parties were discrete and distinct in terms of membership, leadership and ideas. The corporation party were Anglican, Pittite, patriotic Tories, headed by Smythies and a rising generation of middling town traders. The opposition were often dissenters, reform or radical minded and led by families such as the Tabors and Daniells – prominent non-conformists, merchants, professionals and traders. After 1790 Tierney took himself off to represent Southwark, a severe setback for the radical cause in Colchester. Thornton seems to have been an effective borough MP. He actively patronised the town's Sunday Schools, personally presenting sixpence to each child at the annual anniversary celebrations. In the 1796 election a visiting radical Alexander Shepley could make no headway. The deepening crisis in France, and the outbreak of war in 1793 had turned all but the most committed away from radicalism. The Tree of Liberty was however still tended in Colchester by several, mostly non-conformist tradesmen and merchants.[53]

In December 1793, the proclamation against seditious literature produced a prosecution of Richard Patmore, a Baptist baymaker, for distributing several pamphlets and the second part of Paine's *Rights of Man*. Town Clerk Smythies handled the prosecution. Patmore and six other non-conformist tradesmen stood surety for £100 and £200 apiece. The matter dragged through the courts until it was lost on a technicality. The case seems to have been locally notorious; five years later it was remembered as a triumph for patriotism.[54] The anti-corporation group remained sufficiently organised to call a public meeting in 1795 to move for peace with France; a

---

51 See n. 38 above. *London Gazette* 25 July 1789, p. 514, banking partnership between Crickett, Truelove, Kerridge and Whaley in Ipswich dissolved.

52 See note 32 above. Barker,'Dudley, Sir Henry Bate', Colchester Public Library, E. COL 1 324.28, J.B. Harvey collection. The second woman, nicknamed 'Betty Flounder' is accused of having a foul and vicious tongue. She may be Jane Smythies' sister Susan Norfolk who lived with them.

53 *IpsJ* 14 February 1795; 'Friends of Freedom' dinner at the Red Lion in honour of Hardy and Tooke. *ChCh* 3 June 1796; *IpsJ* 26 July 1796; 1796 Poll Book.

54 PRO TS/11.854.2910. Smythies also had a hand in the prosecution of another similar case in Saffron Walden. *IpsJ* 19 January, 13 March, 20 July 1793. ERO D/B 5 Sb6/8 Colchester Borough Sessions Book, 1793. For Patmore, JBB BD/644. Patmore's sureties were his own for £200, Robert Tabor ygr. (JBB BD/852), Timothy Walford upholsterer (BD/901) for £100 each, Isaac Slythe stonemason (BD/1253 and Chapter 3 above), William Cole, surveyor (BD/184) for £200 each, Michael Boyle silkweaver (BD/94) and John Rouse ironmonger (BD/721) for £200 each; L.

debate that was lost by 36 votes to 105. For substantial merchants such as Tabor the wartime inflation as well as the economic hardship of remaining wool workers and other employees can only have helped concentrate their political and religious convictions, though Tory patriotism was far more popular. The pacifist motion was supported by leading non-conformists Robert Tabor and James Halls Esq. Smythies and his brother-in-law Revd Twining opposed.[55]

Non-conformity and political disaffection continued to go hand in hand. The local postmistress included a majority of non-conformists among those she considered disloyal to king and constitution.[56] The eminently quietist and respectable Eld Lane Baptists felt threatened by the prevailing political climate. As their minutes record on 19 April 1793:

> We have been keeping a national fast. The service began at half past ten, concluded quarter past two. Some churches, on account of the nature of the times, had only a short service by the minister alone, but our friends were enabled to pray as that, *had Informers been there* (their emphasis), they must have gone away without their errands.[57]

The outbreak of war with France bound Colchester into a thoroughly national moment of crisis.[58] War brought high prices and inflation, with hardship for some and the increased risk of bankruptcy for every trading family. Its proximity to the Essex coast meant that Colchester was heavily garrisoned until 1804 and fears of invasion, particularly in 1802, led to the flight of many refugees.[59] In 1797, as the invasion threat first materialised, the middling sort had hurried to join the Volunteers, providing their own uniforms and mounts. Middling masculinities were enhanced by this military role; historians of gender have argued how war tends to reinforce gender difference.[60] The rapid growth of volunteer forces across the country was unprecedented, though the historically entrenched abhorrence of a standing army meant that the call to arms was an established part of the freeborn Englishman's ideological baggage. The volunteer forces doubled in size during the first half of 1798 and provided around half of Britain's military manpower and a crucial element in its home defence. The local newspaper is full of movements of regiments, parades and salutes by the Colchester Loyal Volunteers. *Feu de joie* celebrated many royal birthdays and Nelson's victory on

---

54 *cont.*

Blaxhill, *History of Lion Walk Congregational Church* (Colchester, 1939), Appendix 3; NA HO42/213 Elizabeth Manning to Freeling, April 1798. This was a reply from the Colchester postmistress to the Aliens Office on local inhabitants taking the radical paper, *The Courier*. She digressed at length on those she thought disloyal to king and constitution, and commented on the Patmore case. C. Emsley,'An aspect of Pitt's terror', *Social History*, 6 (1981), pp. 155–84.

55 *IpsJ* 2 February 1795; Walker, *Thomas Twining*, letter 168, Thomas Twining to Richard Twining, pp. 428–9; Colchester Public Library, G.O.R. Rickwood, *Annual Register*; JBB BD/400 for James Halls.

56 NA HO42/213 Elizabeth Manning to Freeling, April 1798.

57 L. Spurrier, *The memorials of the Baptist Church, Colchester* (Colchester, 1889), p. 39.

58 H. T. Dickinson, *The politics of the people in eighteenth-century Britain* (London, 1994).

59 J. Gilbert (ed.), *The autobiography and other memorials of Mrs Gilbert* (London, 1876), pp. 172–4.

60 S. Conway, *War, state and society in mid-eighteenth century Britain and Ireland* (Oxford, 2006), p. 120; P. Highgate (ed.), *Military masculinities: identity and the state* (London, 2003); S. Dudink *et al.* (ed.), *Masculinities in politics and war: gendering modern history* (Manchester, 2004).

the Nile occasioned feasting. Theatre audiences called for 'God save the king' and 'Rule Britannia' to be sung repeatedly.[61] Dissenters, evangelicals, the opposition party, working artisan groups and the corporation party all subscribed readily to the Fund for Defence of the Country in 1798. In the crisis, a wide cross-section of the middling sort could find common ground in the cause of patriotism and the defence of home and family. The positive attractions of patriotism combined with a state actively repressing radicalism to mute any political opposition for the duration.[62]

Into the nineteenth century the parliamentary representation was for the most part Tory, though the charismatic radical and reformer, Daniel Whittle Harvey did successfully garner the oppositional vote and occupied one of the Colchester seats for some years. Harvey's success, however, was dependent on the by now larger numbers of London freemen, and as parliamentary reform came nearer he gave up the seat. Meanwhile Colchester corporation became ever more encumbered by the cost and distraction of its own lawsuits. Bitterly fought contests for the mayoralty in 1812 were satirised in the notorious doggerel *The Guild*, whose printer was imprisoned for libel.[63] Subsequently the device of invalid election was argued once again at law and led to the Charter being disclaimed. Unlike in 1742 however, a fresh Charter was immediately obtained. The borough's finances became ever more precarious and debt-ridden even when the 99-year mortgage on the corporation's estates at Mile End ended in 1821 which improved the income from the land to £893 p.a. by 1829. Outside the corporation, the resident freemen remembered the discourse of particularist rights to claim entitlement to the income from corporation lands. Benjamin Strutt, the borough chamberlain, produced a plan to sell the lands and divide the profits among the burgesses. However, demographic growth had left the 480 resident freemen a small minority in a town of over 16,000 population. No longer did the networks of corporation and electoral politics colour social connection across the town. The corporation continued to be a political battle ground for middle-class

---

61 *IpsJ* 5, 12, 19, and 26 January 1793, 17 August 1793, 9 November 1793, 13 December 1794, 18 June 1797, Gilbert (ed.) *Mrs Gilbert*, p. 171; J.E. Cookson, *The British armed nation 1793–1815* (Oxford, 1997), pp. 40, 66, 68; I. Beckett, *The amateur military tradition 1558–1945* (Manchester, 1991), Chapter 3.

62 *IpsJ* 31 March 1798; K. Gilmartin, 'In the theater of counter-revolution: Loyalist association and conservative opinion in the 1790s', *Journal of British Studies*, 41 (2002), pp. 291–328; M. Duffy, 'William Pitt and the origins of the loyalist-association movement of 1792', *Historical Journal*, 39 (1996), pp. 943–62; J. Mori, 'Responses to revolution – the November crisis of 1792', *Historical Research*, 69 (1996), pp. 284–305; L. Colley, *Britons: forging the nation, 1707–1837* (New Haven and London, 1992); L. Colley, 'Whose nation – class and national consciousness in Britain 1750–1830', *Past and Present*, 113 (1786), pp. 97–117; A. Booth, 'Popular loyalism and public violence in the northwest of England, 1790–1800', *Social History*, 8 (1983), pp. 295–313; C. Black, *The association* (Cambridge, Mass., 1963) for the Reevites; J.R. Western, 'The volunteer movement as an anti-revolutionary force, 1793–1801', *Economic History Review*, 71 (1956), pp. 603–14; A. Mitchell, 'The loyalist association movement, 1792–3', *Historical Journal*, 4 (1961), pp. 56–77.

63 M.E. Speight, *Politics in the borough of Colchester 1812–1847*, (PhD thesis, London, 1959), p. 30. The minority party on the corporation published a satirical poem, *The Guild*, which led to the printer Isaac Marsden being imprisoned in the castle in January 1814. Cooper *et al.*, *Colchester*, pp. 161–2; A.F.J. Brown, *Colchester 1815–1914* (Chelmsford, 1980); JBB BD/1111 for Isaac Marsden.

men, including Francis Smythies jnr, who held tight onto the town clerk's office. However it became an increasingly unrepresentative Tory Anglican body and there seemed to be little injustice when it was replaced under the 1835 Local Government Act.[64]

Conclusion

This chapter has reviewed the ways that the governance of the borough was achieved through the incorporation of a widely defined middling sort into its structures and processes. Office-holding was a facet of middling credit; it accrued social, cultural and sometimes economic capital. Borough administration was an intrinsically political affair; the middling sort were deeply involved in local politics. Periodically, politics also involved violence, and not only that of the mob, in pursuit of arguably legitimate political ends. Middling political activity overlapped with office holding and local politics depended on the activities of middling political managers in working up and husbanding political interests. Political interests at some moments cohered into clear and antagonistic local parties, at other periods such interests circulated in a more complex and opaque political soup. In either case the energies of middling political managers were vital to the contest. The discourse of rights and liberties was a key rhetoric of local politics of sufficient flexibility to be both consonant with middling preoccupations with family, business and credit and attractive to poorer burgesses (both resident and outvoters) whose vote was a right with realisable market value. Both wider and narrower currents of change eventually rendered the old corporation and its politics far less relevant to the concerns of early nineteenth-century Colchester. However, across the eighteenth century the sordid detail of the local political struggle was a meaningful arena where middling identities (particularly masculinities) were forged and through which the governance of the town as a whole was conducted.

64 Cooper et al., *Colchester*, pp. 162–3.

Chapter 7

Points to be carried

Introduction

The previous chapter outlined the history of Colchester local politics, though such summaries necessarily neglect the complex texture of political struggle which was an important part of its point. It was in the heavily politicised minutiae of Colchester's public and institutional life, in the formation and maintenance of political interests, in the disposition of the benefits of patronage (sometimes in only minor matters) and the obligations so incurred, and in the (always contestable) solidarities around family, religion and social association that the real business of politics was engaged. Much of this is irrecoverable, but untangling the dense accretion of source material gives at least indirect access to the textures of local politics. To pursue such a method across the eighteenth century would extend this work to a second volume. Consequently this chapter will limit itself to three case studies which bring some of the complexities of local politics into historical view.

The rich old rogue: George Gray, 1739–42

In 1739, as the Tories' majority on the corporation was threatened, they were presented with an apparently fortuitous means of ejecting one of the Whig aldermen and thoroughly discomforting the opposition. An indictment was lodged in Borough Sessions of Epiphany 1739 against George Gray, gentleman plumber and glazier, for sexual assaults against two men. Gray had lived in Colchester 'a great number of years ... during which Time he hath carried on a great trade in Iron, Glass, Lead and other Merchandise'. He owned property around the town including the Red Lion inn. He had been an alderman since his party took over the corporation in 1719. He was the father of Charles Gray, the future Tory MP, who kept quiet during this crisis. The surviving records indicate that Gray's sexuality had long been known, at least in some quarters. He had at least one ready and possibly long-term partner in Thomas Francis, his tenant, a barber then aged about 30 of St Nicholas parish. It was only when John Blatch, a rower, complained of unwelcome advances that the matter came to court.[1]

---

1 George Gray and Thomas Francis, Report to the Secretary of State of Defendants' Evidence to Support their Petition for a Pardon, NA SP 36/50/377 which is the source of this account unless otherwise stated. See also Borough Sessions Book ERO D/B 5 Sb5/3, Sessions Rolls ERO D/B Sr 193, Epiphany 1739, D/B Sr 194 Easter 1739; Assembly Book, ERO D/B 5 Gb7, 13 February 1739, 3 September 1739, 23 February 1740, 1 September 1740, 22 October 1740; *Colchester Journal* 18 August 1739; *IpsJ* 23 February 1740, 3 May 1740; NA King's Bench pleas, KB 28 and index thereto IND 6658: KB 28/150/1, 2 Trinity 13 Geo II, 1739, Gray's pleas of not guilty; KB 28/155/41 Michaelmas 14 Geo II, 1740 and /156/30 Hilary 14 Geo II, 1741, Mandamus to restore Gray to the corporation (there is no mention of the case in the relevant Assize roll, PRO ASSI 35/180/9 Summer 1740); NA C111 Signet Office Ind. 16972, his pardon of 3 May 1740. Assembly Book, ERO D/B 5 Gb7, 13 February 1739.

Gray was indicted for committing sodomitical practices with Francis (who was similarly indicted) and for an assault with intent to commit such practices on John Blatch. The first of these was a capital crime. The offence with Francis apparently took place on 2 October 1738 in a cellar under a house owned by Gray in Church Lane. The cellar was fitted up as a 'Common Cellar ... (that is available to general access) ... for Selling Wine by Retail with Boxes and Seats therein for the Accommodation of persons coming there to Drink'. The act was overheard (not seen) by one John Wright. For the three weeks before the prosecution commenced, a whispering campaign was bruited about the town and attempts were made to secure other witnesses to like acts by Gray. Wright was heard to gloat that he could make £500 out of the matter as well as gaining his revenge on the 'Rich Old Rogue' for an earlier dispute over a house he leased from Gray.

Wright had a lawyer, Jeremiah Howlett, a man apparently fully alive to the possibilities for leverage and manipulation. He bragged around the town, 'We Catcht Them and declared that he and Wright were concerned in the Prosecutions and that if they did not come down Handsomely they would blow them, but if they would come down Handsomely they should hear no more of it.' These remarks were reported in Gray's support by leading Whig tradesmen James Thorn, Benjamin Dikes and Edward Jones. Dikes claimed to have been threatened with a subpoena after resisting a bribe. Howlett used the Old Three Crowns Inn as a meeting place. John Graves, the innkeeper apparently told him, 'Jere, You are very busey in Troubling yourself about Mr Gray and I believe if You would speak the Truth this Affair is a contrivance of Yourself and Wright's to get Money out of the Alderman,' upon which Howlett promised that 'in Case he could get any Money of the Alderman he ... (Wright) ... should have half of it'. Howlett summoned potential witnesses to the Three Crowns and offered ten guineas for evidence against Gray. Although John Bumstead refused to swear to an earlier remark that Gray had reached inside his breeches, Howlett did find a willing witness in John Blatch.[2]

Blatch, like Wright, was a rower and may have been a connection of the Tory alderman of the same name. He swore out an indictment for 'assault with intent to commit'. This applied to two offences, one committed on Mersea Island two years earlier and the second in St Peters parish, Colchester a few days later when (said Blatch) Gray had beat and ill-treated him for refusing sex. Blatch was later somewhat discredited by two witnesses to the Mersea trip who held that both parties were in their sight all day and secondly that the occasion took place six not two years ago. Nevertheless, Blatch's evidence, complete with close anatomical detail, was repeated on the several occasions the case was heard, read out in the Colchester Assembly and cried about the town.[3] Gray and Francis provided recognisances of £200 apiece, and

---

2 JBB BD/870 for James Thorn, grocer and clockmaker, BD/481 for Edward Jones, grocer. Benjamin Dikes was a Quaker and father of wine merchant, Thomas Dikes. See BD/250 for Rose Dikes. These were substantial tradesmen. John Graves was innkeeper at the Old Three Crowns and thus a near neighbour of Thorn and Jones.

3 The original Borough Sessions indictments (Epiphany 1739, see n. 1 above) included one for assault with intent brought by a weaver Samuel Kettle, which was not pursued into the higher courts. Wright, Blatch and Kettle put up £100 recognisance each to appear and give evidence. All the indictments were found at that sessions, but the matter was outside the competence of the

two sureties for each put up £100 a man. At Chelmsford Assizes in August 1739 Gray and Francis were found guilty. On 13 February 1740 the corporation expelled Gray from the aldermen's bench. In his presence the articles of complaint, extending over several ponderous pages, were again read out in full bringing the sexed body into rhetorical visibility in the civic arena of the Moot Hall and inscribing it into the written record.[4] Gray and his friends submitted detailed grounds for a pardon to the Crown via Secretary of State, Newcastle, which was granted after a further hearing at King's Bench that summer. It was a political act when Gray, armed with his pardon and a writ of Mandamus from King's Bench demanded the corporation reinstate him. In an assembly of the mayor, corporation and all freeburgesses a vote was forced on the issue and delay procured by requiring the mayor to take legal advice. Gray obtained a second Mandamus early in 1741, though events were overtaken by the final collapse of the corporation and the order was never implemented.[5]

Gray supporters named in the sources for the case almost invariably voted Whig. James Weatherly (surety for Thomas Francis) voted Tory in 1735 but Whig in 1741. Whatever the opinions and practices of the eighteenth-century male middling sort, it can have been no light matter to give evidence or stand a very expensive surety in support of an accused sodomite. Locating the nineteen Colchester individuals identified with the case in the 1735 and 1741 borough polls, ten Gray supporters (including Thomas Francis) voted Whig. Of these, Thorn and Jones both traded from shops at the upper end of the High Street near the Three Crowns. Thorn was agent for the property sale when Graves' wife sold up the business after his death in 1742. The sources identify more pro-Gray individuals, since the prosecutor's evidence does not survive in detail and the voting record of the anti-Grays is less clear cut. John Wright, the prosecutor, was a Whig voter. The lease that was the original cause of grievance between Wright and Gray had therefore been granted from one Whig to another, and the Tories did not garner his vote in 1741 when the case was still a live issue. Jeremiah Howlett and his father Jeremiah both voted Tory in 1735. A Jeremiah Howlett did, however, vote Whig in 1741. At the same time as the Gray affair, Howlett jnr was also contesting a bastardy order brought against him by St Nicholas vestry before the magistrates' bench of Tory aldermen, a case in which he was eventually successful. This might have soured his attachment to the Tories. At any rate he left Colchester in the early 1740s. Of the five non-voters recorded in the Gray case, four were pro-Gray and one, John Blatch the prosecutor, was against him.[6]

The Gray case is therefore largely explicable as a political manoeuvre. In the prevailing state of local politics, the prosecution was a concerted initiative to bring

---

3 *cont.*

borough court for sentencing. The next sessions, Easter 1739, an officer of King's Bench appeared with two writs to remove the case to the higher court. NA KB 28/150/21, Trinity 13 Geo II, 1739, for Gray's plea of not guilty.

4 Gray's sureties were Cornelius Bogard (JBB BD/89), and Samuel Todd the elder (JBB BD/883), both shopkeepers, and both prosperous Whig non-conformists. Francis' sureties were James Purkes, innholder and Joseph Weatherley, bricklayer.

5 NA SP 36/50/377; KB 28/155/41 Trinity 13 Geo II, June 1740 and KB 28/156/30 Hilary 14 Geo II, January–February, 1741; Assembly Book, ERO D/B 5 Gb7 22 October 1740.

down the alderman. Gray submitted '... that the Prosecutors were encouraged by a Party Interest to Distress ... (him) ... and that they carried on their Prosecutions to make Gain of him'. The refusal of the Mandamus to restore him to office underlined that this was (or rapidly became) a party matter. Gray had been Borough Chamberlain between 1719 and 1725 and was part of the committee appointed in 1713 to sell freedoms to finance the (Whig) corporation's legal expenses. His fall must have seemed particularly sweet to the embattled Tories of 1740.[7] There is no direct evidence that the prosecution was directly organised by Tory aldermen. If Gray and his attorney William Daniel had any hard evidence of a Tory fabrication I doubt they would have scrupled to use it. Gray's petition disputed the fact of the first assault on Blatch at Mersea, but no evidence was brought to contradict the accusation of the second. Neither were any protestations of innocence made over the overheard incident with Francis. The pardon submission argues on legal technicalities only.[8]

There does seem to have been some sexual activity behind the scandal. It is hardly likely that Gray and Francis were the only homosexuals among the Colchester middling sort, and something of that sexual culture is made visible.[9] The sexual relations involved were between an older, richer man and a younger man. Nevertheless, their relationship does not closely accord either with Trumbach's 'pre-1700', model of sex between an adult man and a teenage boy, nor with the succeeding pattern he argues for, that of sex between a man and an effeminate sodomite – Thomas Francis was after all a married man and a father.[10] Between Gray and Francis sexual relations seem to have been part of a much more extensive

---

6 Howlett worked for attorney William Mayhew, for whose leadership of the campaign to regain the Borough Charter in the 1750s see below. The two co-witnessed two wills proved in the archdeaconry courts; Joseph Wheeley, ERO D/ABR 22/113, 1738; Samuel Mahalon, ERO D/ABR 22/178, 1738. He was called before borough sessions repeatedly from Epiphany 1737 on a long-standing dispute over a bastardy order, Borough Sessions Book ERO D/B 5 Sb5/3. He denied paternity of Mary Merring's illegitimate child and refused to pay up. His own recognisance was set at £40. His father stood surety for him of £20. He eventually won the case at King's Bench, Easter 1740, NA IND1/6658/163 not in relevant roll, KB 28/153, Easter 13 Geo II, 1740. Manuscript poll book for Colchester 1747 election in Colchester Public Library, E. Col 1 324.241.

7 L.C. Sier, 'Charles Gray, MP, of Colchester', *Essex Review*, 57 (1948), p. 17.

8 NA SP 36/50/377 argues that the joint indictment deprived Gray and Francis of the benefit of each other's evidence. Secondly Wright is said not to have any case since he did not actually *see* the act in question but merely *heard* sounds which gave him to believe that such an act was in progress.

9 R. Trumbach, 'London's sodomites; homosexual behaviour and western culture in the eighteenth century', *Journal of Social History*, 11 (1977), pp. 1–34, especially p. 21; R. Trumbach, *Sex and the gender revolution, volume 1, heterosexuality and the third gender in enlightenment London* (Chicago, 1998), T. Hitchcock, *English sexualities, 1700–1800* (Basingstoke, 1997).

10 R. Trumbach, 'Sex, gender, and sexual identity in modern culture – male sodomy and female prostitution in enlightenment London', *Journal of the History of Sexuality*, 2 (1991), pp. 186–203; Trumbach briefly summarises his position in R. Trumbach, 'Review of *Sexual suspects: eighteenth-century players and sexual ideology* by Kristina Straub', *Eighteenth-Century Studies*, 26 (1992–3), pp. 342–6 here, pp. 343–4; for a recent overview see K. Harvey, 'The century of sex? Gender, bodies, and sexuality in the long eighteenth century', *Historical Journal*, 45 (2002), pp. 899–916, here pp. 908–11.

relationship. Francis was Gray's tenant; both families came from the nearby village of Nayland and when Gray died in 1747 his will makes no mention whatever of his (Tory and very respectable) son Charles Gray and leaves the greater part of his property to Francis' son George who, of course, shared Gray's Christian name.[11] The location of sexual activity in a 'common' drinking venue or in the great outdoors, and with other men nearby relates it to other kinds of homosocial leisure. This kind of sex was neither heavily concealed nor strictly private. The suggestions by Blatch of physical violence, whether or not factual, were plausible because they reflected something about the power differentials within sexual relationships and the dominant man's use of violence to underline sexual and social authority.

Gray and Francis never denied the sexual activity but defended themselves by asserting that

> THE CHARACTERS of the Def^{ts} were supported not only by a Certificate sign^{d} by forty Persons but by the Affidavits of several Persons that they were Sober Good Men and had behaved with great credit in all their Dealings and without any Colour or Suspicion of any Vicious practice.

Culpability lay less in a man's sexual practice than in his social credit and general reputation. The uses of sexual matters as the ground for political scandal is a historically recurrent phenomenon, and the sexualised language of political insult was a feature of the period. By robbing Gray of the capacity of political action the scandal constituted him as unmanly. Nevertheless this was not the same thing as punishing him for sexual effeminacy. Among middling provincial circles in the 1730s, homosexual practice does not seem to have constituted a defining sexual identity.[12]

The Gray case also gives a comparatively rare glimpse into how such interests were orchestrated, the role of inns as venues for all kinds of organisation (and plotting) as well as the importance of gossip and geographically very localised chatter. The evidence here is partial, of course, as it comes from Gray's supporters, but the social context of the incriminating remarks these witnesses attributed to Wright and Howlett has the believability necessary for the evidence itself to carry weight. It is also rare to see such a comparatively minor figure as Jeremiah Howlett at work and salient that his methods seem not dissimilar from those employed by the higher status political managers seen operating in the following two case studies.

The clamours of the people: William Mayhew, 1747–63

Attorney William Mayhew became a key player in the charter campaign by working up an independent political interest which he used to bargain with parliamentary candidates in return for their undertaking to secure a new borough charter. Mayhew was a Tory who learned his politics before the '45. He was a flamboyant figure who

---

11 L.C. Sier, 'The ancestry of Charles Gray', *Essex Review*, 59 (1950), p. 92; NA PROB 11/755, proved 29 July 1747.

12 J. Weeks, *Sex, politics and society; the regulation of sexuality since 1800* (London, 1989); M. McCormack, 'The new militia; war, politics and gender in 1750s Britain', *Gender and History*, 19 (2007), pp. 403–500, here p. 484; P. Carter, '"An effeminate" or "efficient" nation? Masculinity and eighteenth-century social documentary', *Textual Practice*, 11 (1997), pp. 429–43, here pp. 430–1.

with evident relish badgered, flattered, bullied and cajoled his parliamentary betters in the name of the popular interest, until at last a new reign and political compromise in Colchester brought a new charter.[13] Mayhew used a discourse of political rights to engage the support of the free burgesses. The political importance of arcane institutions to wider political struggles is also evident, in this case the Treasurers of the Common Lands.

After the debacle of 1742 it was virtually a new generation of local politicians who fought the 1747 general election. Charles Gray (Tory) and John Olmius (Whig), both veterans of the 1741 campaign, chose to stand together, hoping to gain their seats without a contest. Their plan was upset, however, by Richard Savage Nassau, a Whig who stood on a campaigning platform of 'A New Charter and No Compromise', in the interest of his uncle the Earl of Rochford (seated at St Osyth). William Mayhew supported Nassau and Gray who topped the poll, instead of the Gray-Olmius compromise.[14]

By 1749 and with no charter forthcoming, Mayhew approached Nassau with an interest evidenced by a petition of 200 signatures (claiming to be able to raise 500 more), asking that he obtain the charter. Charles Gray, a proscribed Tory tinged with Jacobitism, had no pull at Westminster. Nassau replied crossly that he was surprised to hear from Mayhew, whom he did not number among his friends and felt the approach presumptuous as the attorney was not among the town's 'principal Burgesses'. Mayhew was nettled. He replied:

> Who the Princ^{l} Burgesses were of y^{r} Friends, I couldn't distinguish, besides principal persons are not the persons immediately aggrieved, for that reason not so ready to apply for a proper remedy.[15]

He reminded Nassau of the support he and his interest had proffered him at the last election and challenged his honour over election promises about the charter, never alas committed to paper. Mayhew clearly had some interest to poll already in 1747 but was outside the elite Whig circle around Nassau. He was probably then acting principally for Gray and had the second vote of Tory burgesses to retail to Nassau, rather than the unsatisfactory regime Whig, John Olmius. Colchester Tories were adapting to post-1745 political realities and the aftermath of their 1741 defeat. The need was for bargaining and persuasion. Nevertheless, Mayhew drew a blank with Nassau. The correspondence ended and Nassau, apparently a poor attender at the Commons, took the matter no further. His conduct appears to have upset his Whig friends too, and he did not stand again. However, Mayhew and the local Tories, and standing behind them the proscribed Gray, were not about to let the issue drop.[16]

---

13 J. Bensusan Butt, *When Gainsborough painted a Colchester attorney* (Colchester, privately printed, 1978); J. Bensusan Butt, 'A friend to his country: William Mayhew and the recovery of the Colchester charter, 1763', *Essex Archaeology and History*, 18 (1987), pp. 63–74.

14 R. Romney Sedgwick, *The history of parliament: the House of Commons, 1715–1754* (London, 1971), Vol. 2, p. 289, for Nassau; *IpsJ* 20 June 1747; Mayhew to Nassau, 14 October 1749, in J. Bensusan Butt, *A friend to his country* (privately printed version, Colchester, 1972), p. 15.

15 Bensusan Butt, *A friend* (1972).

16 L. Colley, *In defiance of oligarchy; the Tory party 1714–60* (Cambridge, 1982), Chapter 10.

In 1750, a few months after Mayhew's last letter to Nassau, the Charter Club was founded. This association of burgesses in support of a new charter, met at the King's Head Inn. The Charter Club's popular Tory rhetoric of ancient rights and privileges was a constitutionalist call to middling and artisan burgesses to defend their position against a section of property holders. According to a Charter Club Bulletin, 'to Acquaint the *Publick* as to why the *Burgesses* desire a charter' (my emphasis), a charter would give them various powers and institutions so that:

> ... their Estates, their Rights of Common, their Markets, their Tolls, their Quit-rents, their Charities, their Freedoms, their Exemptions, their Fines on Delinquents; and all other their prescriptive and customary Rights, will be preserved and protected.[17]

Without a charter, cash and land value benefits on corporation property, 'to the Amount of £1,000 a Year' fell into pockets not entitled to them, tenants of Borough estates (shopkeepers and Hythe merchants) were excused their rents and were accused of making huge profits pulling down buildings and selling materials, baymakers benefiting from White's Charity monies did not repay the loans, half year land holders were enclosing their lands and vastly increasing their worth. 'Those who dread the Day of Accounting cry out for Peace and Quiet, and no Charter.'[18]

The distinction between the public and the burgesses harmonises with (though it does not replicate) Isaac Slythe's distinction between 'the County' and his family (Chapter 3) and milliner Elizabeth Shillito's contrasting her friends (favoured customers) with the public (Chapter 4). There was never any finite definition or any absolute separation between public and private, but there were innumerable social and rhetorical situations where distinctions were made between the insides and outsides of specific interest groups, networks or institutions. These various 'outsides' hardly amounted to a Habermasian public sphere – they themselves were multiple and overlapping. They did, however, provide a cultural terrain in which there was the potential for public opinion to develop.

There was no distinct socioeconomic divide between pro- and anti-charter factions; many affluent middling traders and leading baymakers were Tories. Pro-charter burgesses were also described as 'having estates'. However, rights over property were bunched together with rights to a local court, to elect officials and MPs to produce a package with which the whole socioeconomic range of voters could identify, to the most indifferent artisan. Add this to the decay of the town fabric that Morant laments, the additional expense incurred and revenue lost to the town through losing its market tolls and subjecting itself to County administration based twenty

17 Bensusan Butt, 'A friend', (1987). White's Charity arose from a bequest to help the woollen industry in numbers of English towns, who received in rotation an annual sum of £25. The slowly accumulating stock of £25 bequests were then lent out on bond for ten-year terms to various bay traders. Bonds could be called in and the money lent to different individuals, but in fact they seem to have been frequently renewed. The charity was administered in Colchester by the corporation and had the effect of increasing the stock of circulating capital within the trade. Morant, *Colchester*, book 3, p. 180. See for example the Assembly Book for 18 May 1733, ERO D/B 5 Gb7, where twelve bonds were renewed and twenty-one new loans made. Three bonds were called in but two of these were immediately replaced by a new loan.

18 Bensusan Butt,'A friend', (1987).

miles distant, not to mention many offices and perquisites that borough organisation could distribute among middling and artisan burgesses, and a constitutionalist campaigning platform of strength emerges.[19]

The advertisement which invited signatures to Mayhew's original petition, while rehearsing these grievances, also lamented the loss of benefit to the burgesses through 'a valuable fishery incroached upon and made common', the loss of grazing rights, 'our cattle are impounded, and no redress to be had', the loss of borough freedom to sons and apprentices and for good measure, 'Our Markets spoiled by Forestallers, Regrattors and Ingrossers'.[20] The identity constructed of the outraged burgess is defined by his rights as a small middling or artisan producer, practising a mixed domestic economy where grazing and fishing rights were important, planning to hand on the business and lifestyle to the next generation and beset by landowners and market entrepreneurs. Such rhetoric blurred the edges of reality for many burgesses, where the declining wool trade was polarising the town's socioeconomic profile, where the half-year grazing was a racket run by a clique of butchers and victuallers, where demographic shifts were already beginning to show up in the declining ratio of Colchester to country and London freeburgesses. Nevertheless lived (or imagined) experience for many middling and artisan burgesses was close enough to this image for it to be an effective rallying call. Colchester's more affluent citizens could operate within county circles and institutions, though they would, of course, corner leading borough positions when available. The loss of the charter above all circumscribed the public role of the smaller man, and it was to him that Mayhew's populist rhetoric appealed. The charter campaign developed the populist stance of the proscribed Tory grouping which lost political impetus and local leadership in the early 1740s. By appealing to the burgesses as a whole (in 1752 the Charter Club was keen to insist that it was not a 'Party Cause') it moved local politics away from the pre-1742 parameters and into a more ambiguous mid-century configuration.[21]

Mayhew's Charter Club was an active presence in Colchester politics as the 1754 election approached. Nationally, both the Jew Bill and the Militia question focused anxieties over national identity, articulated as failures in the gender order.[22] In November 1753 Tory Charles Gray addressed a Charter Club meeting to protest at the Jew Bill.[23] In July 1752 the King's Head Club solicited the attendance of young men not yet registered as freemen at the club every second Monday of the month, to test the size of their interest and 'induce some worthy commoner to bring us a Charter'. In 1753, Isaac Martin Rebow, a young and untried candidate though with exemplary family credentials in Colchester Whig politics, put up against the Gray/Olmius compromise. His campaign accounts show twelve months campaigning organised by a group of non-conformist Whig tradesmen, including that James Thorn who had

---

19 Morant, *Colchester,* book 1, p. 71.

20 *IpsJ* 14 October 1749.

21 *Ibid.*

22 McCormack, 'The new militia'.

23 *IpsJ* 11 August and 17 November 1753.

supported the sodomitical alderman a decade earlier.[24] Mayhew and the Charter Club responded to Rebow's early campaigning in May 1753 with *An Alarum to the Freemen of Colchester ag^{t} Charter Cookery*. This pamphlet warned the freemen that there were plans to petition for a renovated charter which would alter the terms of the old one. It complained,

> If we desire Guardians to our Community let us have them from the best and most experienced of the resident Burgesses not from the dreggs of the people to make the Body deformed, ragged and contemptible – Thus to act will shew you are not the Scoundrells some modern Gent^{n} are pleased to call you, to be purchased at an hours warning by money & drink for any Vile purpose; but men of the generous Mastiffs Quality in the Fable – who can refuse bread from those who attempt to stop your Clamour for an Opportunity to plunder your families.[25]

The burgesses were addressed as resident householders of independent political capability, defending their rights and their families. They were members of a corporate Body which once tall, straight and tested by time, will become deformed through corrupt manipulation. McCormack dates a widening of those social groups who could associate themselves with the idea of political independence to the later eighteenth century.[26] In a popular constituency such as Colchester the Charter campaign was already deliberately including the poorer burgesses in the early 1750s. What exactly was the reform which would lead to the ascendancy of the 'dreggs of the people' is more ambiguous. It is unthinkable that any Whiggish mid-eighteenth-century gentleman such as Isaac Martin Rebow should advocate a really democratic system of borough government. Presumably this was Mayhew's spin on a proposal for something like a £5 or £10 rate-payer franchise which would include the affluent traders and gentry who were not free and exclude the poor artisans who were.

Parliamentary candidates Charles Gray and John Olmius were wary of the Charter Club. Its interest was significant but not sufficient to stop the Rebow campaign. The Club wanted a compromise with both Gray and Olmius committed to regaining the charter on its old terms, but they preferred to stand 'single', which let second votes stray to Rebow. Nevertheless the Club declared itself stoutly for Gray and Olmius and against 'Charter Cookery' and Rebow. By July, 1753 the Rebow interest had opened their own Freemen's Club. It met at the King's Arms in the High Street and ran up bills for entertainment, ribbons from milliner Mary Walford (whose kin voted Whig) and a band to play at the hustings.[27]

By the 1750s Mayhew was a political player of some experience. He had been sadly disappointed in the earlier MP's (Nassau's) conduct and told him so in no uncertain terms. His tactics with Olmius, again across party, were even more forthright and original. He laid a wager with Olmius, 500 guineas to one that Olmius

---

24 Rebow Papers, ERO, Box 2, T/A 491/1.

25 Handbill of 7 May 1753, quoted in Bensusan Butt, *A friend* (1972), p. 16.

26 McCormack, *Independent man*, Chapter 5.

27 See n. 25 above. For the events of this campaign see: *IpsJ* 18 May, 4 and 11 August, 15 September, 6, 13 and 20 October, 17 November, 8 December 1753; 23 and 30 March, 6, 13 and 20 April, 11 May 1754.

would either *not* be elected or, if elected would *not* be petitioned against within fourteen days. In effect this meant that Olmius could buy the support of the Charter Club interest (and by implication his seat) at a bargain price (Rebow's campaign cost him £1,251). If he lost the election Olmius would have reduced his expenses by 500 guineas. If he won the election he lost the wager and the Charter Club were 500 guineas better off to continue their campaign. To be sure of retaining the 500 guineas the Club had to see him returned at the top of the poll to avoid a petition. In other words, Mayhew, who also had Gray's interests to defend, was gambling on beating Rebow into third place. Hence, a popular Tory local interest, clearly without the strength to bring in a second Tory and unsure of its ability to return Gray at the top of the poll, sought to influence a Whig candidate to secure the Charter in its old form.[28]

A Charter Club pamphlet of 17 January 1754 referred directly back to Isaac Rebow's eponymous ancestor who had a hand in procuring the earlier charter from William and Mary, yet at corporation expense, implying that the younger Rebow would not pay his share towards any new petition.

> IX: If 'tis likely, THE SETT OF PEOPLE who OBLIGED an Hon Gentleman ... (Nassau) ... to *Drop his undertaking* to PROCURE A CHARTER and loose His Seat in Parliament rather than suffer Him to PERFORM IT should, with Mr R-B-W at their Head endeavour to procure it?

> X: Who were the persons broke in upon that CHARTER *pretended to be restored by Mr R-B-W's ever memorable* Ancestor; *and* DEPRIVED You all of your RIGHTS & PRIVILEGES for these Twelve Years last past?

The Charter Club were reviving memories of 1741 when Rebow's in-laws (the Martins and the Prices) made sure the Tories lost the election and accusing the same group of dissuading the 1747 MP, Nassau from securing a new charter.[29]

The Rebow party replied in biblical parody; *The First Chapter of the Second Epistle of Elections* imagines the 1754 poll culminating in the triumph of the Young Man from the East (Rebow) over the Old Man (Gray). The old man's party (The Charter Club) composed of the Chief Priests, Lawyers and Tradesmen of Colchester had sold the town for 500 pieces of gold to a wealthy Man from the West (Olmius). By corruption the Old Man won at the scrutiny:

> And it came to pass, when they had quite done, that they put their darling old man into a chair, and carried him through the streets of the town, with musick and dancing: as if they had obtained an honourable victory.[30]

---

28 Bensusan Butt, *A friend* (1972), p. 8.

29 ERO, Morant Papers, D/Y 2/2, p. 349. Local historian G.O. Rickwood interpreted the 1754 election as 'probably a trial of strength between the rival local families of Creffield and Rebow'. G.O. Rickwood, 'The Members of Parliament for Colchester, 1747–1830', *Essex Review*, 8 (1899), p. 227. Charles Gray was backed by his in-laws, the Tory Creffields. The Charter Club understood clearly the continuing interest which was behind the Whig machinations in 1741 when Rebow's maternal grandfather, Matthew Martin and Olmius were candidates, and his relatives the Price brothers, Robert (the recorder) and John, had a hand in managing the election. The pamphlet blames this group for ending Nassau's attempts, however half-hearted, to procure a charter after 1747.

30 ERO, Morant Papers, D/Y 2/2, p. 351.

However, the Young Man triumphed on petition before the 'judges and rulers of the people' and the Old Man 'was seized with horror; insomuch that he could not look this excellent young man in the face' and returned home in shame. For the Rebow party, the chief threat was not Olmius (who disassociated himself from the Charter Club)[31] but Gray. Gray hid behind the Charter Club who used the language of rights and privileges to construct an ostensibly cross-party interest round the issue of the charter, but were in fact utilising the oppositional stance of popular Toryism. The next Charter Club pamphlet blamed a faction of 'Brewers, Distillers, Tavern and Alehousekeepers' (presumably a reference to Rebow's campaign managers Samuel Todd and Thomas Kendall) who dulled the burgesses' sensibilities with drink to the detriment of their families.[32] The iconic Charter Club burgess, the honest freeborn Englishman of small property, was inevitably always a family man.

The rather dangerous game that Mayhew and the King's Head Club were playing, trying to secure Gray *and* Olmius and protesting their stand to be one of issue politics across party lines, finally came unstuck at the polls where Olmius came first (so Mayhew won the 500-guinea wager) but Gray was last. A scrutiny based on the dubious and mutilated borough records reversed Gray's and Rebow's position, the result of which was again up-ended on petition. Gray was out and the Charter Club were faced with Olmius, his equivocal support secured mainly on his promissory note and Rebow, the advocate of Charter Cookery.[33]

The election contest was further enlivened by riot. The town's historian, Philip Morant, was the Colcestrian most likely to have at his fingertips the details of the borough's 'Antient Rights and Privileges'. Notes survive for his letters to Lord Hardwicke explaining the events and legal precedents for a 1753 dispute over the burgesses' half-year grazing rights. Part of the half-year lands was owned by Hardwicke. Burgesses' grazing rights between harvest and planting meant that the land should remain unenclosed. When extant, the corporation officials enforced these rights and collected fines. This policing, notoriously corrupt, had ended with the lapse of the charter in 1742. By the 1750s, few burgesses had cattle to graze and a few butchers and graziers ran the business to suit themselves. The farmers were, of course, keen to enclose.[34] As the election approached, some burgesses had taken legal opinion of William Daniel, the Whig attorney (probably pro-Olmius). He drew up a case on which Tory lawyer George Wegg refused to comment. Morant represents the grazier burgesses as corrupt thugs and racketeers extinguishing the rights of poor tenant farmers 'most of them low in the world'. The grazing right operated from Lammas Day to 2 February. With the calendar change in 1752, Lammas Day had

---

31 *IpsJ* 13 and 20 October 1753. Without the poll book it is impossible to assess the size of Olmius' independent interest. Certainly, there are several crucial broker names missing from the Rebow faction. William Daniel (JBB/BD 220) the lawyer and political manager for the Whigs in 1741 and all his baymaker and attorney relations as well as Michael Hills (JBB BD/446), another clothier, are conspicuous by their absence. Just before the poll the 'Freemen in the Interest of John Olmius' were requested to meet at several inns to process to the hustings, *IpsJ* 13 April 1754.

32 ERO, Morant Papers, D/Y/2/2, p. 349.

33 *IpsJ* 20 April 1754.

34 ERO D/Y 2/2, p. 349–58. These officials were the Treasurers and Drivers of the Common Lands.

moved from 1 to 12 August, yet the graziers insisted on continuing to turn out cattle on the *new* 1 August, when necessary into standing corn.[35] This incident involves a complex of offended rights of both burgesses and farmers, of electoral politics and of cynical popular attitudes to the calendar change.[36]

The source leaves the issue of party ambiguous, though the matter may have been inspired or abetted by the Olmius faction. Against this background, Mayhew's best bet of obtaining a charter was to work on Olmius, whose unpaid promissory note he held. Mayhew's style was at first expansive if direct:

> If Gentlemen had rather spend two or three Thousand Pounds in an Election and forfeit their Character, rather than assist them in their Request MERRY be their HEARTS, and let them be gone. But if they have a Mind to enjoy the Borough in Peace and quietness, let them join in getting a Charter, and I will heartily assist.[37]

After a further fruitless two years of waiting Mayhew was clearly out of patience: 'Nothing renders a man so despicable as the breach of his promise ... If I hear not soon from you, I shall give directions ... (to submit an independent petition) ... and place it to the Account of your Note.' And a few months later:

> You are out of the hearing of the clamours of the people. You publickly assured them you w^{d} use y^{r} utmost Endeav^{rs} to procure them a Charter. Myself and all your Agents by your Permission gave them the same Assurances. We are affronted we are used ill because you don't use any Endeavours towards getting them the thing you promised.[38]

Mayhew's power had limits. Olmius replied in a huff, but he was now prepared to take action. He met privately with Rebow and they agreed to set a Charter petition in motion. However, Mayhew's prestige was dented for this news was communicated not to him but to Phillip Havens, prosperous Quaker baymaker and one of the Rebow party. Mayhew's response, watchful as ever for Charter Cookery, was to reiterate the Club's intention of voting against any reformed charter. The freemen retained a final power of veto. Acrimonious correspondence between Mayhew and Olmius indicate the extent of the rift. Eventually two petitions were sent, apparently one 'cooked' and the other original. Rebow's power base as a sitting MP was enough for him to bargain successfully for his party's measures.

The Privy Council's lengthy deliberations were abridged by the death of George II. The new reign brought (at last) an Irish peerage for John Olmius. In the 1761 election, Rebow and Gray, having jointly promised a charter to the King's Head Club, were returned unopposed. Colchester's compromise period had begun. A fresh charter petition made some attempt to iron out the question of aldermen's majorities in the election of mayors that ended the corporation in 1741, though this was not pressed seriously by either MP and the amendment was lost. It seems that as the price of a cheap, unopposed election Rebow had abandoned any serious plans to reform the

35 *Ibid.*, Morant to Hardwicke on 19 October 1753.

36 R. Poole, *Time's alteration: calendar reform in early modern England* (London, 1998).

37 Mayhew to Olmius, 12 May 1755, quoted in Bensusan Butt, *A friend* (1972), p. 21. See also Mayhew to Olmius of 20 August 1757, *Ibid.*, p. 22.

38 *Ibid.*, p. 10.

charter and at last, in 1763, Colchester received its new charter in the precise form of the old. The town celebrated.[39]

The charter campaign demonstrates how a political interest required careful husbanding over time as well as the complexity of politics with a two-vote franchise, and how electioneering widened to involve riots over the half-year lands. At mid-century the popular Tory constituency used the language of political rights as well as local organisation to maintain political effectiveness during the years of proscription.

Although the eighteenth-century political system demanded the mobilisation of extensive resources to acquire power, the middling sort nevertheless played a crucial role organising the spending of candidates' money. Managers such as William Mayhew carved out political space within the constraints of the local contest and the national disposition of political power. Husbanding political interests was a face-to-face business. Campaign managers knew the voters they canvassed. They provided the treats and also lent financial assistance to candidates through short-term credit. Colchester sources show how political choice and social connection were linked – in the prosecution of George Gray for sodomy in 1740 or the fact that Rebow's campaign managers in 1754 were predominantly non-conformist.[40] The following section pursues these arguments into the later eighteenth century, past the decades of superficial calm and qualified co-operation under the Compromise between Rebow and Gray. Thereafter, as the Compromise weakened and broke, new configurations of local party began to coalesce around the rising generation of political managers.

Points to be carried: Francis Smythies and the Free School election, 1779

In January 1779 the burgesses elected a new Master of Colchester Free (Grammar) School. The school stood in All Saints parish behind the church. It arose from an Elizabethan endowment of real estate including the Three Crowns Inn. This was an extensive property at the top of Head Street facing down the High Street. In 1707 the properties had been transferred to trustees so that the schoolmaster should have the benefit of the rents. The first trustees were an august body of gentry and local notables.[41] In the 1760s two landed local gentry, two town gentry (Mayhew and Gray)

---

39 Namier and Brooke, *The history of parliament, 1754–1790,* Vol. 1, pp. 276–8; Vol. 2, p. 535; Vol. 3, p. 350; Bensusan Butt, 'A friend', (1987), pp. 71–2.

40 S. D'Cruze, *The middling sort,* pp. 372, 405–6.

41 The trustees were: Sir William Luckin bart. Messing, Sir Isaac Rebow kt., Joseph Thurstan, Hope Gifford, John Potter, Nathaniel Lawrence jnr, Thomas Ruse, G. Martin, *The history of Colchester Royal Grammar School* (Colchester, 1947). The primary sources for the Free School election are in the Trustees records, ERO Acc. C16, Trunk 1 unless otherwise cited. The pamphlets and handbills are: 1, *To the freeburgesses of Colchester,* Colchester, 17 November 1778; 2, *To the freeburgesses of Colchester,* this being the address by the trustees signed by Charles Gray, Michael Hills, Samuel Todd, Peter Daniell; 3, *An address to the free burgesses of Colchester in answer to the address from the trustees of the school estate,* Colchester, 9 December 1778; 4, *To the freeburgesses of Colchester,* Colchester, 16 December 1778; 5, *To the freeburgesses of Colchester,* signed by 'A Freeman and a Lover of Truth', Colchester, 26 December 1778; 6, *A fourth address to the freeburgesses of Colchester,* Colchester, 28 December 1778; 7, *An address to the*

and a number of town tradesmen manned the trust. There were equal numbers of non-conformists and Anglicans.[42] By the 1770s, however, only a rump of the previously named Trustees were active. The gentry absented themselves. The trust properties were managed by the Daniell family of lawyers and Charles Gray, with other non-conformist businessmen summoned to form a quorum as required. Dissenting attorney Peter Daniell, the secretary, was at the heart of the administration. This was an odd alliance for Gray, who stayed on presumably both because he was an ex-pupil and because the school was in his home parish.[43]

The cash value of the trust had declined; in the 1720s the Three Crowns lease had been sold for £1,000, though by the 1730s it was leased for only £81 a year. A later leaseholder was advertising it for £30 per annum in 1752 and the purchaser was bankrupted in 1758. The inn was apparently being eclipsed by the nearby White Hart, King's Head and the Three Cups, and never traded as such again. When the lease was auctioned in 1759, non-conformist barber Fisher Walford took it for £11 7s. The properties were extensive but in a very poor state of repair.[44] The next generation of Walfords stayed on at the Three Crowns, improved the property, and ran successful cabinet making and millinery businesses from there. Timothy Walford, the Three Crowns lessor was both a non-conformist and brother-in-law to Peter Daniell.[45]

The master of the Free School since 1723 had been Palmer Smythies, rector of St Michael Mile End, master of the Hospital of St Mary Magdalen and father of the town

---

41 *cont.*

freeburgesses of Colchester, occasioned by an address dated, December 26th, 1778, Colchester, 12 January 1779; 8, *To the freeburgesses of Colcheste, a man may buy gold too dear,* Colchester, 13 January 1779. There are also small handbills by Hewitt, the corporation candidate of 26 October 1778 and 12 January 1779 and by his opponent Duddell of 29 October 1778. Pamphlets will be noted here as Pamphlet 1, Pamphlet 3, and so on.

42 As mortality took its toll, in 1727 and again in 1752, the last surviving trustee had re-conveyed the property to new members to replace the full quorum. By 1760 the local gentry interest on the trustees was filled by Hezekiah Haynes Esq. and Thomas Rawstorn of Lexden (JBB BD/680), together with Rawstorn's son-in-law, Lexden rector James Kilner (BD/503). Charles Gray and William Mayhew snr were the town grandees represented. The balance of the members were town lawyers and businessmen, including baymaker Isaac Boggis (BD/1128). Attorneys William Daniel (BD/220) and Peter Daniell (BD/224), Jeremiah Daniell (BD/979), baymakers Philip Havens snr and jnr (BD/415, 416) and Michael Hills (BD/446) as well as distiller Samuel Todd (BD/883) were non-conformist. There were six non-conformists and six Anglicans in 1760.

43 The active Trustees in the 1770s were baymaker Michael Hills, attorneys William Daniel and Peter Daniell and grocer Samuel Todd.

44 Pamphlets 1, 2 and 3; For the Three Crowns, *IpsJ* 1 October 1743, 17 February 1747, 17 December 1748, 23 September 1749, 20 July 1751, 29 December 1753; 22 October 1757; 4 March 1758; 18 March 1758; Trustees papers Box 2 for the auction and lease to Fisher Walford, also *IpsJ* 6 October 1759.

45 They had both married sisters of the Shepherd family, JBB BD/224 and 901. Mary Walford, milliner, operated from the Three Crowns. She and her husband Michael Boyle later manufactured and sold ribbons there, see: *IpsJ* 8 May 1773, 16 January 1783, 8 May and 23 October 1790, 31 October 1795, 5 April 1799, 12 November 1808, 25 March 1809; JBB BD/94 for Michael and Mary Boyle.

clerk. Smythies held the job until his death on Christmas Day of 1776, though he seems to have done little teaching for some time before.[46] On his death the school properties were found to be in need of repair and the trustees tried unsuccessfully to extract the costs of these from Smythies' estate (not an action likely to endear them to Francis Smythies). Eventually the trustees found £40 from their own pockets to make the place presentable for the new master, the well-known scholar Samuel Parr.[47] Parr seems to have accepted the post under the expectation that the rental income would increase as the result of a plan sponsored by the corporation party to take the management of the property directly into the hands of the master. In this case the office of the trustees would become redundant under suspicion of mismanagement. The dispute between Parr and the trustees seems to have arisen quite early on in his tenure and eighteen months later, when even a full-scale hearing in the Moot Hall failed to secure their removal, Parr left for Norwich.[48]

Masters of the Free School were elected by the free burgesses but a contested election for the post was highly unusual. When Parr left, however, lines of conflict were already drawn between the Free School trustees and an emergent new corporation party led by Francis Smythies (then aged 36), allegedly defending the rights of the town's burgesses and the honour of the late master, Smythies' father. The trustees were accused of mismanagement and peculation. The corporation party appropriated the populist cause and the language of rights against the establishment Trustees. The corporation candidate was Charles Hewitt, a Cambridge divine who had been awarded a gold medal for classical scholarship and taught school in Bristol. William Duddell, a more low-church aspirant and married man who had run a school fifteen miles away at Coggeshall, was proposed by the Trustees and supported by the town's opposition and non-conformist groups. Hewitt and the corporation party campaigned partly on a plan to void the lease agreement on the Three Crowns and thus repudiate the action of the trustees and overturn the outcome of the 1778 Moot Hall enquiry. The trustees were defending their own positions as well as Duddell's candidature.

Thus Charles Gray became hopelessly compromised by finding himself among the opposition ranks. Unambiguous Whig and Tory labels are difficult to attribute. The divide was partially high:low church, as the trustees supported evangelical Duddell, partially corporation:opposition along similar lines to the 1768 general election contest (the opposition political manager of 1768, William Seaber was again at work in 1778) and partially Tory:Whig as Charles Gray found himself opposing the corporation officials, nominally at least appointed through Whig MP and recorder, Isaac Rebow. Whig mayor Thomas Clamtree had been in office during the summer and early autumn of 1778 as the dispute between Parr, the departing master, and the trustees moved to its climactic public hearing at the Moot Hall. The corporation party claimed

---

46 Trustees Papers, March 1723. Palmer Smythies' candidacy was opposed by Jeremiah Daniell, Whig alderman, largely on the grounds of his plurality of livings and offices. His assistant at the school was Revd Thomas Twining.

47 L.W. Cowie, 'Parr Samuel (1747–1825)', *Oxford Dictionary of National Biography* (Oxford, 2004), www.oxford.dnb.com/view/article/72236, accessed 9 September 2007.

48 J. Johnstone (ed.), *The works of Samuel Parr LLD,* (London, 1828), Vol. 8.

Parr (known as the Whig Dr Johnson) as one of their own, and he was certainly on friendly terms with their leading actors.[49] On this issue the town's non-conformists no longer supported Isaac Martin Rebow, once the triumphant 'young man' of the 1754 election.

A pamphlet war was waged between the autumn of 1778 and the poll in mid-January 1779. Most of the trustees' pamphlets seem to have been written by Peter Daniell, and the corporation party's by Smythies who derided the Trustees' candidate, Duddell, as 'Methodist, Fanatic, Enthusiast'.[50] In the bad-tempered closing stages of the campaign Smythies was ironical over what he supposed was the Duddell evangelical brand of (true) religion:

> Shall I tell you what *true Religion* is? – It is the religion of the *imagination* and the *passions*, Gentlemen; the religion of long prayers, long sermons, dismal bawling, lamentable tones; – nothing to be heard but sighs and sobs – nothing to be seen but tears, wet handkerchiefs, and whites of eyes; – all *faith*, and no *reason* – all *feeling*, and no *effect*.[51]

How easy it was to paint a methodistical conspiracy between non-conformist lawyer Daniell, low-church Duddell and Daniell's non-conformist brother-in-law, the lessee Walford, with Charles Gray implicated in this plot to deprive honest Anglican free burgesses of their rights. The corporation party's popular Anglicanism was to develop into Pittite Toryism in the 1780s and 90s. The campaign marked Gray's unofficial retirement from public life. He had begun his electioneering life in Colchester as the champion of the popular Tory interest. He was to end it when the victorious corporation party paused in their triumphant progress around the town to halloo and catcall outside his door. He declined to stand in the general election the following year, leaving the field clear for the Whigs, who, albeit briefly, gained both parliamentary seats.[52]

It is difficult to discover the complex and subtle re-patterning of social political networks. What shows most is the emergence of new broker figures. The Free School election brought Smythies into the public arena as a champion of the school, the burgesses and their rights. It proved a milestone in his public career, when he acted unrestrained by the borough grandees. His practice as town clerk had already demonstrated to middling officials that he had a mind and ambitions of his own. The Trustees complained they were 'respectable Men assassinated in the dark; Stung by Secret Calumny and made the butt of a Boy's Ambition'.[53]

The debate over the merits of the candidates revolved around different styles of education. Both clerics were masters of arts and could produce testimonials from their universities and other clergy. The corporation party argued that Hewitt's testimonials came from the higher clergy and were therefore more valuable, but their trump card was his Gold Medal in Classics. Being a grammar school, skill in the classics was vital.

---

49 Walker (ed.), *Thomas Twining*, letter 52, pp. 160–2, Twining to Samuel Parr, January 1779. See also Johnstone (ed.), *Samuel Parr*.

50 Pamphlet 3.

51 Pamphlet 6, pp. 2–3.

52 Twining to Parr, January 1779, see n. 49 above.

53 Pamphlet 4.

The trustees countered with Mr Duddell's superior moral capabilities in guiding the moral development of the town's youth. They cited his wife and children; a moral man was a family man. Instead of the classics, the trustees emphasised the enlightenment virtues of scientific, organised and rational instruction. They argued that education should train the child for a civic role in adulthood. A properly educated adult was 'instructed in the principles of Civil Liberty and religious Love'. What was at stake was not only the individual future of the child but his future social identity as one who should be 'useful to others and to ourselves', and who was part of 'the still increasing ties that bind Society to Society and State to state'. In other words, by combining instruction and morality, the purposes of education were to produce individuals with a public role, citizens it may be added, not only of a 'private' provincial borough but of society and state.[54] By contrast, the corporation party engaged the burgesses' interest in the traditional way, with the prospect of a threat to their rights. The corporation pamphleteer insisted 'that the rights of the school, and of the schoolmaster ... are indeed also your own rights'.[55] These rights were being extinguished by the corruption of the trustees and must be reasserted by exercising the right to vote – for the corporation candidate. These are populist, proprietorial rights akin to the rallying cry of 1741 and 1754. There was clearly a good audience for this argument as the election result proved. In contrast, the Trustees (representatives of the non-conformist middling sort) were moving the discourse onto slightly different ground.

The trustees' last broadside links the familiar trope of rights with Liberty (rather than liberties) in the manner already employed by the opposition in the 1768 election. They accused the corporation party of threatening to turn opposing burgesses out of home or employment (the opposition burgesses, too, were by implication family men); 'Not daring to let every Man exercise that Liberty he is lawfully intitled (sic) to ... they themselves, would (if they could) starve him that dares to oppose *the Body*.' The body corporate had become something corrupt, rather than the upright and wholesome body of freemen imagined by William Mayhew in the 1750s. They continued, 'Nor think it a Compliment due to our Worshipful Governors, that we must always yield passive Obedience and Non-resistance.'[56] At this point the trustees' rhetoric approaches popular radicalism.

The heat of the contest divided the coalition of the trustees and, to the cost of Gray, allowed a more radical voice to emerge which tied in the local debate to wider currents of political thought. It blended the tenets of popular radicalism with a view of citizenship and society which was more comprehensive and widely drawn than the traditional view which linked rights, citizenship and particularism. The new arguments seem to have come from the middling, non-conformist, Whiggish and professional sector in the person of Peter Daniell and his likeminded trustees whose connections can be linked to the radical or reform cause in later decades. While there were those who would make these arguments in Colchester of 1779, there were comparatively few prepared to listen. Interest, the corporation network, the reputation of

---

54 *Ibid.*

55 Pamphlet 1.

56 *Ibid.*

schoolmaster Palmer Smythies, the energetic campaigning of his son, and the old language of rights combined to win the day. Duddell conceded when, with the votes standing 487 to 470 in favour of the corporation candidate, Hewitt, word arrived that 100 more Hewitt voters were on the road.[57]

Smythies' victory parade also stopped to harangue opposition manager William Seaber, who appeared at his first-floor window to acknowledge the attentions of the crowd.[58] In 1768, Seaber had introduced the outsider candidate Alexander Fordyce against the Compromise, and for the first time in Colchester rights had been linked to Liberty rather than liberties. The Compromise had succeeded then, despite strong local opposition support. Just over ten years later, old age and a changing political climate left the Compromise shaken and divided. The corporation party now freely catered to populism, which in 1768 had been an opposition tactic. We do not know the part of the other Whig and corporation grandees in the issue. Rebow (himself an old man), William Mayhew and Ennew (Rebow's man of business) took no part. The struggle for local power nevertheless still seized on every available opportunity for its subject matter. As the corporation pamphleteer explained,

> But why cast reflections on the innocent Trustees? ... They did not, I suppose, take a *bribe*. I believe them. But they must know very little of the motives, which induce men's conduct, who suppose, that money is the sole mover in the mind of a man of law, or of trade. They must know very little of *borough manoeuvres*, who do not know, that there are sometimes *points to be carried*, in which pecuniary considerations are totally out of the question.[59]

We have the word of Thomas Twining, a partisan if acute observer, that the election proved more than commonly divisive among the middling sort and town gentry. As well as the isolation of Gray, the election caused a serious row about money between trustees Peter Daniel and affluent Whig baymaker Michael Hills, which ended any sympathy Hills may have had for the opposition cause.[60] The election may have had longer-term consequences for Peter Daniell. His public status cannot but have been damaged when his candidate was defeated. It is clear from the trustees' accounts that there were no funds to fight an election campaign. Although there is no proven connection, it might be significant that Daniell went bankrupt a few years later.[61]

Conclusion

The hard-fought and sometimes dirty infighting that characterised Colchester local politics in the eighteenth century was no new departure. Corporation politics had been

---

57 *IpsJ* 22, 29 January 1779; see n. 49 above.

58 Twining to Parr, n. 49 above.

59 Pamphlet 3.

60 Twining to Parr, n. 49 above. Michael Hills voted for the Tory candidate Edmund Affleck in the 1781 election.

61 However, the strength of Peter Daniell's local interest is revealed in that he suffered no outright material loss. His practice and property were saved largely by a substantial mortgage granted him by Timothy Walford. No doubt he also drew support from his connection at Lion Walk where he was a trustee and deacon. He practised in Colchester until his death in 1792. JBB BD/224 and 901.

at least as tough in the Stuart period and in other eighteenth-century provincial towns political life similarly lacked magisterial dignity. Colchester politics had two main dimensions, firstly the control of the borough, its institutions, office and perquisites and secondly the scrapping over parliamentary elections. In this large, popular borough, contested elections were comparatively frequent and often hard-fought. Control of the process of election was vested in the corporation, hence control of the corporation meant significant pay-offs. Power and patronage was always a matter of negotiation. Elections were hugely costly and depended on local political managers to get in the vote. Aspiring and sitting members of parliament had to remember their obligations to those who helped them to their seats if they wanted to keep their power base intact. The promulgators of the 1835 Local Government Act (among others) looked back on most eighteenth-century corporations as corrupt and inefficient. If unreformed boroughs could appear shambolic and self-serving, there were nevertheless real gains in terms of power and status as well as in the prestige of the town at stake which could produce hard and sometimes bitter struggles over superficially trivial matters (who taught at the local grammar school) or apolitical (an alderman's sex life) ones.

The energies of the middling sort, as office-holders, burgesses, political managers and (whether voters or not) as partisan observers, gossipers and string-pullers were crucial to the operation of borough politics. Politics conceived as the exercise of rights by independent (manly) citizens both provided a flexible and utile rhetoric for the local struggle, appropriated until the 1760s by the Tory ('Country') opposition, attached for a while by anti-Compromise interests with one ear to the Wilkite agitations in London and then pounced upon by an emerging new corporation party which in the changing political climate of the 1780s and 90s found that rights talk sat comfortably with political virtues realised through Pitt and patriotism. For the (in part non-conformist) Colchester opposition, rights became configured with Reform and Liberty, but this was a rallying cry which came into its own for a brief period only in the early nineteenth century with the career of radical Daniel Whittle Harvey – and then mostly due to his ability to round up the popular radical artisan vote from the London-resident burgesses.[62]

62 A.F.J. Brown, *Colchester 1815–1914* (Chelmsford, 1980).

Chapter 8

Disorder and dependence

Middling disorder

Three overlapping (and now contested) metanarratives have suggested, firstly, that processes of modernisation involved a decline in interpersonal violence.[1] Modern masculinities as well as respectable identities more generally have arguably become more reticent in their uses of interpersonal violence. According to Norbert Elias, developing states sought a monopoly of legitimate violence and elites came to displace their physical aggressiveness into competition for the goods accompanying elite status. According to these arguments, as the state developed criminal justice institutions, 'civilised' behaviour as a social practice became internalised by ever wider social groups and as a result, over the *longue durée* populations became less violent.[2] Because interpersonal violence has historically been a practice of more men than women, these changes have been gendered, and because they have been argued to have originated in the upper or middle classes, the argument is also classed. Secondly, as discussed in Chapter 3, it has been argued that the spaces and practices of domestic life, including violence, became normatively more secluded from the gaze and interference of other people.[3] This argument is qualified by the third proposition,

---

1 T. Gurr, 'Historical trends in violent crime: a critical review of the evidence', *Crime and Justice: An Annual Review of Research*, 3 (1978), pp. 3–23; M. Eisner, 'Long-term trends in violent crime', *Crime and Justice: An Annual Review of Research*, 30 (2003), pp. 83–142. For England, the debate focused around homicide rates. L. Stone, 'Interpersonal violence in English society, 1300–1980', *Past and Present*, 101 (1983), pp. 22–33; J.A. Sharpe, 'The history of violence in England', *Past and Present*, 108 (1985), pp. 206–15 and L. Stone, 'The history of violence in England: some observations: a rejoinder', *Past and Present*, 108 (1985), pp. 216–19. On the eighteenth century in particular see R.B. Shoemaker, 'The decline of public insult in London 1660–1800', *Past and Present*, 169 (2000), pp. 97–131; R. Shoemaker, 'Male honour and the decline of public violence in 18th-century London', *Social History*, 26 (2001), pp. 190–208.

2 N. Elias, *The civilizing process: the history of manners and state formation and civilization*, E. Jephcott (trans.) (Oxford, 1994). A large amount of work in violence history has been influenced by Elias, for example, P. Spierenburg, *Men of violence; gender, honour and rituals in modern Europe and America* (Colombus OH, 1998); E.A. Johnson and E.H. Monkkonen, *The civilization of crime: violence in town and country since the middle ages* (Chicago, 1996); M.J. Wiener, *Men of blood: violence, manliness, and criminal justice in Victorian England* (Cambridge, 2004). Discussions of the Elias thesis include P. Spierenburg, 'Violence and the civilizing process: does it work?', *Crime, Histoire et Societés*, 5 (2001), pp. 87–105; J. Carter Wood, 'It's a small world after all? Reflections on violence in comparative perspectives' in B. Godfrey, C. Emsley, and G. Dunstall (eds.), *Comparative Histories of Crime* (Cullompton, 2003), pp. 36–52; S. Carroll, 'Introduction' in S. Carroll (ed.), *Cultures of violence: interpersonal violence in historical perspective* (Basingstoke, 2007), pp. 1–46.

3 L. Stone, *Family, sex and marriage in early modern England*, 2nd edn (Harmondsworth, 1979); R. Chartier (ed.), *Passions of the renaissance* (Cambridge, Mass., 1989), Vol. 3 in P. Aries and G. Duby (eds.), *The history of private life*; the key studies for a more nuanced discussion of the historical

that the growth and refinement of criminal justice criminalised ever more areas of interpersonal violence including that within the 'private' family.[4] In so doing it made the domestic violence of poorer people particularly visible, so much so that wife-beating became perceived as a characteristic of the Victorian poor and the violence of those of higher social status was partially concealed.[5] Eighteenth-century urban society and the emergent middle classes have been identified as important to all these changes.

More recently, historians have found such metanarratives to have limitations in historical explanation. As Chapters 3 and 5 above have suggested, the connections between family, gender, domesticity, privacy and trajectories towards modernity are now understood to be far more complex and uneven than earlier assumed. The connections between declining violent crime and a civilising process in the eighteenth century also now seem less robust in some areas. Druh Warhman accepts the pattern of increased reticence but interprets reductions of interpersonal violence on London's eighteenth-century streets not in terms of state control but because of shifting behaviour patterns more appropriate to metropolitan living and the social utility of increasing reticence in the crowded and anonymous urban space.[6] Joanne Bailey has made a detailed and comprehensive critique of models of the increasing privacy of domestic violence by the later eighteenth century. Shoemaker, for example, argues that later eighteenth-century London men were curtailing their outdoor (public) violence against both family and other men, and confining their 'private' violence against wives and other intimates within doors. Bailey queries Shoemaker's elision between outdoors:indoors and public:private. She points out that domestic space was not necessarily private at this period; even more affluent households contained ever-

---

3 *cont.*

development of middle-class domesticity in early nineteenth-century Britain remain: L. Davidoff and C. Hall, *Family fortunes, men and women of the English middle class, 1780–1850* (London, 1987); C. Hall, *White, male and middle class: explorations in feminism and history* (Cambridge, 1992); L. Davidoff, *Worlds between: historical perspectives on gender and class* (Cambridge, 1995). For fuller citation of the field see Chapter 3 above n. 3.

4 M.J. Wiener, *Men of blood.* On the more targeted use of violence by the criminal justice system the classic texts remains D. Hay *et al.*, *Albion's fatal tree: crime and society in eighteenth-century England* (Harmondsworth, 1975); on the growth of the criminal justice system see i.a. J.M. Beattie, *Crime and the courts in England 1660–1800* (Oxford, 1986); J. Innes and J. Styles, 'The crime wave: recent writing on crime and criminal justice in eighteenth-century England' in A. Wilson (ed.), *Rethinking social history. English society 1570–1920 and its interpretation* (Manchester, 1993), pp. 201–65; I. Gilmour, *Riot, risings and revolution: governance and violence in eighteenth-century England* (London, 1992); D. Hay and F. Snyder (ed.), *Policing and prosecution in the English courts 1750–1850* (Oxford, 1989); *P. King, Crime, justice and discretion in England 1740–1820* (Oxford, 2000), useful overview discussion pp. 1–14; P. King, *Crime and law in England 1750–1840* (Cambridge, 2006). General historical overviews, J.A. Sharpe, *Crime in early modern England; 1550–1750* (Harlow, 1999); C. Emsley, *Crime and society in England 1750–1900* (Harlow, 1996).

5 A. James Hammerton, *Cruelty and companionship; conflict in nineteenth-century married life* (London, 1992).

6 D. Wahrman, *The making of the modern self: identity and culture in eighteenth-century England* (New Haven and London, 2004).

watchful servants. Neighbours were not deterred from intervention because of notions of family privacy, though they might refrain for other reasons. Some men (and sometimes their victims) might, however seek to conceal their violence, especially where it so far exceeded the accepted norm of 'correction' of dependents as to jeopardise the social credit of the household.[7] Shepard and Harvey argue that from the seventeenth century the available modes of masculinity valorising physical restraint came to signal better class status.[8] Bailey suggests that violent middling men with both a cultural investment in politeness and the resources to afford domestic accommodation more conducive to concealment had both motive and opportunity to keep their violence from view and thus preserve their respectability. Furthermore, '... the features of rank and reputation were tied in to a range of factors such as occupation, material living standards, and urban or rural environment' all of which depended on the nature and extent of industrialisation and urbanisation in particular localities.[9] What then were the uses of indoor and outdoor violence in a provincial town such as Colchester?

The association of modernity with the growth and organisation of the criminal justice system and the progressive criminalisation of (visible) violence is also undergoing further historical exploration. Peter King outlined Essex magistrates' increasing use of imprisonment rather than fines for minor assaults between the 1780s and 1820s as well as the focus of the courts on the violence of working people. His later work has further complicated this picture by delineating the degree to which discretion and the input from complainants and other parties shaped the administration of justice at this period. Criminal justice had an important local dimension.[10] Therefore, although this limited local study cannot be expected to make a decisive intervention in major historical debate, it makes a contribution to the mapping of such particularities. There are certainly examples of violence and disorderly conduct among the Colchester middling sort into the early nineteenth century, both indoors and out. There is also, however, evidence from the local summary courts that the policing of disorder shifted by the 1800s. This chapter will

---

7 J. Bailey, '"I dye [sic] by inches": Locating wife beating in the concept of a privatization of marriage and violence in eighteenth-century England', *Social History*, 31 (2006), pp. 273–95, here p. 274; R. Shoemaker, *Gender in English society 1650–1850: The emergence of separate spheres?* (London, 1998); M. Hunt, 'Wife beating, domesticity and women's independence in eighteenth-century London', *Gender and History*, 4 (1992); S.D. Amussen, '"Being stirred to much unquietness": Violence and domestic violence in early modern England', *Journal of Women's History*, 6 (1994), p. 70; S.D. Amussen, 'Punishment, discipline, and power — the social meanings of violence in early-modern England', *Journal of British Studies*, 34 (1995), pp. 1–34. See also E. Longfellow, 'Public, private, and the household in early seventeenth-century England', *Journal of British Studies*, 45 (2000), pp. 313–34.

8 K. Harvey, 'The history of masculinity, c.1650–1800', *Journal of British Studies*, 44 (2005), pp. 296–311; K. Harvey and A. Shepard, 'What have historians done with masculinity? Reflections on five centuries of British history, c.1500–1950', *Journal of British Studies*, 44 (2005), pp. 275–80.

9 Bailey, 'I dye [sic] by inches', p. 294.

10 P. King, 'Punishing assault: the transformation of attitudes in the English courts', *Journal of Interdisciplinary History*, 27 (1996), pp. 43–74; P. King, *Crime, justice and discretion*; P. King, *Crime and law*, Chapters 1 and 8.

first look more closely at middling interpersonal violence and will then shift perspective to discuss the management of disorder and the preoccupations of the local petty sessions.

Middling individuals who adopted cultures of politeness were not necessarily debarred from participation in popular culture, something that (for example) the extensive literature on the fairly broad social composition of the eighteenth-century mob makes clear.[11] They rather extended their range of cultural expression. As Carter suggests, politeness was in part an aspiration and different social contexts could legitimate less refined behaviour.[12] I argued in Chapter 5 that polite social practices were characteristic of much that is recoverable about the Colchester middling sort, and yet Chapters 6 and 7 also showed plenty of instances where local politics included disorder and violence. The memoirs and correspondence that survives for Colchester middling families tends to emphasise emotional investment and the value placed on domestic life (Chapter 3). However, middling household and intimate power relations throughout the century could also be delineated by physical violence. Some people who (in terms of their social standing, their possessions as divulged for example in property sales or wills, and sometimes their character and activities where these can be recuperated) seemed to be firmly attached to polite culture, could also behave violently. Robert and Elizabeth Kendall were high-street drapers and Quakers. They chose an ornamental sword as part of their smart interior décor and hung it over the marital bed. In a bout of (unfounded) jealousy Kendall seized it from the wall and used it to attack and wound the apprentice apothecary he thought was enamoured of Elizabeth.[13]

Revd William Smythies, Rector of Alpheton in Suffolk and Vicar of St Peters Colchester in the 1760s and 70s, was half brother to Francis Smythies the town clerk and to Elizabeth Twining.[14] On 15 July 1765 he was bound over to keep the peace towards his wife, Anna Dorothea née Carleton. It seems little coincidence that three months earlier an action had been entered by Humphrey Carleton (Anna Dorothea's brother) against William Smythies for principal and interest of £270 on a bond. Smythies' violence was positioned at the intersection of family, credit and masculinity.[15]

Thomas Hedge came from the 'persistent' clockmaking family of All Saints, but

11 R. Shoemaker, 'The London mob in the early 18th-century', *Journal of British Studies*, 26 (1987), pp. 273–304; D. Wahrman, *The making of the modern self: identity and culture in eighteenth-century England*, (New Haven and London, 2004); see also Chapter 2 above, n. 72.

12 P. Carter, *Men and the emergence of polite society: Britain 1660–1800* (London and New York, 2001), p. 11.

13 J. Bensusan Butt, *Benjamin Strutt, William Cole and James Fisin* (Colchester, privately printed, 1994), p. 18; JBB BD/1012, Robert Kendall.

14 See Table 3.3 above.

15 Colchester Sessions Book, ERO D/B 5 Sb6/3. He was not only violent towards her, for on 14 March 1771, ERO D/B 5 Sb5/4, he was also presented to the court for assaulting William Lawrence, a labourer. Thursday Court Book, ERO, D/B 5 Cb2/37, 25 April 1765 for Humphrey Carleton action, also 23 October 1777 Philadelphia Peagram widow and Philadelphia Berney widow brought an action against him for 14s, the balance of accounts between them.

later became a successful coachmaster; he and his partners ran mail and passenger coaches between London and East Anglia. He served four times as mayor and died in 1814, 'much respected'. He prosecuted his first wife Sarah and she was bound over to keep the peace towards him on 27 April 1778, finding two £10 sureties. For several years Thomas and Sarah Hedge had lived at 93 High Street, but on the death of Thomas' elder brother had moved into the Hedge family premises in March 1778. Sarah's sureties were subsequently increased to £50 and when in April 1783 she was unable or unwilling to supply sureties and she was gaoled in the castle for a year. Hedge's use of the courts to solve his marital difficulties was but one aspect of a generally litigious character and he also prosecuted two cases of theft and one of assault.[16]

Surgeon Richard Tomkins moved to Colchester in 1787, selling a previous practice at Bildeston, Suffolk. He lived first in Culver Street and then at 71 High Street, a five-bedroom house which he had fitted up 'at considerable expense'.[17] Tomkins seems to have been a comprehensively violent man. He swore profane oaths at William Keymer, the printer.[18] His wife Ann prosecuted him for beating her on 6 May 1793. In 1794 he dragged his servant Sarah Seagrave upstairs by the hair and kicked her several times, for which he was fined 1s.[19] The evidence is too scant to read much into the 'upstairs' here, except perhaps the gender dependencies underlying his abuse to all women household members. In 1800 he also broke a window belonging to widow Elizabeth Bennell of St Runwald.[20] Meanwhile his wife had separated from him in April 1799 and finally survived him. Her will mentions a deed of separation. She had returned to Wormingford, the home of her father John Ratford, farmer, deceased.[21]

Sarah Seagrave is just one example of servants and apprentices in middling households who experienced violence sufficient for them to bring it to the borough petty sessions. Samuel Balls had let himself to Revd William Shillito of St Mary-at-the-Walls for 1s 6d per week. He complained to the court when Shillito 'abused him very much by taking him by the arms, shaking him several times, flinging him down on the floor and turning him out of doors'.[22] Thomas Barnes the brewer at Sheregate Steps also saw fit to punch his servant Ann Cockerill.[23] John Sadler, apprenticed to Samuel Rouse, currier and leather cutter of St Botolphs, complained that on a Saturday evening his master 'knocked him off a chair on which he was sitting ... several times and turned him ... out of the house without suffering him to finish getting his supper and .. obliges ... him ... to sleep in a worse bed than he did at the commencement of

---

16 B. Mason, *Clock and watchmaking in Colchester, England* (Colchester, 1969), pp. 315, 337–8.

17 *IpsJ* 18 November 1786, 9 February 1800.

18 ERO, P/CoR 16, 2 July 1792.

19 ERO D/B5 Sr325, Sessions file Michaelmas 1794.

20 ERO P/CoR 22a 12 June 1800, deposition of Elizabeth Bennell; ERO P/CoR17, 13 September 1794, deposition of Sarah Seagrave.

21 ERO A/BR 31/422, 1818.

22 ERO P/CoR 17, 17 January 1794, deposition of Samuel Balls.

23 ERO P/CoR 12, 24 January 1789, deposition Ann Cockerill.

his apprenticeship'.[24] Servants and apprentices were integral to the household family and the violence they describe (being pulled by the hair, being put out of doors, being flung down on the ground) bears significant similarities to that of abused wives. Household relationships, including those of violence, followed lines of power and dependence, and not only those of gender. Because these cases came to the sessions it can be assumed that they exceeded the violence against dependents that could be justified as 'correction'. Comparatively few incidents of violence against household dependents figured in the local courts and offer little helpful evidence as to the frequency with which domestic relations were violent ones. Such cases persisted across the century and bear strong similarities to studies of domestic violence in subsequent periods; the possibility of such violence has been a striking historical continuity, and as these examples show, not only among the labouring and artisan classes.[25]

Substantial middling men could also be violent out of doors. John Malby, coachmaker, was prosecuted for assault on at least three occasions. Malby traded in the High Street and owned property behind North Hill worth £500.[26] James Hamilton, innkeeper and coachmaster was prosecuted twice.[27] James and Sarah Halls, High Street fishmongers and grocers assaulted two women, throwing one down and beating her and striking the other in the face with a cloth. Although lower middling sort, artisan and labouring women are a significant minority of those accused of assault at petty and quarter sessions (see below) it is less common for more prosperous middling women to be so prosecuted. Occasionally the sons of the ostensibly respectable found themselves in court. Alderman Edward Capstack's son William was prosecuted in 1786 for tipping 'oyl etc. ... from the window of the workshop of Mr Edward Capstack, currier' spoiling the coat of William King, a cooper, who 'was walking through St Nicholas churchyard on the common footpath'.[28]

---

24 ERO P/CoR 22a, 11 August 1800, deposition of John Sadler.

25 E. Foyster, *Marital violence: an English family history, 1660–1857* (Cambridge, 2005); Bailey,'I dye [sic] by inches'. For the seventeenth century, see for example Longfellow, 'Public, private'; S. Amussen, 'Punishment, discipline, and power — the social meanings of violence in early-modern England', *Journal of British Studies*, 34 (1995), pp. 1–34, and her '"Being stirred to much unquietness": violence and domestic violence in early modern England', *Journal of Women's History*, 6 (1994), pp. 70–90. Nineteenth-century studies include A.J. Hammerton, *Cruelty and companionship: conflict in nineteenth-century married life* (London, 1992); S. D'Cruze, *Crimes of outrage; sex, violence and Victorian working women* (London, 1998), Chapter 4; E. Ross, '"Fierce questions and taunts": married life in working-class London, 1870–1914', *Feminist Studies*, 8 (1982), pp. 4–27; A. Clark, *The struggle for the breeches: gender and the making of the British working class* (Berkeley, 1995), Chapter 3. Of the vast criminological literature, historical continuities are evident in (for example), K.A. Kelly, *Domestic violence and the politics of privacy* (Ithaca, NY, 2003), pp. 1–50.

26 ERO P/Co R 22a, 10 October 1800, deposition William Biggs; D/B 5 SB 5/5 recognisances for Malby to answer for assaults appear in Epiphany 1779 and Midsummer 1784 Quarter Sessions; JBB BD/55; ERO Acc 47 CPL.

27 Sessions files ERO D/B 5 Sr 245, Midsummer 1774, Sr 245 Michaelmas 1785 (not found); Sessions Book ERO D/B 5 Sb 5/6, Midsummer 1789; JBB BD/402.

28 ERO P/Co R11a, 21 August 1786. Capstack had officially taken his son apprentice on 7 September 1785 (no fee). On 7 August 1788 William Taylor was bound apprentice for £52 10s

In 1774 John Savage, a physician who ran a freshwater baths in the Colne, assaulted Ann Gull tearing her handkerchief and apron. The same year, High Street glover Thomas Tillett committed a similar assault on Elizabeth Taylor, 'tearing the cap off her head'.[29] These assaults seem to be sexually motivated, something made far more explicit in a case of 1804 involving John Killingworth Bowland, the proprietor of the Three Cups (rated £50 in 1795) as well as a house in Crouch Street. He survived bankruptcy in 1798 and apparently continued to prosper.[30] In 1804 he met with heavily pregnant Mary Ann Haward, a soldier's wife, on a December Friday evening. Bowland 'took hold of ... (her) ... and pulled her backwards and requested her to walk with him, which ... (she) ... objected to but he then put his hand up ... (her) ... coats and materially hurt the lower part of her belly'. She called her husband who was walking some yards behind and rescued her. The assault was sufficiently serious for some sentinels on local guard duty to arrest Bowland and for the physician Richard D. Mackintosh to treat her with hartshorn. She remained ill in bed for the remainder of her pregnancy.[31] Women walking the streets could be assumed to be sexually available by even ostensibly respectable men.

These cases came to court, so were clearly held to be exceptionable by the prosecutor and not infrequently the witnesses, though where found they attracted only minor punishment. Such violence seems not to have severely undermined these men's middling status. Sometimes there were exceptional reasons; attorney Samuel Wall made repeated attacks on pastry cook James Wellum. Matters came to a head when Wall burst into the White Hart coffee room and threatened the proprietor and assembled customers with a drawn sword, and he was adjudged to be a lunatic 'with lucid periods'.[32] Given that criminal prosecution at this period was part of a wider and negotiable grid of means for obtaining redress for grievance, it is impossible to recover the numbers of comparable incidents that did not enter the written record. These examples are deliberately chosen from the more prosperous middling sort. Not all of the individuals cited here necessarily used violence regularly, but still did so on at least one occasion that came to court. The patterns of such violence, particularly that at home, were necessarily inflected by the material and social environments that came with comparative prosperity, but still have congruities with the violence of the poor, which is discussed further below.

The disorder of the middling sort also took other forms. Anecdotes of the borough corporation drunk and incapable at its annual dinner, or of the sexual peccadilloes of the local Exciseman may be exaggerations but would lose their satire if they were

---

28 *cont.*

and on 12 May 1794 Capstack's nephew Samuel Lufkin paid the much reduced fee of £5. ERO Acc 905, Box 1, index of apprentices from Colchester Borough Servants and Apprentices Register.

29 ERO P/Co R5 4 October 1774, deposition Elizabeth Taylor. JBB BD/880, Thomas Tillett.

30 JBB BD/1180, John Killingworth Bowland; *London Gazette* 28 April, 7 July, 24 November 1798.

31 ERO P/CoR 24, 9 February 1804.

32 JBB BD/911 Samuel Wall; ERO P/CoR 4, 3, 23 and 27 June, 2 and 11 July and 17 December 1774; Borough Quarter Sessions Book D/B 5 Sb5/4 (indictments and recognisances transcribed at the back); Sessions Rolls D/B 5 Sr245 Midsummer 1774, D/B 5 Sr247 Epiphany 1775; NA C/211/27/W91, *De Lunatiko Inquirendo* re Samuel Wall snr.

completely implausible fabrications. Stephen Hooker, a fairly prosperous 'chymist and druggist' with High Street premises was a non-conformist and apparently a participant in polite associational culture with a taste for genteel artefacts. He may also have been a kleptomaniac:

> His propensity to thieve he indulged in a long time without suspicion, and many petty thefts were attributed to others, of which he was the perpetrator. He at last stole a gold watch of great value from Mr Nathaniel Hedge ... (the clockmaker).
>
> Being from other circumstances suspected, a plan was laid to detect him, and at a Club at the Red Lion Inn, a wager was proposed by which everyone present was obliged to produce their watches, Hooker, not suspecting any design, and rendered callous to detection by frequent escapes, most inadvertently produced his among the rest. It was recognised and immediately claimed by Hedge, Hooker begged for mercy, and forbearance to expose him, delivered up the watch, and was suffered to retire to his home, The next morning he quitted Colchester for America, and was never afterwards heard of.[33]

This is an uncorroborated source, though Hooker did suddenly disappear from the local record.[34] The anecdote was credible because the incident was contextualised within polite associational culture where such a discovery would collapse the credit and reputation of such a middling tradesman. Hooker may have been behaving badly, but if so he escaped any criminal sanction. He did not become an object of formal policing. The remainder of this chapter turns its attention to the aspects of local governance that managed disorder and in so doing positioned Colchester's poorer inhabitants as incipiently disorderly.

Policing

In the heyday of the bay trade the wool workers were a large and (when it counted) cohesive group. In 1715 a major strike brought the town's economic life to a temporary halt. Colchester had its share of grain riots in the eighteenth century, the most serious being in 1740, 1772 and 1789. During 1740 there was a string of incidents stretching over two harvests, where wagons taking grain for distant sale or export through the Hythe were stopped. Other rioters broke into a barn where flour was stored prior to shipment.[35] Riot was not uncommon, either large scale or a fairly

---

33 ERO Acc 905, Box 2, *Bland's Anecdotes*, p. 84.

34 JBB BD/480 Stephen Hooker, chymist and druggist. Though Bland is incorrect in the maiden name of his wife, Hooker certainly disappeared suddenly from Colchester between 1776 and 1780 (years for which parish rates are available) while Mrs Hooker remained. His death was not reported and Hannah Hooker is referred to as 'Mrs' not 'Wid' in subsequent records. She was the owner of the property on the corner of Pelhams Lane and of 39 High Street in 1783 (Land Tax) but lived elsewhere. In 1784, for one year only she was occupier of 50 High Street (rated 10).

35 ERO D/B 5 Sr 189, Epiphany 1738, Presentment Thomas Gossard, weaver, (fined 6d) for with others, forcible ejectment of Widow Hutton from her house. Gossard pleaded to the case in Epiphany 1739 sessions (D/B 5 Sr 193) when his recognisances included Guy Hutton. Perhaps the dispute had been resolved in the interim. For 1740 riot see, *IpsJ* 22 April, 17 and 25 May, 14 June, 29 November, 13 December 1740. Of the sizeable literature on the grain riot, see E.P. Thompson, 'The moral economy of the English crowd in the eighteenth century', *Past and Present*, 50 (1971), pp. 76–136; Rude, 1972; J.M. Beattie, *Crime and the courts in England 1660–1800* (Oxford, 1986), p. 202 *et seq*; see also Chapter 2 above n. 72.

limited affairs. To take three examples from the 1730s, William Lane and James Minks with 'other malefactors' broke into a house and ejected its occupant James Pavett. Lane's relation had defaulted on a mortgage and rights to the property were ambiguous so the quarter sessions did not convict. When borough leather searchers seized a quantity of shoes in a campaign to control the business of unapprenticed traders, the son and friends of the woman cordwainer rioted and rescued the shoes. As noted in Chapter 2, around a hundred people turned out for a riot over gin duty in 1738.[36] In 1779 eight young men were prosecuted for a riot that involved a spree of window smashing at the upper end of the High Street.[37] In 1794 half a dozen artisans set upon gentleman Thomas Hussey.[38]

Like most eighteenth-century towns, Colchester lacked any very efficient policing mechanisms. The governing group were constantly forced into accommodation with the lower middling sort, the artisans and the poor who were seen as the chief perpetrators of disorder. None of the indictments against the gin rioters were found. Quarter sessions arbitrated between weavers and employers in 1736, laying down terms and conditions of work in favour of the weavers. The corporation petitioned the Secretary of State for assistance in dealing with grain riots in 1740 and 1772. The authority of the borough constables was not infrequently challenged. Constables' periodic clean-up campaigns, targeting disorderly houses, lewd women or short weights and measures, seem to indicate that generally, offences went uncontrolled. Four lewd women were, for example, prosecuted in 1799 but apparently none in 1794.[39] James Birchly was an active constable, frequently chivvying dealers in short weight and harbourers of inmates as well as the Gin Mayor rioters. In 1735 he prosecuted one disorderly alehouse too many. Victualler James Hudson, backed up by other aggrieved tradesmen, wrote the following letter:

> Mr Burchwel tho' you Indicted me Last Year You think to do the same now but if you do take care of yourself and Ben Barnes the same. N.B for I will ... (?) ... the Indictment and will know who it is that doos the same for you are a busy fellow.[40]

Barnes, Tory weaver and victualler of St Nicholas parish, was another busy constable. Hudson got off on both counts. In 1745 Constable Lewis Salmon was indicted at county sessions for failing to do his duty and sort out a disturbance at ten o'clock at night in Holy Trinity parish. However incompletely, incorporation of superior artisans

---

36 ERO D/B 5 Sr 183; Will John Selly, ERO 480 CR 14, 1736, Will John Lane ERO 463 CR 14, 1736. Presentment for rescuing shoes siezed by the Leather Searchers from Anne Hewes, trading as a cordwainer, ERO D/B 5 Sr 182, Easter 1736; gin mayor riot, ERO D/B Sr 191, Midsummer 1738; Patrick Dillon, *The much-lamented death of Madam Geneva: the eighteenth-century gin craze* (London, 2002).

37 ERO D/B 5 Sb5/5, Epiphany 1779 sessions, recognisances of John Kendall, Isaac Kendall and others.

38 ERO D/B 5 Sr 523, Easter 1794, indictment of Robert Blyth, Henry Mason, Robert Candler and others.

39 ERO Sessions Files D/BD/B5 Sr 322–5 for 1794; Sessions Book D/B Sb 5/7 for 1798–1812.

40 ERO D/5 Sr 179, Midsummer 1735.

and the middling sort into local office-holding came to define the poor as those who were policed and hence excluded from full citizenship.[41]

The dividing line between the governed and those participating in the processes of governance was a socially and culturally significant one in eighteenth-century Colchester; it was nevertheless always potentially permeable. Even the more substantial middling sort could sometimes find themselves prosecuted. Sources also show individuals clustered around this dividing line; the borough constable zealous in policing disorderly houses who lacked the skills of literacy, or those sworn to their settlements who had paid rates not directly to the vestry but via their employers or landlords. As Chapter 4 argued, the uncertainties of the market could bring bankruptcy to the most circumspect business. Mortality and morbidity, old age, accident or injury, emotional conflict, too many (or too few) children, poor judgement in business or social life were also among the myriad possible threats to the middling household. Such risks generated much anxiety because they had real power to undermine family respectability and material security and thus push a middling household across the line from independence into the ranks of the governed.[42]

This chapter will explore the construction, operation and meanings of the line between governed and governors by looking more closely at the operation of the two lowliest institutions of governance; petty sessions and the parish vestry. Eighteenth-century quarter sessions, improvement commissioners and even some corporations may well have been larger players in the field of local governance, and have been argued from several directions to have taken the lead in modernising local government. However, if capillary power is most discernible at the peripheries, in the quotidian and mundane workings of systems, then it is arguably in the albeit incomplete and erratic records of the humbler institutions of local administration that the line between governors and governed was made, challenged and defended. Governance intruded into poor and artisan families. A few men were jailed for beating their wives and others who left families chargeable to the poor rates served hard labour.[43] In close focus, this dividing line is shown to be frequently articulated by violence. Furthermore, many of the key themes that previous chapters have argued were crucial to the middling sort (the family, intimacy and domesticity, materiality and consumption, credit and association) reappear in the gendered narratives of the governed. The reiteration of such narratives was a micro-technology of governance, inscribed in its written records, which interpellated individuals' dependencies by both class and gender. Arguably, avoiding the necessity of having your story so inscribed, or at the very least achieving an authoritative (and reticent) position in the narrative, was a key attribute of middlingness.

---

41 County Quarter Sessions roll ERO Q/SR 682, 8 October 1745.

42 J. Bailey, *Unquiet lives: marriage and marriage breakdown in England, 1660–1800* (Cambridge, 2003); M.R. Hunt, *The middling sort: commerce, gender, and the family in England, 1680–1780* (Berkeley and London, 1996).

43 For example, ERO Sessions Book D/B 5 Sb 5/6; Gaol Kalendar, Midsummer 1789 includes John Knopp sentenced to a month's hard labour for having 'having gone away and left family chargeable'; D/B 5 Sb 5/4, Goal Kalendar includes Guy Hutton in Epiphany 1769 and William Moor in Midsummer 1769, both released on entering sureties to keep the peace towards their wives.

Table 8.1
Petty sessions cases by decade

	1759	*1774*	*1784*	*1794*	*1804*
interpersonal violence (ipv)	51	50	30	31	33
master and servant cases (m/s)	10	16	9	6	1
military, desertion, billeting etc. (mil)		3	5	6	16
miscellaneous (misc)		4	2		
prostitution and vagrancy (mor)	10	4	8	10	
poor law (pl)	23	79	96	110	73
property crime (prop)	31	13	7	4	5
traffic, market, nuisance, other regulatory offences (reg)	3	2	7	1	22
Total	128	171	164	168	150

Table 8.2
Petty sessions cases by decade as percentages

	1759 %	*1774* %	*1784* %	*1794* %	*1804* %
interpersonal violence (ipv)	39.8	29.2	18.3	18.5	22.0
master and servant cases (m/s)	7.8	9.4	5.5	3.6	0.7
military, desertion, billeting etc. (mil)		1.8	3.0	3.6	10.7
miscellaneous (misc)		2.3	1.2		
prostitution and vagrancy (mor)	7.8	2.3	4.9	6.0	
poor law (pl)	18.0	46.2	58.5	65.5	48.7
property crime (prop)	24.2	7.6	4.3	2.4	3.3
traffic, market, nuisance, other regulatory offences (reg)	2.3	1.2	4.3	0.6	14.7
Percentage	100.0	100.0	100.0	100.0	100.0

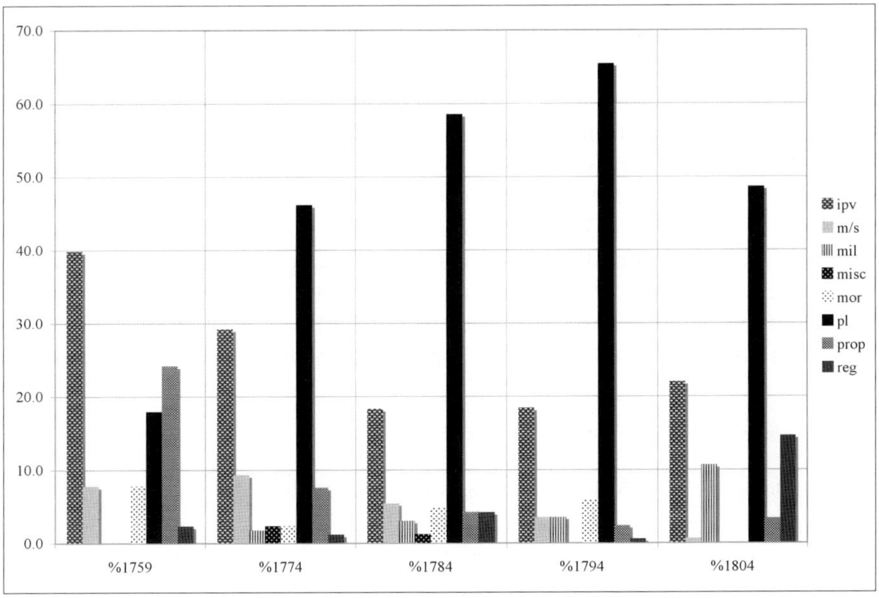

Petty sessions: business and usage

Borough petty sessions were held at least twice weekly before a bench of one to three borough justices. During the period when the charter was in abeyance Charles Gray, as county magistrate, held separate sittings of Lexden and Winstree sessions. Petty sessions heard a narrower range of matters than the quarter sessions, mostly assault, very minor thefts, poor law and vagrancy cases and some regulatory offences over traffic, market and the billeting of soldiers. However, frequency, accessibility and cheapness meant that petty sessions were well used by people in search of speedy restitution of injury but also as an adjunct of local government to police the (physical and sexual) disorder of the working classes, to manage poverty and welfare and to regulate the streets in terms of both wheeled traffic and pedestrian nuisances such as beggars. Felonies went straight to quarter sessions, as did prosecutions for nuisances that involved the Law Inquest, contested bastardy orders, cases where people were confined in the gaol and some assaults. However, the majority of people who encountered the Colchester courts did so by coming first to the petty sessions.[44] Petty sessions deposition books were in small, handy, quarto size. Not all depositions confine themselves to a page, but most do. The stories depositions relate are therefore fairly brief. In criminal or regulatory cases they are accusatory narratives, told by complainants or witnesses. In settlement, bastardy and many other poor law cases they are confessional or justificatory narratives told by someone seeking relief. Depositions were written by a clerk or officer and signed by the witness and the justice(s). Although many are expressive circumstantial vignettes, they can be formulaic, particularly later in the century. If such formulae obscure some of the texture of the events behind the case, they also indicate the normative assumptions of the law. Only at the end of the century is there any indication of the outcome of the case.

The survival of Colchester petty sessions depositions is incomplete for this period, beginning with a few (principally from 1758 and 1759) from the Lexden and Winstree sessions that heard Colchester business and continuing with an increasingly full series from the reconstituted borough sessions from the 1770s. This discussion draws on depositions from 1758, 1759, 1774, 1779, 1784, 1789, 1794, 1800 and 1804.[45] For indications of trends over time a sample of all depositions for 1759 and then at ten-year intervals (1774, 1784, 1794 and 1804) was used, comprising 901 depositions in all. This sample was amplified by available non-poor law cases in the remaining years.[46] The overall profile of cases at Table 8.1 shows an increasing case load across the later eighteenth century, with a small decline in 1804.

Presenting each category of case as a percentage of the total number of cases in

---

44 Sessions Books ERO D/B 5 Sb5/4, 5, 6, 7, 8. Sessions Files ERO D/B5 Sr series.

45 Lexden and Winstree Petty Sessions Book, ERO P/Lwr 1. Compared with Colchester Borough Petty Sessions, a stray volume for 1764 (P/Co R 1) and regular survivals from the 1770s (P/Co R 2 et seq) show an essentially similar picture. The only earlier surviving petty sessions book (P/Co R1a) is an anomaly containing only settlement cases, the bulk of which were heard by Charles Gray on 18 January 1745, mostly from St Martins parish.

46 ERO P/Lwr 1 and 4, 1758–9; P/Co R 8, 10a, 10b, 12, 13, 17, 18, 22, 22a, 24, 25.

Table 8.3
Gender of deponents

	1759	*1774*	*1784*	*1794*	*1804*
women	35	42	29	48	33
men	93	129	135	120	117
all	128	171	164	168	150

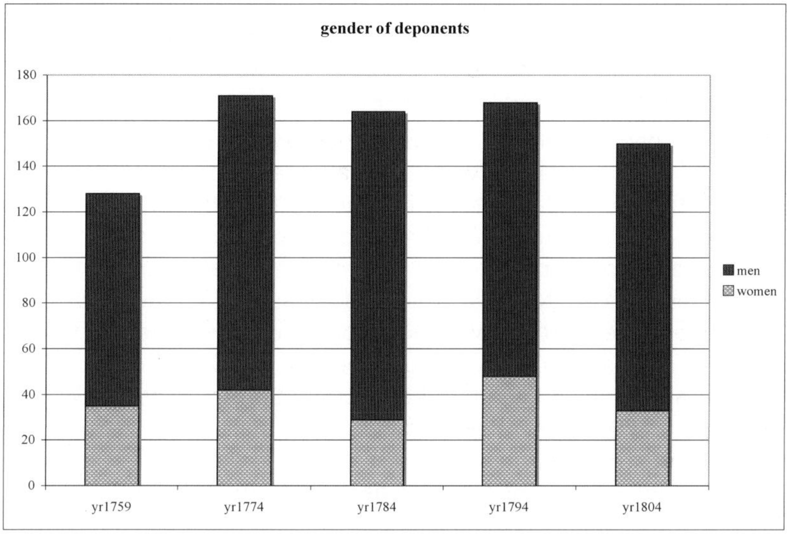

Table 8.4
Deponents signing by mark

	1759	*1774*	*1784*	*1794*	*1800*	*1804*
signed by mark	68	82	54	56	29	48
shaky signature	3	3	5	0	0	2
all cases that year	128	171	164	168	100	150
% signed by mark	53.1	47.9	32.9	33.3	29	32

that year highlights a trend already apparent in the raw figures. Interpersonal violence and poor law cases predominate in all years, but there is a shift in emphasis from the former to the latter over time (Table 8.2). This sample covers a chronology of population growth and the decline in the staple industry. Thus, in 1759 the majority of people milling around in the Moot Hall had come to court to protest at an assault or other grievance. In 1794 the majority were people who had been brought to the sessions as part of the process of securing immediate (or occasionally future) parish relief for themselves, and their families.

Property cases were a small percentage of the depositions. Most property crime was indictable and went straight to quarter sessions. The larger total in 1759 is due to petty sessions being used to take depositions when a gang of horse thieves operating between London and north-east Essex were apprehended. Cases between master and servant (disorderly or absconded apprentices or occasionally masters) decline from a low starting point. The regulation of morals, represented here as the swearing of 'prophane' oaths and the occasional apprehension of lewd women (prostitutes) show low but fluctuating totals, testifying to the very sporadic attempts to prosecute

Table 8.5
Numbers of parish and borough officers among petty sessions deponents

Year	*Depositions made by borough or parish officer*	*% of all depositions that year rounded to whole numbers*
1759	15	12
1774	24	14
1784	36	22
1794	14	8
1804	21	14
Total	161	

in such matters. Especially when Colchester was a garrison town in the 1790s the very few depositions against lewd women clearly bear no relationship to the actual incidence of prostitution.[47] Cases involving the military (billeting, deserters, or the refusal of Colchester carriers to have their vehicles commandeered for baggage duty) unsurprisingly show up more strongly during the Napoleonic period. The few regulatory offences (market tolls, weights and measures, traffic) show a small but significant increase in the more crowded town of the early nineteenth century.

Women were a consistent minority of between 20 and 39 per cent of deponents in any sample year and were a slightly greater proportion in years of particularly high case load (1774 and 1794). Petty sessions was not a male preserve. A small minority of women made detailed depositions about sexual and domestic violence as well as the female deponents in cases of common assault and poor law matters. A few men who beat their wives spent short periods in gaol. Women and men saw petty sessions as a means to address grievance, however, as I will argue, women tended to occupy positions of greater comparative dependency in the growing number of poor law cases.[48]

The comparative social range of individuals making depositions at petty sessions is indicated by the high proportion of those signing by mark, declining from a little over half in 1759 to around a third in 1804.

Depositions by officials (overseers, constables, churchwardens or other officers) using the court as part of their duties are not surprisingly a significant minority of the totals (Table 8.5). However, when juxtaposed to the changing case profile, an increase in regulatory and poor law cases over time did not mean a leap in the number of depositions by officials. The majority of poor law cases required individuals to speak 'for themselves' and thus produced the confessional narratives that made visible the domesticities and dependencies of the poor.

Deponents normally gave their place of current residence, for the most part in Colchester, except for a larger minority of out-of-town residents coming to the Lexden

47 T. Henderson, *Disorderly women in eighteenth century London; prostitution and control in the metropolis, 1730–1830* (London, 1999); S. Lloyd, '"Pleasure's golden bait": prostitution, poverty and the Magdalen hospital in eighteenth-century London', *History Workshop Journal*, 41 (1996), pp. 51–70.

48 R. Connors, 'Poor women, the parish and the politics of poverty', in H. Barker and E. Chalus (eds.), *Gender and society in eighteenth-century England* (Harlow, 1997), pp. 126–48.

Table 8.6
Deponents' location

	1759	*%**	*1774*	*%*	*1784*	*%*	*1794*	*%*	*1804*	*%*
In parishes	29	23	47	27	58	35	68	40	46	31
Out parishes	16	13	32	19	51	31	22	13	53	35
Liberties	4	3	3	2	12	7	21	13	12	8
Colchester unspecified	43	34	87	51	40	24	55	33	36	24
Country	32	25	2	1	3	2	2	1	3	2
London	4	3								
Total	128		171		164		168		150	

and Winstree sessions in the 1750s. Decennial samples are affected by changing in reporting practices[49] so the data defies close analysis of trend. However, within Colchester where a parish is specified, town parishes far outnumber the liberties. The larger figure for the liberties in 1794 is attributable to Lexden sorting out poor law settlements and bastardy cases at the height of the military garrison. Furthermore, parishes within the walls contributed more cases than those outside it, despite contemporary perceptions of greater poverty in the 'outparts' of the town.[50] The division between 'in' and 'out' parishes did not necessarily accord with 'rich' and 'poor'. St James and St Peter included both affluent neighbourhoods near the town centre and poorer areas at the bottom of North and East Hills. St Martin and St Nicholas likewise combined prosperity with working people living in courts and alleys behind the main streets. The poor were 'always with' the middling sort and town gentry who paid parish rates. Very many of them were also within a short walking distance of the justices at petty sessions. The weavers of St Giles and St Botolphs could be riotous, but also used the sessions. For example, the Orrin family show up several times. William Orrin had been born and bought up there. One night in The Pig in St Botolphs he assaulted Hannah Cowell, wife of another weaver. William Orrin was married to Jane. A few years later she and others 'made a riot' in the dwelling house of Mary Lay. In that same incident, Sarah Orrin (wife of James, weaver) also complained of Mary Orrin (wife of John, carter) who threw water over her.[51]

Familiarity with the sessions seems to have encouraged repeat usage, though this phenomenon operated differently depending on individuals' social status and institutional position. True, middling tradesmen who were prosecuted for assault, such as John Malby, also took their turn as overseer. Given their material position,

49 Parishes were specified more commonly in the later decades of the century when more poor law cases were heard.

50 Morant, *Colchester*, book 2, p. 130 commented that there were insufficient ratepayers in the small parish of St Giles to meet its poor law expenses. *IpsJ* 17 May 1740.

51 ERO P/CoR 10b, 1784 (undated), examination of William Orrin; P/Co R 13, 29 October 1789, examination of Sarah Orrin; P/CoR10a, 26 January 1784 deposition of Hannah Cowell; P/Co R 13 9 October 1789, deposition of Mary Lay. The family seems to have become more respectable in the next generation. Christopher Orrin was overseer in St Giles in 1800 and 1804, P/Co R 22a. 8 July 1800, examination of William Blackwell and P/Co R 25, 3 July 1804, deposition Christopher Orrin.

interpersonal violence that could be represented as a manly affray did not substantially undermine their social status.[52] The Smythies family, relations of the Town Clerk, were unsurprisingly confident in using the sessions. Francis Smythies was also collector of duty for riding and carriage horses and presented James Hamilton, innholder and coachmaster, for non-payment. He swore depositions for two other traffic offences concerning carts. As billet master in 1794, he presented a fraudulent claimant for a billet. He also twice presented beggars, and a victualler in 1784 for swearing 'four prophane curses "Damn you" meaning him this examinant'. (One's sympathies might lie with the victualler.) It is not surprising that the town clerk should make ready use of the sessions; it is the more interesting to encounter depositions by his brother Revd John Smythies, presenting a tenant for abandoning premises rented from him leaving arrears of rent, and his relation Carleton Smythies Esq, reporting a further traffic offence in 1789.[53] The Colchester town gentry did not make a regular practice of reporting minor regulatory infractions.

Minor office-holders such as constables and overseers were also comparatively frequent deponents for matters concerning their office, but in some cases there is also a greater readiness for them and their connections to come to court as deponents in other matters. William Bugg, a shopkeeper, was St Botolphs overseer who presented rates defaulters three times in 1804.[54] His wife Susan had complained of an assault in August 1794.[55] Almost three months previously she had been standing at her door when Abraham Ray, St Botolphs, millwright '... held a lighted serpent in this examinant's face in consequence of which this examinant ran her arm through a pane of glass and cut it in a terrible manner that she was under a surgeon's hands for more than a month'. The fact that this deposition differs from the 'several violent blows' that most assaulted deponents complained of and that Susan had taken three months to come to court separates it from the majority of cases. This was a case brought only after lengthy consideration and probably some informal negotiation. James Albra was a borough constable and John Albra was sergeant at mace. Each were deponents in petty sessions on a couple of occasions on matters concerned with their official duties. In addition, Phoebe Albra, James' wife, complained in 1779 of five profane oaths sworn by Ann Smith.[56]

The tendency for repeat appearances by people whose official role (or that of their

---

52 ERO Sessions Book D/B 5 Sb 5/4, Epiphany 1769, Malby, as St Peters overseer, presented Daniel Bruce for neglect of family.

53 ERO P/Co R 13 September 1788, deposition of John Smythies; P/Co R 10a 6 March 1784, deposition of Edward Holton; P/CoR 5, 12 September 1774, P/Co R10b 18 August and 4 November 1784; P/Co R 17, 17 March 1794, depositions of Francis Smythies; P/Co R 13, 18 November 1789, deposition of Carlton Smythies. Carlton Smythies was the son of William Smythies, the surgeon and hence great grandson to Francis Smythies' father, Palmer Smythies. Carlton Smythies' mother remarried to the Colchester MP Edmund Affleck. JBB BD/810 William Smythies 2, BD/5 Edmund Affleck.

54 P/Co R 25, 26 April, 11 June, 6 August 1804.

55 P/ Co R 17, 20 August 1794.

56 Depositions of John Albra, P/Co R 12, 8 May 1779 and P/Co R 18, 16 December 1794 when he was a sergeant in the West Essex Militia; Phoebe Albra, P/Co R 8, 4 June 1779; James Albra, P/Co R 12, 25 May 1789 and P/Co R 18, 1 November 1794.

kin) arguably strengthened their confidence in the sessions is mirrored by people who appear more than once but in less favourable positions. Sarah Bruce was examined as to an illegitimate child in February 1774, and the following May complained of an assault by labourer William Kilbourn.[57] Elizabeth Lee was examined twice about an illegitimate child in 1794, naming a soldier. While she was pregnant she also came to court to complain of an assault by another soldier 'in her father's house' by whom she was 'struck on the shoulder and pushed ... over the settle'. She had, she said, been much hurt and ill ever since.[58] While an overseer's or constable's wife might use the sessions to discipline the disorderly, Elizabeth Lee and Sarah Bruce's repeat appearances say more about their comparative disadvantage and vulnerability. In de Certeau's terms, the dividing line fell between those who used the sessions strategically along the lines of dominant dispositions of power and those more marginalised individuals whose experience of the courts was far more tactical.[59]

Yet another logic explains the two appearances of James Triggs, innkeeper at the Red Lion. When constable William Ball came snooping round the inn yard on a Sunday morning in 1788 to see if there was any drinking going on during church service hours Triggs ejected him by main force.[60] Early in 1789 Triggs lost his temper with one of the soldiers billeted on the inn. As the soldier was hanging around in the inn kitchen, one January morning, 'the said James Triggs did then and there violently assault (him) by taking him by his coat and pushing him against the dresser in the said kitchen and taking him by the collar and pushing him out of the house.'[61] Billeting could be a tiresome and costly business for busy innkeepers. These two cases make greater sense in the context of the prevailing political history of that year. The radical George Tierney had won a by-election in 1788 in the teeth of an organised Tory corporation party (Chapter 6). Tierney's political interest focused on the Hand in Hand Club which met at the Red Lion. Triggs' tenure at the inn did not last long after Tierney's defeat in the general election of 1790. Petty sessions was, it seems, an additional site of local party conflict.[62]

Petty sessions: violence

In line with research on interpersonal violence in other locations, most of these depositions were assault cases between people known to each other.[63] The degree of relationship ranged from married couples, through apprentices, neighbours and

---

57 P/Co R 4 12 February and 20 May 1774.

58 P/Co R 17, 5 March, 7 April, 28 August 1794. The baby was delivered in the house of William Lee, St Runwald. This seems to have been William Lee, carrier previously innkeeper at the Wagon and Horses. JBB BD/519.

59 M. de Certeau, *The practices of everyday life* (London, 1984).

60 P/Co R 12, 22 May 1788, Examination of William Ball.

61 P/Co R 12, 7 January 1789, Examination of John Carr drummer 63rd regiment of foot.

62 JBB BD/888 entry for James and Ann Triggs, victuallers; Chapter 5 above n. 53, Chapter 1 n. 72.

63 Among many possible references, see P.J.R. King, *Crime and law in England*, Chapter 7; R.B. Shoemaker, 'The decline of public insult'; J.E. Archer, '"Men behaving badly"?; maculinity and the uses of violence, 1850–1900' in

drinking companions to apparently slighter acquaintance. The assailant was always named, though (as in some outdoor sexual assaults) it is not clear whether the complainant knew the victim previously or whether the name was hunted out afterwards for the purpose of the deposition.

The declining number of interpersonal violence cases in this sample could be taken as a fragment of evidence of a civilising process. However, the limited size of the sample, the short time frame as well as institutional factors such as the comparative informality of the petty sessions and its formulaic reporting practices, would make any such conclusion over ambitious. Allowing for incomplete years in the sources (1758, 1779) the downward trend in interpersonal violence seems erratic, reversible in the bad economic year of 1789 but not in the inflationary period of the 1790s. There is no evidence of increased effectiveness of policing by the early 1800s, though the military may have dealt with some violence concerning soldiers. At the same time, populations, military and civilian, were growing. The working classes were rather differently constituted in 1800 compared to 1750 given the decline of the bay trade, though even in the 1750s cloth trade workers held no monopoly of violence.[64] Furthermore, as argued above, interpersonal violence was not a practice confined to Colchester's poor even though artisans and working people were the large minority of those involved in assault cases. In fact, reading the evidence here against studies of interpersonal violence in English towns at both earlier and later periods, it is the continuities of patterns of violence rather than any shifts in incidence that stands out.[65] In short, while it is unsafe to conclude that these figures demonstrate anything about incidence, they do show the declining significance of interpersonal violence in projects of governance in Colchester in relation to the management of poverty via the poor law.

There is a pronounced temporality to the interpersonal violence described in these depositions. The day of the week is discernible in between 11.7 per cent and 26.9 per cent of violence cases in any year, though there is no clear chronological trend in the rate of reporting (Table 8.7). The time of day is evident in from 10 to 47 per cent of cases (Table 8.8). As other historians have found, violence could often be associated with leisure time when people were congregating together (indoors or out depending on the season) and, as is not infrequently evident, people had been drinking. The categories of night and evening seem to overlap, and taken together 'after dark' violence is a significant proportion of the assault cases.[66] Although hardly consistent,

---

63 cont.
S. D'Cruze (ed.), *Everyday violence in Britain, 1850–1950* (Harlow, 2000), pp. 41–54; B.S. Godfrey, S. Farrall and S. Karstedt,'Explaining gendered sentencing patterns for violent men and women in the late-Victorian and Edwardian period', *British Journal of Criminology*, 45 (2005), pp. 696–720.

64 Deponents with baytrade occupations in violence cases numbered four in 1758, one in 1759, four in 1774, two in 1779, eight in 1784, none in 1788, six in 1789, one in 1794 and none in 1800 and 1804.

65 For example, compare R. Shoemaker, *Prosecution and punishment: petty crime and the law in London and rural Middlesex, 1660–1725* (Cambridge, 1991); J.A. Sharpe, *Crime in early modern England; 1550–1750* (Harlow, 1999), pp. 71–4. See also n. 60 above.

66 Depositions are not always clear what they mean by night as opposed to evening. Some specify night as around 7 pm and others count evening as 9 pm. There are only one or two cases in

Table 8.7
Interpersonal violence cases by day of the week

	1758	*1759*	*1774*	*1779*	*1784*	*1789*	*1794*	*1800*	*1804*	*Total*
Monday (M)	2	5	12	2	2	5	3	6	7	44
Tuesday (T)	1	0	5	2	2	10	4	4	5	33
Wednesday (W)	1	1	4	1	3	8	7	5	4	34
Thursday (TH)	0	1	5	1	6	5	2	4	5	29
Friday (F)	2	2	5	6	4	5	5	3	3	35
Saturday (S)	1	5	14	9	6	5	3	10	6	59
Sunday (SS)	1	1	1	1	1	2	3	3	0	14
not specified	11	36	4	3	6	12	4	3	3	81
total interpersonal violence cases	19	51	50	25	30	52	31	38	33	329

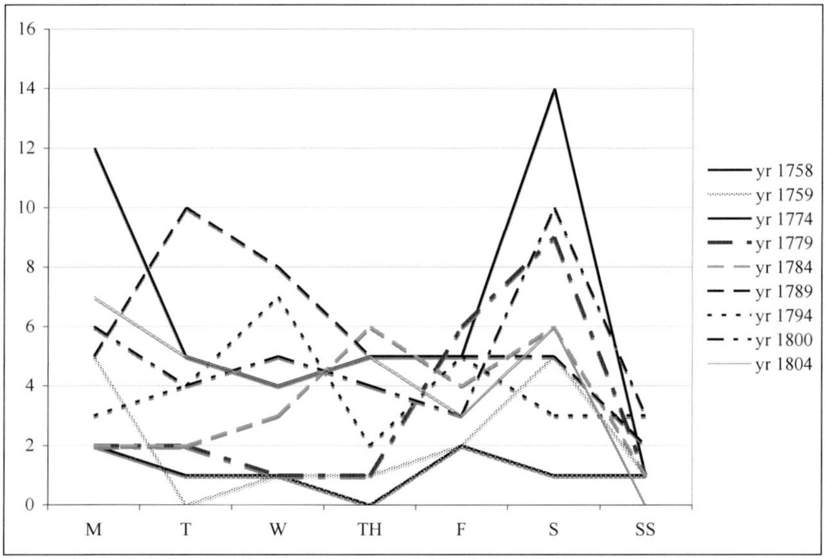

Table 8.8
Interpersonal violence cases by time of day

	1758	*1759*	*1774*	*1779*	*1784*	*1789*	*1794*	*1800*	*1804*	*Total*
morning		3	4	3	4	4	1	7	3	29
afternoon	1		9	3	1	4				18
evening/night	2	1	4	1	5	4	3	7	2	29
	4	10	14	7	5	11	10	3	4	68

cases show a tendency to cluster around the end of the week and the end of the day.

The second striking temporal feature of interpersonal violence cases is the rapidity with which they came to court, evidencing the utility of a sessions close to hand. While, of the cases where the day of the assault is specified, 15.8 per cent in 1758 and 13.7 per cent in 1759 came to the less frequent Lexden and Winstree sessions within thirty-six hours. However between 35.5 per cent and 52 per cent came to the town sessions within thirty-six hours in all other years except 1784. Here the low of 10 per cent seems to be mostly accounted for by recording practices.

Interpersonal violence happened at all times of the day and on all days of the week

Table 8.9
Depositions sworn within 36 hours

	1758	1759	1774	1779	1784	1789	1794	1800	1804
depositions made within 36 hours	3	7	26	9	3	23	11	18	12
all interpersonal violence depositions	19	51	50	25	30	52	31	38	33
percentage	15.8	13.7	52.0	36.0	10.0	44.2	35.5	47.8	36.4

Table 8.10
Location of interpersonal violence

	House	Inn	**Total indoors**	Parish	Street	Field	**Total outdoors**	All interpersonal violence
1758	6	2	8		3	1	4	19
1759	9	14	23	2	10	2	14	51
1774	5	1	6	1	3	0	4	50
1779	1	3	4	3	3	3	9	25
1784	9	4	13	0	0	0	0	30
1789	11	2	13	9	2	1	12	52
1794	5	1	6	11	3	0	14	31
1800	3	0	3	11	2	1	14	38
1804	3	0	3	10	1	0	11	33
	52	27	79	47	27	8	82	330

but there was an opportunity effect; the violence coming to the sessions was frequently to do with social interaction around leisure which included violence as an immanent possibility. Frequently, people then made a rapid resort to this accessible court.

The location of violence can be discerned in 175 depositions (53 per cent of all the 330 violence cases in the sample, Table 8.10). Distributing these 175 across the categories of house (violence within domestic space, or at the door, or damage to a house in particular breaking windows), inn, street, parish and field (any rural or agricultural location) shows a complex and varied distribution. Field is a small fraction of the total throughout. Street and inn make up a large minority of cases in the 1750s, but are progressively less prevalent later in the century. House is a larger category than any of these, but nevertheless also declines over time. Deponents were more loquacious early in the century and gave fuller details in all kinds of cases. In contrast, the pattern of recording the parish of the assault increases in the later decades of the eighteenth century.

The figures may well, however, be demonstrating a change in reporting practices rather than a change in the location of violence. Depositions stating that 'x assaulted me in St Nicholas' seems to have been a shorthand for 'in the street in St Nicholas' — common assault often took place in neighbourhood space. Even in the most formulaic depositions, an assault at home is indicated by the (indignant) complaint of violence 'in my own house'. To speak (or to be made to speak) of one's 'own' house connotes domesticity and family and the disruptions caused by interpersonal violence. The few cases of intra-household violence (between husband and wife or master and apprentice) are distributed across the period. Much violence at home was not a matter for the law. The decline in 'home' violence is associated with fewer depositions complaining of incursions by argumentative or riotous neighbours.

Rather clearer profiles are obtained for location by combining parish, street and field into an 'outdoors' category, leaving house and (albeit contentiously) inn to comprise a category for 'indoors'. In this combination depositions addressing outdoor violence rise over the chronology as 'indoor' violence declines. The proportion of violence cases which indicate location is also higher for later decades and the 1750s than between 1774 and 1789. Although these conclusions are necessarily tentative, it seems that as over time depositions concerning interpersonal violence become less frequent, the more typical assault described is an 'outdoors' assault. Indoor violence, comprising here mostly assaults in or damage to dwelling houses, pales in the routine business of governance. At the same time, the family concerns of working people were being more strongly represented in petty sessions in poor law depositions where people were either directly requesting relief or considered likely to be a future charge on the rates.

Petty sessions: poor law

The data examined here dates from the period after the ending of the borough's Workhouse Corporation had centralised poor relief in the town. Consequently relief was a parish affair and fragmented across the numerous small administrative units. The institutional history was inscribed upon the memories and biographies of the recipients of relief, who were moved from place to place. As Ann Clarke said when examined as to her settlement in 1758, because 'the parishes had been divided, she was removed' to another part of the town.[67]

John Bugg's settlement examination of 1784 is not untypical of those who locate their settlement through apprenticeship and employment.[68] Bugg came from the village of Wormingford, where his father was settled. Since he was thirteen, Bugg had passed through a series of short-term farm service engagements in the rural parishes north of Colchester, and the examination recited these in chronological order. Little Horkesley farmer Clear Saddler had paid him £3 for the year 'as nearly as he can recollect as to the wages'. Bugg was a particularly mobile worker, but for all required to give one, the formal settlement examination required a concerted act of memory. The list of employments was so long as to encourage Bugg or perhaps more probably the clerk who was taking the deposition to summarise ('Let himself several times afterwards but never continued a year in any one service') making sure to fill in the details of the last annual service to Samuel Taylor, which secured Bugg's settlement and that of his wife Eleanor, in Lexden. The requirements of the poor law shaped the narrative of people's biographies. Especially at the moment when relief was being requested, such narratives shaped identity.

Edward Harvey said he had been born in St James, Colchester where his father's settlement was. About twelve years previously he had been apprenticed for seven years to Thomas Cooper, Threadneedle Street, London hairdresser, where he served five years 'but ... during all that time ... slept in the parish of Shoreditch. Then his master gave up his business and released the examinant who came to Colchester and

67 P/Lw R 1, 4 August 1758, deposition Ann Clarke.

68 P/Co R 10b, 11 November 1784.

let himself to Geo Weatherley, St James, barber and perukemaker at 3s per week and stayed about a year and three quarters and then enlisted himself in HM East Essex Regiment of Militia.' He had no other settlement and had a wife Ann and child Mary Ann, five months old.[69] For a journeyman, even with an apprenticed trade, work was not necessarily stable. Service in the militia, the regular regiments or at sea were a not infrequent resource for men when other work dried up or paid less well. St Martins parish had apprenticed Robert Tracy to a Colchester weaver in 1779. A couple of years later, 'when the Bay trade failing, his said Master had no employment', Tracy spent a few months trying to pick up journey work in the bay trade in Coggeshall, but there was little available and he re-apprenticed himself to a Harwich fisherman. After about a further year he broke those indentures and served in a man of war for eighteen months or so before returning to cloth work in St Peters and marrying. By 1784 Tracy was juggling jobs between baymakers. That his settlement was taken at that point seems to indicate that St Peters overseers saw the likelihood of a charge to the poor rates now that he had married. Tracy's is just one of a number of examinations which retell the history of the declining bay trade at the level of individual experience.[70]

These many stories of work and migration were tied into histories of family, firstly since a child's original settlement was inherited from her or his father (or mother if illegitimate) and secondly since examinations always included details of wives and/or children who would have a settlement claim on the father's parish. Unsurprisingly, in a number of women's settlement examinations the themes of work and family are even more closely intertwined. Susan Sparrow (examined in 1794) had come to Colchester from the village of Bures St Mary (about fifteen miles away) when she married, thus exchanging a settlement through her father to one in St Martins Colchester acquired through her husband. After he died she established a settlement in St Mary-at-the-Walls through six years of domestic service, and handed this on to her fifteen year old daughter, Rachael.[71] In Ann Clark's case the parish and the family together shaped her employment history. She came from Aldham and her father had died before she was born. Upon her mother's second marriage the parish had intervened to let her for a year's service to her step-father, John Samson, gardener of St Peters Colchester. Presumably because the parish was involved there was a written agreement and she drew wages 'at different times, taking only a few pence at once'.[72]

Examinations often demonstrate the ambiguous status of women's employment. Sarah Bilton had been apprenticed by her parish (St Botolphs) to George Wright, weaver of St Nicholas but after only nine days she had been transferred to Robert Wright his father, who kept the Cock and Pye inn on North Hill.[73] Sarah received

---

69 P/Co R 10b, barber, St Leonard, undated in November 1784.

70 P/Co R 10b, 9 June 1784, examination Robert Tracey and deposition of James Mansfield ygr, baymaker of 5 August 1784, complaining that Tracey had 'taken employment with another master'.

71 P/Co R 17, 1 February 1794, examination of Susan Sparrow.

72 P/Co R10a, 5 February 1784, examination of Ann Clark.

73 1768 Poll book. JBB BD/103 entry for Henry Mason, brandy merchant. Robert Wright was left the option to purchase the Cock and Pye for £400 in Mason's will. George Wright, his son, was Mason's godson.

wages but also clothes, linen and washing. After 'some words' with Wright she worked elsewhere for a month but soon returned though Wright would no longer pay her wages. She left again after six months when he still refused to pay her, though after a bout of illness when she lived off parish relief she did manage to get 8d per week from Wright for over a year until she 'went into St Giles as a journeywoman until taken ill by a fever'. Shortly after St Giles returned her to St Peters, 'and she being then very ill and the weather very cold the overseer of St Peter ordered her to be taken care of'.[74] Being introduced into service as a parish apprentice, Sarah Bilton's identity as a wage earner was never secure. Although her subordinated place in Robert Wright's household at the Cock and Pye was pretty continuous, her claims there were limited; she needed the 'care' of the parish when she could not work through illness. For Sarah Bilton the parish alternated with her employer as the source of her subsistence. Her settlement narrative is one of marginality and the tactical juggling of dependencies.

If women outside a family household were particularly materially vulnerable, even married couples could find their independence disintegrate before the scrutiny of the poor law. Jabez Hemstead described himself as a weaver in 1784, but seems to have moved in and out of the trade between a number of jobs in service. Apart from a two-year period when he worked for All Saints baymaker Thomas Boggis, his employers were not in the cloth trade and were located in Colchester, Sudbury, Kelvedon and London. These were all short-term positions of a few months each, so his settlement remained in All Saints. He married Mary Middleton in London in 1776. Back in Colchester, the Hemsteads hit hard times. The overseer of Holy Trinity complained that Hemstead had gone away and left his wife chargeable in May of 1784. The following month he was back but at the charge of the parish. Presumably at this point they were removed into All Saints. In August Mary Hemstead was in All Saints, subsisting on the parish but Jabez was jailed in the castle for having left her 'chargeable'.[75] The Hemsteads seem to be one of several examples of tactical desertions where a man leaves his wife and often children to the care of the parish, risking imprisonment to secure a subsistence and reneging on the masculine duties of provider. The ideal of middling household identity was by contrast one of independence based on material sufficiency and normative gender roles.

Eleanor Turner's examination further demonstrates the fragilities of working people's family structures. During her first marriage she had lived in Colchester, and when her husband died had obtained a certificate to move to Boxted to live with her brother-in-law by whom she had three children, marrying him only subsequently in London. The family then lived in Colchester for around ten years until she was widowed for a second time. By this time in early middle age she was living with the last (and probably the only legitimate) child of her second marriage (Susannah aged

---

74 P/Co R 4, 20 June 1774, examination Sarah Bilton. See also her father's settlement examination, P/ Co R 4, 14 November 1774, examination of James Bilton.

75 P/Cor R10a, 1 June 1784 and P/Co R 10b, 10 June 1784; P/Co R 10b, 9 August 1784, deposition Thomas Watts overseer of All Saints and 24 June 1785, deposition Daniel Rudkin, overseer Holy Trinity. Sessions Book D/B 5 Sb 5/5, Gaol Kalendar 5 October 1784; P/CoR 22a 19 December 1800, deposition of Mary Blackwell, assaulted by Widow Hemsted of All Saints by a blow on the ear.

eighteen months) as well as an 'abandoned child' of around the same age.[76] This was unsurprisingly a household that was falling to the charge of the parish rate. Women's lower wages as well as their child-bearing made them more likely to encounter the poor law in a dependent role.[77] Hitchcock argues that changing sexual practices across the eighteenth century made penetrative heterosexual sex a more common behaviour, increasing the risk of illegitimate pregnancy. Evans suggests that single mothers seeking aid from the London Foundling Hospital increasingly used seduction narratives to emphasise their sexual passivity and constitute themselves as suitable recipients of charity.[78] Women's vulnerabilities were real risks, but also learned positions.

Not all individuals and households covered by Colchester settlement examinations were such obvious cases of dependency. Even those with a more secure material underpinning at some stage of the life cycle could subsequently meet with poverty and energetic overseers seem also to have occasionally taken settlement examinations from incomers on general principles. As well as apprenticeship and service, the payment of poor rates in a parish also established settlement. A number of examinees claimed to have paid rates in the past. Carpenter George Turnor had earlier paid rates on a watermill and house in Lavenham and served as surveyor of that parish, but was still called to give his settlement in St Peter's Colchester.[79] Samuel Moore, cordwainer, had paid rates for a house worth £10 per year in Holy Trinity and served as parish constable for two years, but was examined when he moved to the next-door parish of St Mary-at-the-Walls.[80] However, it seems that small rate-payers did not always pay in their own names. In the 1740s baymaker Isaac Boggis had deducted poor rates from the wages of weavers whom he employed.[81] Isabella Dowson, widow, paid poor rates for almost two years in All Saints, 'though she believes her name never put into the rate but that the same continued in the name of the former occupier of the house'.[82] James Ruse, tailor, paid the St Martins overseer 5s rates in 1792, but could not 'say whether was entered in the poor rate book or not'.[83] James Ratcliff was in gaol in 1779 and was examined because his wife and children were therefore chargeable. In an example which also shows women's

76 P/Co R 12, 8 May, 1789, examination of Eleanor Turner.

77 Connors, 'Women and the poor law'; M. Hanly, 'The economy of makeshifts and the poor law: a game of chance', in S. King and A. Tomkins (eds.), *The poor in England 1700–1850: an economy of makeshifts* (Manchester, 2003), pp. 76–99; T. Hitchcock *et al.* (eds.), *Chronicling poverty; the voices and strategies of the English poor 1640–1840* (London, 1997).

78 T. Hitchcock, *English sexualities, 1700–1800* (Basingstoke, 1997); T. Evans, '"Unfortunate objects": London's unmarried mothers in the eighteenth century', *Gender and History,* 17 (2005), pp. 127–53.

79 P/Co R10b, 6 September 1784.

80 P/Co R 10b, undated 1784.

81 P/Co R 1a, 4 July 1746, examination of John Cook: 'As he believes and well remembers that he used to carry home his father's weaving work to Mr Boggis who used to deduct money out of his father's wages for what he had paid for his father to the poor rates.'

82 P/Co R 10a, 9 January 1784.

83 P/Co R 17, 27 January 1794.

responsibilities for household expenditures he claimed that 'his wife about a month ago paid a poor rate to the overseer of St Martin for the house he then occupied, paid in the name of Thomas Gilson his landlord'.[84] Misfortune, old age, indigence or other difficulties meant that independence could not necessarily be guaranteed throughout the life cycle. Furthermore the relaxed recording practices of overseers (who each only served a short term) and the complex circulations of cash and value in a specie-poor economy created ambiguities around the claims to independence of artisans and the lesser middling sort. Such people therefore occupied a liminal position between the independent rate payer and the dependent pauper.

Even for those deponents with some better claim on independence (in the past if not in the present) examinations taken for the poor law remained confessional narratives. They divulged family histories, economic sufficiencies and insufficiencies and either stated or anticipated dependence. Particularly (but not exclusively) for women with illegitimate children they were tales of wayward sexuality. The poor law deposition was a narrative about work and its relationship to family or its absence and (if only by implication) intimacy. It constituted dependence and women's economic vulnerabilities reinforced this as a feminised subject position.

Parishes, poor relief and the family

The parish vestry was the forum for rate payers to determine the administration of local affairs. In All Saints, rate payers signed vestry minutes in strict order of precedence generally headed by 'Charles Gray Esq', thus inscribing local social hierarchies on the records of governance. The heaviest workload of parish administration fell on the overseers of the poor. Viewed in close focus the operation of the poor law meant more than simple social control.[85] It also provided many headaches for the overseer who had to dip into his own pocket to meet expenses in advance of collecting the rate. St Giles overseer Christopher Orrin was presented after he tried to persuade William Buckingham and pregnant Lydia Watts to marry, and so avoid her baby being chargeable to the rates. He apparently offered to pay for the wedding breakfast.[86] A sense of the embedded relationship between the overseer and his parish survive in the correspondence of St Leonards overseers.[87] The correspondence includes letters between overseers, their business clerks also undertaking parish matters, the keeper of the house of correction, attorneys giving legal advice and other interested parties. Many letters between parishes indemnified each other against the cost of relieving poor who were chargeable elsewhere. Apart from rate collection, keeping accounts and paying weekly collections, the overseer

---

84 P/Co R 8, 6 May 1779.

85 T. Hitchcock,'A new history from below', review of T. Sokoll (ed.), *Essex pauper letters, 1731–1837, History Workshop Journal,* 57 (2004), pp. 294–8; T. Sokoll, 'Negotiating a living: Essex pauper letters from London, 1800–1834', *International Review of Social History,* 45 (2000), pp. 19–46; T. Sokoll (ed.), *Essex pauper letters, 1731–1837* (Oxford 2001).

86 Buckingham's settlement was in St Botolphs. ERO D/B 5 Sr/323, Easter 1794; n. 44 above.

87 St Leonard's overseers' correspondence ERO D/P 245; Connors,'Women and the poor law', p. 134.

needed to keep a weather eye on the poor of the parish and their incipient needs and ruses. Overseers also dealt with local JPs, courts and other borough and parish officials. Office-holding was a matter of practical experience and social connection.

Ephraim Shillito, the Keeper of the House of Correction, wrote to the St Leonards overseer, Jonathan Tabor in 1765, leaning on the parish to admit the settlement and accept the costs of relief of a woman in the House of Correction whom Shillito was keen to get off his hands. Poor Law administration was coloured by patronage and connection. Behind Shillito was Charles Gray, Shillito's patron and the magistrate who committed the woman to the castle in the first place, who had 'Examined me very Particularly about the Prisoner'. Welfare was also a matter of business. Shillito concludes, 'You'll find a great deal Less charge at any other Place where she may be Confin'd, than can be done by Yr Servt, Ephraim Shillito.'[88] Furthermore, poor relief involved the proximate management of dependency. Shillito had, he said, provided her with clothes and was 'now Nurse and Doctor to her' though we may perhaps perceive the work of his wife, Elizabeth, hidden behind these assertions.

Household, family and their dependencies were closely imbricated in the day-to-day operation of poor relief. Sarah Neave of Halesworth wrote that she and her elderly husband would no longer keep a troublesome parish apprentice and his mother. She complained that both were lazy and bad-tempered.[89] The Neaves had extended their household to take on the boy and his mother, but now ejected them. Overseers were keen to keep costs down and this could threaten the integrity of dependent families; George Nutter the vestry clerk threatened the Bocking (Essex) vestry that St Leonards would send Benjamin Murrells and his 'aged and infirm' wife to the House of Industry in Suffolk if Bocking vestry removed them to St Leonards.[90]

The correspondence mixed the social and familial with business. 'Official' letters include personal greetings and remembrances to family and friends. Apart from overseers of distant parishes, most of the letter writers in the St Leonards correspondence were known to each other. Letters refer to friends and business contacts in London and elsewhere. Indeed, St Leonard's papers include a letter to his mother from the overseer's son, away in service, miserable, hard up and playing on her sympathy to make his peace after some row with his father. Business and family letters are not dissimilar in style and as this survival indicates, were kept together.

James Watts, a carrier or broker (and a ready letter writer) gave the St. Leonards overseers a particularly hard time over 1768 and 1769. Watts had been a violent husband and then had left Colchester for London leaving his wife Sally and the three

---

88 ERO D/P 245, 20 March 1765. See also All Saints Vestry Minutes, D/P200; Overseers' general correspondence, St Botolphs parish D/P 203/18/1, 1750–1850.

89 St Leonards overseers' correspondence, ERO D/P 245, Sarah Neave to John Oathwaite, 25 August 1778.

90 *Ibid.*, John Bartholemew to George Nutter, vestry clerk, Bocking. Bartholemew replied that St Leonard planned to send the Murrells to the House of Industry in Suffolk, 'where we intend sending all those that are beholden to the parish.' See A.F.J. Brown, *Chartism in Essex and Suffolk* (Chelmsford, 1982), for later protests at the larger more centralised workhouses which operated in Suffolk.

children chargeable to the parish.[91] St Leonards attempted to collect four shillings a week from Watts for maintenance, and when this was not forthcoming, to have him committed for vagrancy, since he was out of the parish without a certificate. They were able to achieve neither end. Watts had, he said, been unable to find work in Colchester and had gone up to London and around the Home Counties to make a new life. Far from being penitent, he complained hotly of the parish's threats and refused to comply with their demands. As a 'nature born Englishman' he resented what he described as the threats of the parish officers; in a personal and family concern Watts drew on a language of imperilled rights and the illegitimate extension of power. He represented himself as the aggrieved party; 'I am very sensible that had I been well used and had good words instead of bad ones that the Parish of St Leonard need not (have) Disbursted any money upon my acc[t], but as it is they must trust till I am able to pay.'

Watts did not intend (he said) to return to Colchester, and regarding his wife remarked, 'I shall not take the Trouble of Coming eighty miles to kill a fool and be hang[d] into the bargain.'[92] Violence continued to inflect his (now rhetorical) relationship with his own family. But in the same letter he drew attention to the family of the overseer. He opens his letter to overseer John Bartholomew with a recommendation that had he, 'minded your own and not interfer[d] into other people's Affairs I believe it would have been better for you and your family' which gives an especially truculent tone to his closing valediction, wishing that 'all your good family are well'.

Watts subsequently bid farewell to Sally by letter, planning (he said) to leave for Jamaica. He had contracted a second bigamous marriage in London, where he had 'the happiness of a Very good companion and plenty of Cash', to a lady among whose attractions was £500 of her own. Watts drew up a written will in the form of a letter to Sally dividing his second wife's money between the children of his first marriage. Meanwhile, no doubt, St Leonard's overseers were having to support Sally and the children. Family is thoroughly entangled in Watt's largely self-authored narrative, where it is marked by the intersections of violence and money. Watts' family romance was laid open to scrutiny because he refused the tenets of household respectability. His ironical will is a hollow rebuttal of his failure to provide for his family. He addressed the 'gentlemen' of the St Leonards vestry less in their official function but as (somewhat better off) business colleagues and family men. Watts may have been a tongue-in-cheek opportunist but the fact that such a conception of the parish was available within the prevailing social imaginary gives some insight into the everyday negotiations involved in governance at parish level. Watts' blustering attempts to

91 ERO Sessions Book D/B 5 Sb 5/4, Epiphany 1769, Gaol Kalendar. Watts was jailed overnight until he entered into recognisances to keep the peace towards his wife.

92 *Ibid.*, Watts to Thomas Barnes, innkeeper at the Three Horseshoes, St Leonard, 20 July 1769; Watts to John Bartholomew, merchant (Chapter 4), 30 July 1769. Also William Mayhew probably to Bartholomew, 10 August 1768, giving legal opinion that the parish had grounds to arrest Watts. Watts to his wife, two undated letters. One containing disposition of property, the other saying he plans to go to Jamaica, both apparently written 1768–9.

invoke *their* family responsibilities batters against the divide between governors (who did indeed send family remembrances in business letters and filed complaints from their teenage sons with the parish correspondence) and those they governed.[93]

Conclusion

The process of governance in eighteenth-century Colchester was complex, uneven, wide-ranging and always subject to challenge at its peripheries. It operated across a heterogeneous array of institutions and involved a significant sector of the middling sort and town gentry. Petty officialdom also included more substantial artisans. The practices of government also took in the work of wives and became incorporated into the range of activities of middling households and forming one component of their credit. Circulations of cash as well as social interaction moved in and out of the field of governance. A sometimes permeable social and cultural divide operated between those who participated in some way in the processes of governance and the working classes of the town whose greater material insecurity situated them outside the governing group and subjected them to intervention and sometimes punishment. The processes of governance invited and compelled the production of narratives of disorder and dependence which opened up the families and households of the governed to scrutiny and record. The always-present risks to material sufficiency and family social and emotional stability could jeopardise middling respectabilities, revealing the limitations of politeness, undermining credit and positioning middling individuals disadvantageously in the business of governance. Socially visible cultures of violence provided a problem for governance, particularly since the majority of interpersonal violence cases involved artisans or the poor. However, violence was by no means a social practice confined to the lower orders. While in theory violence undermined the claims of middling individuals to participation in polite culture it remained an entrenched part of the social practice of certain men.

93 *Ibid.*, Watts to his wife, two undated letters.

Chapter 9

The indefatigable Mr Strutt

Figure 9.1 E.P. Strutt, *Benjamin Strutt* watercolour, *c.* 1806. Reproduced by kind permission of Colchester and Ipswich Museums Service

Benjamin Strutt was a man whose appearance and demeanour inscribed him in people's memories; both Ann Taylor and Henry Crabb Robinson left accounts of him and his son E.P. Strutt included his likeness among the series of caricatures he drew in the early 1800s. The Taylor sisters knew Strutt as the odd but likeable father of their teenage friends. Ann Taylor remembered that

> His fine grey head and dark penetrating eyes made his appearance singular and interesting, while a marked scowl and a taciturn austerity seemed intended to express a high disregard of society in all its forms of external elegance and conventional politeness — intended, I fancy, to express all this, but, to my thinking, it did its business awkwardly.[1]

1 J. Gilbert (ed.), *The autobiography and other memorials of Mrs Gilbert,* 2nd edn (London, 1876), Vol 1, p. 143.

To the Victorian cataloguer of the borough records, who knew Strutt through his copious diminutive handwriting and careful Chamberlain's accounts, he was the 'indefatigable Mr Strutt', the most commendable and most far-seeing borough officer during the last decades of the old corporation, dedicated to the cause of urban improvement.[2] Crabb Robinson, serving as a lawyer's clerk, thought Strutt was 'the only superior person I knew at Colchester. I stood in fear of him and his sarcasms.'[3] Strutt was Whig/radical in politics and apparently atheist in religion. He made his living as a scrivener and a political agent. He was also 'artist, musician, antiquary, poet, and author, an amateur in each'.[4] Among a number of publications he wrote a town history. As borough reformer, pedestrian, man of business, domestic man, historian and intellectual, Benjamin Strutt reflects the themes of this study as they coalesced at the end of its chronology.

Strutt was the son of a Clacton schoolmaster, born in 1754. He came to Colchester in 1769 as apprentice of William Mayhew jnr, who was first Deputy Recorder and then Recorder and High Steward. According to Crabb Robinson, Strutt's early apprenticeship left him much free time. Mayhew had business as a bencher at Grey's Inn and as Recorder of both Ipswich and Aldeburgh. Strutt used this leisure firstly to pursue an extensive course of self-education and later to make interventions in borough politics. Strutt's Whiggish connections extended to the Revd Nicholas Corsellis, landed gentleman from nearby Wivenhoe, for whom Strutt acted as agent in the 1780s, attempting to negotiate a settlement of the debts Corsellis was owed by Francis Smythies.[5] Strutt first figured in borough politics during the mid-1780s, mostly as Mayhew's agent[6] but after Mayhew's death became a political manager in his own right, acting for George Tierney, the radical candidate in the 1788 and 1790 elections. A letter to *The World* newspaper comments that Tierney's agent 'after having strutted his hour of importance on the stage, is enraged to find himself reduced to his primitive insignificance'.[7] Strutt's politics were sufficiently well known for the local postmistress to include him among the 'Known Leading Disaffected men in this Town'.[8] Politically, therefore, Strutt opposed Frank Smythies and the then dominant

2 Harrod, H., *Repertory of the records and evidences of the borough of Colchester* (Colchester, 1865).

3 Crabb Robinson papers in Dr William's Library, quoted by J. Bensusan Butt, *Benjamin Strutt, William Cole and James Fisin* (Colchester, privately printed, 1994), p. 37.

4 Gilbert, *Mrs Gilbert*, Vol 1, p. 143.

5 ERO D/DHt E24, correspondence between Strutt and Francis Smythies re the stamp duty.

6 *IpsJ* 26 February 1785 for the satirical advertisement of the 'COMMITTEE for collecting Evidence in support of the C— ELECTION give this public notice, that they will continue to sit at the house of Shining Jemmy, known by the sign of Neptune's Nag, every evening next week, in order to receive information … As facts will be difficult to obtain, any probably circumstance will be admitted. … (anyone) … who is a good hand at EVIDENCE COINING will meet with every possible encouragement.' The Neptune's Nag was the Seahorse in All Saints, and its landlord was James Green. The pseudonymous committee are recognisable as middling tradesmen, and its secretary was said to be BEN VELLUM. For a fuller explanation of the politics behind this see S. D'Cruze, *The middling sort in provincial England: politics and social relations in Colchester 1730–1800* (PhD thesis, Essex, 1990), p. 438.

7 *The World*, 9 September 1790.

8 Elizabeth Manning to Aliens Office, NA HO/42/213, 26 April 1798.

corporation party during the French Wars when radicalism seemed tantamout to disloyalty. Strutt's business acumen and reforming energies were nevertheless to raise him from 'primitive insignificance' in the politics of the early nineteenth-century borough.

Strutt was a familiar figure on Colchester's streets, where his

> ... duffle coat its collar rears,
> To screen the mouth, the chin, the nose, and ears;
> ...
> With solemn pace, he treads the streets,
> And seems to grudge to look at those he meets[9]

Pedestrian, solitary, preoccupied and provincial, walking the streets of a garrisoned town in wartime, Strutt was a particular kind of flaneur.[10] His *History* carries the traces of his walks around Colchester. He paced the graveyards; his second volume includes full listings of monumental inscriptions. His description of the town's market is written from the perspective of one who regularly walked the High Street.

> The flesh market is now held in the principal street, and, to the great annoyance to individuals even in the foot path. A custom however obnoxious and absurd still prevailing, and in spite of cleanliness, decency, and public benefit, likely to continue. The herb market, tho' in 1529 ordered to be held from the Lion to St Nicholas's church, is kept from that inn to Pelham's lane, notwithstanding the former situation is preferable. The fish market was formerly kept at the New Hythe, but now is held in the butchery, — a place from its native stench and filth sufficiently offensive, but aided as it is by the exalted effluvia of decayed fish; becomes ten times worse, and were it not sometimes washed by a timely shower, would go near to occasion the worst of putrid disorders.[11]

Strutt's offended gaze was that of a vegetarian and an urban improver. From both perspectives the market represented things out of place — the literal and symbolic pollution of sound governance. This view of Colchester is contemporary with but very different to Ann Taylor's more sentimental geographies (Chapter 2). Strutt's antiquarianism might have been romantic, but the past was not to get in the way of environmental improvement.

In 1807, during his first term as Borough Chamberlain Strutt put forward a *Plan for improving the common or half-year lands*. The half-year lands and the burgesses' right of common had recurrent potential for causing political upset (Chapters 6 and 7). By 1807 the grazing rights were of little use to most burgesses and most of the land was leased out at a very low return. Strutt proposed selling off the land as opportunity arose. The proceeds, placed in 3 per cent Consols returned the freemen around 16s

---

9 S. Bridge, *The Guild* (Colchester, 1814), quoted in Bensusan Butt, *Benjamin Strutt*, p. 28; J. Cooper *et al., The borough of Colchester* (Woodbridge, 1994), pp. 161–2. B. Strutt, *The History and description of Colchester* (Colchester, 1803).

10 J. Walkowitz, *City of dreadful delight, narratives of sexual danger in late-Victorian London* (London, 1992), pp. 16–17. The concept of the *flaneur* needs some scaling down from Baudelaire's and Benjamin's original conceptions to fit into Colchester's provincial townscape. Nevertheless it still conveys the modern, bourgeois, masculine, observing and reforming gaze that Strutt turned onto Colchester's streets.

11 Strutt, *History*, Vol 1, pp. 78–9.

per year instead of as little as 8d under the old scheme.[12] He was Common Councilman and Assistant in 1818 and also sat as one of the Improvement Commissioners, by that time very much the more efficient institution.[13] In that role he intervened to improve the water supply and close several old insanitary wells, including the so-called King Coel's pump at the top of the High Street.[14] In 1807 he had been instrumental in procuring a 'substantial Oak Chest for the purpose of depositing the Common Seal, Charters and other matters' to be locked by four keys respectively held by the four Borough Claviers, since 'for the lack of this a mortgage had been granted to Thomas Lowten, and the whole transaction appeared to be for the furtherance of party views and purposes'. This referred to the legal bill run up with London attorney Lowten to defend Frank Smythies' assumption of the Recordership against the wishes of the previous Recorder, Strutt's old master William Mayhew. Smythies and Lowten were business partners and the bill of £2,000 was only eventually paid in 1822, long after both of them were dead.[15] Strutt's oak chest looks both forward and backward in time. It revives earlier corporation practice and restored purpose to the moribund Claviers' office. It was a partisan gesture. Like his other interventions, it also moved on from the past in the direction of more efficient and bureaucratic town governance.

The early nineteenth century corporation was increasingly unrepresentative — there were only 480 resident burgesses in a town whose population was now over 16,000.[16] During Strutt's period of office a vociferous burgesses' rights party squabbled with the Tory corporation. Had he lived, he would doubtless have supported the petition against the corporation in favour of the 1835 Local Government Act. Strutt followed the established middling route into office and local politics. He expanded his credit and reputation by so doing. His career coincided with a period when his politics put him in opposition to the locally dominant Tories and when population growth and social change had made the corporation an increasingly irrelevant and inefficient institution. His agendas seem to be as much about better government as about individual advancement and he was able to make some headway by using the battered edifices of local administration.

Strutt put together the deal between the Borough, the Norwich Company of Comedians and himself and other subscribers to build a new theatre in 1812, big enough to hold an audience of over 1,000. His forty shares produced an income of £200 a year.[17] The first production was Shakespeare's *Cymbeline*, a reference to Cunobelin the ancient leader who ruled from Colchester. *Cymbeline* is in many ways a story where the restoration of family underpins a 'British' state. The Improvement Commissioners used the proceeds of the last night production that season (*Catherine*

12 Bensusan Butt, *Benjamin Strutt*, pp. 26–7; T. Cromwell, *The history and description of the ancient town and borough of Colchester*, two vols (Colchester, 1824), pp. 261–2; Cooper *et al.*, *Colchester*, p. 165.

13 M.E. Speight, *Politics, in the borough of Colchester 1812–1847* (PhD thesis, London, 1959).

14 A. Phillips, *Ten men and Colchester* (Chelmsford, 1985), p. 12.

15 Bensusan Butt, *Benjamin Strutt*, p. 27.

16 R.G. Thorne, *The history of parliament: The House of Commons 1790–1820*, Vol. 2, p. 158.

17 Bensusan Butt, *Benjamin Strutt*, p. 24.

and Pettruchio — another show which examined contested gender relations in families) to fund the removal of an unwanted impediment to orderly urban space located just outside its door — the town gate at St Botolphs.[18]

Strutt followed the well-trodden path for eighteenth-century middling men with legal training as a man of business and was to act in this capacity for Elizabeth Mayhew. William Mayhew snr (Elizabeth's father) had extended his credit in no small part through property he controlled as executor.[19] William Mayhew jnr, Strutt's old master, had altered his will in 1787, two weeks before he died. The codicil (in Strutt's hand) left the bulk of his property to his mistress, Sarah Campling, and her three-year-old daughter, leaving only a residue to his sister Elizabeth who was nevertheless named as executor together with attorney William Francis. She took the matter to Chancery and repeatedly demanded exact accounts from Sarah Campling, whose inheritance dwindled to nothing. Crabb Robinson, then a clerk in attorney William Francis' office noted that one day they 'looked over Mayhew's papers for amusement.'[20] Strutt acted for Sarah Campling and became a trustee of her daughter Harriet's 1807 marriage settlement with Thomas Courtney. Whatever his successes in borough government, Strutt seems to have encountered more complications in this capacity. After his death his estate owed £600 to the trust. By taking on the family and legal complications of the Mayhews, Strutt seems to have undermined the credit of his own family.

Strutt had married Caroline Pollett, the daughter of a Colchester apothecary, in London in 1779.[21] The couple had two sons and three daughters. Caroline Strutt died in 1795. His poem, apparently accompanying the gift of her watch to a daughter makes clear his affective investment in family relationships:

> BY THIS GILT TOY, which marks each hour that flies
> Watched thy anxious Mother thy couch beside
> While dewy slumbers clos'd thy infant eyes;
> To whose sad Memory the ceaseless tide
> Of my sad tears down flow, & as they rise
> Obtrusive hope and joy are scattered wide

When the Taylor sisters knew the family, Strutt's mother also lived there and his unmarried sister Sarah Charlotte kept house. The two elder daughters died in their early twenties, apparently of consumption, something Ann Taylor blamed on the family's vegetarianism. This does seem to have been a household that pursued domestic gentility; there was no family business to absorb the labour of daughters and sons. To the extent that Ann Taylor's recollections are reliable, the Strutt household saw the pains and grief of middling family life but apparently none of its possible violence; Richard Tomkins the surgeon who beat up his wife and servant lived next door (Chapter 8).

The Strutts lived at 70 High Street just uphill from The Minories. The house has a

---

18 ERO Acc 905, Box 2, MS 'Colchester Theatre'; T. Cromwell, *Colchester*, Vol. 2, pp. 340–1.

19 Through his executorship of Thomas Harrison's estate. Chapter 4 above, n 18.

20 26 September 1792, quoted in Bensusan Butt, *Benjamin Strutt*, p. 23.

21 JBB BD/1126 Hugh Bernard Pollett.

classical red-brick front, but Ann Taylor remembers some unconventional internal renovations that challenge formulations about increased family privacy and the growing rationalisation of domestic space.

> The house was rendered as antique in appearance as it could be. In the centre was what was used as a music hall, occupying two stories in height, and hung round with pieces of old armour, weapons and similar curiosities. One of the upper chambers opened into the hall, not by windows, but literally, the whole side being removed. It was defended only by a low balustrade, so that the daughter whose room it was, might, as she lay in bed, have found her dreams disturbed by the spectral appearances of shield, helmet, and breastplate gleaming under the moonlight falling on them from a skylight in the roof.[22]

Jane and Ann Taylor spent their last night in Colchester with the Strutts and were excited to be the first to sleep in a new room with a 'gothic bed'. Gothicism in house design was a minor fashion in early nineteenth-century Colchester. Strutt's liking for the gothic and the antiquarian went further and marked much of his scholarly and artistic activity. It was a taste which seems to have been about cultures of sensibility and the rejection of politeness in its rule-bound (and provincial) form.

Chapter 5 located Strutt among a group of energetic young friends hung up on Ossian, philosophy, writing and art. At that time he painted in oils and nursed (unfulfilled) ambitions to 'be two degrees above Sir Joshua'. From his early twenties Strutt was publishing engravings and dry point, the earliest of which was probably the map of the 1648 Colchester siege in 1773. The romance of the past, as well as an aversion to tyranny (in the person of Fairfax) made the siege an absorbing theme which occupied 125 pages of Strutt's first, 276-page, volume of his *History of Colchester*. He also painted the execution of the royalist leaders, Lucas and Lisle, their heroic martial masculinities dwarfed by the bulk of the castle.

Like Morant, Strutt's *History* is a vehicle for political comment. Strutt closes his historical narrative in fairly short order after the Siege, though James II's interference with borough charters are a further manifestation of tyranny in a country, 'the boast of which is a conservation of public and private rights, and the general principles of political liberty.'[23] On the whole Strutt paid more attention to liberty as an abstract concept than to an accumulation of 'public and private rights'. Liberty took on new kinds of emphasis in a garrison town during the French wars, for political radicals as well as Tories. Strutt concludes by celebrating the 1688 revolution and its historical consequences which included peace, economic and social progress and greater national cohesion. His own political experience seems to be referenced when he comments

> The walls and gates of the feudal burgh, shorn of its battlements, were thrown down, to admit at every avenue, the flux and reflux of internal wealth. The repair of highways, and opening rivers choaked by neglect, rendered every corner of the kingdom easy of access, whether for pleasure or merchandise; and served well to connect and consolidate the pecuniary interest of the burghs, with that of the metropolis.[24]

---

22 Gilbert (ed.), *Mrs Gilbert*, Vol. 1, p. 142. Traces of these renovations remained on the staircase in the 1980s, Bensusan Butt, *Benjamin Strutt*, p. 24.

23 B. Strutt, *Colchester*, Vol 1, p. 272.

24 *Ibid.*, p. 276

Nevertheless, this apparent celebration of change and modernity is abruptly foreshortened in his next and concluding sentence:

> Thus connected and consolidated, ...(the)... importance ...(of popular boroughs)...is reduced; their historical facts of less moment, and no longer disjunct and independent; but like the ancient Baron removed from his primitive dignity to a menial attendance upon royalty, are become the degraded appendages of a proud and overgrown capital, and involved in the vortex of its corruption.[25]

For Strutt in 1803, modernity proved a disappointment, since national integration led not to the improvement of independent local government but its subsuming into metropolitan vice.

By the end of Strutt's life, however, the town made a favourable impression on its next historian, Thomas Cromwell, who lauded its paving and gas lighting, numbers of brick-fronted 'capital messuages' in the principal streets. The untidy market shambles had been in part cleared from the centre of the High Street and an indoor market built (much disliked by traders). There were new, prestigious residential developments outside the town walls along Lexden Road together with a new hospital. There was the new theatre in Botolph Street. Churches and the castle had been renovated. The town pillory and the cage had been removed and public whipping of felons ended in 1823; punishment was no longer an urban spectacle. There was still some industry near the town centre in the form of an iron foundry but it was tucked away behind the High Street and its products in the form of elegant iron columns on the new Corn Exchange graced the town centre.[26] Spatial and architectural changes had been the product of economic change, of changes in governance, and of shifts in urban public culture. Cromwell was a commercial writer who borrowed his history from Morant. However, because his impressions on contemporary Colchester were born of swift observation and consultation with a few prominent citizens, including Strutt, his book says much about how the Colchester of the 1820s wanted to present itself – as a progressive, well-ordered town. It was an over-optimistic view. There was still much for urban improvers to tackle, since population was now growing and water supply, sanitation and drainage had not much troubled the builders of new housing.[27]

The aim of this study has been to track such visually apparent alteration in the town fabric back to the middling sort who both produced and consumed the tangibles and intangibles of eighteenth-century urban culture, who were part of the structures and institutions of urban governance and who both gained and lost as Colchester's economy moved. Provincial towns were important to eighteenth-century society and culture, and the middling sort were in many ways at the heart of such towns, helping shape and investing in the distinctive urban identity of each. In Colchester, the borough, parish and the neighbourhood contextualised the histories of trading and professional families who persisted over generations and arguably were a distinctive feature of this slower-growing town. Even among the 'persistents', the most affluent

25 *Ibid.*

26 Cromwell, *Colchester*, Vol. 2, p. 305, A. Phillips, 'Early Colchester foundries', *Transactions of the Essex Archaeological Society*, 14 (1982), pp. 102–10.

27 Phillips, *Ten men*, pp. 11–13.

merchants and professionals extended their activities and their credit over a wider geographical area. The 'fine folks' who graced genteel social occasions included local landed gentry who used the town as a social and cultural arena, provided custom for its traders and could exercise some patronage, but who were far from controlling its government and politics. Even the town and local gentry who did involve themselves in the borough depended on the middling sort to maintain that interest. At the opposite end of the social spectrum, the vicissitudes of economic change made geographic mobility a frequent subsistence tactic of the poor. It was the institutional imperative of the poor law as much as familial attachment that tied labouring people to place. The Colchester middling sort positioned themselves on the uphill side of the always porous but nevertheless salient divide between those who were attached to governance through office-holding and rate-paying and those whose more tenuous hold on independence constituted them as the objects of governance. This political and administrative distinction mirrored that equally opaque boundary between the polite and the 'meaner sort of people'.

If the middling sort can be tracked through the history of eighteenth-century Colchester, then family organised much of what they did and how they thought about it, not least because family was a vital foundation of credit. Credit was the solvent of social and economic relations as well as of political and administrative ones in a large borough that required officers. Office-holding was characteristic of middling masculinities but its duties were folded into household activities and so involved the labour of women as well as men. Politeness, as an arena of cultural production and reproduction and as a mesh of embodied social practice, even (or perhaps especially) as it settled into rule-based etiquette, was appropriated by the middling sort. Together, family, credit and politeness were the common denominators of the eighteenth-century Colchester middling sort across divisions of religion, politics and affluence, through which they dealt with currents of historical change mostly emanating from outside and which led to the decline in the town's staple industry. These were secular economic and demographic growth which moved the regional focus of the urban network north and west, the growing markets for East Anglian grain especially in London, the increasing integration of national markets for goods, credit and money, and the changing national political contexts wrought by the growth of empire, war and the calls for parliamentary reform which shifted the eminently useful discourse of rights and liberty towards popular radicalism.

Bibliography

Primary sources

Manuscript

The John Bensusan Butt (hereafter JBB) collection of research material is located at the Essex Record Office, Chelmsford (hereafter ERO) reference Acc 905.

The manuscript material in Acc 905 that is not available elsewhere, as well as correspondence, unpublished papers and lectures and the draft entries for the *John Bensusan Butt Biographical Dictionary of Eighteenth-Century Colchester* (forthcoming 2008) include:

Bland H. D, 'Colchester Anecdotes', unpublished manuscript

Report on the Records of Winsley's Charity, J. Bensusan Butt to P. Daniell, Clerk to the Trustees. 27 December 1969

Correspondence between J. Bensusan Butt and the Librarian, United Grand Lodge of England, Freemasons Hall, London WC2, 1965 and 1972

Notes on Deeds of numbers of properties including Headgate House, Cullingford's Stationers and St Mary's Cottage, all in private hands and originally lent by the owners

Notes on the records of Colchester Charity School, originals now lost

Plans and photographs of The Minories, c.1950 and a number of other eighteenth-century houses

The following list of primary sources includes those consulted directly for this study and those accessed via notes in the JBB collection. All records are located in ERO unless otherwise stated.

Parish records for Colchester

All Saints (D/P 200): Registers, bapt. and bur. 1682–1793, 1793–1812, mar. 1682–1754, 1754–73, 1774–92, 1792–1806, 1807–12; Churchwarden's rates 1763–1870; Vestry minutes 1686–1859; Overseer's rates 1776–1841 and Accounts 1745–1800

Holy Trinity (D/P 323): Registers, bapt. 1696–1723, 1723–1812, bur. 1696–1732, 1732–1812, mar. 1696–1730, 1731–53, 1753–1812; Overseer's rates 1794–1805; Overseer's accounts 1747–77; Survey and plan of the parish by Cole and Hale of 1818 (T/M 268)

St Botolph (D/P 203): Registers, bapt. 1682–1716, bur. 1680–1799, 1800–12; Churchwarden's rates 1785, 1791, 1797, 1805 and Accounts 1759; Vestry minutes 1752–82; Overseer's rates 1745–9, 1753–1800; Overseer's accounts 1746–1800; Correspondence on applications for poor relief from 1755–1830

St Giles (D/P 324): Registers, bap. 1692–1781, 1781–1812, bur. 1699–1781, 1779–1812, mar. 1693–1754, 1754–92

St James (D/P 138): Registers, bapt. 1695–1727, 1727–82 (inc bur.), 1783–1812 (inc bur.), mar. 1727–54, 1754–1812; Churchwarden's rates 1776, 1782–7

St Leonard (D/P 245); Registers, mar. 1754–1807; Churchwarden's bills 1725–1815; Overseer's bills 1747–1830; Overseer's accounts 1746–54, 1763–9, 1773–83; Overseer's correspondence c.1740–c.1820

St Martin (D/P 325): Registers, bapt. 1735–1812, mar. 1735–59, 1760–93, 1793–1814

St Mary-at-the-Walls (D/P 246): Registers, bapt. 1731–90, 1791–1812, bur. 1732–90, 1791–1812, mar. 1726–54, 1754–82, 1782–1803

St Nicholas (D/P 176): Registers, bapt. 1695–1768, bur. 1696–1768, bapt. and bur. 1769–1812, mar. 1754–1812; Overseer's rates 1757, 1766, 1773–1800

St Peter (D/P 178): Registers, bapt. 1732–82, 1781–1812, bur. 1781–1812 (microfilm), mar. 1732–54, 1782–1812; Overseer's rates 1764–83, 1798–1802; Settlement and apprenticeship papers 1722–c.1820

St Runwald (D/P 177): Overseer's rates 1745–9, 1753–4, 1766–1804

Wills proved in Archdeaconry of Colchester and the Commissary of London (Essex and Herts) held at ERO, 1735–1800. Viewed either in the registers (ERO D/ACR and D/ABR) or in the original (ERO D/ACW D/ABW).

Administrations in the same jurisdictions, 1735–1800. Viewed either as bonds (D/ACWb, D/ABWb) or in the Register of Probate (D/ABAc, D/ACAc).

Colchester borough records

Assembly Book, D/B 5 Gb 6–9
Borough Quarter Sessions Books, D/B 5 Sb 4–6, and Files D/B 5 Sr 158–369
Borough Petty Sessions, 1745–1800, P/CoR1, 1a, 2–25

Lexden and Winstree petty sessions

Colchester Sittings, P/LWR/1 and P/LWR/4

Rebow papers

Transferred from Colchester Public Library (CPL), Acc 47, Boxes 1–5
Records of Rebow family's tenure of Harwich lighthouse, D/U 59, D/AB2, D/Ht B2, D/QS116

Essex militia records

L/V/4/2–10

County quarter sessions 1735–1800

Rolls Q/SR, Bundles Q/Sb, Q/SBb, JP Lists Q/JL, Order Books Q/SO

Land tax assessments

Colchester and neighbouring parishes, Q/RP

Records of Colchester Free School

Acc C16 Trunk 1, Boxes 1 and 2
The pamphlets and handbills included there are:

1. *To the freeburgesses of Colchester*, Colchester, 17 November 1778
2. *To the freeburgesses of Colchester*, this being the address by the trustees signed by Charles Gray, Michael Hills, Samuel Todd, Peter Daniell
3. *An address to the free burgesses of Colchester in answer to the address from the trustees of the school estate*, Colchester, 9 December 1778
4. *To the freeburgesses of Colchester*, Colchester, 16 December 1778
5. *To the freeburgesses of Colchester*, signed by 'A Freeman and a Lover of Truth', Colchester, 26 December 1778
6. *A fourth address to the freeburgesses of Colchester*, Colchester, 28 December 1778
7. *An address to the freeburgesses of Colchester, occasioned by an address dated, December 26th, 1778*, Colchester, 12 January 1779

8. *To the freeburgesses of Colchester. a man may buy gold too dear*, Colchester, 13 January 1779

Also small handbills by Hewitt the corporation candidate of 26 October 1778 and 12 January 1779 and by his opponent Duddell of 29 October 1778

Charity records

Winsley's Charity Bonds ERO D/Q 30/4/8
Winnock's Charity leases ERO D/Q 30 & 31

Non-conformist records

Eld Lane ERO D/NB/4/1–2
Lion Walk Miscellaneous Papers
Registers of Lion Walk, Eld Lane, Stockwell, Methodist chapels, to 1815, microfilm in ERO

Round papers

D/DR, D/DRb, D/DRc, D/DRe, D/DRh, especially D/DR/T28 and D/DRe T28/24, for Hollytrees
Acc C15 Box 1 Gray's Diary
D/DR/B1, B1a Box 16, Gray's accounts
D/DRbZ1–7 Gray's correspondence
D/DRc B1–10 legal and professional papers
D/DRc F74–79, Gray family funerals at F77
D/DRc F17 Gray to Creffield
D/DRet/F38–9; Horatio and Susan Cock domestic papers and accounts

Gray Mss

D/DRg, especially D/DRg4, correspondence

Michael Hills' accounts

D/DCm/222

Corsellis papers

D/DHt E24–6, 32, estate and family especially:
Stamp Duty farm D/Dht E24
Colchester Customs house D/DHt T72/114

Smyth family papers

Correspondence D/DEl/f15 and D/D/fg/Z1
Estate accounts D/D T/B/224/5

Morant papers

D/Y/2/1 and 2/2

Miscellaneous deeds

Duffield's coal yard leased from the Corporation D/DU 518/5
D/De/T162 Deeds of the Bowling Green, Colchester
D/Del/T/6 Deeds of property owned by Bawtree family
D/Da/T/714a Deeds of Cross Keys Inn
D/Q 31/3/4, D/Du/441/89, D/Du/559/88 Deeds of various Colchester properties.

Collection of deeds and papers originally held in Colchester Public Library now transferred to

ERO, Acc 47, including:
Deeds of Fleece or White Lyon CPL654
30 High Street, CPL 619, CPL 649
112 High Street, CPL 638
Freshfield Brewery, St Botolphs, CPL 957
Tabor estates at Hythe, CPL 933
Rootsey family property, CPL 747–53
25–28 Queen Street, 1743–1845, CPL 629
Berryfield, George Wegg, CPL 628
Marriage Settlement, James Round to Thamar Creffield, CPL 278
Will George Wegg, 1776, CPL 280
Will John Selly, Brewer, 1736, CPL 286
Revd John Halls, CPL289ff

Mss transferred from library of Essex Society for Archaeology and History

Manuscript Poll Book for 1735
Bankruptcy Papers for James Lovett, 1810

Manuscript sources in Colchester Public Library

Rickwood collection of mss. including: Annual Register; listings of Colchester Corporation; Notes on the Daniell family
Rebow Scrapbook
Gray notebook with Jacobite toasts
Duncan J; 'The Early Days of Methodism in Colchester, The visits of John Wesley and also its Beginnings as a Circuit', unpublished manuscript notes, 1971
Crisp's Index to Essex Marriage Licences
Crisp's Transcripts of Colchester Monumental Inscriptions

Manuscript sources in National Archives

King's Bench: KB 11/35; KB 28/153–62, 1735–42; Ind 6658, index to KB 28
Treasury Solicitors, TS 11
State Papers Domestic, SP 36 and 37
Home Office Papers, HO 42
Index to Apprenticeships, IR 17
PCC Wills PROB 11
Assize Indictments, Eastern Circuit, ASSI 35
PRO Signet Office C 111 Ind 16792, Pardon of George Gray
PRO C 211/27/W91; de Lunatico Inquirendo, Samuel Wall, attorney, Colchester, 1775; C 211/27/S146 de Lunatico Inquirendo, Mary Seaman, Colchester, 1806

Printed

Act … For repairing roads leading from the Western Part of the parish of Shenfield to Harwich … (and) … from Chelmsford … to Sudbury … (and) … from Margaretting to Maldon … (and) … from Colchester to Langham, 1746, ERO Acc 305
Act for … Cleaning and making Navigable the Channel from the Hithe at Colchester to Wivenhoe, 8 George II Decimo Tertio, 1739 and the Channel Act of 1780, ERO Acc 306
Boyd's Index of Essex Marriages
Extract of a letter from a lady in Colchester to her friend in town (London, 1768)
Bentham, J., *Correspondence of Jeremy Bentham*, Christie, I (ed.) (London, 1968)
Bridge, S., *The guild* (Colchester, 1814)
Chelmsford Chronicle

Colchester Journal
Colchester Borough, *Poll Books*, 1741–1830
Cromwell, T., *The history and description of the ancient town and borough of Colchester*, two vols (Colchester, 1824)
Forster, N., *Grace without enthusiasm, a sermon* (Colchester, 1781)
Gilbert, J., (ed.), *The autobiography and other memorials of Mrs Gilbert*, 2nd edn (London, 1876)
Gray, C., *Considerations of several proposals lately made for the better maintenance of the poor* (London, 1751)
Ipswich Journal
Morant, P., *The history and antiquities of the most ancient town of Colchester* (Colchester, 1748)
Morant, P., *The history and antiquities of Essex* (Colchester, 1768)
Salmon, W., *Palladio londoniensis or London art of building* (London, 1734)
Strutt, B., *The history and description of Colchester*, two vols (Colchester, 1803)
Twining, T., *A selection of Thomas Twining's letters 1734–1804: A record of a tranquil life*, Walker, R.S. (ed.) (Lewiston, 1991)

Secondary sources

Oxford Dictionary of National Biography (Oxford, 2004) [viewed online at www.oxford.dnb.com]
Amussen, S.D., 'Punishment, discipline, and power — the social meanings of violence in early-modern England', *Journal of British Studies*, 34 (1995)
Amussen, S.D., '"Being stirred to much unquietness": Violence and domestic violence in early modern England', *Journal of Women's History*, 6 (2) (1994)
Anderson, B.L., 'Provincial aspects of the financial revolution in the eighteenth century', *Business History*, 11 (1969)
Anderson, B.L., 'Money and the structure of credit in the eighteenth century', *Business History*, 12, (1970)
Appleby, J.H., 'Robert Dingley FRS, 1710–1781, merchant, architect and pioneering philanthropist', *Notes and records of the Royal Society of London*, 45 (1991)
Appleby, J.H., 'Mills, models and magdalens — the Dingley brothers and the society of arts', *Royal Society of Arts Journal*, cxl, no 5427 (1995)
Archer, J.E., '"Men behaving badly"?; masculinity and the uses of violence, 1850–1900' in S. D'Cruze (ed.), *Everyday violence in Britain, 1850–1950* (Harlow, 2000)
Bailey, J., *Unquiet lives: marriage and marriage breakdown in England, 1660–1800* (Cambridge, 2003)
Bailey, J., '"I dye (sic) by inches": Locating wife beating in the concept of a privatization of marriage and violence in eighteenth-century England', *Social History*, 31 (2006)
Barker-Benfield, G.J., *The culture of sensibility: sex and society in eighteenth-century Britain* (Chicago, 1992)
Barker, H., *Newspapers, politics, and public opinion in late eighteenth-century England* (Oxford, 1998)
Barker, H., *The business of women: female enterprise and urban development in northern England 1760–1830* (Oxford, 2006)
Barker, H. and Chalus, E., (eds.), *Gender in eighteenth-century England* (Harlow, 1997)
Barry, J., *The cultural life of Bristol, 1640–1775* (DPhil thesis, Oxford, 1985)
Barry, J. and Brooks, C.W., *The middling sort of people: culture, society, and politics in England, 1550–1800* (London, 1994)
Barry, J., 'Bourgeois collectivism? Urban association and the middling sort' in Barry and Brooks (eds.), *The middling sort of people* (London, 1994)
Barry, J., 'Provincial town culture 1640–1780: Urban or civic?' in Pittock, J.H. and Wear, A. (eds.), *Interpretation and cultural history* (Basingstoke, 1991)
Beattie, J.M., *Crime and the courts in England 1660–1800* (Oxford, 1986)

Beckett, I., *The amateur military tradition 1558–1945* (Manchester, 1991)

Behagg, C., 'Custom class and change; the trade societies of Birmingham', *Social History*, 4 (1979)

Benham, H.A., *Once upon a tide* (Colchester, 1955)

Benham, W.G., 'The Dunthornes of Colchester', *Essex Review*, 10 (1901)

Bennett, J.M., 'Women's history: a study in continuity and change', *Women's History Review*, 2 (1993)

Bensusan Butt, J., 'Jane and Ann Taylor as engravers', *East Anglian Magazine*, 21 (1961)

Bensusan Butt, J., 'Living in style in eighteenth-century Colchester', text of lecture given 22 February 1967

Bensusan Butt, J., *When Gainsborough painted a Colchester attorney* (Colchester, privately printed, 1978)

Bensusan Butt, J., 'George Wegg of East Hill House, text of lecture given 22nd October', (1981)

Bensusan Butt, J., *All Saints' Colchester in the eighteenth century* (Colchester, privately printed, 1989)

Bensusan Butt, J., *Charles Shillito, Oliver Goldsmith* (Colchester, privately printed, 1994)

Bensusan Butt, J., *Benjamin Strutt, William Cole and James Fisin* (Colchester, privately printed, 1994)

Bensusan Butt, J., *Magens and Read, Gainsborough and Mayhew, James Deane and Charles Gray* (Colchester, privately printed, 1994)

Bensusan Butt, J., *Moses Cooke and Moses Griffith* (Colchester, privately printed, 1994)

Bensusan Butt, J., *Yorick Smythies and W.R. Bigg* (Colchester, privately printed, 1994)

Bensusan Butt, J., *The house that Boggis built*, revised edn, (Colchester, 1972)

Bensusan Butt, J., 'An introduction to William Cole', *East Anglian History Workshop*, 2 (1981)

Bensusan Butt, J., 'A friend to his country: William Mayhew and the recovery of the Colchester charter, 1763', *Essex Archaeology and History*, 18 (1987)

Bensusan Butt, J., 'A Gallery of High Stewards', *Essex County Standard*, 6 and 20 October 1967

Bensusan Butt, J., 'The Gallant Story of Admiral (Sir Edmund) Affleck (MP)', *Essex County Standard*, 7 December 1962

Berg, M., *The age of manufactures 1700–1820* (London, 1985)

Berg, M., *Luxury and pleasure in eighteenth-century Britain* (Oxford, 2005)

Berg, M, and Clifford, H, (eds.), *Consumers and luxury: Consumer culture in Europe 1650–1850* (Manchester, 1999)

Berg, M. and Eger, E. (eds.), *Luxury in the eighteenth century, debates, desires and delectable goods* (Basingstoke, 2003)

Berry, H., 'Polite consumption: shopping in eighteenth-century England', *Transactions of the Royal Historical Society*, 6th Series, 12 (2002)

Berry, H., 'Prudent luxury: the metropolitan tastes of Judith Baker, Durham gentlewoman', in Sweet, R. and Lane, P. (eds.), *On the town: women and urban life in eighteenth-century England* (Aldershot, 2003)

Black, C., *The association* (Cambridge, Mass., 1963)

Black, J. (ed.), *Culture and society in Britain 1660–1800* (Manchester, 1997)

Blaxhill, L., *The history of Lion Walk Congregational Church* (Colchester, 1939)

Blaxhill, L., *Nonconformist churches of Colchester* (Colchester, 1946)

Bohstedt, J., *Riots and community politics in England and Wales 1790–1810* (Cambridge, Mass., 1983)

Bohstedt, J., 'Gender household and community politics: women in English riots, 1790–1810', *Past and Present*, 120 (1988)

Bohstedt, J., 'The moral economy and the discipline of historical context', *Journal of Social History*, 26 (1992)

Booth, A., 'Popular loyalism and public violence in the northwest of England, 1790–1800', *Social History*, 8 (1983)

Borsay, A., 'A middle class in the making: the negotiation of power and status at Bath's early Georgian General Infirmary', *Social History*, 24 (1999)
Borsay, P., 'The English urban renaissance; the development of provincial urban culture, 1680–1760', *Social History*, 5 (1977)
Borsay, P., 'Culture, status and the English urban landscape', *History*, 68 (1982)
Borsay, P., 'The rise of the promenade: the social and cultural use of space in English provincial towns c.1660–1800', *British Journal of Eighteenth-Century Studies*, 4, (1986)
Borsay, P., *The English urban renaissance: culture and society and the provincial town* (Oxford, 1989)
Borsay, P. (ed.), *The eighteenth-century town, 1688–1800* (Oxford, 1990)
Boulton, J., 'Going on the parish: the parish pension and its meaning in the London suburbs 1640–1724' in Hitchcock, T., Sharpe, P. and King, P. (eds.), *Chronicling poverty: the voices and strategies of the English poor 1640–1840* (London, 1997)
Bourdieu, P., *Outline of a theory of practice*, trans. Nice, R.T. (Cambridge, 1977)
Bourdieu, P., *Distinction: A social critique of the judgement of taste* (London, 1979)
Brewer, J., 'This, that and the other; public social and private in the seventeenth and eighteenth centuries', in Castiglione, D. and Sharpe, L. (eds.), *Shifting the boundaries: transformation of the language of public and private in the eighteenth century* (Exeter, 1995)
Brewer, J., and Styles, J. (eds.), *An ungovernable people: the English and their law in the seventeenth and eighteenth centuries* (London, 1980)
Brewer, J., *The sinews of power: war, money and the English state, 1688–1783* (London, 1994)
Brewer, J., *The pleasures of the imagination: English culture in the eighteenth century* (London, 1997)
Brewer, J, and Porter, R. (eds.), *Consumption and the world of goods* (London, 1993)
Briggs, N., *John Johnson architect and county surveyor for Essex* (Chelmsford, 1991)
Britnell, R.H., *Growth and decline in Colchester, 1300–1525* (Cambridge, 1986)
Brown, A.F.J., *Colchester in the eighteenth century* (Colchester, 1969)
Brown, A.F.J., *Essex at work 1700–1815* (Chelmsford, 1969)
Brown, A.F.J., *Essex people, 1750–1900* (Chelmsford, 1972)
Brown, A.F.J., *Colchester 1815–1914* (Chelmsford, 1980)
Brown, A.F.J., *Chartism in Essex and Suffolk* (Chelmsford, 1982)
Brown, F.E., 'Continuity and change in the urban house: developments in domestic space organisation in seventeenth-century London', *Comparative Studies in Society and History*, 28 (1986)
Burley, K.H., 'The economic development of Essex in the later seventeenth and early eighteenth centuries', (PhD thesis, London 1957)
Burney, F., *Evelina, or, a young lady's entrance into the world. In a series of letters* (London, 1779)
Calhoun, C. (ed.), *Habermas and the public sphere* (Cambridge, MA, 1992)
Carroll, S. (ed.), *Cultures of violence: interpersonal violence in historical perspective*, (Basingstoke, 2001)
Carroll, S., 'Introduction' in S. Carroll (ed.), *Cultures of violence: interpersonal violence in historical perspective* (Basingstoke, 2007)
Carter Wood, J., 'It's a small world after all? Reflections on violence in comparative perspectives', in B. Godfrey, C. Emsley and G. Dunstall (eds.), *Comparative histories of crime* (Cullompton, 2003)
Carter, A.C., *Getting, spending and investment in early modern times: the English public debt in the eighteenth century* (London, 1968)
Carter, P., *Men and the emergence of polite society; Britain 1660–1800* (London and New York, 2001)
Carter, P., '"An effeminate" or "efficient" nation? Masculinity and eighteenth-century social documentary', *Textual Practice*, 11 (1997)

Carter, P., '"Men about town": representations of foppery and masculinity in early eighteenth-century urban society' in H. Barker and E. Chalus (eds.), *Gender in eighteenth-century England* (Harlow, 1997)

Castiglione, D. and Sharpe, L. (eds.), *Shifting the boundaries: transformation of the language of public and private in the eighteenth century* (Exeter, 1995)

Chalkin, C., *The provincial towns of Georgian England* (London, 1974)

Chalkin, C., 'Capital expenditure on building for cultural purposes in provincial England 1730–1830', *Business History*, 21 (1980)

Chalkin, C. and Haviden, M. (eds.), *Rural change and urban growth 1500–1800* (London, 1974)

Charlesworth, A. and Randall, A.J., 'Morals, markets and the English crowd in 1766', *Past and Present*, 114 (1987)

Chartier, R. (ed.), *Passions of the renaissance* (Cambridge, Mass., 1989), Vol. 3 in Aries, P. and Duby, G. (eds.), *A History of private life*

Chartres, J.A., *Internal trade in England 1500–1700* (London, 1977)

Clark, A., *The struggle for the breeches: gender and the making of the British working class* (Berkeley, 1995)

Clark, P., *Country towns in pre-industrial England* (Leicester, 1981)

Clark, P., *British clubs and societies, 1580–1800: the origins of an associational world* (Oxford, 2000)

Clark, P. *et al.* (eds.), *The Cambridge urban history of Britain* (Cambridge, 2000)

Clark, P. (ed.), *The early modern town* (London, 1976)

Clark, P. (ed.), *The transformation of English provincial towns, 1600–1800* (London, 1984)

Clark, P. and Slack, P. (eds.), *English towns in transition, 1500–1700* (Oxford, 1976)

Clayton, P., *Angel lodge, no 51, Colchester: 250th anniversary celebration 12 December 1985* (Colchester, 1985)

Cody, L.F., 'The politics of reproduction: from midwives' alternative public sphere to the public spectacle of man-midwifery', *Eighteenth-Century Studies*, 32 (1999)

Colley, L., 'Whose nation — class and national consciousness in Britain 1750–1830', *Past and Present*, 113 (1986)

Colley, L., *Britons: forging the nation, 1707–1837* (New Haven and London, 1992)

Colvin, H.M., *A biographical dictionary of British architects, 1600–1840* (New Haven, Conn, 1995)

Connors, R., 'Poor women, the parish and the politics of poverty' in H. Barker and E. Chalus (eds.), *Gender and society in eighteenth-century England* (Harlow, 1997)

Conway, S., *War, state and society in mid-eighteenth century Britain and Ireland* (Oxford, 2006)

Cookson, J.E., 'The English volunteer movement of the French wars, 1793–1815 — some contexts', *Historical Journal*, 32 (1989)

Cookson, J.E., *The British armed nation 1793–1815* (Oxford, 1997)

Cooper, D. and Donald, M., 'Households and "hidden" kin in early nineteenth-century England: four case studies in suburban Exeter, 1821–1861', *Continuity and Change*, 10 (1995)

Cooper, J. *et al.*, *The borough of Colchester*, Vol. 9, *The Victoria county history of Essex* (Woodbridge, 1994)

Copeland, E., 'Defoe and the London wall: mapped perspectives', *Eighteenth Century Fiction* (1998)

Corfield, P.J., *The impact of English towns, 1700–1800* (Oxford, 1982)

Corfield, P.J., 'Class by name and number in eighteenth-century Britain', *History*, 72 (1987)

Cox, J. and Cox, N., 'Probate 1500–1800: a system in transition' in Arkell, T. *et al.* (eds.), *Till death do us part: understanding and interpreting the probate records of early modern England* (Oxford, 2000)

Crowley, J.E., 'The sensibility of comfort', *American Historical Review*, 104 (1999)

Cruickshank, D. and Burton, N., *Life in the Georgian city* (London, 1990)

Cruickshanks, E. and J., B, (ed.), *The Jacobite challenge* (Edinburgh, 1988)

Cruickshanks, E. (ed.), *Ideology and conspiracy: aspects of Jacobitism, 1689–1759* (Edinburgh, 1982)
D'Cruze, S., 'To acquaint the ladies; women traders in Colchester c.1750–c.1800', *Local Historian*, 17 (1986)
D'Cruze, S., *Crimes of outrage: sex, violence and Victorian working women* (London, 1988)
D'Cruze, S., 'The eighteenth century attorney as political broker; the case of Francis Smythies', *Essex Archaeology and History, Transactions of the Essex Society for Archaeology and History*, 19 (1988)
D'Cruze, S., *'Our times in God's hands', religion and the eighteenth century middling sort, a study of Colchester*, Studies in Essex history (Chelmsford, 1990)
D'Cruze, S., *The middling sort in provincial England: politics and social relations in Colchester 1730–1800* (PhD thesis, Essex, 1990)
D'Cruze, S., 'The middling sort in eighteenth-century Colchester: independence, social relations and the community broker', in Barry, J. and Brooks, C. (eds.), *The middling sort of people, culture, society and politics in England, 1550–1800* (Basingstoke, 1994)
Darnton, R., *The great cat massacre and other episodes in French cultural history* (New York, 1984)
Daunton, M., Review of 'Victorian insolvency: bankruptcy, imprisonment for debt, and company winding-up in nineteenth-century England', *Journal of Modern History*, 70, (1998)
Davidoff, L., 'Life is duty, praise and prayer', *Fawcett Library Papers*, 4 (1981)
Davidoff, L., 'Mastered for Life: servant and wife in Victorian and Edwardian England' in *Worlds between: historical perspectives on gender and class* (Cambridge, 1995)
Davidoff, L., *Worlds between: historical perspectives on gender and class* (Cambridge, 1995)
Davidoff, L. *et al.*, *The family story: blood, contract and intimacy, 1830–1960* (London, 1999)
Davidoff, L., 'Gender and the "great divide" — public and private in British gender history', *Journal of Women's History*, 15 (2003)
Davidoff, L. and Hall, C., *Family fortunes, men and women of the English middle class, 1780–1850* (London, 1987)
de Certeau, M., *The practices of everyday life* (New York, 1984)
de Certeau, M., 'Practices of space' in M. Blonsky (ed.) *On signs* (Baltimore, 1985)
Deane, P., *The first industrial revolution* (Cambridge, 1979)
Derry, W., *Dr Parr; a portrait of the Whig Dr Johnson* (Oxford, 1966)
Dias, R., 'A world of pictures: Pall Mall and the topography of display 1780–99', in Ogborn, M. and Withers, C.W.J. (eds.), *Georgian geographies: essays on space, place and landscape in the eighteenth century* (Manchester, 2004)
Dibdin, C., *The musical tour of Mr. Dibdin; in which, previous to his embarkation for India, he finished his career as a public character* (Sheffield, 1788)
Dickinson, H.T., *Liberty and property: political ideology in eighteenth-century Britain* (London, 1977)
Dickinson, H.T., *The politics of the people in eighteenth-century Britain* (London, 1994)
Dillon, Patrick, *The much-lamented death of Madam Geneva: the eighteenth-century gin craze* (London, 2002)
Dobson, C.R., *Masters and journeymen* (London, 1980)
Donnison, J., *Midwives and medical men: a history of the struggle for the control of childbirth* (London, 1988)
Doolittle, M., 'Close relations? Bringing together gender and family in English history', *Gender and History*, 11 (1999)
Downe, M., 'Interview with the daughter of the last of the bay makers', *Essex County Standard*, 25 March 1893
Dudink, S. *et al.* (eds.), *Masculinities in politics and war: gendering modern history* (Manchester, 2004)
Duffy, I., 'Betting on lives: the culture of life insurance in England, 1695–1775', *Albion*, 32 (2000)

Duffy, I.P.H., *Bankruptcy and insolvency in London during the industrial revolution* (London and New York, 1985)
Duffy, M., 'William Pitt and the origins of the loyalist association movement of 1792', *Historical Journal*, 39 (1996)
Dyer, A., 'Urban housing', *Post-Medieval Archaeology*, 15 (1981)
Hellmuth, E, (ed.), *The transformation of political culture: England and Germany in the late eighteenth century* (Oxford, 1990)
Eisner, M., 'Long-term trends in violent crime', *Crime and Justice: An Annual Review of Research*, 30 (2003)
Elias, N., *The civilizing process: the history of manners and state formation and civilization*, trans. Jephcott, E. (Oxford, 1994)
Elliott, P., 'The origins of the "creative class": provincial urban society, scientific culture and socio-political marginality in Britain in the eighteenth and nineteenth centuries', *Social history*, 28 (2003)
Ellis, J., 'Georgian town gardens', *History Today*, 50 (2000)
Ellis, J.M., *The Georgian town, 1680–1840* (Basingstoke, 2001)
Emsley, C., *British society and the French wars, 1793–1815* (Basingstoke, 1979)
Emsley, C., 'An aspect of Pitt's terror', *Social History*, 6 (1981)
Emsley, C., *Crime and society in England 1750–1900* (Harlow, 1996)
Erickson, A.L., *Women and property in early modern England* (London, 1993)
Evans, T., '"Unfortunate objects": London's unmarried mothers in the eighteenth century', *Gender and History*, 17 (2005)
Everitt, A. (ed.), *Perspectives in English urban history* (London, 1973)
Farries, K., *Essex windmills, millers and millwrights*, Vol. 2 (Edinburgh, 1984)
Finn, M., 'Men's things: masculine possession in the consumer revolution', *Social History*, 25 (2000)
Finn, M., 'Women, consumption and coverture in England, c.1760–1860', *Historical Journal*, 39 (1996)
Finn, M.C., *The character of credit: personal debt in English culture, 1740–1914* (Cambridge, 2003)
Foyster, E., 'Creating a veil of silence? Politeness and marital violence in the English household', *Transactions of the Royal Historical Society*, 6th series, 12 (2002)
Freeman, L., *Character's theater: genre and identity on the eighteenth-century English stage*, (Philadelphia, 2002)
French, H., '"Ingenious & learned gentlemen" — social perceptions and self-fashioning among parish elites in Essex, 1680–1740', *Social History*, 25 (2000)
French, H.R., 'Social status, localism and the "middle sort of people" in England 1620–1750', *Past and Present*, 166 (2000)
French, H., 'The search for the "middle sort of people" in England, 1600–1800', *Historical Journal*, 43 (2000)
Geertz, C., 'Thick description' in C. Geertz (ed.), *The interpretation of cultures* (London, 1975)
Gilmartin, K., 'In the theater of counterrevolution: loyalist association and conservative opinion in the 1790s', *Journal of British Studies*, 41 (2002)
Gilmour, I., *Riot, risings and revolution: governance and violence in eighteenth-century England* (London, 1992)
Godfrey, B.S. *et al.*, 'Explaining gendered sentencing patterns for violent men and women in the late-Victorian and Edwardian period', *British Journal of Criminology*, 45 (2005)
Goodwyn, E.A., *A century of a Suffolk town: Beccles 1760–1860, part 1, 1760–1815* (Ipswich, 1965)
Goose, N., 'English pre-industrial urban communities', *Urban History Year Book* (1982)
Goose, N., 'The "Dutch" in Colchester: the economic influence of an immigrant community in the sixteenth and seventeenth centuries', *Immigrants and Minorities* (1982)
Goose, N. and N. Evans, 'Wills as an historical source' in T. Arkell *et al.* (eds.), *When death do us*

part: understanding and interpreting the probate records of early modern England (Oxford, 2000)
Goose, N., 'The rise and decline of philanthropy in early modern Colchester: the unacceptable face of mercantilism?', *Social History*, 31 (2006)
Gregory, J., 'Christianity and culture: religion, the arts and the sciences in England 1660–1800' in J. Black (ed.), *Culture and society in Britain, 1660–1800* (Manchester, 1997)
Gregory, J., 'Homo religiosus': masculinity and religion in the long eighteenth century, in Hitchcock, T. and Cohen, M. (eds.), *English Masculinities 1660–1800* (London, 1999)
Gunn, J.A.W., *Beyond liberty and property; the progress of self-recognition in eighteenth-century political thought* (Kingston, Ontario, 1983)
Gurr, T., 'Historical trends in violent crime: a critical review of the evidence', *Crime and Justice: An Annual Review of Research*, 3 (1978)
Habermas, J., *The structural transformation of the public spheres*, trans. Burger T. and Lawrence, F. (Cambridge, MA, 1989)
Hammerton, A.J., *Cruelty and companionship: conflict in nineteenth-century married life* (London, 1992)
Hanly, M., 'The economy of makeshifts and the poor law: a game of chance', in King, S. and Tomkins, A. (eds.), *The poor in England 1700–1850: an economy of makeshifts* (Manchester, 2003)
Hanson, J., *Decoding homes and houses* (Cambridge, 1998)
Harris, S.C., 'Clearing the stage: gender, class, and the freedom of the scenes in eighteenth-century Dublin', *Publications of the Modern Language Association of America*, 119 (2004)
Harrod, H., *Repertory of the records and evidences of the borough of Colchester* (Colchester, 1865)
Harvey, K., 'The century of sex? Gender, bodies, and sexuality in the long eighteenth century', *Historical Journal*, 45 (2002)
Harvey, K., 'The history of masculinity, c.1650–1800', *Journal of British Studies*, 44 (2005)
Harvey, K., 'Review of *The independent man; citizenship and gender politics in Georgian England*', Institute of Historical Research, Review no. 530 (2006), http://www.history.ac.uk/reviews/paper/harvey.html
Harvey, K. and Shepard, A., 'What have historians done with masculinity? Reflections on five centuries of British history, circa 1500–1950', *Journal of British Studies*, 44 (2005)
Harvey, K., 'Spaces of erotic delight', in Ogborn, M. and Withers, C. (eds.), *Georgian geographies: essays on space, place and landscape in the eighteenth century* (Manchester, 2004)
Hay, D. and Snyder, F. (eds.), *Policing and prosecution in the English courts 1750–1850* (Oxford, 1989)
Hay, D. *et al.*, *Albion's fatal tree: crime and society in eighteenth-century England* (Harmondsworth, 1975)
Henderson, T., *Disorderly women in eighteenth century London; prostitution and control in the metropolis, 1730–1830* (London, 1999)
Higgs, E., 'Women, occupations and work in the nineteenth century censuses', *History Workshop Journal*, 23 (1987)
Highgate, P. (ed.), *Military masculinities: identity and the state* (London, 2003)
Hill, B., *Servants: English domestics in the eighteenth century* (Oxford, 1996)
Hill, F., *Georgian Lincoln* (Cambridge, 1966)
Hitchcock, T., *English sexualities, 1700–1800* (Basingstoke, 1997)
Hitchcock, T., *Down and out in eighteenth-century London* (London, 2004)
Hitchcock, T., and Cohen, M., (ed.), *English masculinities, 1660–1800* (London, 1999)
Hitchcock, T., 'A new history from below: review of T. Sokoll (ed.) *Essex Pauper Letters 1731–1837*, *History Workshop Journal*, 57 (2004)
Hitchcock, T., 'Begging on the streets of eighteenth-century London', *Journal of British Studies*,

44 (2005)
Hitchcock, T., *et al.* (eds.), *Chronicling poverty: the voices and strategies of the English poor 1640–1840* (London, 1997)
Holderness, B.A., 'Credit in a rural community, 1660–1800', *Midland History*, 3 (1975)
Holderness, B.A., 'Credit in English rural society before the nineteenth century', *Agricultural History Review*, 24 (1976)
Holderness, B.A., *Pre-industrial England; economy and society, 1500–1750* (London, 1976)
Holman, P., 'The Colchester partbooks', *Early Music*, 28 (2000)
Hoppit, J., 'Financial crises in 18th-century England', *Economic History Review*, 39 (1986)
Hoppit, J., 'The use and abuse of credit in eighteenth-century England' in M. N. and R.B. Outhwaite (eds.), *Business life and public policy*, (Cambridge, 1986)
Hoppit, J., *Risk and failure in English business, 1700–1800* (Cambridge, 1987)
Hoppit, J., 'Attitudes to credit in Britain, 1680–1790', *Historical Journal*, 33 (1990)
Hoppit, J., 'The myths of the south sea bubble', *Transactions of the Royal Historical Society*, 6th series, 12 (2002)
Hunt, M., 'Wife beating, domesticity and women's independence in eighteenth-century London', *Gender and History*, 4 (1992)
Hunt, M.R., *The middling sort: commerce, gender, and the family in England, 1680–1780* (Berkeley and London, 1996)
Innes, J., 'The King's Bench prison in the later eighteenth century: law, authority and order in a London debtor's prison' in J. Brewer and J. Styles (eds.), *An ungovernable people: the English and their law in the seventeenth and eighteenth centuries* (London, 1980)
Innes, J. and Styles, J., 'The crime wave: recent writing on crime and criminal justice in eighteenth-century England' in A. Wilson (ed.), *Rethinking social history. English society 1570–1920 and its interpretation* (Manchester, 1993)
Jewson, C.B., *The Jacobin city; a portrait of Norwich in its reaction to the French revolution* (Glasgow, 1975)
Johnson, E.A. and Monkkonen, E.H., *The civilization of crime: violence in town and country since the middle ages* (Chicago, 1996)
Johnstone, J. (ed.), *The works of Samuel Parr LLD* (London, 1828)
Joscelyne, C., 'Medical practice and medical theory: smallpox in Britain during the long eighteenth century' (PhD thesis, Essex, 1990)
Kelly, K.A., *Domestic violence and the politics of privacy* (Ithaca, NY, 2003)
Kelsall, A.F., 'The house plan in the later seventeenth century', *Post-Medieval Archaeology*, 8 (1974)
King, P.J.R., 'Crime, law and society in Essex, 1740–1820' (PhD thesis, Cambridge, 1984)
King, P., 'Decision-makers and decision-making in the English criminal law, 1750–1800', *Historical Journal*, 28 (1984)
King, P.J.R., 'Urban crime rates and borough courts in eighteenth-century Essex — the impact of local court availability', *Historical Journal*, 22 (1987)
King, P., 'Edward Thompson's, contribution to eighteenth-century studies — the patrician plebeian model re-examined', *Social History*, (1996)
King, P., 'The summary courts and social relations in eighteenth-century England', *Past and Present* (2004)
King, P., 'Punishing assault: The Transformation of attitudes in the English courts', *Journal of Interdisciplinary History*, 27 (1996)
King, P., *Crime, justice and discretion in England 1740–1820* (Oxford, 2000)
King, P., *Crime and law in England 1750–1840* (Cambridge, 2006)
King, S. and Tomkins, A. (eds.), *The poor in England 1700–1850: an economy of makeshifts* (Manchester, 2003)
Klein, L.E., 'Gender and the public/private distinction in the eighteenth century — some questions about evidence and analytic procedure', *Eighteenth-Century Studies*, 29 (1995)

Klein, L.E., 'Politeness and the interpretation of the British eighteenth century', *Historical Journal*, 45 (2002)
Klein, L., 'From courtesy to civility: changing codes of conduct in early modern England', *Social History*, 25 (2000)
Klein, L., 'Luxury in the eighteenth century: debates, desires and delectable goods', *History Workshop Journal*, 57 (2004)
Kobialka, M., 'Words and bodies: a discourse on male sexuality in late eighteenth-century English representational practices', *Theatre Research International*, 28 (2003)
Kowaleski Wallace, B., 'Women, china and consumer culture in eighteenth century England', *Eighteenth-Century Studies*, 29 (1995)
Kross, J., 'Mansions, men, women, and the creation of multiple publics in eighteenth-century British north America', *Journal of Social History*, 33 (1999)
Langford, P., *The excise crisis society and politics in the age of Walpole* (Oxford, 1975)
Langford, P., *A polite and commercial people: England, 1727–1783* (Oxford, 1989)
Langford, P., *Englishness identified: manners and character 1650–1850* (Oxford, 2000)
Langford, P., *Public life and the propertied Englishman, 1689–1798* (Oxford, 1991)
Langford, P., 'The uses of eighteenth-century politeness', *Transactions of the Royal Historical Society*, 12 (2002)
Langton, J., 'Urban growth and economic change from the late seventeenth century to 1841' in P. Clark (ed.), *The Cambridge urban history of Britain*, Vol. 2, *1540–1840* (Cambridge, 2000)
Laslett, P., *The world we have lost* (London, 1965)
Laslett, P. and Wall, R. (eds.), *Household and family in past times* (Cambridge, 1972)
Laver, H., 'The last days of baymaking in Colchester', *Transactions of the Essex Archaeological Society*, new series, 10 (1906)
Lemire, B., 'Consumerism in pre-industrial and early industrial England; the trade in secondhand clothes', *Journal of British Studies*, 27 (1988)
Lemire, B., *The business of everyday life: gender, practice and social politics in England, c.1600–1900* (Manchester, 2006)
Lloyd, N., *A history of the English house from primitive times to the Victorian period* (London and New York, 1975)
Lloyd, S., 'Pleasing spectacles and elegant dinners: conviviality, benevolence, and charity anniversaries in eighteenth-century London', *Journal of British Studies*, 41 (2002)
Lloyd, S., '"Pleasure's golden bait": prostitution, poverty and the Magdalen hospital in eighteenth-century London', *History Workshop Journal* (1996)
Longfellow, E., 'Public, private, and the household in early seventeenth-century England', *Journal of British Studies*, 45 (2006)
Macleod, E.V., 'The problem of the active citizen: conservative reactions to the French revolution in Britain', *Annales historiques de la Revolution Française*, 342 (2005)
Mah, H., 'Phantasies of the public sphere: rethinking the Habermas of historians', *Journal of Modern History*, 72 (2000)
Markham Lester, V., *Victorian insolvency: bankruptcy, imprisonment for debt, and company winding-up in nineteenth-century England* (Oxford, 1995)
Marshall, J.D., *The autobiography of William Stout* (Manchester, 1967)
Martin, G., *The history of Colchester Royal Grammar School* (Colchester, 1947)
Martin, G., *The story of Colchester* (Colchester, 1959)
Mason, B., *Clock and watchmaking in Colchester, England* (Colchester, 1969)
Mason, S., *Essex on the map* (Chelmsford, 1990)
Mason, S. and Bensusan Butt, J., 'P.B. Scalé: surveyor in Ireland, gentleman of Essex', *Proceedings of the Hugenot Society*, 24 (1988)
Mccormack, M., *The independent man: citizenship and gender politics in Georgian England* (Manchester, 2005)
Mccormack, M., 'The new militia: war, politics and gender in 1750s Britain', *Gender and History*,

19 (2007)
Mckendrick, N. *et al.*, *The birth of a consumer society* (London, 1982)
McNay, L., 'Gender, habitus and the field — Pierre Bourdieu and the limits of reflexivity', *Eighteenth-Century Studies*, 16 (1999)
Meldrum, T., 'Domestic service, privacy and the eighteenth-century metropolitan household', *Urban History*, 26 (1999)
Meldrum, T., *Domestic service and gender 1660–1750: life and work in the London household* (Harlow, Essex, 2000)
Mighall, R., *A geography of Victorian gothic fiction: mapping history's nightmare* (Oxford, 1999)
Miles, M., 'The money market in the early industrial revolution; the evidence from West Riding attorneys, c.1750–1800', *Business History*, 23 (1981)
Mitchell, A., 'The loyalist association movement, 1792–3', *Historical Journal*, 4 (1961)
Money, J., 'Taverns, coffee houses and clubs; local politics and popular articulacy in the Birmingham area in the age of the American revolution', *Historical Journal*, 14 (1971)
Money, J., *Experience and identity, Birmingham and the West Midlands 1760–1800* (Manchester, 1977)
Money, J., 'Freemasonry and the fabric of loyalism in Hanoverian England', in E. Hellmuth (ed.), *The transformation of political culture: England and Germany in the later eighteenth century* (Oxford, 1990)
Mori, J., 'Responses to revolution — the November crisis of 1792', *Historical Research*, 69 (1996)
Morris, R.J., 'The middle class and the property cycle during the industrial revolution', in T. Smout (ed.), *The search for wealth and stability* (London, 1979)
Morris, R.J., 'Voluntary societies and British urban elites, 1780–1850: an analysis', *Historical Journal*, 24 (1983)
Morris, R.J., 'Clubs, societies and associations' in F.M.L. Thompson (ed.), *The Cambridge social history of Britain, 1750–1950, Vol. 3* (Cambridge, 1990)
Morris, R.J., 'Civil society and the nature of urbanism: Britain, 1750–1850', *Urban History*, 25 (1998)
Muldrew, C., 'Credit and the courts — debt litigation in a 17th-century urban-community', *Economic History Review*, 46 (1993)
Muldrew, C., 'Interpreting the market — the ethics of credit and community-relations in early-modern England', *Social History*, 18 (1993)
Muldrew, C., 'The culture of reconciliation: community and the settlement of economic disputes in early modern England', *Historical Journal*, 39 (1996)
Muldrew, C., '"Hard food for Midas": cash and its social value in early modern England', *Past and Present*, 170 (2001)
Muldrew, C., '"A mutual assent of her mind"? Women, debt, litigation and contract in early modern England', *History Workshop Journal*, 55 (2003)
Muldrew, C., *The economy of obligation: the culture of credit and social relations in early modern England* (Basingstoke, 1998)
Namier, L. and Brooke, J., *The history of Parliament: the House of Commons 1754–1790* (London, 1964)
Nenadic, S., 'Middle rank consumers and domestic culture in Edinburgh and Glasgow, 1720–1840', *Past and Present*, 145 (1994)
Newman, A.N., 'Leicester House politics 1750–60', *Camden Miscellany*, 23 (1969)
Nixon, E., *Mary Wollstonecraft; her life and times* (London, 1971)
O'Day, R., *The professions in early modern England, 1450–1800: servants of the commonweal* (Harlow, 2000)
Ogborn, M., *Spaces of modernity: London's geographies, 1680–1780* (New York, 1998)
Ogborn, M. and Withers, C.W.J., *Georgian geographies: essays on space, place and landscape in the eighteenth century* (Manchester, 2004)

Outhwaite, W., *Habermas: a critical introduction* (London, 1994)
Owens, A., 'Inheritance and the life-cycle of family firms in the early industrial revolution', *Business History*, 44 (2002)
Owens, A., 'Property, gender and the life course: inheritance and family welfare provision in early nineteenth-century England', *Social History*, 26 (2001)
Owens, A. *et al.*, 'A measure of worth: probate valuations, personal wealth and indebtedness in England, 1810–40', *Historical Research*, 79 (2006)
Page, W. and Round, H. (eds.), *The Victoria county history of Essex* (London, 1907)
Patterson, A.T., *A history of Southampton* (Southampton, 1966)
Pedley, M.S., *The commerce of cartography: making and marketing maps in eighteenth-century France and England* (Chicago, 2005)
Penfold, J., *The history of Essex County Hospital, Colchester, 1820–1948* (Colchester, 1984)
Phillips, A., 'Early Colchester foundries', *Transactions of the Essex Archaeological Society*, 14 (1982)
Phillips, A., *Ten men and Colchester* (Chelmsford, 1985)
Pinches, S., 'Women as objects and agents of charity in eighteenth-century Birmingham', in Sweet, R. and Lane, P. (eds.), *On the town: women and urban life in eighteenth-century England* (Aldershot, 2003)
Plumb, J.H., *Chatham* (London, 1953)
Plumb, J.H., *Walpole,* two volumes (London, 1956)
Plumb, J.H., *England in the eighteenth century*, 2nd edn (Harmondsworth, 1983)
Pocock, J.G.A., *Virtue commerce and history, essays in political thought and history, chiefly in the eighteenth century* (Cambridge, 1975)
Pocock, J.G.A., 'The varieties of whiggism from exclusion to reform: a history of ideology and discourse' in Pocock, J.G.A., *Virtue, commerce, and history: essays on political thought and history, chiefly in the eighteenth century* (Cambridge, 1985)
Poole, R., *Time's alteration: calendar reform in early modern England* (London, 1998)
Poovey, M., *Uneven developments: the ideological work of gender in mid-Victorian England* (London, 1989)
Porter, D. and Porter, R. (eds.), *Patient's progress: doctors and doctoring in eighteenth-century England* (Oxford, 1989)
Porter, R., *English society in the eighteenth century* (Harmondsworth, 1982)
Porter, R., 'Seeing the past', *Past and Present*, 118 (1988)
Porter, R., 'The new eighteenth-century social history' in J. Black (ed.), *Culture and society in Britain 1660–1800* (Manchester, 1997)
Priestly, U. and Corfield, P., 'Rooms and room use in Norwich housing', *Post-Medieval Archaeology*, 16 (1982)
Radcliffe, W., 'Thomas Tunmer and a forgotten spa', *The Practitioner*, 193 (1964)
Radcliffe, W., 'The Colchester medical society, 1774', *Medical History*, 20 (1976)
Randall, A, and Charlesworth, A, (eds.), *Markets, market culture and popular protest in eighteenth-century Britain and Ireland* (Liverpool, 1996)
Renton, S., 'The moral economy of the English middling sort in the eighteenth century, the case of Norwich in 1766 and 1767' in A. Randall and A. Charlesworth (eds.), *Markets, market culture and popular protest in eighteenth-century Britain and Ireland* (London, 1996)
Rickwood, G.O., 'The members of parliament for Colchester', *Essex Review*, 7 (1899)
Rickwood, G.O., *Bygone Colchester* (Colchester, undated)
Romney Sedgwick, R., *The history of Parliament: The House of Commons, 1715–1754* (London, 1971)
Ross, E., '"Fierce questions and taunts": married life in working-class London, 1870–1914', *Feminist Studies*, 8 (1982)
Royal Commission for Historic Monuments of England, *North east Essex* (London, 1922)
Rudé, G., *Wilkes and liberty* (Oxford, 1962)

Rudé, G., 'Popular protest in eighteenth century Europe' in Fritz, P. and Williams, D. (eds.), *The triumph of culture; eighteenth century perspectives* (Toronto, 1972)
Rudé, G., *The crowd in history; a study of popular disturbances in France and England 1730–1848*, 2nd edn (London, 1981)
Rule, J., *The experience of labour in eighteenth century industry* (London, 1981)
Rule, J. (ed.), *British trade unionism 1750–1850, the formative years* (London, 1988)
Rule, J., *Albion's people: English society, 1714–1815* (New York and London, 1992)
Russo, M., *The female grotesque, risk, excess and modernity* (New York, 1994)
Ryan, M., 'The public and the private good — across the great divide in women's history', *Journal of Women's History*, 15 (2003)
Sant, A.V., 'Historicizing domestic relations: Sarah Scott's use of the "household family"', *Eighteenth-Century Fiction*, 17 (2005)
Schmidt, A.J., 'The country attorney in late eighteenth-century England: Benjamin Smith of Horbling,', *Law and History Review*, 8 (1990)
Sharpe, J.A., 'The history of violence in England', *Past and Present*, 108 (1985)
Sharpe, J.A., *Crime in early modern England; 1550–1750* (Harlow, 1999)
Sharpe, P., 'Gender in the economy: female merchants and family businesses in the British Isles, 1600–1850', *Histoire Sociale-Social History*, 34 (2001)
Sharpe, P., 'A woman's worth: a case study of capital accumulation in early modern England — women and property relationships in medieval and early modern England', *Parergon*, 19 (2002)
Sharpe, P., 'Population and society 1700–1840' in P. Clark and D.M. Palliser (eds.), *The Cambridge urban history of Britain*, Vol. 2, *1540–1840* (Cambridge, 2000)
Shoemaker, R., *Gender in English society 1650–1850: the emergence of separate spheres?* (London, 1998)
Shoemaker, R., 'Male honour and the decline of public violence in 18th-century London', *Social History*, 26 (2001)
Shoemaker, R.B., 'The decline of public insult in London 1660–1800', *Past and Present*, 169 (2000)
Shoemaker, R., 'The London mob in the early eighteenth century', *Journal of British Studies*, 26 (1987)
Shoemaker, R., *Prosecution and punishment: petty crime and the law in London and rural Middlesex, 1660–1725* (Cambridge, 1991)
Sier, L.C., 'The Blue Coat school in Colchester', *Essex Review*, 54 (1940)
Sier, L.C., 'Charles Gray, MP of Colchester', *Essex Review*, 57 (1948)
Sier, L.C., 'The ancestry of Charles Gray', *Essex Review*, 59 (1950)
Sills, A., 'Eighteenth-century cartographic studies: a brief survey', *Literature Compass*, 4 (2007)
Smail, J., 'Credit, risk, and honor in eighteenth-century commerce', *Journal of British Studies*, 44 (2005)
Smail, J., *Merchants, markets and manufacture; the English wool textile industry in the eighteenth century* (Basingstoke, 1999)
Smail, J., 'The culture of credit in eighteenth-century commerce: the English textile industry', *Enterprise and Society*, 4 (2003)
Smith, H., *All men and both sexes: gender, politics and the false universal in England, 1640–1832* (University Park, PA, 2002)
Smith, J.R., *The borough of Maldon 1688–1768; a study in English urban history* (MPhil thesis, Leicester, 1981)
Smith, R.D., *The middling sort and the politics of social reformation, Colchester 1570–1640* (New York, 2004)
Smythies, R.H., *Memorials of the Smythies family* (London, 1912)
Sokoll, T., 'Negotiating a living: Essex pauper letters from London, 1800–1834', *International Review of Social History*, 45 (2000)

Sokoll, T. (ed.), *Essex pauper letters 1731–1837* (Oxford, 2001)
Speight, M.E., *Politics, in the borough of Colchester 1812–1847* (PhD thesis, London, 1959)
Spierenburg, P., *Men of violence; gender, honour and rituals in modern Europe and America* (Colombus OH, 1998)
Spierenburg, P., 'Violence and the civilizing process: does it work?', *Crime, Histoire et Societés*, 5 (2001)
Spufford, P., 'Rural credit in seventeenth-century England', *Annales-Histoire Sciences Sociales*, 49 (1994)
Spurrier, L., *The memorials of the Baptist church, Colchester* (Colchester, 1889)
Stallybrass, P. and White, A., *The politics and poetics of transgression* (London, 1983)
Stephenson, D., *The book of Colchester, a portrait of a town* (Buckingham, 1978)
Stirk, N., 'Arresting ambiguity: the shifting geographies of a London debtors' sanctuary in the eighteenth century', *Social History*, 25 (2000)
Stobart, J., 'The economic and social worlds of rural craftsmen-retailers in eighteenth-century Cheshire', *Agricultural History Review*, 52 (2004)
Stone, L., *Family, sex and marriage in early modern England*, 2nd edn (Harmondsworth, 1979)
Stone, L., 'Interpersonal violence in English society, 1300–1980', *Past and Present*, 101 (1983)
Stone, L., 'The history of violence in England: some observations: a rejoinder', *Past and Present*, 108 (1985)
Styles, J., '"Our traitorous moneymakers", the Yorkshire coiners and the law, 1760–83,' in Brewer, J. and Styles, J. (eds.), *An ungovernable people: the English and their law in the seventeenth and eighteenth centuries* (London, 1980)
Summerson, J., *Architecture in Britain 1530–1830* (Harmondsworth, 1983)
Sweet, R., *The writing of urban histories in eighteenth-century England* (Oxford, 1997)
Sweet, R., *The English town 1680–1840: government, society and culture* (London, 1999)
Sweet, R., 'Antiquaries and antiquities in eighteenth-century England', *Eighteenth-Century Studies*, 34 (2001)
Sweet, R., 'Topographies of politeness', *Transactions of the Royal Historical Society*, 12 (2002)
Sweet, R., 'Women and civic life in eighteenth-century England', in Sweet, R., and Lane, P. (eds.), *On the town: women and urban life in eighteenth-century England* (Aldershot, 2003)
Sweet, R., and Lane, P. (eds.), *On the town: women and urban life in eighteenth-century England* (Aldershot, 2003)
Tadmor, N., *Family and friends in eighteenth-century England: household, kinship, and patronage* (Cambridge, 2001)
Tadmor, N., 'Women and wives: the language of marriage in early modern English biblical translations', *History Workshop Journal*, 62 (2006)
Tadmor, N., 'The concept of the household-family in eighteenth-century England', *Past and Present*, 151 (1996)
Thale, M., *The autobiography of Francis Place, 1771–1854* (Cambridge, 1972)
Thompson, E.P., *The making of the English working class* (Harmondsworth, 1963)
Thompson, E.P., 'The moral economy of the English crowd in the eighteenth century', *Past and Present*, 50 (1971)
Thompson, E.P., 'Eighteenth-century English society, class struggle without class', *Social History*, 3 (1978)
Thorne, R.G., *The history of Parliament: The House of Commons 1790–1820* (London, 1986)
Tilly, L., 'The food riot in France', *Journal of Interdisciplinary History*, 1 (1971)
Todd, B., 'Freebench and free enterprise: widows and their property in two Berkshire villages', in John, C. and Hey, D. (eds.), *English rural society, 1500–1800: essays in honour of Joan Thirsk* (Cambridge, 1990)
Tosh, J., 'English politeness: conduct, social rank and moral virtue, c.1400–1900', *Transactions of the Royal Historical Society*, 12 (2002)
Triffit, J.M., *Politics and the urban community; parliamentary boroughs in the south west of*

England 1710–1730 (DPhil thesis, Oxford, 1985)
Trumbach, R., 'London's sodomites; homosexual behaviour and western culture in the eighteenth century', *Journal of Social History*, 11 (1977)
Trumbach, R., 'Sodomitical subcultures, sodomitical roles, and the gender revolution of the 18th-century — the recent historiography', *Eighteenth-Century Life*, 9 (1985)
Trumbach, R., 'Sex, gender, and sexual identity in modern culture — male sodomy and female prostitution in enlightenment London', *Journal of the History of Sexuality* (1991)
Trumbach, R., 'Review of *Sexual suspects: eighteenth-century players and sexual ideology,* by Kristina Straub', *Eighteenth-Century Studies*, 26 (1992)
Trumbach, R., *Sex and the gender revolution*, Vol. 1, *Heterosexuality and the third gender in enlightenment London* (Chicago, 1998)
Vaisey, D., (ed.), *The diary of Thomas Turner* (Oxford, 1985)
Vickery, A., 'Golden-age to separate spheres — a review of the categories and chronology of English women's history', *Historical Journal*, 36 (1993)
Vickery, A., *The gentleman's daughter: women's lives in Georgian England* (New Haven and London, 1998)
Vickery, A., 'His and hers: gender, consumption and household accounting in eighteenth-century England', *Past and Present*, supplement vol. 1 (2006)
Wahrman, D., *Imagining the middle class: the political representation of class in Britain, c.1780–1840* (Cambridge, 1995)
Wahrman, D., 'Percy's prologue: from gender play to gender panic in eighteenth-century England', *Past and Present*, 159 (1998)
Wahrman, D., *The making of the modern self: identity and culture in eighteenth-century England* (New Haven and London, 2004)
Walkowitz, J., *City of dreadful delight, narratives of sexual danger in late-Victorian London* (London, 1992)
Walter, J., and Braddick, M.J. (eds.), *Negotiating power in early modern society: order, hierarchy, and subordination in Britain* (Cambridge, 2001)
Walter, J. and Wrightson, K., 'Dearth and the social order in early modern England', *Past and Present*, 71 (1976)
Walter, J.D., 'Grain riots and popular attitudes to the law: Maldon and the crisis of 1629' in J. Brewer and J. Styles (eds.), *An ungovernable people: the English and their law in the seventeenth and eighteenth centuries* (London, 1980)
Weatherill, L., *Consumer behaviour and material culture in Britain, 1660–1760* (London, 1998)
Weber, W., 'The fabric of daily life and the autobiography of John Marsh', *Huntington Library Quarterly*, 59 (1997)
Weeks, J., *Sex, politics and society: regulation of sexuality since 1800* (London, 1989)
Western, J.R., 'The volunteer movement as an anti-revolutionary force, 1793–1801', *Economic History Review*, 71 (1956)
Whitridge, P., 'Landscapes, houses, bodies, things: "place" and the archaeology of Inuit imaginaries', *Journal of Archaeological Method and Theory*, 11 (2004)
Wiener, M.J., *Men of blood: violence, manliness, and criminal justice in Victorian England* (Cambridge, 2004)
Willan, T.S., *The English coasting trade 1600–1750* (Manchester, 1967)
Williams, D., 'Morals, markets and the English crowd in 1766', *Past and Present*, 104 (1984)
Williams, N., *Contraband cargoes: seven centuries of smuggling* (London, 1959)
Williamson, T., *Polite landscapes: garden and society in eighteenth-century England* (Stroud, 1995)
Wilson, A., 'Conflict, consensus and charity: politics and the provincial voluntary hospitals in the eighteenth century', *English Historical Review* (1996)
Wilson, K., 'Empire, trade and popular politics in mid-Hanoverian Britain; the case of Admiral Vernon', *Past and Present* 121 (1988)

Wilson, K., *The island race: Englishness, empire and gender in the eighteenth century* (London, 2003)

Wilson, K., 'Urban culture and political activism in Hanoverian England: the example of voluntary hospitals' in E. Hellmuth (ed.), *The transformation of political culture: England and Germany in the late eighteenth century* (Oxford, 1990)

Wilson, K., 'Citizenship, empire, and modernity in the English provinces, c.1720–1790', *Eighteenth-century Studies*, 29 (1995)

Wilson, K., *The sense of the people: politics, culture, and imperialism in England, 1715–1785* (New York, 1995)

Wilson, R.G., *Gentleman merchants; the merchant community in Leeds, 1700–1830* (Manchester, 1971)

Wiskin, C., 'Urban businesswomen in eighteenth-century England' in Sweet, R. and Lane, P. (eds.), *On the town: women and urban life in eighteenth-century England* (Aldershot, 2003)

Woodfine, P., 'Debtors, prisons, and petitions in eighteenth-century England', *Eighteenth-century Life*, 30 (2006)

Wrightson, K., *English society 1580–1680* (London, 1982)

Wrightson, K. and Levine, D., *Poverty and piety in an English village; Terling 1525–1700* (New York, San Francisco, London, 1979)

Wrightson, K., *Earthly necessities: economic lives in early modern Britain* (New Haven, CT, 2000)

Wrigley, E.A. and Schofield, R., *The population history of England 1541–1871; a reconstruction* (Cambridge, Mass., 1981)

Wrigley, E.A., 'Urban growth and agricultural change: England and the continent in the early modern period' in P. Borsay (ed.), *The eighteenth-century town* (London, 1990)

Wrigley, E.A., *Poverty, progress and population* (Cambridge, 2004)

Yonemoto, M., 'The "spatial vernacular" in Tokugawa maps', *Journal of Asian Studies*, 59 (2000)

General Index

For individuals living in Colchester in the eighteenth-century see Name Index below. Modern academics and other historical figures (e.g. John Wesley, Jeremy Bentham) are indexed here.

Name Index

Individuals living in, or closely associated with Colchester in the eighteenth century. For other historical figures (e.g. John Wesley) and modern academics, see General Index.